THERE ARE MORE LIKE ME

THERE ARE MORE LIKE ME

Search, Reunion, and Synchronicity in Adoption

DOUGLAS B. HENDERSON, PH.D.

Cover Photos

"Doug's Stages of Life"

Baby, ca. 1947
School Boy, ca. 1954
College Graduate, 1968
Graduate School Student, 1973
Happy Old Guy, 2024 (*credit*: Pat Sinnott)

I dedicate this book to
Wayne Lerand, Bob Andersen, and Jack Marvin,
all friends, and also fellow mental health professionals,
each from the adoption world,
and all who fought the good fight.

And to my parents,
Eleanor L. Henderson, and Douglas P. Henderson.
They lived long enough to meet my birth family, to share my joy,
and to see this book as it was in 1998. Without them, I would not
be who, and where, I am today.

Henderson Family ca. 1965 L to R: Me, Dad, Mom, Dave

TRIGGER WARNING

This book deals with a number of my behaviors, including date rape, marital infidelity, drunken driving, and excessive use of pornography. Some people, me included, find these behaviors to be unacceptable and disturbing.

I believe these bad decisions are related to both my adoption and my alcoholism. They are some of the reasons I wrote this memoir.

The effects of adoption impact my life on a daily basis, and I have been sober since June 17th, 1978.

—DBH

C O N T E N T S

INDEX OF NAMES

Listed by first name.

Douglas Palmer Henderson, Dad. Changed the diapers, chased the ghosts, checked the homework, and cheered the victories. (D) (A1, A7)

Dorissa Flanagan, adoptee psychologist from Milwaukee, one of the "Adoptee shrinks."

Eleanor Lewis Henderson, Mom. Changed the diapers, chased the ghosts, checked the homework, and cheered the victories. (D) (A1, A7)

Frank Hermon, a friend since elementary school. We travelled in Europe together. (D) (G1)

Herbert Dixon, Pearl's husband, father of Keith. (D)

Howard Mullett, "Uncle Henry," known to the family as "Uncle Junie," oldest brother of Bill, married to D'Nelle. (both D) (C9, C10)

Jack Marvin, adoptee, psychologist, adoption activist, AAC Officer, and all-around good human. (D)

Jack Quist, adoptee singer-songwriter, I assisted him at the AAC Conference in Las Vegas, 1995.

Jane Mullett, Bill's ex-wife, divorced when Bill's drinking got out of control. (D) (C2, H2)

Judy McCann, friend since college, when we dated briefly, lost contact, and reestablished a friendship at our tenth reunion. I visited her frequently in Hoboken, NJ.

Katherine Edwards, birthmother I met in New York City, and eventually assisted with her search back in Wisconsin.

Kathy Werrick Largey, girl next door in childhood, adopted, closely attached to my mom. (F1, F2)

Keith Bruce Dixon, son of Pearl and Herbert, married to Kathy, parents of Derek and Stephanie, my birth brother. (D5-D7, H3, I2, I4, I6, J6)

LaVonne Stiffler, birth mother, friend, author of *Synchronicity and Adoption*, was responsible for my appearing on television. (D)

Linda Day, adoptee, birth mother, adoptive mother, second AID President.

Linda Horvatis Luxenberg, a neighbor, playmate, friend from first grade through high school.

Marcia Van Brunt, social worker in Rhinelander, WI. Owned a clinic that was both a licensed mental health clinic and an adoption agency. Married to Bart Bartholomew. (Both D)

Margaret, my first wife from 1973 to 1985. A psychologist, now remarried with a family.

Marlou Russell, adoptee psychologist, met at AAC conferences, helped me in many ways, author of *Adoption Wisdom: A Guide to the Issues and Feelings of Adoption*.

Martha Pointer, faculty member at my university, with whom I had a relationship.

Mary Flynn, Bill's third oldest daughter, birth sister. (C2-C5, J3, H1-H3, J3)

Mary Margaret Shanley, sister of Bill Mullett, birth aunt. (D) (C10)

Mary Towers, dated in graduate school, lost our virginity together, lived together, and I behaved like a jerk.

Maureen Kenmore, my first "girlfriend," in grade seven. Married to Robin Kenmore, a high school friend.

Melinda Warshaw, adoptee friend, a mystic and very spiritual, pushes me toward growth, author of *A Legitimate Life: A Forbidden Journey of Self-Discovery*. Introduced to me by LaVonne Stiffler.

Mike Indian, Mike has been a friend since high school. I stayed with Mike and Karen while doing my search in the Buffalo area. (G1, G2)

Mike Solly, has been a friend since high school. I stayed with Mike and Carolyn in Chatham, NJ, when I went to the ALMA meeting, after which I called my birth mother.

Molly Gold, Bill's second oldest daughter, birth sister (C1-C3, C11, H3, H4, J2), widow of Jim Gold (D) (C11)

Nancy Masters Ghoston, my longest serious "girlfriend" relationship, from grade nine on and off through my senior year in college.

Phyllis G. McCoy, a spiritual channel from Minnesota. I met her through Marcia and Bart in Rhinelander, and Susan and I and had several sessions with her. Author of *The Primer: Channeled Guidance from God and the Masters*.

Pearl Belschner Dixon, my birth mother. (D) (D1-D4)

Robin Kenmore, a high school friend. Married to Maureen Kenmore, my first "girlfriend."

Sally Albertson, Bill's secretary, who helped with arrangements at his death, and with my first reunion, with my birth sister, Susan Hannen.

Sarah, reporter for the local newspaper with whom I had a brief relationship shortly after my divorce.

Shannon Poole, adoptee friend, family therapist.

Sue Werrick, girl next door in childhood, adopted, she and I were playmates. (F2)

Susan Gingrasso, my wife (after 14 years of "dating"), mother of Carch. (E1, E2)

Susan Hannen, Bill's oldest daughter, birth sister, first birth relative I ever met. (C1-C3, C10, J1)

Tom and Cindy Little. Tom has been a friend since college, was a college fraternity brother, and Cindy is his high school sweetheart. I was their best man and have visited them often in Connecticut.

Tom McGowan, adoptee friend and psychologist, co-led session on adopted males with me, Baltimore AAC meeting, 1996.

Tom Rowe, Psychology Department colleague. We published some work (together with our students), on synchronicity.

Wayne Lerand was Psychology Department Chairperson when I was hired. He was a counseling psychologist, adoptive father, and fellow survivor of testicular cancer. Wayne and Judy Lerand (both D) are the parents of Andrea and Christopher.

TIME LINE

1940–2024

1940
November: My parents marry.

1946
October: I am born.

1950
April: My brother Dave is born.

1958
I am told that I am adopted.

1962
Winter: Nancy and I first begin to date.

1964
June: I graduate from Kenmore East Senior High School.

1966
Summer: Nancy and I begin to date more seriously.

1967
Winter: Nancy and I are pinned.

1968
June: I pay a surprise visit to Nancy's college, and I get a surprise of my own; I graduate from St. Lawrence University with a B.S. in psychology; **September**: I start graduate school at The Ohio State University.

1970

Winter: I meet Mary, we date through the spring, and live together in the summer; **September**: I start my internship year in clinical child psychology in Chicago.

1971

September: I return to Columbus, meet Marjorie and Margaret, and date Marjorie; **November**: I stop seeing Marjorie and start to date Margaret.

1973

February: Margaret and I become engaged; **August**: I graduate from The Ohio State University with a Ph.D. in clinical child psychology. **September**: I marry Margaret; **October**: I start service in the U.S. Army in San Antonio.

1974

January: I finish service in the U.S. Army and return to Columbus. **March**: I start work in The Ohio State University Department of Pediatrics at Columbus Children's Hospital.

1976

September: I start work in the Psychology Department at the University of Wisconsin–Stevens Point.

1978

June: I stop drinking for the last time.

1981

May: I have testicular cancer and have surgery and chemotherapy during **June, July,** and **August**. I begin to think about searching.

1982

August: I learn my parents know more about my adoption than they had previously told me.

1983

January: Margaret and I separate; **March**: Bill, my birth father, dies. **May**: I talk to my parents about my adoption, and attend my 15th college reunion; **June**: I do my search, talk to my birth mother, and meet my birth sisters; **July and August**: I begin to write Part One, and some of Part Two, of this book.

1984

April: Margaret and I divorce; **April-July**: I date Martha;
October: I present at my first adoption conference, AAC Midwest
Regional/AID State Conference in Eau Claire;
December-January 1985: I date Sally.

1985

January: I start the Stevens Point chapter of AID; **February**: Susan
and I meet.

1986

April: AAC conference in Milwaukee; **June**: I start consulting at
Northern Family Services.

1988

January-June: I spend spring semester in Madrid, Spain.

1989

April: I stop consulting at Northern Family Services.

1990

April: AAC conference in Chicago.

1991

June: Susan and I visit Uncle Henry in northern New York State.
June: I call my birth mother about a health problem and
get rebuffed.

1992

April: AAC conference in Philadelphia, I call my birth brother
Keith; **May**: I am elected State President of AID; **August**: Susan
and I visit Keith and Kathy in Western New York

1993

April: AAC conference in Cleveland.

1994

April: AAC conference in New Orleans; **June**: I am filmed for
Unsolved Mysteries; **October**: I appear on *Unsolved Mysteries;*
December: I am filmed for *The Other Side.*

1995

January: I appear on *The Other Side*; **April**: AAC conference in Las Vegas; **September**: I am filmed for *Sightings*; **October**: I join the AAC Board of Directors; **November**: I am elected to the AAC Executive Committee.

1996

April: AAC conference in Baltimore; **August-December**: I have a sabbatical leave to write this book.

1997

January-May: Susan, Carch and I spend the spring semester in London; **January**: *Sightings* appearance airs just after we leave for London; **August-December**: I have a sabbatical leave to finish this manuscript.

1998

April: AAC Conference in Seattle; **August**: I meet with Michael Austin, learn of Version Two of my adoption; **August**: Susan and I marry; **Fall**: I lose contact with Keith and my birth sisters.

1999

January: I suspend work on this book for many years.
April: AAC Conference in McClean, VA.

2000

April: AAC Conference in Nashville, TN.

2001

April: AAC Conference in Anaheim, CA; **May**: I retire after 25 years teaching at the University of Wisconsin–Stevens Point.

2002

April: AAC Conference, Philadelphia, PA, receive AAC President's Award; **September**: 2002 Biennial Adoption Conference, "The Life-long Adoption Journey: Through the Eyes of the Adopted," St. John's University, Queens Campus. I make connections there with other adoption experts and am invited to submit three papers to the *Handbook of Adoption*, and to assist in writing the introductory chapter.

2003

April: AAC Conference in Atlanta, GA.

2007
Publication of the *Handbook of Adoption*.

2010
I am invited to make a presentation at the male adoptees monthly group telephone call.

2013
June: I develop a variety of health problems. My health begins a long and varied decline, not correctly diagnosed as chronic Lyme's Disease until 2016.

2015
I register with 23andMe.

2016
June-August: I finally see Lyme's specialists and begin a slow recovery. Long-term Lyme's continues to the present time.

2020
Spring: Covid suspends or ends most of my social and service activities. I develop a case of personal anomie, which outlasts the pandemic.

2024
April: Susan refocuses me on this project.

CHAPTER 1

Begin Here!

Welcome! You are about to read a book that I wrote for both entertainment and educational purposes. I want to provide you with an interesting story, and in the process, to help you to learn about the life-long effects of adoption, and about the nature of synchronicity. If my book was only a novel, or only an educational work, perhaps an introduction such as this would not be necessary, but since the book has aspects of both a story and a text, reading this chapter will give you more solid ground on which to begin.

My adoption, search, and reunion story takes place mostly between my birth in October 1946, and the essential end of my search (and of the original writing of the manuscript), in 1998. The majority of the work on the manuscript took place during a 2-semester sabbatical leave from teaching in the Psychology Department at the University of Wisconsin Stevens Point (UWSP) in the fall semesters of 1996 and 1997. I spent the spring semester of 1997 co-leading a group of UWSP students in London, England. The original plan had been to complete the work and submit the manuscript for publication during the summer of 1998.

Several developments caused this schedule to self-destruct. You will read more later about the biggest issue, but that issue raised the possibility that much of my work had been in vain. Unfortunately, I did not have time to work on resolving that problem, since I had to return to full-time teaching in January of 1998, at the end of my sabbatical leave. Another daunting event was a lone critical review of my manuscript from an author who was widely known at the time, and whose disapproval would have been a serious impediment to publication. That was very disheartening, and I just set the book project aside and returned to work. About that same time, the Gods of careful saving and finance

1

were smiling on me, and it began to look as if I could afford to retire sometime in my mid-to-late fifties, which was only a few years away. I planned to get back to my book during retirement, when I assumed I would have more time.

Happily, I was able to retire at 55, in the spring of 2001. Also happily, retirement rapidly became so full and so enjoyable that I didn't even have time on rainy days to work on the manuscript. Some of these enjoyable things included: carpentry and construction; rock collecting, cutting, and polishing; shooting professional fireworks shows; riding my UTV; and heating our home and my cabin with wood I cut from my own 44 acres, 15 miles from Stevens Point. Retirement was great for the first 12 years.

Then, in 2013, I developed significant health problems which remained a mystery until 2016, when I realized it was Lyme's disease. Treatment has been an ongoing experience, with occasional returning symptoms that may last the rest of my life. Retirement and life were still good, just more challenging. In 2015, I registered with 23andMe, and my genetic history information showed me that I could have continued work on my book in 1998. However, I just didn't have the desire, or the energy, to do that, and the manuscript remained untouched on my computer. In 2020, Covid hit, and as with most of us, virtually anything I did that involved other people, and that was most everything, came to a sudden stop. Between 2020 and 2022, I spent considerable time managing and working on my 22 acres of woods which were due for a harvest under Wisconsin's Managed Forest Law. Then in 2023, I received a grant from the U.S. Fish and Wildlife Service to convert an 18-acre fallow farm field into an oak savanna and prairie. I worked to clear that field through the summer of 2024. During that time, health problems also made it difficult do some physical things that I used to be able to do easily. Unfortunately, even as Covid restrictions gradually melted away, I still did not get my mojo back. My wife, Susan, saw this and suggested I look again into getting my book published.

In April of 2024, we visited the UWSP Cornerstone Press 40th anniversary event, and there she "bribed" me with the gift of a $20 book I was interested in if I would agree to get back to work and finish my own book project. I guess either I sold my soul pretty cheaply, or I knew a good deal when I saw it!

Since the majority of my search and reunion, as well as most of the writing of this book, came to an end in 1998, most of the book other than the first and last chapters, are written as though it was still 1998.

In the last chapter I have included follow-up information, and a couple of synchronistic experiences that I had between 1999 and 2024, as well as updates, where available, on people who are, or were, part of my story.

Here in Chapter 1, I will present definitions of important terms which appear throughout the book, but may not be fully explained until you get to the sections of the book which more resemble a textbook (primarily Parts Three through Five). There is also information about two important people who appear in those portions of the book which more resemble a novel about my search and reunion (Parts One, Two, and portions of the remaining three parts), but who are not introduced in detail until later on.

At the front of the book is an index of names and a timeline. At the back of the book in the appendix you will find a list of further resources, a list of my publications, and an annotated map of the Buffalo and Western New York area. These may be useful to consult as you read.

IMPORTANT ADOPTION-RELATED TERMS

Adoptee: The individual who is adopted. Use of the term "adopted child" is discouraged because "adopted children" in many ways are never allowed to grow up. Children, adolescents and adults are all adoptees for all of their lives, no matter what their age may be.

Adoption triad: The three primary parties to an adoption: The adoptee, the birth parents, and the adoptive parents. Some would add, as a fourth party to the adoption, the legal system.

Adoptive parents: The persons who gain and raise a family member through the adoption process. To most adoptees these people are "my parents," or just plain old "Mom" and "Dad." They were there to change the diapers, chase the ghosts, check the homework, and cheer the victories. The term "real parent" is avoided by most in the adoption triad because the idea of "real" parents suggests that other parents, particularly the birth parents, are unreal.

Birth parents: The persons who are the biological/genetic parents of the adoptee. Some prefer to use the term biological or genetic parent, which are also acceptable, but this emphasis may be somewhat misleading. The role of the birth parent covers more than just the biological and genetic dimensions. Birth parents, especially birth mothers, also share with the adoptee their pregnancy and birth experiences, which we are learning are increasingly important. "First parent" is another term that is coming into more frequent use. We avoid using "real parents" in referring to birth parents for the same reasons we avoid using it for adoptive parents: it suggests that other parents are unreal. "Natural parents" is also avoided because it suggests that adoptive parents are unnatural.

Open adoption: A newer type of adoption, in which the birth and adoptive families are known to each other, in contrast to the much more historically typical "closed" adoption, where these parties remain anonymous. The "open" concept was introduced in the 1970s, and has since grown to include the majority of infant adoptions in the U.S.. Open adoptions are believed to be healthier for the adoptee than closed adoptions

Reunion: The meeting of biological relatives who have been separated by the adoption process. The term reunion may strike some as unusual, especially when used to apply to birth relatives whom adoptees have never met, such as siblings born after adoptees left their birth family, It certainly seemed an unusual term to me. However, at least with our birth mothers, we adoptees were "in union" with them while we were in their wombs, thus, when we meet as adults, it is a re-union.

IMPORTANT SYNCHRONICITY-RELATED TERMS

Chance: simple pairing, or even sequential occurrence, of random events. Chance occurs without an apparent or seeming cause, and occurs with varying frequencies, from very high and likely to very low and unlikely (at least seemingly sometimes even close to zero). The outcome of chance may vary from extremely positive to extremely negative. Chance is not sought out, rather it just happens. Chance has no meaning or significance on its own, and although meaning and significance may be imposed after the fact, meaning and significance are not present in the occurrence of the chance. Another way to think of chance is that it produces effects along a continuum known as the "bell" or "normal" curve.

Serendipity: an event that is unsolicited, similar to chance (because it is happened upon or discovered accidentally), but, unlike chance, serendipity has a beneficial outcome. Serendipities are, by their nature, pleasant, and are not sought out, or caused by any particular factor such as a field or a spiritual factor. They may have a long-term and meaningful effect, but they are not thought to be "caused" in the scientific sense. It may be thought of as "good luck."

Coincidence: simply two things that happen at the same time. They may be desirable or not. Coincidence does not indicate causality and some definitions specifically state that there is no causality present.

Coincidences may or may not be synchronistic. If the two items that occur together do not have meaning or significance for those involved it remains coincidence. Note that I use both "celestine" and "coincidence" frequently in this book, partly because I was not fully aware of the concept of synchronicity until a fair way into my reunion process. Also, sometimes I was not really aware that an event was more than coincidence until some later point. A typical reaction to coincidence might be "hunh!."

Celestine: A term used by James Redfield to describe "our world as a field of spiritual energy, adaptable to our thoughts, feelings, and behaviors all centered around giving." Redfield wrote a series of books, the first of which is *The Celestine Prophecy: An Adventure*. I started reading the series in 1993, while I was conducting my search. The ideas I found there have influenced my spiritual development greatly. The term "field" is also used by others, such as Carl Jung, in defining synchronicity, to describe an over-arching level of connectedness. I see a good deal of similarity between the terms celestine and synchronicity.

Synchronicity: The occurrence of highly unusual events which have personal meaning to the people experiencing the events. Synchronicity is felt to be more than simple chance because the events seem to be so perfectly planned, appropriate, or meaningful, as to defy any belief in their occurrence merely at random. However, we are also hard-pressed to explain their occurrence by the generally accepted understanding of "cause and effect." Synchronicity was first defined by the psychoanalytic therapist and philosopher Carl Jung, who indicated that it was incorrect to say that synchronistic events were "caused" by each other. Nor were they "caused" by a third occurrence, element, phenomenon or factor, or by any other kind of causation as it is usually defined. Jung believed in an overarching "level" or "field" of unity which is difficult, if not impossible, for we humans, especially western, logically trained, and scientific, to perceive or understand. The term "field" is also used by others, such as James Redfield in defining celestine, to describe an over-arching level of connectedness.

This "field" idea is difficult for traditional scientists to accept, or was, until the advent of quantum physics, which has demonstrated unexpected and hard to explain connections. For example, given two atomic particles, created by the splitting of one particle in half, with the particles travelling in opposite directions, a physical effect on one particle causes a similar reaction in the other particle. Somehow, there was "communication" or "a relationship," or "a connection," or "a field" between the two particles. This phenomenon, weak and still not totally understood, was called by Einstein "spooky attraction at a distance."

Jung sets aside the traditional ideas of cause and effect, and states it is the dimension of meaningfulness that is the most important attribute of synchronicity. Without meaningfulness, there is mere chance. Many people believe that one can increase the synchronicities in their life by techniques such as attending to the environment, mindfulness, setting intentions, and engaging in personal observation. I see a good deal of similarity between the terms synchronicity and celestine. In this book, when I use the phrase "It just happened" that is often describing an event which, at the time it was occurring, was so "rare," "perfect," and "helpful" that I suspected more than just coincidence or serendipity was happening. I often suspected synchronicity.

IMPORTANT CHARACTERS

Though most characters are introduced as they appear more or less chronologically in the story of my adoption, search, and reunion, two need a separate introduction. In February 1985, I started to date Susan Gingrasso, the head of the dance program at the University of Wisconsin–Stevens Point. We had both been divorced in 1984. When we met, our relationship became very strong very quickly. Details of our relationship are presented in Chapter 22, titled "If Marriage Doesn't Work, Let's Try Another Way." Susan was, and remains, a very important part of my life. I have been in a relationship with her longer, and feel more closely connected with her, than with any other woman I have ever known, although as you will see our relationship has not been without its challenges. Susan was present for several important portions of my search. Therefore, introducing her here at the beginning of the book avoids confusion about her identity, or interruption of the story for an introduction, later on.

Susan has a son, Carch, born in 1980, who was just under five years old when we met. I know Carch, and have watched his growth into a man, better than any other child I have ever known. He is as close to a son as I will ever have, although you will see that, as with my relationship with his mother, our relationship too was not without its challenges.

I believe that the three best things I've ever done are sobriety, search, and Susan, with the priority depending on my mood. Buying my land and building my cabin is a solid fourth. Hopefully the publication of this book will be in the top five!

PART ONE
THE SEARCH

CHAPTER 2

I Decide to Search

Version One: A boy about 12 years of age asks his mother as she puts him to bed one night "Was I adopted?" His mother and father had anticipated his question, and they had agreed to talk with him together about his adoption when he was old enough to understand. Not wanting to lie to him however, his mother answers his question truthfully by herself, even though his father has not yet arrived home from a business trip. The boy, when told he was adopted, begins to cry uncontrollably, and his father, just getting home, has to help to calm the boy by holding him. The boy goes upstairs to bed and cries himself to sleep.

Version Two: A boy about 12 years of age, looking for his lucky number, asks his mother as she tucks him into bed, what room she was in at the hospital when she had him. His birthday, October 14, is too close to the number 13 to be lucky, and surely his mother will remember the "lucky number" of the room she occupied when he was born. The boy's mother takes him downstairs to see his father, telling the father about the question which he had just asked. Looking at his watch, the father says "it's too late to tell him tonight, let's talk about it tomorrow." The next night the boy's parents tell him his mother did not go to the hospital to have him because he was adopted. They go on to tell a story, both sad and happy, about wanting a baby and not being able to have one; about waiting years and wanting a special baby; about getting a phone call; about hasty preparations; about joy; and about love. The boy goes upstairs to bed and cries himself to sleep.

Version one is his parents' memory of how the boy discovered he was adopted, and version two is the boy's own memory of the event. Some aspects of truth are more important than others. We may never know which version of these memories is more accurate, and perhaps we don't really need to know exactly how he found out about his adoption. The most important aspect of truth here is that a very basic fact about himself was not revealed to the boy for 12 years. Another important truth is that the next morning the boy woke up and didn't think about his adoption again for nearly ten years.

I was that boy. I am now a man, but in the eyes of many I will always be a boy, an "adopted child," never having the right to see my own birth certificate or to know the truth of my own origins. This is the story about how I finally came to know my truth: about how I found answers to questions I never knew I had; about how I had to overcome obstacles both in myself and in others; and about the unexpected role of synchronicity in my life. This is the story of the best thing I have ever done for myself: the story of my search for and reunion with my birth family, and this is the story of what being adopted has meant to me.

How different was my childhood than the childhood of other children because I was adopted? This is a hard question to answer, since I never experienced anything other than my own childhood. I don't think I was aware of any difference I ascribed to being adopted, either before or after I learned about my adoption (A1-A6, B1, B2). In fact, in the 1940s, one of the purposes of the secrecy that kept me from being told I was adopted was precisely in order to keep my childhood from being negatively affected by my adoption. This secrecy was practiced "for the good of the child." To the extent my childhood was "average," perhaps the secrecy surrounding my adoption somewhat served its intended purpose. To the extent the secrecy had effects that were not good for me, perhaps a more truthful approach would have been more desirable.

I was neither the most nor the least popular in my school. I had friends, girlfriends, and acne at the appropriate ages, and I think I had about the same kind of relationship with my parents as most of my friends seemed to have. All through high school I was told I was not living up to my potential. My grades went up every semester during my four years at St. Lawrence University, from barely above straight C to barely below a straight A, with several semester appearances on the Dean's List. After a freshman year in which I majored in drinking and partying, I joined the fraternity known on campus as "the intellectuals," and decided on either psychology or sociology as a major. By my senior year I realized I would have to go on to graduate school to complete my education, and psychology, rather than social work, seemed more to my liking. I began work on a Ph.D. in clinical child psychology at The

Ohio State University in Columbus, and during my second year had a house-mate named Bob Young, a fellow student in the same program.

Late one beer-filled night we got into a discussion about Bob's adopted younger sister, who had recently expressed a desire to search for her birth family. Bob said, "I think my sister's need to know about her birth family is fine. In fact, it's completely natural. I'm curious about them too."

I said, "Why would anyone even think about poking around in the past like that? What do you think she's going to find, she's the queen of the May? Isn't she grateful she was adopted and loved by good parents?"

Bob wondered "Why *wouldn't* someone want to know about their history? I sure would."

"Don't you think she's hurting your parents by going off looking for a new family? I know my parents sure would be hurt if I ran off and did something like that!"

Bob didn't realize until then I was adopted, and when he found out, he began to ask me more and more pointed questions about my experiences. "When did you find out?" "At about 12 or so."

"How do you feel about being adopted?" "What do you mean, how do I feel? I'm just happy I was taken out of a bad situation and given a good home."

"Well, how do you know it was a bad situation?" "It HAD to have been, or I wouldn't have been adopted in the first place!"

Bob asked "Don't you want to find out why you really were adopted and how you were conceived?" I said "You know what, I've never even thought about it, and I have no interest in looking for, or meeting anyone from, my birth family. The best thing they ever did for me was to give me up for adoption!" My voice rose as I began to get more and more agitated at Bob's questions. Before long I was in a state of great anger, gesturing and pounding on the table. When Bob mentioned the fact I might have another whole family out there somewhere, I shouted "I already HAVE a family! They love me, and I love them, and I have no need to know anything more!" Eventually (Bob was pretty drunk also) he saw he had touched a nerve, and backed off.

Perhaps it was only the beer and the hour that led to my rage. But, just perhaps, with all of my education in psychology, I should have been aware of myself enough to realize I was protesting too much. I was arguing not as much with Bob as with myself, trying to convince myself I really didn't care about my adoption. I think that night was the first time I had ever seriously, and consciously, thought about my birth family, and I was obviously not yet ready to deal with the idea of meeting them, since just thinking about them sent me over the edge. I should have seen I was denying the importance of something that was in truth really important to me, and had been for a long time. I just wasn't ready to see this yet.

There could have been any of a number of issues about my adoption that were difficult for me to handle, and all of them were very much hidden from my conscious awareness. At that time, it was the fact I had not known I was adopted that was the most notably bothersome. In addition, since my parents had spoken to me little if at all about my adoption since the night they told me, I had consciously sensed that, for whatever reasons, my adoption was not a topic with which they were comfortable. I did not want to display the appearance of being disloyal or ungrateful to my parents, and searching for my birth family appeared that way to me. Around the time of the outburst with Bob, a significant change in my political and spiritual beliefs evolved in relationship to my adoptive family.

Throughout high school, and largely through college, my political beliefs tracked pretty closely to those of my parents. Our party affiliation was Republican, and I voted for Richard Nixon the first time I was able to vote for president. Most St. Lawrence students had a fairly conservative viewpoint, and my enrollment in the U.S. Army Reserve Officer Training Corps (ROTC) only furthered my conservatism (B3). At Ohio State I found a much more liberal atmosphere, and was marching around The Oval (the center of the campus) on May 4, 1970, protesting for Black Student rights, when the Kent State killings happened. This was an eye- and mind-opening experience for me.

Spiritually, I also tracked closely with my parents. For a while in High School, I even wanted to be a minister. I assisted in services at our Presbyterian church, and preached at least one Youth Sunday sermon. In college, a required freshman class, The History of Western Faith and Reason, pretty much killed my faith in organized religion. I learned how much of what I had been taught as "The Sacred Word of God" turned out to be what I thought of as little more than encrusted old social and health customs, primarily from the Jewish tradition. I also realized once the "old customs" were stripped from virtually all major religions, they boiled down to the same basic message, which I saw as some variation of the Golden Rule, or perhaps in a broader sense, karma: what you give to the world you will get back. I retained my belief in God, but perhaps based on the teaching that what we do to the least important person, we do to God, I decided there was a little bit of God in every human being. I began to believe I could best practice my particular set of religious beliefs on a daily basis throughout my life rather than just on Sunday mornings in a particular building, with a particular religious label.

While visiting my family and friends in Buffalo during December 1969, I became increasingly uncomfortable around my parents. I don't remember whether this was before or after my conversation with Bob, but it might well have been shortly afterward. Under the influence of more liberal students on the Ohio State campus, I had begun to let my hair grow long, and they noticed this right away.

Christmas was difficult, and shortly before New Year's I decided to leave Buffalo and go to Detroit where Terry, a high school friend, lived in a commune. I arrived there early on the afternoon of New Year's Eve, and spent that evening with Terry and his friends. Prior to that, I had had several chances to try one of the "funny little cigarettes" that many of my friends were smoking, but I had courteously turned them down. That night I decided it was time to give this new form of recreation a try. Unlike Bill Clinton, I inhaled! By the end of the night, rather than being good and drunk, I was good and high.

Everyone slept late on New Year's Day, and it wasn't until almost lunchtime that life began to return to the commune. I found my way to one of several bathrooms and proceeded to take a shower and, after the shower, to shave. Just as I began shaving a young woman who I vaguely remembered from the night before came in. We smiled, and I said hi. She said "You're Doug, right? I said Yes. She introduced herself and then casually undressed and got into the shower.

I continued equally casually shaving, as if this was something that happened to me every day, although this was my second "first experience" within 12 hours! By the time she was out of the shower and drying off, the mirror had fogged up, and I was having to wipe it off to see myself. And of course, to see her as well.

Having recently started one new recreational behavior (marijuana smoking, not mirror peeping!), I guess I was ready to stop an old behavior, and that morning was my last shave for many years as I began to grow my beard. A day or two later, I made my way back to Columbus where the winter quarter was about to begin.

You will read later about a dinner I had in Columbus with Carol, the daughter of one of my mother's high school friends. Our mothers had been pressing us to meet and after our dinner, I realized that she might well report the experience to her mother, who might then tell my mother, and in the process might mention my beard.

I realized it was going to be unwelcome news and decided I wanted my parents to hear it directly from me, rather than thirdhand. Very soon after that dinner, perhaps even the next day, I called my parents. Dad was on one extension and mom on another (A1, A7). After the pleasantries, and after telling them about the dinner with Carol, I told them about my beard, and things took a significant change of direction. My father swore, said "Maybe someday you'll have some good news for me" and hung up the phone. My mother stayed on the line but started crying, asking me "Why would you want to do such a thing?" The result of the call was my realization that I was going to have to do things that pleased me, and not to worry about what my parents would think of either what I did, or of me.

A couple of weeks went by with no further contact, and since my mother had historically been writing me a letter every week or so since I left for college, I knew there had been a disruption in the flow. After a couple of weeks, I wrote them a letter stating that this was a decision I was making for my life, that if this decision was going to result in family disruption, it would not be me that was cutting them off, but they who were cutting me off. I also suggested that were I to come home with a woman who I had chosen to marry I would hope that they would accept my choice and not try to overrule it.

I received separate responses from each of them in short order, probably written and mailed the day they received my letter. Both mom and dad's letters had variations of the idea that they loved *me*, but not necessarily everything that I chose to *do*. I quickly wrote them back, thanking them for their letters and at least for the moment the issue was settled.

In the fall of 1971, I had started a one-year psychology internship at Michael Reese Hospital in Chicago before adoption became a conscious issue for me again. An idea of how much I had changed in the years between 1968 and 1973 can be seen in photos B4-B7. I experimented with a mustache in 1975 (B8), but by 1977, I had settled on a "look" and a hobby that I liked (B9). Surprisingly, in 1988, I came home from Wisconsin to find my dad sporting a full beard! (A7). Oddly enough, he and I never really seriously spoke about it, other than jokingly, as in me saying "Who IS that guy?" Mom suggested privately to me that it was his way of accepting who I had become.

During the early part of my internship, I learned I would soon be expected to participate in an all-day "encounter group" as part of a course in group therapy. I did not wish to be in the encounter group, and asked Dr. Vita Krall, my internship supervisor, to be excused from having to take the class. She told me I needed to talk to the course director, a very sharp female staff psychiatrist who I barely knew. I made an appointment with her, and then had an anxiety attack in her office when she asked me to explain why I didn't "think I needed to learn about group therapy." As a result of the anxiety attack, I was not only required to attend the group therapy course, but was also referred to a social worker at the University of Chicago Hospital for personal therapy. Ruth Spaulding was to be but the first of many therapists I would see. About six weeks into our work, I mentioned in an off-hand way at the end of a session that I was adopted.

I knew even then as a graduate student and psychology intern that therapists, especially psychoanalytically oriented ones such as mine, were supposed to maintain a cool, rather detached, and unemotional manner. As I recall, when I told Mrs. Spaulding I was adopted, she nearly fell out of her chair, leaning forward and asking me if I didn't think that was an important enough piece of information about myself that I should have told her sooner. I told her I didn't think being adopted was particularly important. Her response, destined to be a monumental understatement, was "I think we have an issue to discuss during our next session." For the next several months we worked on my feelings about being adopted, and I discovered adoption was a major issue in many areas of my life.

One of the first issues we addressed was related to my conversation with Bob Young about his adopted sister. I began to see, as I should have at the time it happened, that the intensity of my angry reaction to hearing about her desire to search revealed my own strong feelings about searching myself. I felt guilty for even thinking about my birth family. One Friday afternoon during a session about my adoption I expressed some anger at my parents for withholding the fact of my adoption from me. I don't remember whether I said directly that I was feeling guilty for these thoughts, or whether Mrs. Spaulding just saw it in my behavior. What I do know is I went home that afternoon, got dressed and left my apartment to go out to a bar for the evening. I had not yet had anything to drink, and so cannot blame what happened on any impairment due to alcohol. While waiting for a traffic light to change, I thought I could sneak between the back of a bus in front of me, and a Volkswagen "bug" waiting to my left, and thereby pull ahead of the bus when the light changed. I slowly eased my car between the two stopped vehicles. Quietly, and with clean surgical precision, using the left rear bumper of my car like a scalpel, I pulled the entire right front fender off of the bug!

Just a year earlier I had my first major auto accident in which I had hit a car that ran a red light in front of me, doing thousands of dollars of damage to both vehicles. That car's driver had been both drunk and uninsured, and so my insurance company ended up paying for the damage to my car, even though the accident had not been my fault. I didn't want my company to find out about this accident, especially since this one *was* my fault. So early the next week I settled privately with the Volkswagen's owner by paying him $250 in cash, an amount less than my premiums would have risen had I notified my insurance company and had them pay for the damage. At that time my month's rent was $200, and my monthly stipend for the internship was barely more than $300 after taxes. Two hundred and fifty dollars hurt.

The next Friday afternoon, when my therapist asked how things had gone since we saw each other last, I rolled my eyes and groaned, telling her of my "bad luck" and describing the auto accident. Without losing a breath or batting an eyelash, she asked me what I thought had made me want to punish myself that way. I had no idea what she meant by "punish," and so after a few moments of silence, she suggested we pick up where we left off last week. When I couldn't remember what we had been talking about, she reminded me I was expressing anger at my parents over my adoption. I still couldn't see the connection until she asked me "And what often happens to children who are angry at their parents?" My reflexive and immediate answer was "They get punished," which I followed shortly with "Oh, my God!" I had punished myself for my angry thoughts at my parents by having a "safe," but expensive, accident. We talked for a few sessions about why I should feel *so* guilty about simply wanting to know where I came from. This was about as far as we took the search and reunion-related aspect of my adoption. My therapy ended along with my internship, and I returned to Ohio State in the fall of 1972, with a beginning-level awareness about the wide-ranging, and largely unconscious, importance of my adoption in my life.

Once back on campus, I met Margaret, a first-year graduate student in the same program in Clinical-Child Psychology which I was completing. We dated for most of her first (and my last), year of graduate school, and decided to marry in the fall of 1973, just after I was scheduled to finish work on my Ph.D. We seemed to have more than our share of problems and I spent over half of the next 12 years in both joint marital counseling with Margaret, and in my own personal therapy. My adoption came up on several occasions, and with several different therapists, as an issue, although not all of the therapists were equally aware of the dynamics of adoption, or of how they could affect our marriage. I, however, began to see being placed for adoption by my birth mother, and my not finding out from my adoptive mother I was adopted until I was older, were both related to my inability to trust women in general, and women intimately related to me in particular. As time progressed my inability to trust became a dominant focus of both my own therapy and of our marital counseling.

In the fall of 1976, as I was about to turn 30, I took a job as an Assistant Professor of Psychology at the University of Wisconsin–Stevens Point. Margaret stayed in Columbus to finish her dissertation, after which, in November of that year, she joined me in Stevens Point. We had anticipated Margaret might have to work at some distance from Stevens Point, and one or both of us to have to commute a considerable distance to work each day. However, Margaret found a job as a clinical-child psychologist in the Portage County Mental Health Clinic, located in what was then the county's only hospital, just a block from my office at the University. We often drove to and from work together, and in good weather could even ride our bikes. I'm sure on the outside we looked to be a happily married modern dual-career couple. Unfortunately, problems in our relationship continued.

Several times in my twenties and early thirties, often as a result of my continuing although intermittent therapy, I asked my parents to tell me what they knew about my adoption. The questions were difficult for me to ask, especially since what I really wanted to know was both how I came to the Henderson family, and how I came to leave my birth family. I'm sure my questions were equally difficult for my parents to answer. Each of the times I asked I was told a variation of the same story. After a heartbreaking series of five miscarriages and a still-born full-term boy, my mother asked her physician to think of her if he ever had a patient who could not keep her baby. About a year later, when they got the call saying there was a baby boy they could have "if you want him" they immediately said yes, sight unseen, and asked how soon they could come to see me. There was such unrestrained joy and excitement right after that phone call my father nearly burned down their house by forgetting to close the damper on the coal furnace when they rushed out to the hospital to meet me for the first time. Two weeks later I joined them and we became a family of three. Four years later my mother became pregnant and successfully carried the baby to birth. My brother, Dave, made us a family of four (A1-A6, F1, F2).

Every time I heard that story I cried. I love my parents so much that I was reminded of the pain they went through in trying to have their own biological children. The story also reminds me of how much I was wanted and loved by them. Since I have mentioned my parents also have a younger son who is their biological child, I never felt they treated us any differently, other than me being the older one, and I have no doubt they love us both equally, although in ways, differently.

However, aside from the history of how the Henderson family came to be, my parents told me little of how I came to leave my birth family. What they did tell me was the generic information that was told to many adoptees from the 1940s: "Your birth parents were in good health and they must have loved you very much to have given you up." The inherent contradiction in the idea of loving a baby so much that you give the baby to strangers initially did not strike me as odd. While I enjoyed hearing about how I came to be a member of my family, the questions I had about my birth family remained unanswered. At that time, I had not yet realized just how important the answers to those other questions were to me, but during these years I still wanted to know my "other" history.

I gradually began to wonder just how a birth mother could love her baby so much she gave it away. I later learned that, perhaps to avoid the contradiction inherent in "loving-and-giving-away," there was another common variation of the "how-you-came-to-our-family" story during the 1940s and 1950s. That variation, given to adoptees, and often to their adoptive parents by the adoption agency, involved a "tragic accident in the laboratory at the medical school both of your birth parents attended," or a "terrible auto crash," or a fire, or some other similar (and non-existent), catastrophe. The death of the birth parents both solved the loving-and-giving-away problem, and helped make the birth family appear inaccessible.

Even though I still had unanswered questions, perhaps nothing would have changed from the situation that had evolved by the time I was in my mid-thirties except for my discovery of a painful lump on my left testicle in early May 1981. In the space of one week, I changed from an apparently healthy 35-year-old man to a hospitalized cancer patient. As I spent the summer of 1981 traveling back and forth from my home in Stevens Point to hospitals and doctors' offices both there and in Madison, a common fact of life for adoptees became increasingly problematic to me: the virtually complete absence of any family medical history. My major treatment was at the Wisconsin Clinical Cancer Center (now the Carbone Center), located at the University of Wisconsin Hospital in Madison. Since this was a teaching hospital, several times a day, students in various health care professions would enter my room to practice taking a health history. Each time they began to ask about my family medical history, I would have to tell them I was adopted at birth, and had no information to give them. There would then be a short pause as they skipped over sometimes several pages of the form. The importance of what I was unable to provide began to weigh heavily on me. I began to realize unless I did something extraordinary to get the information, those pages would remain forever blank.

I had a lot of time to think that summer. Although I never would want to go through the experience again, one cannot encounter cancer, and go through two major surgeries (my gall bladder was also removed), and three months of chemotherapy, without doing some serious thinking about one's place in the world. Most of these thoughts were not specifically about my adoption, but as I evaluated and reevaluated the various pieces of my life, I developed an increasing awareness that I was not, as the dominant adoption lore of the 1940s and 1950s would have me and my parents believe, "just like other people." *Other* people had a medical-genetic life history as well as a social-psychological one. *Other* people knew who they were and from where they came as a matter of course. *Other* peoples' lives were filled with living relatives, and stories or photos of previous generations. Many things of crucial importance beyond medical history, were missing in my life.

All through that summer of chemotherapy treatments my parents had wanted to come to Wisconsin to visit me, and I had held them off, not wanting to have them be forced to stay in a hotel while I was in the hospital in Madison, and not feeling very much like having company when I was at home. By the end of the summer, however, I was looking forward to the prospect of the end of my chemotherapy. Additionally, Margaret, who had spent the whole summer doing an excellent job of nursing me, and who had been suffering along with me, needed a break. We invited my parents to visit for a while, and Margaret took off with a friend for a well-deserved weekend in northern Wisconsin.

By that time, I had lost all of my hair, weighed some 20 pounds less than I had in May, and looked so different from my usual self that friends who saw me on the street would frequently walk by without recognizing me. I soon stopped saying hello to them to spare them the embarrassment of having to avoid an awkward silence while they figured out how to not say I looked so bad they hadn't even recognized me. Much later I would learn from friends of my mother that, for the first split second, even she did not realize the stooped figure, slowly walking up the stairs from the family room to greet them when they arrived at our house, was me.

Although my cancer treatment was devastating in its effect on my appearance, the treatment fortunately had the same effect on the cancer cells, and therapy was ultimately successful. At the time I was being treated I had been told I had a 90% chance of complete recovery, and my parents had been told the same information, and yet I don't think any of us really believed I would recover because testicular cancer had long been a highly fatal disease. The cisplatin I was given raised overall survival rates for testicular cancer from 10% to 90% had only been in use in the U.S. for a short period at the time, and most of the general public had not yet heard of it. In the absence of certainty or knowledge, we make up something to replace what we do not know, and we may well fear the worst. I certainly looked like the walking dead by the time my parents saw me.

After a visit that was as good as one could be under the circumstances, Mom and Dad left to go back to Buffalo, and I set about returning to a normal life. During the summer and fall of 1981, the relationship between Margaret and I actually improved. The seriousness of the ill-ness itself, the enforced inactivity on my part, the sacrifices of time and plans, and the increased contact with family and friends had all acted to draw us closer together. However, as my health and energy returned, I began again to spend more and more of my time with the various community, professional, and student groups with which I had previously been heavily involved. Our marital problems returned, and we again began marital counseling.

By the summer of 1982 I was nearly completely recovered from the physical trauma of my cancer. My head, facial, and body hair had grown back, and I looked and felt pretty much like my old self. So, we invited my parents to visit us again, knowing that seeing me in my immediate post-chemotherapy state had been very hard on them. Their reaction when they first saw me was one of unrestrained joy. Mom hugged and kissed me, and Dad ran up the walk to hug me, telling me I looked great, and he had always liked the look of a beard on a man. I could not let his remark go by without giving Dad a more-or-less-good-natured ribbing, since my decision to grow a beard as a graduate student in 1970 had resulted in what was the first serious rift ever between me and my parents. That is if you don't count catching me smoking—or trying to—in high school! After the excitement of the first sight of me had waned, we had a good visit, catching up on all that had happened over the past year.

One afternoon during that visit Dad was smoking his pipe on the back deck, and Mom asked to take a walk around the yard with me. As we walked to the front of the house, she told me how glad she was I was recovering so well. Then she said she realized I had asked in the past about my adoption, and added Dad had "a piece of paper with a name on it." If I ever wanted to know more, I'd have to make a point of asking him about the paper, since she didn't know whether he would tell me otherwise. I realized Mom couldn't even say the words "adoption papers," for those were surely what my father had. On a sunny afternoon sometime in July 1982, my whole perception of myself, my parents, and my world shifted.

I thanked Mom for telling me, and said I'd have to think about what to do next. After my parents went back to Buffalo, I began to try to deal with what Mom had told me. There were many levels on which the information was distressing. In addition to not having been told about my adoption until I was about 12, now I felt I had been lied to for an additional 24 years. Several of my friends have told me they feel I am being harsh on my parents when I use the word "lie" to describe what the friends characterize as "just not telling you everything they knew."

American history since at least the 1970s, includes any number of national events in which the whole truth was with-held from the citizens, or in which affirmative lies were told. Without much difficulty at all I can name events such as Watergate, Iran-Contra, and revelations of the hidden behaviors of nationally known television preachers and politicians. More recently there was the number of U.S. soldiers who were exposed to chemicals in the Gulf Wars. And, of course, we now have the story of a President and candidate for reelection who told multiple lies and was reelected anyway. Our country has also had to face the question of whether the "withholding of information," the practice of not "telling the whole truth" or telling a selected part of the truth, is the same thing as telling a lie. Passively leaving information out and actively telling a lie are at opposite ends of a continuum, but are they all equally wrong? As a country we seem not to have been able to answer this question with consistency and certainty.

However, I can say with certainty for me in 1982, discovering I had not been "told the whole truth" *felt* very much like having been told a lie. There was more information than I had been led to believe. The fact that a potentially life-threatening illness was needed to get my mother to break the silence was not particularly comforting. The problems I had previously experienced with trust came rushing back again. Even though I was assured all of the "withholding" had been done with my best interests in mind, the fact was, again, someone close to me had revealed information I had not previously known existed. How would I ever trust I had really been told the complete story now? Might there be yet more information "out there"? What further problems might have to arise to shake *that* information loose?

In addition to the psychological issue of difficulty with trust, there was also now the distinct possibility that with "a name" I might be able to find my birth family and fill in those missing pages in my medical history. If I were able to find the person(s) who knew my medical history, what would I discover of my social history? How was I conceived? Why had I been surrendered for adoption? Did I have birth brothers or sisters somewhere? Finding answers to these questions was not only an exciting but also a very frightening possibility. I would have to approach my father in order to get the information he had, and that was an extremely distressing thought. Mom had broken a 36-year silence, and I worried about Dad being mad at her when he found out she had told me. I took these questions both to Margaret, and to the therapists who Margaret and I were still seeing for marital counseling.

I will never know exactly what part my mother's disclosure played in the course of our marriage, but finding out my parents had withheld major information from me for some thirty-plus years couldn't help but have affected my ability to trust other closely related people. In early January 1983, after more than nine years of marriage, and just six months after Mom had told me about Dad having my adoption papers and my birth mother's name, Margaret and I separated. Although blaming the separation entirely on issues surrounding my adoption would be both unfair and untrue, to say my feelings about being adopted had no effect on my marriage would be equally unfair and untrue. After the separation, I continued to get individual therapy, and a dominant issue in my therapy was what to do about the information my mother had given me.

After a spring filled with sometimes painful therapeutic work, I decided I had to know my missing medical history, which had been made important to me during my cancer experience. Perhaps more importantly though, as I looked at whether I wanted to make my marriage work, I also realized that to feel complete I also needed to know my missing social and psychological history. My ability to trust others, especially those close to me, was impaired, but in addition, my basic self-concept was also flawed. Therapy helped me see I had all sorts of illogical, but very real fears about my basic worth as a human being. Why would a mother "give away" her baby? What was wrong with me that she didn't want to keep me? If there was nothing wrong with *me*, then what was wrong with *her* that she would give up her baby? After all, what more important, even sacred, connection was there than love between a mother and her child? While my attention at that time was focused on my birth mother, many years later I realized that I also had many similar questions about my birth father. We will return to that issue later.

I could tell myself intellectually that my birthmother may not have "given me away" *voluntarily* at all. I could also say to myself that the reason she surrendered me probably had nothing to do with what kind of person I was, nothing to do with what kind of person she was, and everything to do with her life situation. However, at the feeling level, I still viewed myself as defective in some very basic way. Not knowing the full truth allowed my worst fears to run amok. As I worked through my self-concept problem, I slowly came to realize the strength of both my reluctance to hurt my parents by bringing up the subject of my adoption, and of the fears and fantasies I had about the unknown. I came to realize the fears and fantasies were hurting me more than either the hurt I might cause my parents by asking them, or the hurt of finding out the truth of my origin, no matter how bad my truth might turn out to be. I *had* to approach my parents. I *had* to search. I *had* to know. Finding my truth became a matter of finding myself.

On a Sunday night in the late spring of 1983, after I had made my decision to search, I just happened to tune late into a Stevens Point radio call-in show on which the guest was Katrina Maxtone-Graham, the author of *An Adopted Woman*, released mere months earlier, in January 1983.She talked about her search, and what the process had meant to her. Not knowing where she was adopted, I was only half listening to the specific search hints she gave, and more attending to her description of how she felt about her search. I was thinking whatever she was saying about searching specifically would probably not apply to me since I needed to search in New York State. She talked about the Adoptees Liberty Movement Association (ALMA), and then added the fact that the location of the ALMA headquarters in New York City was fortunate for her. Since she was born in New York State, her search also needed to take place there, and the ALMA people had known the New York laws very well.

Suddenly I became quite attentive to the details of what she was saying about her search process, and wished I had listened more carefully from the beginning. I learned that the New York State adoption system was at that time, one of the most closed in the country. Nothing from the original birth certificate, or any other documentation of an adoption, such as the court order, the health or social history of the birth family, was available to adoptees of any age without a court order. Katrina suggested that the best place to start was with one's adoptive parents. If they had any helpful information, which they often did, some of the expensive and time-consuming legal processes could be avoided, and going through the court system might not even be necessary at all. The specific news about the difficulties of searching in New York was discouraging. However, the fact that Katrina had ultimately been able to find the information and the people she had been looking for suggested I had at least some hope of success myself. Even though the specific search information was helpful, hearing Katrina talk about how connected she felt once she found her history was perhaps the most valuable portion of the show for me. I even called in to the show to talk to her myself. I was surprised at the coincidence that she had information on the very state in which I had to search, but didn't give this coincidence much more thought at the time. I was then more concerned about how I was going to approach my parents with what I knew would be a very difficult question for all of us.

My therapy continued, and I began to work out the specific language with which I would ask my parents about the questions I still had about my adoption. I rehearsed strategies with my therapist, trying to anticipate possible responses from my parents, including both what I hoped for and what I dreaded. Planning my reaction to the positive possibilities was rather easy, but I felt I had to be prepared for negative reactions also. What if Dad denied knowing anything more than he had already told me? What if he got angry at Mom for telling me there was more information they hadn't yet told me? What if he told me he knew more but felt I shouldn't be told? What if he said "let the past be the past and forget about it"? What if Dad thought my asking about my adoption meant I did not love him? What if . . . ? The possibilities on the dark side were frightening, but I had to be prepared to make the best of any situation, and I was *not* going to let the possibility of an unpleasant reaction deter me from making the request.

I spent a good deal of time in therapy working out my resentment at being told less than the truth, moving from angrily calling what they had done lying, to understanding the reasons for their behavior and wanting not to hurt them, back to anger, then back to understanding, then to wishing the whole thing would just disappear. I knew, however, that whatever I did, the problem, and the questions, would not disappear. As the spring semester of 1982 drew to a close, I made plans to go to Buffalo. I would first stay with my long-time friends Mike and Karen Indian (G1, G2) to talk to them about my decision, and then go to Grand Island to talk with my parents.

I left Stevens Point just hours after my final grades were turned in, and drove all night to get to Buffalo. Mike is a friend from high school and I had grown even closer to him over the years since graduation. He teaches high school history and psychology, understands much about human behavior, and he knew me well. After I recovered from the drive, we talked into the late hours for a couple of nights about my reasons for wanting to search, how I might go about searching, and how to bring up the subject with my parents. By the third day at their house, I was feeling guilty about the fact that for the very first time since I left home for college, I had come back to Buffalo without telling my parents I was in town. I decided it was time to talk to them, and I was ready.

On Sunday afternoon I called home, and when Mom answered the phone, she asked immediately where I was. I tried to hide the guilt, and responded that I was in town at Mike's, and would be there shortly. By coincidence, Mrs. Werrick, our next-door neighbor from the home where we had lived for many years, was there visiting my parents at the time I called. Due to my father's work, my family had moved around quite a bit in a relatively short time when I was young. Although the school I attended from second grade through 6th grade was the one in which I had started kindergarten, we had moved three different times while I was in kindergarten and first grade. When we finally settled in the house on Claremont Avenue, we lived in a typical neighborhood of working-class baby boom families. There were probably 25 to 30 children living within a block of my house. My brother Dave (five years younger than I) and I were members of a play group of about a dozen children from six families, and three of those families went to the same church my family attended.

Mrs. Werrick was the mother of Kathy and Sue, the "girls next door" for the entire 11 years we lived on Claremont Avenue (F1, F2). They were each one year older than my brother Dave and I. The Werricks attended the same church as our family, and their younger daughter, Kathy, had become very close to my mother over the years. As we grew up, the Werrick girls and the Henderson boys had our share of shifting friendships, fights, and forgiving. In various combinations, often with other kids in the neighborhood, we rode bikes, roller skated, built forts in the basement, the back yard, and nearby fields, cooked meals, played games, war, house, and cowboys and Indians with each other. Thus, we were probably the prototypic next-door neighbors, except it just so happened that both Kathy and Sue were also adopted! Their adoption was a fact I had not thought very much about, and might not have even been told for many years, especially since when we first moved next to them, I did not even know I was adopted myself. Even after I found out about my own adoption, I don't remember talking about the topic much with either Kathy or Sue. Even though both of them had always known about their adoption, we all "knew" discussions of adoption were unwelcome, at least in the Henderson home.

Hearing Mrs. Werrick was visiting my parents at this particular time was quite a shock. I was going to be visiting several friends after my college reunion (the surface reason for my trip east) and had already planned to include a visit to Kathy and her husband in Pennsylvania if at all possible. Some time would pass however, before I would learn that part of the reason my mother told me about "the name" Dad had in the first place, was because Kathy had shared with my Mom the very positive results of her own search and reunion with her birthmother. I talked briefly on the phone with Mrs. Werrick, faintly hoping that somehow, she would still be there when I got home, and that her presence would in some way make my questioning of Dad easier. I packed up my things, left Mike and Karen's and arrived home about an hour after I called.

CHAPTER 3

First Search: To Find My Birth Mother

On the afternoon of Sunday, May 29, 1983, I first learned specific information about my birth parents. When I got home, Mrs. Werrick had already left, and I was on my own with Mom and Dad. Very shortly after we got my luggage into my room and things started to settle down, I told my parents "I have something important to discuss with you. Could we sit in the living room and talk?" They said "certainly." We went to the living room, and I took a deep breath and began the speech I had rehearsed in therapy for months.

"I have been planning the conversation we are about to have for a long time, and I realize this may be difficult for all of us. I only ask that you listen to all of what I have to say first, without asking any questions, and then when I am done you can say whatever you want to and ask me any questions at all." They agreed, and I'm sure they wondered, with that introduction, just what was coming next!

"I love you both, and I always will, no matter what has happened in the past, or might happen in the future. When I was in therapy in the early 1970s, during my internship in Chicago, I discovered being adopted was much more important to me than I ever realized. I'm sure you remember I have asked you several times over the last few years for you to tell me what you knew. And you've been very good about telling me the story of how I came into our family. I love hearing that story, even though it makes me very sad because of how much pain you went through. The problem is what I really have wanted to know all along was what had happened to me before I came to our family." So far so good! My parents were listening carefully, and I was discovering that once I had begun, I had less of a problem saying what I wanted to say than I had feared. Apparently I was sufficiently prepared for what

I was doing. I only hoped I would be able to deal with whatever their response might be when I was finished.

"During my cancer experience I realized how important my medical history is to me." I described the experience of seeing all of the blank pages of medical history being turned by the medical personnel, and told them my illness had brought my adoption issues to the forefront. "Through the therapy Margaret and I have had, I have come to see adoption-related issues as part of what has caused us to have so much trouble in our marriage. In fact, I'm not sure we'll be able to work things out. My adoption has also caused me to have a lot of problems in how I feel about myself."

Now I had to bring up the most sensitive issue of all: Mom's breaking of the news to me about the existence of, and the information on, my adoption papers. "After talking to Mom last summer, I now realize there is still more information you have. I think it is probably my adoption papers, and I need to find out everything that you know. I know you were doing what you thought was best for me by not telling me about my adoption until I was older, but my life started out with some pretty important secrets. Because of that secrecy, I have always had a hard time learning to trust people, and learning last summer about the existence of still more things I didn't know has been eating away at me. I have been working in therapy a long time just to even have this talk with you."

At this point I was so scared I'm sure my voice was shaking. A long-standing rule in my family had been not to talk about unpleasant things, and I had just broken that rule. But I had come this far, and I had to complete what I had started. "If I am going to be mentally healthy again, there must be no more secrets." At that point I had finally gotten through my long-rehearsed presentation. I told them I was through saying what I had wanted to say.

I held my breath, proud of myself for having gotten that far, but not knowing what their reaction would be. I knew I would have to control myself for just a little longer, in the event Dad, who was really the person I was speaking to, attempted to evade my questions, to deny having any more knowledge, or to otherwise not respond to my needs. His response was short, simple, and *very* sweet:

"What can we do to help?"

My immediate thought when Dad responded as he did was total relief. I didn't have to deal with him having any of the responses I had feared. I hoped that because of my therapy I was ready to respond to any of Dad's potential negative reactions in a healthy manner, but I didn't need to. I realized I must have been able to convince him that my questions weren't about whether there was enough love in our family, or about whether they had been good parents to me. While I was having these thoughts, my own answer to his question was fairly immediate.

"You can tell me everything you know, now, so I can go on with my life without the fear of any more secrets coming out in the future."

Immediately Dad said "All right. Your birth mother's name was Belschner, she was 20, Catholic, and a resident of Lockport. She worked as a domestic and was of German background. All I know about your birth father is his age was 18." Mom spoke up for what I think was the first time since I had begun the conversation, saying "And they were both in good health."

As Dad began to tell me what he knew, I was surprised, not just that he was telling me, but at the wealth of what he knew. I couldn't believe he had all of these facts on the tip of his tongue, and briefly wondered how long they had been sitting there, unspoken. I had really expected at best he would say something like "OK, tomorrow morning we'll go to the safe deposit box and get out what we have." The fact that the information was right there and tumbling out at me made me wonder whether Dad hadn't somehow known my questions were coming, and prepared for them. Had Mom shared with him our conversation in Stevens Point while he smoked his pipe? I wondered how difficult having had to keep the information secret for all of these years had been for him.

As he was speaking, I realized I wanted a pencil and paper, and fast, to write all of what I was hearing down. Then, I thought "No, I won't forget what he's telling me. I've been waiting to hear this information for too long." I also think I was afraid to interrupt him, perhaps for fear that any interruption would give Dad time to realize just what he was saying, and to change his mind and stop talking! Or maybe this was a dream, and I would wake up!

By the time Dad had finished speaking tears had run down my cheek and disappeared into my beard. I stood up, walked across the living room and gave both Dad and Mom a long heartfelt hug, thanked them, and told them I loved them. I then realized I wanted to let them know in a very specific and concrete way that our relationship had not changed because of what had just happened. I decided the best thing to do was to behave in exactly the same way as I always did when I came back for a visit. I smiled through the tears, and said "And now how'd you like to go downstairs for a drink? This question, usually asked by my father, and the drink(s) that followed the question, had always been part of the ritual family greeting process once my bags were in my room when I came for a visit. Even after I had stopped drinking alcohol, we'd still go downstairs to the family room, where Dad always had a fire built and ready to light, to have drinks and a talk. Only my drink had changed to a Coke. So, we went downstairs once again. Even though I had immediately told myself I would not forget what Dad had told me, the experience of finding out so much so quickly was quite a surprise. When we went downstairs for our ritual drink Mom and Dad and I talked a lot about our family and my childhood. I was so grateful their response had been so supportive that I actually felt closer to them that evening than I had in a long time. The rest of the evening was so laden with positive emotion, that by the time I went to bed that night I discovered I had forgotten what my birth mother's last name was!

For the next couple of days, I tried to continue to be, if anything, more attentive and at home more often than usual, to assure my parents there was not going to be any major change in our relationship. I continued to be thrilled to get the information about my birth family, and to be even more thrilled the process had gone so smoothly. Although I was not yet totally sure, I was pretty certain of what I would want to do next. I still had serious questions about my medical history, and knew I had an even more important need to know about why I had been given up, who my birth parents were, what they were doing now, did I have any brothers, sisters, cousins, and much, much more. That Sunday afternoon I had taken the necessary first step, and asked the difficult questions. My father had answered with my birth mother's name, and quite a bit of information about her. Unfortunately, I had forgotten her name, and relaxing around the house for a few days did not bring my memory back. I made the decision to search, but first needed to get (again) my birth mother's name.

Four days later, Thursday, June 2nd I took the next step which was to go to the Erie County Office Building and inquire about obtaining my records. I knew getting much, if anything from the records on file with the county would not be possible, but I needed a place to begin. Perhaps my naiveté about searching explains what happened next, but I thought, "why not just plain ask them what they have on file?" So I did. After finding the correct office, I identified myself to the secretary there, and told her that even though I knew the records were closed, I was going to find my birth family. I asked if she could tell me what records were there, and how I would go about getting access to them. She informed me I would need a court order to get access to my adoption order, and that all I would find out from the order would be my birth mother's name. She told me the process of getting a court order was by no means guaranteed, and since hiring a lawyer to request the order would also cost me a minimum of $300, she suggested that if I had any other source of access to the information, I should use that source. She essentially advised against using the legal system, especially when there was no guarantee I would get the court order, or that the order would produce any useful information. I was surprised she didn't seem to be aware, as I was by then, that the adoptee's birth name, or the name of the birth mother, were both pieces of information that were not only essential for searching but also the hardest to obtain.

I then asked her to give me whatever she could, and she asked me for my year of adoption. Not thinking, or perhaps not hearing, clearly, I instead gave her my year of birth: 1946. Returning with a piece of paper, she handed the paper to me, and I saw the name "Liebowitz, 10-23-46." Not quite sure of what I was seeing, afraid to believe that the name my father had given me was wrong, and fearful of not getting any more answers, I told the woman my birthday was not the 23rd but the 14th of October. She again asked for my last name, and said she wanted the year my adoption was finalized, not the year of my birth. She left again and returned, handing the paper to me with a laugh, saying she should have noticed the Henderson she had looked up before was a girl!

As she handed me the paper, she smiled, winked, and wished me good luck in my search. As I walked away, I noticed that on the back of the paper she had written "Belschner June 19, 1947." Immediately I recognized the name my father had given me four days earlier. Although this was the first time someone I didn't know had gone out of the way to help me in my search, I was to find there would be many more of these instances in the future.

Before going back to Grand Island for the evening though, I took advantage of being three blocks from the main Erie County Public Library. The library was a relatively new one, replacing an old turn-of-the-century brick building I remembered going to in high school to work on term papers. Although I had used the new library for term papers several times when I was home from college on vacation, I was not entirely familiar with it. I found an employee who helped me to find the city directories, and as we talked, we shared memories of the old Grovesnor Library where she had worked before the present building was built. I was comforted to find someone who shared a piece of common past with me as I began to look for my own unique past. Our shared memories of the old building reminded me that even though I had not lived in Buffalo for many years, I still had strong psychological roots there.

Our conversation over, I returned to my search and spent three hours going through the Lockport City Directories for the years 1937 to 1956. I found no one with the last name of Belschner, as it was spelled on the paper I had been given at the courthouse. There was an Alice M. Belchner (spelled without the letter s), who lived at two different addresses in Lockport from 1939 to 1955. She was employed for the entire time as a stenographer for the Niagara County Department of Social Services, and had a "Glorian Belchner," identified as a student, living with her in 1947. At the time I found the Belchner name I did not know her first name. I thought Glorian could be a female name. Might Glorian be my birth mother? I copied down the addresses of the Lockport Catholic High and Elementary schools, and decided that on Friday I would go to Lockport (on my way to Rochester for a lunch with Linda Horvatis Luxenberg, an old friend who I had known since we were both in 1st grade) to begin my search in earnest.

Of course, I had realized as soon as I had forgotten my birth mother's last name that I could always ask my father to tell me her name again. I chose not to ask because I didn't want to appear too interested in the information, or to perhaps create a situation that was less enjoyable than the first time. Being given her last name by the court clerk was an unexpected blessing, allowing me to begin looking for her that day. Relieved, I thought I would not have to approach my father again. That is until I ran into the lack of any Belschners in Lockport, and the presence of a family named Belchner. I decided to answer the questions about my birth mother's first name and the spelling of her last name. That evening, I asked Dad if I could see my actual adoption papers.

Dad walked back to their bedroom, to his dresser, and took out the old leather folder of important family papers. When he reached into one of the upper drawers, I knew what he was going to get because I remembered sneaking looks into that drawer as a small child. From next to his naturalization papers, he took out several pink sheets of onionskin paper with carbon-copy typewritten information on them, and began to read aloud to me from the beginning of the first page. Impatient to get past the legal language, I moved around next to him and scanned the page looking at each filled in blank line for the name "Glorian Belchner" only to find the name "Pearl Belschner." For each question answered, another seemed to rise in its place. Why was there a difference in the spelling of the last names? If Pearl Belschner (D1–D4) was my birth mother, who were Glorian and Alice Belchner? I realized I would need to go to Lockport to get the next answers, and that finding those answers would probably also lead to another set of questions.

On the topic of when and how I found out I was adopted, there is an interesting possibility here. When Dad got out the leather folder, I clearly remembered, when I was alone in the house as a child, sneaking into my parents' room and looking at all sorts of things there. Based on these forays into what I knew was forbidden territory, I knew my father's naturalization papers were in the folder, as well as their marriage license and some other legal papers. I have to acknowledge the distinct possibility that I had also seen my *adoption* papers in the same folder when I was a child, but didn't remember, or understand, what was in them. While I have no conscious memory of knowing I was adopted before my parents told me at about 12 years of age, I possibly "knew" on some level much earlier, especially if I had found those papers during my childhood snooping. At any rate, adoptive parents (perhaps all parents!) should realize that nothing that is kept in the home can remain a secret, since children in general, and perhaps adopted children in particular, seem to derive great pleasure from going through their parents' "private" things! The joy of searching through "private" things is corroborated by many adoptees with whom I have spoken.

The next morning, Friday, June 3rd, I left my parents' home on Grand Island to attend my 15th college reunion. I got to Lockport (about 25 miles east of Buffalo) about 8:45 am, knowing I had to leave by about 10:30 to get to Rochester for lunch with Linda. My first stop, at DeSales High School was an attempt to get a copy of the yearbook for the year I guessed my birth mother might have graduated from high school. Perhaps because DeSales was my first stop and I was nervous, or perhaps because I was intimidated by the priest who walked out of the principal's office and watched me intently, things did not go well. The secretaries seemed suspicious of me, and were not very talkative, although after they told me the school did not graduate a class until 1950, one secretary volunteered that she had lived in the city all of her life and never knew a family by the name of either Belchner or Belschner.

Although the difference in the spelling of names had puzzled me, I had more or less assumed there was a typographic error somewhere, and that the people I was seeking were the Alice Belchner family, whose home from 1941 to 1955 was on Harvey Avenue, which was my next stop. I had determined from analyzing city directories that across the street, there still lived the retired son of the family who had owned that home during all the years the Belchners had lived on Harvey. I thought I could probably get information from him about the Belchner family.

I was also assuming Pearl and Glorian were siblings, and I had been giving both spellings of the last name each time I did a records inquiry. I felt I was on the right track. I experienced a strange sensation walking down the street where I assumed my birth mother had grown up, and where I assumed she had lived while carrying me. As I walked down Harvey Street, the houses, the trees, even the cement blocks in the sidewalks all seemed to be especially alive. I found myself wondering again and again "Did *she* see this?" Did *she* play here?" No one answered my knock on the door of the neighbors, and just for curiosity I knocked at the old Belchner home also, with the same results. Upon seeing the neighborhood, I discovered a public elementary school was located about four houses away on an intersecting street, so I made an inquiry there. The secretary and principal both talked to me, but they had no recollection of any children by either family name in their school. They suggested I go to the school administration building to ask the "census office" for records which would tell me if there had ever been children named Belschner or Belchner enrolled anywhere in the system.

I was becoming more confident of my story and more relaxed by now, having decided that "doing a genealogy and looking for members of a branch of my family I just discovered existed" sounded perfectly reasonable. After all, I was in a very real sense doing exactly that. At the school administration office, my third office stop of that morning, I was told Glorian was male and had graduated from Lockport High in 1944. My hypothesis about Pearl and Glorian being siblings changed when the census office said they had no record of any other children in the family. I then thought Pearl was perhaps a cousin or other relative from somewhere else who had come to Lockport to live while she had her baby. Checking the other spelling of the name, I discovered there were never any children by the name of "Belschner" enrolled in the Lockport public school system. Finding no Belschners was disheartening. I began to think that perhaps the Belschner spelling was a typographical error, though typos would seem to be unlikely to occur in something as important as adoption papers. The time was then about 10:15, and I felt I had only 15 more minutes before I should leave for Rochester, so my last stop was going to be the county social services office, where

I hoped to find someone who had worked with Alice during her 1939 to 1955 employment there.

Another cooperative secretary there told me she didn't recognize the name Alice Belchner, and that there were only two employees, both women, with seniority dating back to 1955, who were still working there. Since they were both off of work that day the secretary tried to call them on the phone, and got no answer at either home. She then ran both versions of the last name through the county welfare computer just in case any family members had applied for public assistance. Thankfully perhaps, no matches appeared.

I told her I had to leave (since the time was now 10:30) and asked if she thought the ladies would write to me if they remembered anything about Alice. She said she thought so, and when I gave her my address it just so happened that her nephew had graduated from the University of Wisconsin–Stevens Point in 1974! (I began teaching there in 1976.) After we made the expectable comments about the world being a small place, and exchanged some small talk about the University and the City of Stevens Point, she further suggested that, since I was from so far away, I might want to stop at the county civil service office to look at Alice's personnel records, which might have a forwarding address for her last check if she were no longer employed by the county. Since I was already late, I barely had time to consider what a coincidence we had just experienced, finding that someone in Lockport, New York would have a nephew who just happened to have graduated from a small state university campus five states and nearly 1000 miles away in Wisconsin, where I just happened to teach.

Although the civil service office was on the other side of town, and in the wrong direction to get me off to Rochester on time, I decided to go there anyway, since working in person has always been easier for me than working by phone or letter, and I hoped I could make up the lost time on the road to Rochester. When I arrived, the secretary there told me I'd have to make out a formal "Request to View Public Records," which I completed, listing "Alice M. Belchner (Belschner)" and the Harvey Avenue address. I explained there was "a difference in spelling of the name in different family documents" and she said she would check both versions. Adding the other spelling, by now, seemed to be a futile exercise. I had gotten no positive responses to the "Belschner" spelling at any of the previous four offices I had checked, and I almost didn't bother to write the name in. Perhaps there had indeed been a "typo" and although that still seemed unusual, the existence of a typo was fast becoming my working hypothesis.

The records request had to be approved by a supervisor who was on the phone, so the clerk and I made small talk for a while, and I told her that I understood the necessity for safeguarding private records since for three years I had been the secretary of a licensing board back in Wisconsin. We passed the time by talking a little bit about the challenges of working with the public. When her supervisor got off of the phone and signed off on the form, she left to check the records. Shortly she brought back Alice Belshner's work card, and I found little new information there.

As I packed up my papers and asked her for directions out of town toward Rochester, the clerk said "by the way, I did get a match on the other spelling, but the matching person was a much older man, who had worked as a night watchman in Wilson much more recently. You wouldn't be interested in that one would you?" I was surprised, since this was the first positive response to the Belschner spelling, so I said, "Sure, why not." She short-cut the paperwork time by having me add "Clarence Belschner" in the blank line below "Alice M. Belchner" on the original form, saying "no one will ever know his name wasn't there originally."

At about 10:50 am on Friday, June 3rd, I viewed the work card of a 79 year old man from Wilson, New York, a small town, 10 miles west of Lockport and 25 miles north east of Buffalo, on the shore of Lake Ontario. He had worked there for Niagara County as a part-time night watchman from 1969 to 1979, starting at age 64 and retiring at 75. I scarcely had time to realize what I had found since I was in such a hurry to get on with the rest of my vacation. I jammed the paper into my folder, thanked the clerk for her help, and raced off to Rochester.

For the next 11 days I was immersed in vacation activities, many of them associated with my college reunion. Fifteen years earlier, in 1968, I had graduated from St. Lawrence University in Canton, New York. So much had happened since then. I had gotten my doctorate in psychology and was now employed. I had been married, and was now separated. I had had cancer, and was now apparently well on the road to recovery. I had been a problem drinker, and was now sober. Yet, despite all of these external changes, somehow, as I drove north along Interstate 81, I felt I had changed very little on the inside. The return to the St. Lawrence campus was enjoyable, and though the fraternity house where I lived had been razed to build a swimming pool, and the

Psychology Building where I had studied had been replaced by a new dining hall, the stately beauty of the old campus was comforting with everything else that had been, and was still going on, in my life.

After the reunion I drove through Eastern New York and several adjoining states, visiting with friends from elementary school through college, as well as with relatives. I thought a lot, especially while driving, but did little, about my search, other than to tell several of the friends I stayed with about my experiences to that point. As I drove around the east coast, I did wonder whether Clarence Belschner could be my grandfather. I had time to think about people's ages. I added my age and my birth mother's age and realized Clarence *could* be Pearl's father, but the importance of this idea still didn't sink in. I guess I just needed some time to digest all of the new information I had recently learned.

CHAPTER 4

First Contact

About a week and a half after the reunion I found myself walking on 42nd Street in New York City on the afternoon of a hot sticky Monday, June 14. I had planned to leave for my next stop, near Philadelphia, on Tuesday. Drenched in sweat, I debated two choices. I could take the train back to Chatham, New Jersey, where I was staying with Mike and Carolyn Solly. Mike is a high school friend, and they had a pool, so I could spend the rest of the day in cool relaxation. Or I could try to look up the Adoptees Liberty Movement Association (ALMA). I had heard Katrina Maxtone-Graham talk about ALMA on the radio program about adoption search in Stevens Point just before leaving home. I was actually doing my search partly as a result of listening to Katrina.

I remembered the ALMA headquarters was located in New York City, so I stopped at a phone booth and looked up "adoption" in both the yellow and white pages. A phone call to something called the "ALMA International Reunion Registry" went unanswered. As I thought about the word, the idea of a "reunion" somehow didn't seem to be right. I felt I had never really known my birth mother in the first place, so why would I use the term "reunion"? Perhaps I had the wrong organization. I nearly dismissed the whole idea in favor of a swim, but decided to stop at the Public Library and check the *Directory of Associations*. There I found a description of ALMA, and the same phone number which I had earlier tried unsuccessfully.

I found a phone booth on the ground floor of the library and dialed the number once more. The phone rang for a long time and again was not answered. That seemed unusual for a national organization, but at mid-afternoon on a hot summer's day, I thought perhaps the office had closed. The address was on 7th, which I thought was down at the south end of Manhattan, perhaps near the World Trade Center. To get back to New Jersey, I would have to take a subway and transfer to the Port Authority Trans-Hudson train not far from there, and so I thought perhaps, if the walk wasn't too long, I'd try to find the office. If I did, I might leave my name and address under the door, asking them to send me literature.

Before leaving the library to get on the subway I thought I'd use the rest room in the library, public rest rooms being in short supply in Manhattan. Fifteen minutes later I *finally* found my goal, back up on the 3rd floor next to the reference room in which I had started. By the time I was back on the ground floor near the phone booths, I thought for some reason perhaps someone had returned to the ALMA office, so I dropped another dime in the phone (ten cent phone calls were then one of the few bargains left in New York City) and tried again.

I got an answer on about the fourth ring. Had I dialed the wrong number earlier? The woman who answered told me she was just an answering service, and therefore she couldn't help me much, either with directions to the office or with information about the organization. The woman did say that she thought someone was currently in the office. If I called right back, rang once, hung up, then right away called again, she would let the phone call go through to the office. I should then let the phone ring until the person who was in the office answered.

I thanked the woman, hung up, looked for another dime, and discovered I had only nine cents in change. The security guard at the library door was most unhelpful, as were the several passersby, who undoubtedly thought I was panhandling or running some sort of a money-changing scam. I finally found a cleaning woman who was willing to take my dollar for 75 cents worth of change, and I placed the one-ring call, hoping the five-minute delay in finding a dime would not confuse the woman at the answering service. She was not confused, and, and upon redialing the ALMA number the phone rang a few times and I got an answer.

Jean Andersen, the woman who answered, was cordial and gave me some information about the group, but said she couldn't talk for long since she had a newsletter deadline to meet that afternoon. I asked whether I could come to the office to get some printed matter or whether mailing the material to me would be easier for her. She said mailing *would* be easiest for her since she would be in and out of the office for the rest of the afternoon. I gave her my name and address, and almost said to go ahead and mail the information to me in Stevens Point. The pool at my friends' house in New Jersey was seeming more and more appealing as the temperature in the phone booth rose.

Instead, just for curiosity, I asked her what cross-streets were closest to the office, again thinking I might walk over before taking the train across to New Jersey. I expected her to say between 1st and 2nd Ave., or between 5th and 6th Ave., and was surprised when she said "between 54th and 55th!" The office was not on 7th *Street*, which was at the other end of the island, but on 7th *Avenue*, and thus only ten blocks away from where I was slowly cooking in the phone booth.

I told her I would walk up to the office, since suddenly the day didn't seem so hot after all! Jean said if she went out of the office, she would put my name and address on an information packet which she would tape to the door. If I hadn't picked the envelope up by the end of the day, she would then mail it to me at home. As I walked up 7th Avenue toward the ALMA office, I could feel excitement building within me. Now I was getting somewhere. Now I was going to hook up with an organization composed of people like me who were looking for their birth families. I hoped to talk to Jean briefly at least, and perhaps even join the organization right on the spot if joining sounded like something that would help rather than waiting to get back to Stevens Point and then sending a check. The ALMA office was on the top floor of the building, and the elevator, which itself was an oven, only went to the floor below, so as I walked up the last flight of stairs I didn't know if I was sweating more from the heat or from the excitement.

I was deeply disappointed to see a thick envelope with my name taped to the door, since I understood that to mean Jean had gone out. I looked through the information briefly in the heat, and decided because there was quite a bit to read, I'd be more comfortable going back to Mike and Carolyn's in New Jersey and reading the material by the pool. I had closed up and stuck the envelope in my back pocket and had turned to leave, when a little internal voice told me to try knocking on the door anyway. Just maybe there was someone in there. It just so happened that, to my surprise (and relief—the office was air conditioned!) the door was opened by Jean, the woman I had talked to earlier. She had gone out, left the envelope on the door, and returned, leaving the envelope there, since she expected to be going out again soon.

As Jean and I talked, I discovered ALMA had a public telephone call-in night for search help every Thursday evening, just three days away. They would have their last meeting (open to members only) before the summer season on that coming Saturday, June 18. Jean told me if I joined the group, I could attend the meeting and meet others still involved in their searches as well as some of those who had "found." I decided I would cancel out on a student research meeting in Wisconsin for Monday June 20, to stay in Chatham for at least three more days so I could take part in the Thursday night phone consultation. Perhaps I would then also stay on for the Saturday meeting. I decided to join ALMA right then, signed over a Travelers Check for a one-year membership, and hurried back to New Jersey to try to cool off, to talk my friends into a few days more hospitality, and to prepare for the next step in my search.

Perhaps I shouldn't have been surprised when, in the ALMA office, Jean told me the Saturday meeting was in a place called the Williams Club. After all, coincidences were beginning to happen more frequently now, and returning to the Williams club was just one more small one. I believed it was more a simple convenience than anything particularly profound. Four days earlier I would have had to ask for detailed directions to the Club, never having been there, or even heard of it, before, but three days earlier, on Friday, I had met my friend Mike there for lunch! At least if I decided to stay for the meeting I'd know where I was going.

Thursday night's phone call from Chatham to the ALMA Registrar in New York was helpful, both in terms of specific information, and moral support. The registrar, Carl Zimmer, had found his own birth family, and was really the first adoptee I had spoken with (not counting my brief radio call to Katrina in Stevens Point) in any detail who had done so. He gave me much information on where to look and how to go about looking that I expected would be very useful. When I told him about the name match with Clarence Belschner, he was not particularly encouraging, suggesting that I write Mr. Belschner a letter telling him I was doing a "*Roots*-type genealogy search" and asking if Pearl Belschner was related to him. Carl suggested enclosing a self-addressed envelope, and added "most of the time people use the stamp to send in their electric bill and you never hear from them, but it's worth the try anyway."

After an hour on the phone with Carl, I thought I'd check "information" in Wilson to see if there was a phone still listed in his name, since the number from the Niagara County Civil Service Office in Lockport was current only as of 1979. To my great surprise and excitement, I found a phone number still listed, and at the same address he had in

1979! Could Clarence Belschner, my grandfather (if that's who he was), still be alive? I decided to stay in the New York area for the Saturday ALMA Meeting, planning to leave Chatham that morning, drive into the city, attend the meeting, and then go on to visit other friends in the Philadelphia area that night.

Saturday, June 18 started on an ominous note, one I certainly hoped was not prophetic. When I got into my Jeep to drive to New York, nearly late already from saying good bye to yet another set of friends, the battery was dead. I had left the glove compartment open the night before when I was getting out a map. A quick jump start, from Mike's rather more impressive BMW, and I was on my way to a day I could not possibly have anticipated a mere three weeks earlier. As I parked at the Port Authority Terminal and walked across town to the Williams Club, I was a jumble of emotions and thoughts. I knew no one who would be there, since both of the people in ALMA who I had so far talked to (Jean and Carl) would not be at the meeting. Florence Fisher, the founder and President of ALMA, about whom I had at least read, would not be there either. All sorts of possibilities both exciting and scary, and none of them very realistic, passed through my thoughts. What would the experience be like? Who would I meet? Might my birth mother or birth father even be searching for me? Would, perhaps, one or both of them be there?

The meeting room upstairs in the Williams Club was large, with perhaps 100 chairs set up in rows. As I came into the room, I saw many places open to sit, and I chose, again for no particular conscious reason, to sit on the left side of the room, taking one of several empty seats. I listened to the conversations taking place around me, and realized that the two women seated immediately behind me were also at their first meeting, and were just introducing themselves. I turned around and joined in their introductions. For the first time ever, I found myself talking to a birth mother about what the experience was like for her to have given up a child for adoption. Her name was Katherine Edwards, and she was searching for a daughter she had given up some 20 years earlier. I was moved to hear about the adoption process as seen through the eyes of a birth mother. Even though she was much younger than my own birth mother would be, she still had gone through the experience. I was deeply touched to hear she wanted to search, and she still wanted contact long after what was clearly a painful experience. Before the meeting even started, I already felt coming had clearly been worth my while. Through ALMA, in just three days, I had talked with an adoptee who had searched and found, and a searching birth mother, both brand new experiences. I could already tell the day was going to be very good.

Then, as we talked, I discovered an amazing fact. I learned that here, at a meeting in New York City, some 1300 miles from my home in Stevens Point, I had accidentally seated myself right in front of Katherine, a birth mother who had grown up in Wisconsin Rapids, a town also some 1300 miles from New York City, but only 21 miles from my Wisconsin home! The "coincidences" were beginning to pile one on top of another. Katherine had gone to live in a maternity home in Eau Claire, Wisconsin, to give birth. She then moved away from Wisconsin some years later, and now lived in New York City. The rather profound experience of "accidentally" meeting this particular birth mother was only one more indication of another, and different, aspect of my search. An "accident" had occurred, an accident which would eventually interweave my search with other lives, other searchers, and other stories. My personal and professional lives would eventually intermingle with each other in a way that would leave the line between work and the other parts of my life fuzzy at best. Not realizing any of these future developments at that time however, I took down Katherine's phone number and address, as well as some information about the birth daughter she was seeking, and promised to get back to her when I returned to Wisconsin.

The ALMA meeting that began shortly was specifically a "Search Workshop." The schedule included individual consultations with ALMA volunteers, group discussion sessions comprised of people involved in similar kinds of searches, and a closing panel discussion in which several members were asked to share their perceptions with the whole group. The small-group discussion was exciting, hearing others who were involved in the same task as I was, and there was much mutual help given. Emotional support and emotional times were shared. My individual consultation happened to be with Laurel Cohen, the ALMA volunteer who was chairing the meeting in the absence of the organization's founder, Florence Fischer. When I told Laurel what I had found so far in my search, she shocked me by saying "Doug—you're in! What are you waiting for? Get on the phone and call Clarence Belschner and find out if he's your grandfather—then call your birth mother!" Hearing the next step described in such simple and concrete terms was a shock, as if that was really all I had to do, and as if my reunion was really going to be that easy!

I asked Laurel "What should I use as a cover story with Clarence? What if Pearl herself answers the phone?" Laurel gave me some good specific suggestions. "With Clarence or whoever answers the phone, tell them you are looking for an old friend of your mothers. Ask if there is a Pearl Belschner who is a member of their family. If the answer is yes, find out how you can reach her." This advice seemed to fit in with my desire not to lie (or at least not to tell outrageous lies!) or to pretend I was someone I was not. I told Laurel "I definitely don't want to stir up problems by revealing too much about who I am too soon, or at all if the situation isn't right." Laurel further suggested I should "Be especially careful not to say anything that might reveal any secrets. Don't tell too much to anyone about who you are, or when, or how, you are connected with Pearl. Since the only person who you can be absolutely sure knew about you was Pearl, you should reveal yourself only to her, and only after determining that she has sufficient privacy, and time, to be able to talk to you. Ask her whether this is a good time to talk, and if it's not, ask when you can call back that would be better." I thanked Laurel for this advice, and began to think seriously about where and when I could call Clarence Belschner.

When the time came for the last portion of the meeting—the panel discussion—Laurel asked me, perhaps since I was a psychologist, to participate and share my feelings and experiences with the group, which I felt both happy and honored to do. That brief presentation, the first of what was to become many I would give about adoption, was another indicator that a major new area of both my personal and professional life was opening up.

After the meeting ended there was an excited buzz of new friends exchanging addresses, wishes of good luck, and hugs. Laurel asked me what I was going to do now. "I guess I'll get a roll of dimes and find a quiet air-conditioned pay phone and make some important phone calls." Laurel said I shouldn't make these calls from a pay phone and asked if I didn't have some place where I could make the calls in a more comfortable environment. When I explained I was on route to the Philadelphia area, she offered her home phone, in Summit, New Jersey (which just happened to be immediately next to Chatham where I had just been for a week!), and was not far out of the way from my intended route to Pennsylvania.

I followed her home, and at about 5:30 the afternoon of Saturday June 18, 1983, made my first call, to Clarence Belschner in Wilson, New York. An elderly, and friendly sounding, woman answered the phone (was this my grandmother?) and when I asked for Clarence, she said, "just a minute" and put him on!

"Hello, Mr. Belschner. My name is Doug Henderson, and I live in Wisconsin at the moment. Long ago in school my mother was friends with a Pearl Belschner and Mom has lost her address. I'm visiting in the area, and am wondering if you are related to Pearl?"

When he replied, "Well yes, Pearl would be my oldest daughter." I nearly jumped out of my skin! Clarence Belschner *was* my grandfather, and yet I dared not identify myself to him for fear of causing trouble—something I did *not* want to do.

"Do you think you could give me her address?"

He said, apparently referring to his wife, "She takes care of that kind of thing." Then, his voice slightly fainter, "Get Pearl's address for this fella." Clarence and I made small talk about the weather while he waited for "her"—the woman who had answered the phone—his wife—my grandmother!—to get the address. I could hardly believe what was happening.

She came back on the line and after asking somewhat suspiciously "what was your story again?" Satisfied, she told me Pearl had married, her husband worked for a cable television company and they moved around a lot due to his work. She gave me a Florida address and I thanked her, telling her my mother would be very happy, and we were about to hang up. Suddenly I realized I didn't know Pearl's married name, and I would likely have a hard time finding a phone number for her that afternoon with only an address. I was ready to complete my search *now*, and couldn't bear the thought of having to wait any longer! I asked if perhaps there was a phone number I might have, and after a minute more of looking, she gave me a phone number. I thanked her and hung up—high as a kite—one call down, so far so good!

I took a deep breath, hugged Laurel, tried to calm both my voice and my pounding heart, and dialed the number. BUSY!!! Busy again five minutes later. At least someone was home, but oh, the frustration. We went downstairs, for me to try to eat. Over pizza, we wondered whether the line was busy because Pearl's mother, who had seemed somewhat suspicious of me, was calling her to warn her about my call. Laurel's children came home, and they talked excitedly about a movie they were going to see later that night. The normal functions of life go on I guess, at least for Laurel and her kids. The movie they were going to see was "E. T.," which was odd, considering I sometimes felt a certain degree of kinship with E. T. I too felt as though I came from outer space. You might say I was, even at that moment, trying to "phone home" myself!

I tried to call once more from the kitchen.

This time the phone rang.

A woman answered.

"Could I speak to Pearl please"

"Yes, This is Pearl"

"My name is Doug Henderson, and I live in Wisconsin now, and I'd like to talk to you in confidence about a very important matter. Is this a good time to talk?"

"No, it's not"

"Well could you give me a time when I could call back, and we'd have some time to talk in private"

"Does this have something to do with sales"

"No this has nothing to do with sales, it has to do with something that happened a long time ago when you were very young"

"I think I know what it is, and I think I know who you are."

My heart was racing with excitement, and I think I just said "Well hello!"

"How did you find me?"

"My adoptive parents recently told me they had your name, and I just talked to your parents in Wilson. Your mother gave me this number."

"You didn't tell them who you were, did you?"

"No, I didn't because I don't want to cause you any problems."

"Thank goodness you didn't tell them. You see my father doesn't know about you. And neither does my son."

"Well, I would really like to talk to you more, but you said this was a bad time to talk. Is there another time or another number where I could call you?"

"What did you say your name was again?"

"Doug Henderson"

"Oh. That's not the family name I thought you had. And where are you from?"

"Right now, I live in Wisconsin, but I grew up in the Town of Tonawanda, and my parents now live on Grand Island."

"That's not where I thought you grew up, either. What do you do now?"

"I'm a professor at the University of Wisconsin in Stevens Point, Wisconsin"

"My goodness, a professor! You know I only went through the eighth grade. School was just hard for me. Your parents must be very smart."

"My mother is very well-read and encouraged me to work hard in school."

Pearl had originally said I had called at a bad time to talk, and the first time I asked about calling back she ignored the question, obviously wanting to go on talking. I was on a cloud being able to talk to her, but I didn't want to cause any problems, so I asked again. "But I don't want to disrupt anything right now. Is there another time I can call back that would be better for you to talk?" She ignored the question again.

"Did you have a happy childhood?"

I answered her question, and she asked many more questions about what my life had been like for the past 37 years. I asked her about what she did, where she had lived, and said I had some health questions I needed to ask her. I asked about any diseases in the family, and told her about my cancer, which concerned her greatly. One of the most touching moments of the conversation for me was her statement about how she never had forgotten me.

"I don't believe a week has gone by when I haven't thought of you. In fact I thought about you yesterday. I wondered whether you had lived a good life, and if you were even alive now."

We shared information about our families, about health, education—specifics of which I now can't remember except for the excitement of listening to her voice, learning about who she was, and more about who I was. I told her I would send pictures of myself when I got home, and asked her if she would send me some of her. She replied "Well I don't have any with me here in Florida, and I don't even have many at home, but I'll see what I can find. I've put on some weight lately, and I don't like cameras very much."

Although I now had loads of information I had never before known about my birth mother, I still had essentially no information about my birth father other than his age at my birth. I had been alerted at the ALMA meeting that morning, and was already aware as a natural consequence of thinking about a search, that the question of how and when adoptees should ask their birth mother about the identity of their birth father is a very difficult one. As the birth mother shares the story of her pregnancy, the situation may be clear without the adoptee even needing to ask, but birth mothers sometimes gloss over the actual circumstances of the pregnancy as well as the identity of the birth father. So far in our conversation, Pearl had done just such glossing over.

One of the risks that must be acknowledged when an adoptee decides to search is that unpleasant information, and memories that are painful to one degree or another will almost certainly result. Some discomfort may well revolve around the birth father. Pregnancies that lead to an adoption are often a result of "young love" and lack of preparation or knowledge of birth control, but some may have been the result of rape or incest. The birth father may have been someone the birth mother knew very well, someone she trusted, such as a teacher, or even a family member, or someone with whom she was barely acquainted, or not at all. Perhaps even any of several men could have been the birth father, and the birth mother may need to see the adoptee to assist her in identifying the birth father. And, regardless of who he was, the birth father may also have already died.

Realizing the sensitive area I was opening up, I asked Pearl "What can you tell me about my birth father?"

"His name was Bill Mullett (C7–C9), but you're a little late in your attempt to find him. He just died, last March, I think in Buffalo where he had lived for the last several years."

I counted on my fingers. I had started my search just three months too late!

"Can you tell me why he died?"

"I don't really know for sure, but I heard he wasn't taking very good care of himself."

Her answer rang some warning signals for me, but I just set them aside for the time being and asked her what he did for a living. She wasn't sure of his employment either, having only occasionally kept in touch with Henry, his oldest brother. She thought that for a while he was in "child welfare."

"That's really interesting because I'm a child psychologist!" Thus, the first of many questions I was to face, very personally, about "nature vs. nurture" was raised.

I had one more major question I wanted to ask. "Would you be willing to tell me how it was that you and Bill didn't stay together and keep me?"

"Yes, I can tell you that. I was 20, and engaged to Bill. When I found out I was pregnant he told me it was all right, that we would just marry sooner than we planned. I went home to tell my mother and she got very angry at me, and yelled at me. She then went into town and into Bill's house, where she yelled at him and called him names. She told him he had to do right by me and marry me. Then she came back out to our house, we lived in the country, and told me I had to leave because it would kill my father if he found out I was pregnant, and he might even kill me. So, I went into town and moved in with Bill's family, but he changed his mind and said he wouldn't marry me, if my mother hated him that much. His brother Henry took me to the hospital when you were born, and took care of me afterward."

She said, "I wasn't too surprised you had contacted me because I've heard of others doing the same thing. I'm glad you found me."

Hearing Pearl was glad I had called her made me very happy. I didn't want to move too fast, so I didn't press for an immediate meeting, especially since the distances involved, between Florida and Wisconsin, would probably make any meeting difficult.

At some point in the conversation Pearl asked, "Is Rockford, Illinois anywhere near Stevens Point?"

"Rockford is about a three-hour drive south of Point."

"My husband will be working there during this coming fall."

I hedged my next statement, leaving her to make the move when she felt ready, but said "I would like to think about meeting then. Why don't we talk about that later on?"

We had talked by then for about an hour, and I had gotten an avalanche of new information. I still wanted to ask her about the son she mentioned, who didn't know about me either, but as much as I wanted to continue the conversation, I began to feel overwhelmed. Pearl seemed to be also ready to end the conversation. We agreed to write and to send pictures, exchanged addresses, and said good bye.

When I hung up the phone, I was in a state difficult to describe. I was absolutely blown away at the fact I had just talked to my birth mother, and rather than rejecting me she had actually said she was glad I had contacted her! The information I got about how she became pregnant and surrendered me was not the best of all possible stories, nor was the death of my birth father, but the overall story was better than a number of the alternatives I had feared, such as rape, incest, or an unknown birth father.

Laurel reminded me her own search had led her to her birth mother's grave, a fact I had heard at the meeting that afternoon, but had since forgotten. I was again struck by how appropriately Laurel's experience prepared her to work with me. Laurel said I would probably find that even though I had never met him, I would need to do some grieving over Bill's death. While I was already saddened that he had died before I got the chance to meet him, the more dominant emotion right then was total joy at having made what I thought of as a successful contact with Pearl. Sadness over Bill's death had not really set in yet, but I tucked Laurel's advice away, hoping to remember it when the time came. I tried to calm myself down and eat some more now-cold pizza, thanked Laurel for her help, and headed off for the next stop on my vacation. I knew I was a far different person than I had been when I left Chatham for the ALMA meeting that morning. Now I knew where I came from. I had roots. I felt more connected to the world. I knew today had been a special day, and my life would never be the same again. I already had much less in common with E. T.

CHAPTER 5

Second Search: Back to Buffalo

$\mathbf{M}$y original vacation plans were to return to Stevens Point by the weekend of June 19-20, but my search had thrown that timetable off considerably. On Saturday June 19th I was still in New Jersey, and I was now intensely involved in my search. One stop I still wanted to make for certain was in Wellsboro Pennsylvania to talk to Kathy Largey, who had grown up as Kathy Werrick, next door to me on Claremont Avenue, and was also adopted. I knew she had sought out her birth family several years ago, and I understood her experience had been good. I was hoping to be able to spend several days visiting with her and talking also with her adoptive mother, who had moved to Wellsboro, about their reactions to Kathy's search and reunion, and about my parents' probable reactions to my own search.

After I visited a college friend who had not been able to attend the reunion, and Nancy, an old girlfriend, and her family in the Philadelphia area, I headed to Wellsboro. Because of my new and still uncertain timetable, I decided to cancel the meeting with my students, which was originally set for June 20, and had already been postponed to June 26, in order to relieve all time pressure on my search. I believed I would then have no commitments which would force me to return home until well after the July Fourth weekend. I called the department secretary back in Stevens Point, shortly after I arrived in Wellsboro, since she would need several days to contact all of my students in order to change the research meeting again.

Late in that spring, I had told the director of an educational play on child sexual abuse, in which I frequently acted as one of the characters, that should the play be accepted as part of Stevens Point's 125th anniversary celebrations during the week of July Fourth, I would be in town to play my part. I was on the Portage County Council for Human Sexuality that had commissioned the play and had sponsored performances of the play in schools and churches throughout Wisconsin. Ironically, I had come up with the idea to apply to the city to put the play on as part of the July Fourth week schedule in the first place. However, at the time we applied in early spring there were no funds available to cover the cost of staging such a production. The Sexuality Council had been little inclined to raise the necessary money, and so the performance would not likely occur. I was only ruling out a long shot when I asked the secretary to check with the play director on Monday, June 20. I arranged to call back on the morning of Wednesday, June 22, to confirm that all of my research students had been contacted, and to check on the status of the play.

I then continued my visit with Kathy, her husband Gale, and her mother, Mrs. Werrick, who had been very close to me throughout my childhood years. (Mrs. Werrick had been visiting my parents barely three weeks earlier on the Sunday afternoon that I had the conversation which started me on my search.) I told Mrs. Werrick about my conversation with my parents the afternoon after she had left, and I asked her how she thought my parents would react to my having searched and found. She thought my mother, at least, would be very happy for me, but couldn't predict my father's reaction. We both acknowledged that Dad was a proud and private man, and might not be comfortable with the idea of "sharing" me with others. I asked her to not mention anything to my parents until I had had a chance to tell them myself, and she agreed.

We talked at length about Kathy's search and reunion. Both Kathy and her (adoptive) mother had met Kathy's birth mother, and Kathy had been very involved with an adoption search support group in Pennsylvania, even appearing on a television show about searching. These initial discussions were helpful in putting my experiences into context, and helped me resolve to seek out my birth father's family. After watching a tape of Kathy's TV show, and after yet more searching of my own heart about what to do next, I decided to return to Rochester, to try to locate more information about my birth father. There I hoped to stay with Linda Luxenberg, from Claremont Avenue, while I searched for my birth father's obituary, which I hoped would contain more information about his family.

On Tuesday June 21 I arrived in Rochester and called Linda. She was surprised to hear from me, especially since we had eaten lunch together just three weeks earlier, on the day I had (at that time unknowingly) found my birth grandfather's name. Another small blessing of the search experience was the chance to talk with Linda for a longer period of time, since she was only able to take a shortened lunch hour on the day of our previous meeting. We sat up late talking about everything from our memories of childhood, to our marriages (hers ended, mine in trouble), to our parents, our careers, and my search.

The next morning was June 22, and after saying good bye to Linda again, I headed off to the Rochester Public Library to find a Lockport paper, and hopefully an obituary for my birth father which would direct the next step in my search. Not only were there no Lockport papers in the library, but when I looked for a Buffalo paper (where Pearl had seen the obituary) I found they kept only the current week's Buffalo papers. I left the library and made the previously arranged call back to my office in Stevens Point to check on the cancellation of the research meeting and on the status of the play. I was told that financial support had unexpectedly developed, and a performance of the play was scheduled for Tuesday, June 28. Worse still, due to an almost entirely new cast, I would have to be at a rehearsal on Monday, June 27.

I was crushed since I was beginning to think I would need to drive beyond Lockport and into Buffalo itself to get information, which I presumed would then lead me back to Lockport or its environs. I asked the department secretary to contact the director again to ask whether she could find a way to get me out of the play. I was beginning to fear more and more that I would have to keep the play commitment and cut my search short. She told me she might have difficulty contacting the play director, a non-traditional student with several young children who lived off-campus, especially since she had needed several calls to reach her the first time. We wondered aloud how and when the secretary could tell me about the play director's response to my desire to drop out of the rehearsal and performance, which was at that time less than a week away. Just then the department chairperson walked into the office, and, on learning I was on the telephone, asked to talk to me about some pressing department business.

Typical of the way "coincidences" had occurred throughout the search, as the chairperson and I were about through talking, who should stop in the office to check on a summer school course but the play director herself! As I talked to her that morning (June 22), I had no idea what was going to happen later that day and night, but I already knew I wanted to get out of my commitment to the play. She told me she would have great difficulty finding a replacement, but she would try.

In order to attend a June 27 rehearsal, my return trip to Stevens Point would need to begin on Saturday, June 25, leaving me potentially just two to three days to locate and meet my birth father's family, so I decided to head immediately off to Buffalo. There I could get the obituary and hopefully use that information to locate other birth relatives. I made plans to call the play director at her home the next day, and left for the hour-long drive to Buffalo.

Returning to the new main library in downtown Buffalo was an exciting experience. I remembered not just the beginning of my search there barely three weeks earlier but also trips to the old library. The continuity and unchanging nature of the books in that institution, even though the building they were housed in had changed, contrasted markedly with the speed of recent developments in my own life.

I made my way to the microfilm area, obtained the microfilm with the *Buffalo News* for March 1983, and ran the film ahead to Monday, March 7, the day Pearl had mentioned when talking of my birth father's death. No William Mullett was listed. I was dismayed, fearing a lapse in her memory might necessitate my going through many reels of obituary notices, but I advanced the reel to Tuesday, March 8. I scanned the alphabetic listings, and there it was! I rapidly skimmed the notice—"husband of . . . , dear father of Susan (C1–C3, C10, H1–H4, J1), Mary (C2–C5, H1–H3, J3), Molly (C1–C3, C11, H3–H4, J3), Amy (C5, C6, J4) . . ." I had four sisters! The obituary next mentioned Bill's surviving brothers and a sister. I had uncles, and an aunt! The church in which his funeral was held was less than five miles from the home on Claremont Avenue where I grew up!

I sought out the microfilm staff person to try to talk her out of enforcing the large sign which read "24 Hour Waiting Period on all Photocopies from Microfilm" which was prominently posted on every wall of the room. Upon hearing I wanted only one copy of an obituary notice, she agreed to make the copy for me as soon as she was free, and I returned to the machine to re-read the obituary notice, and to think about what to do next.

I scanned the other obituaries for March 7, idly wondering who else had died that day. In addition to the alphabetized list of standard obituaries, I saw some larger notices in the form of news stories which described the lives of prominent people in more detail. They seemed to be for people who had died several days earlier, and I wondered if my birth father might have been someone who would rate such a notice. "Don't be silly" I thought, why inflate your ego? "Why should your birth father be special?" But the same little voice that had so often guided my search said "If you don't look you won't find out." I moved the film ahead one more day to Wednesday, March 9.

At the top of the obituary page I saw the headline: "William Mullett, 54 Dies; was aide to Administrative Judge," and there, embedded in the article, was a picture of my birth father! I was looking at the first photo of a birth relative that I had ever seen! I searched the postage-stamp-sized image for familiar features, and thought I saw my cheekbones. My eyes danced over the two columns of information. He had died in the Buffalo Veterans Administration Hospital. From my bed as a child, I had often watched the blinking red aircraft warning lights on top of that building as I fell asleep. The Hospital was close to the University of Buffalo campus, and I could also see the campus clock tower, and often hear the hourly bells. Both the VA Hospital and the University were also less than five miles from where I grew up. Irony and coincidence were beginning to become all too familiar. As I waited for the (now two) copies to be made, I contemplated what to do next.

There was of course the paper trail of documents left behind when anyone died, which Carl Zimmer, the ALMA Registrar, had told me about, and that was one avenue of attack. Much more exciting was learning about the existence of the four sisters and various other blood relatives identified in Bill's obituary, and I decided to look for them. I received the copied obituaries and called Mike and Karen Indian. Mike was out, and I filled Karen in on recent events, asking her if I could stay with them that night if the need arose. Karen assured me I could, and I made my way back into the room in which the city directories were kept.

Comparing the names of my sisters in the obituary with a current Buffalo City Directory, I found no listings for either Susan or Amy, one for Molly, and five possibilities for Mary. I began to be concerned that my sudden appearance, especially only three months after Bill's death, might cause problems for his family, yet I desperately wanted to contact them. The fact that according to his obituary Bill had a long career in the family courts, and had served for over ten years as aide to the chief supervising judge of District Court, gave me a place to start. I decided to contact the judge or his chief aide or law clerk, request confidentiality, and tell my story. I would ask who in the family I should contact, and how that contact might best be done.

CHAPTER 6

Reunion: There Are More Like Me

I arrived at lunch time at the Judge's chambers, a short drive from the library and just across the street from the County Clerk's office I had visited at the start of my search just three weeks before. The receptionist was out, but a bailiff told me the Judge had some time open on his schedule to see me during the afternoon, and I decided to wait. As I sat in the sweltering solarium outside his top floor chambers, I wondered what would lie ahead. Would the family be happy to see me or would they reject me, especially so soon after his death? Would they suspect my motives? Believe my story? Who even knew of my existence? Would I look like them? Would we like each other? I grew restless and decided to walk the two blocks to City Hall and obtain a copy of Bill's death certificate, more for something to do than for any information the certificate might have. After a 15-minute wait there, I was informed that certificates on all deaths in the Buffalo Veterans Administration Hospital were maintained at the Hospital, and not by the Buffalo City Clerk. Oh well, at least I got some fresh air.

Back on the 14th floor of the County Hall of Justice, people were returning from lunch. As I waited, I watched those people, realizing some of them must have known Bill very well, wondering if any of them gave me a second glance, if any of them noticed any resemblance, if any of them would believe, or even perhaps know about, my story.

At length a young man introduced himself to me as Pat, identified himself as the Judge's chief aide and asked about the nature of my business. I asked if we could speak privately, and he took me to his office. As we sat down his phone rang, and I had a few moments to appreciate the view of Lake Erie and compose myself. When I told him I had a personal, non-legal issue to raise with Judge Kane, and I did not wish to discuss the issue with anyone else, Pat said the only way the Judge would see me was if he thought the issue merited the Judge's time. I realized I would have to tell my story to Pat. With a deep breath and a trembling voice, I told of my conversation with Pearl, and of her identification of Bill as my birth father. I asked who in the office knew Bill's family well enough to know who I should contact, and could also be trusted not to make the story the topic of office gossip. He picked up his phone as I finished and made a call.

"Al, this is Pat. Have you got a few minutes? I have someone here I'd like you to meet. Good, we'll be right over."

We walked a short distance to the office of Al Gerke, where Pat introduced me, suggested I tell Al my story, and left, after telling me Al was a close friend of Bill's and had been a pallbearer at his funeral. As I told my story to Al, he listened in silence, looking at me carefully, judging me. When I finished, he asked if I had any proof—any documentation of the truth of my story. I told him all I had to link myself to Bill Mullett was my birth mother's story, and offered him my faculty photo identification card and Wisconsin driver's license as proof of my current identity. Later in the conversation I realized that, of all the possible people I could have been talking to, those working in the county court office would certainly have easy access to the court records containing my original birth certificate, and perhaps even to my sealed adoption records. I suggested that if he had any doubt, he could certainly get any documentation he needed to check me out.

We talked for a few minutes and I asked some of the questions I had. I learned Bill was proud of his Irish heritage, and he marched each year in the St. Patrick's Day Parade. I learned about my four sisters. The oldest one had been married, and they all were living in North Buffalo. Although Al did not know their exact ages, he gave me a general idea—31, 27, 24 and about 11. The youngest, Amy, who I later learned was 9 at the time, still lived with their mother in Kenmore. Bill and his wife Jane (C2) had divorced several years earlier, and Bill had lived in an apartment off of Englewood Avenue before going into the hospital. As I listened, I discovered yet another "coincidence"—all of the locations Al mentioned where Bill and his family lived, as well as the V. A. Hospital where he died, were within five miles of my childhood home on Claremont Avenue, and some of them were within only a few blocks!

As I talked with Al, I began to get a picture of the kind of person Bill was, and the picture seemed very positive—he was kind, a hard worker and had a good sense of humor. The most important question I had for Al had been incubating ever since Pearl told me that, although she didn't know the exact cause of his death, Bill "hadn't been taking very good care of himself." I was startled to hear Al use almost the very words Pearl had used to describe the reason for Bill's death. The phrase was one I had in the past heard people use to describe a drinking or drug abuse problem, so I asked Al directly if Bill had a drinking problem. His response shook me to the core. An almost immediate "No" was followed by a long pause. Al continued, hesitantly, "Well, he certainly liked to drink. I mean he was *really* social when he . . ." Al's voice trailed off, and after another brief pause, as if he was deciding what to say, he completed the thought: "Well, I guess if the truth were told, it was probably his drinking that killed him."

Suddenly, hearing Bill had died of alcoholism, the reality of my genetic history struck home. Just five days earlier I had completed the fifth year of my own sobriety. In the late 1970s I realized I was an alcoholic on the road to serious trouble, and I had finally managed to stop drinking (for the last of many times!) in mid-June of 1978. Increasingly over the past year there had been a little voice within me that said "Come on, Doug, our license plates call Wisconsin "America's Dairyland," but you know Wisconsin is really 'The Beer State.' You make people uncomfortable when you turn down a beer. Go ahead and have one now and then. *It won't kill you.*" Hearing my birth father died at 54 of alcoholism, and remembering the increasingly frequent messages from that little voice within me, made me realize having that beer probably WOULD kill me. This thought broke open an emotional dam, and I began to sob, shaking not so much out of specific sadness at having lost Bill, as out of a deep and profound emotional experience which I could deal with at that time only in that way.

There were to be other tears over the next few days—tears of sadness, of joy, of pure intensity of feeling, but these first tears really caught me by surprise. Then I recalled Laurel's words, the afternoon I first talked to Pearl, about needing to mourn Bill's death. At the time, having just found my birth mother, I was so excited and happy that any kind of grief seemed far in the future. The future, at least the grieving part, had suddenly arrived. The immediate effect of hearing about Bill's alcoholism in Al's office was to bring me from the thinking level to the feeling level with a jolt. The effect of my crying on Al, I believe, was to make him think, "If he's not really Bill's son he is certainly a good actor."

After I composed myself, he made a phone call to another staff member, Sally Albertson, asking her to come in. Al told me she had been Bill's secretary. Again, I told my story to her, and asked both she and Al which of my sisters they thought would be the best for me to contact. I learned that both Al and Sally were very cautious and protective of the family. Susan, the oldest, had taken charge of the funeral arrangements along with Sally, and continued to be involved in post-mortem affairs. Sally thought Susan should be my initial contact with the family. Susan, however, had an infant child, and had just been through another traumatic experience. The night after she returned to Buffalo from a "get-away-from-dad's-death" trip to Aruba, the sister of her best friend had committed suicide. Sally felt the pressure of my appearance right now might be too much too soon.

Al and Sally suggested I write a letter to Susan, explaining my story and asking her whether she wanted to meet, and what she wanted to do next. I objected to writing a letter, pointing out that Stevens Point was a 17-hour drive from Buffalo, and that a meeting at some later date might be quite difficult to arrange. I was so close now I couldn't imagine leaving without some sort of direct contact. I suggested the family might want to meet me, and might be as frustrated as I to learn I had not visited them when I was in town. Sally volunteered to contact Susan for me, to explain my story to her, and to ask if she and my other sisters wanted to see me. We decided that having Sally call Susan was a good course of action.

As we talked in Al's office, Sally told me more about Bill's family. She said she thought Bill badly wanted a son, and that he may have hoped that Amy, the youngest daughter, would be a boy. We became curious as to whether Bill himself even knew about me. A realization hit me for the first time: I might well be the son he always wanted, and never had a chance to raise. I broke down in tears again. Several times during the conversation Sally left the room. I had assumed she was leaving to attend to work matters. Sally told me later she was leaving because my story was causing her to break down in tears, and she didn't want to cry in front of me and Al.

Presently Sally and I went to her office where our conversation continued, as I filled Sally in on more details of my life and search. I again reassured her, as I had Al and Pat, that my desire was not to cause pain or hurt, and I did not want my appearance to become the topic of office gossip. I was searching because I had to answer some basic medical and psychological questions as a long-delayed step in my own identity formation. She seemed reassured and shared with me her perceptions of Bill as both his long-time secretary and friend. He was good-hearted, sometimes to a fault, worked hard to help the Judge and other staff members, and "didn't have an enemy in the world." She showed me his death certificate on which the most immediately important information was the cause of death: liver failure (cirrhosis) and complications of liver failure. As I sat in her office, Sally called Susan to arrange to meet that evening.

"Susan? Hi dear, this is Sally. How are you doing? . . . Fine. Well there's been an issue come up regarding your father. It's nothing bad, but I need to talk to you about it as soon as I can, and I don't want to talk over the phone. Do you think you can get Molly and Mary to come over to my house tonight to talk? OK. Now don't worry. It's not bad news—I'll tell you all about it tonight." She gave Susan directions to her house.

Yet another coincidence arose as I listened to the directions. Sally began her directions near the University of Buffalo campus on the north side of the city. She described a route which led past the church I had attended with my family for 15 years, down Niagara Falls Boulevard past a point no more than six blocks from my old home on Claremont Avenue, and then north to her house on Blackstone Boulevard. I found Sally lived just a few blocks from where I knew I would be staying that night with Mike and Karen. Yet another place that was very important in my search turned out to be within five miles of my childhood home! Her house was very close to a restaurant where I had occasionally gone after basketball games in high school. I flashed back on happy memories of "group dates," and marveled at how so many different threads of my life were coming together in ways I never had even dreamed about.

Sally said good bye to Susan, and I called Karen Indian and filled her in on the developments. Karen said of course I could stay with them that night. Sally and I exchanged phone numbers, and she told me she would call me at the Indian's house after talking to my sisters, "one way or the other." Sally's language suggested to me there was apparently some doubt in her mind about whether or not my birth sisters would want to meet me. The time was, by then, close to 4:00 p.m., and Sally said she would call me after 8:00 p.m. I had some four hours to make the 45-minute drive north to the Indian's house.

I decided to take some time to visit Bill's grave since Sally had given me a funeral mass card which identified the plot in Forest Lawn Cemetery where he was buried. President Millard Fillmore (a nearly life-long Buffalo resident, who was also assassinated there), is buried in Forest Lawn, and also Red Jacket (an early Native American guide, after whom the street my parents lived on is named). In addition, at that time I also had two grandparents and an uncle buried there. I thought a visit to Bill's grave might be a chance to calm myself and think. At any rate, the cemetery was an easy stop on my way from downtown Buffalo to the north suburbs where so much of my life had been centered.

However, as I drove north on Delaware Avenue, I began to feel lonely—to feel the need to share the experience with someone. Not knowing what my grave-side reaction might be, I thought to have someone else going along with me might be a good idea. Mike had been very supportive of my search, and I felt I could be comfortable with him no matter what happened, and so I drove on past the cemetery to Mike's house, and during dinner filled Mike and Karen in on the developments during the three weeks since I had last been in Buffalo.

For everything about my search to have worked out perfectly would seem impossible, and the time for a change of luck had perhaps arrived. After dinner Mike and I went back to Forest Lawn. There was no one in the cemetery office, the security guard knew nothing about the numbering system, and there were relatively few markers by which to guess plot numbers. We were unable to locate Bill's grave, even though we had the section and plot number. We were able to find the correct section, but after about a half hour of walking around, looking at the headstones on all the new graves, we gave up and returned to Mike's. By then I was already convinced that since finding Bill's grave hadn't worked out, that part of the process just wasn't meant to happen yet and so, although I was disappointed, I felt I could wait for the time to be right. Besides, there was another event involving the living to which I was already looking forward with increasing excitement.

We arrived back at Mike's at 7:30. Eight o'clock was the time at, or after which, Sally had said she would call, and as the appointed hour came closer my anxiety rose. At 7:45 I began to wait in earnest anticipation, thinking perhaps they would be so excited as to try calling early, even though I had told Sally not to expect me to be at Mike's before 8:00 p. m. Eight o'clock came, and went, as did 8:15 and 8:30. In the absence of knowledge, I began wildly imagining what might be happening. I became convinced my sisters had been upset, had not wanted to talk to me, and had made Sally uncomfortable about calling me while they were still in the room. Finally, at about 8:40, the phone rang. Karen answered, and the call was for me. Sally was on the line.

"Doug, you have a sister over here who is just going to burst if she doesn't get to see you in five minutes."

I needed no encouragement, told her I'd be there in less than that, and I didn't need directions since I'd heard her give them to Susan earlier in the afternoon. I left almost at a dead run for my car. As I went out the door, Karen too asked if I needed directions and I said no and took off. A minute or two later I was hopelessly lost—the street "one street west from Niagara Falls Boulevard" was named "Wynwood," not "Blackstone!" I tried Sally's number from a nearby gas station phone and the line was busy.

Mike and Karen have an unlisted telephone number, and while I waited for Sally's line to clear, I thought I'd try to get through to them. In the excitement of the moment, I couldn't remember the number, and I went through my wallet several times, unsuccessfully trying to find the slip of paper on which I had written their number. Sally's line was still busy, and I went back to my car to drive back to Indian's house to start over, making sure I had a set of good written directions. I opened my car door only to find the paper with their number sitting in plain sight on my dashboard. I had put the number right where I couldn't miss it! I generally have pretty good "sense" about myself as far as managing important property. However, I have also, on occasion, been known to spend several minutes looking for a writing implement when I was holding one in my mouth. I was thankful that this time my good sense of organization paid off.

I returned to the phone booth and called. Karen answered the phone and told me I had to go one more block south, cross Brighton, and *there* the first street west of the Boulevard would be correct since all of the street names changed at Brighton. I was off again, not knowing what to expect. On the way I had time to wonder why Sally had said I had "a sister" waiting there for me. Had the others not wanted to see me? But now there was no more time to worry or wonder. As I drove up to the house on Blackstone, I saw Sally out in front, and next to her was a young woman in a long summer dress.

I still get teary thinking of the next few minutes. Meeting face to face with the first birth relative you have ever known is something I suspect only fellow adoptees who have been there can even begin to appreciate: to be in one's thirties, and never before having seen someone who looks like you. Words can describe what we did and said, and those words are here, but there is simply no language with the power to describe the feelings from that evening. In the years since that night, I've told the reunion story to friends and family, and to all sorts of other groups consisting of everyone from mental health and adoption professionals, to my university students, to all sides of the adoption triad, and every time the emotions of that evening rush back.

I think Sally said something like "Doug this is your sister. Susan this is your brother." but I wasn't really listening. Susan and I stood, stared for a moment, said hello, hugged tentatively, then stepped back to just look at each other. Susan asked if we could be alone for a few minutes, which was exactly what we needed. For perhaps the next half an hour we sat on Sally's front porch, both of us talking a mile a minute. Mostly we were asking and answering questions, but occasionally we stopped to ask one or the other to take off their glasses so facial features could be more easily seen. I had expected to see a female version of me, and I later learned Susan had expected to see a younger version of her father brought back to life, so our perceptions took a while to come in line with reality. As we looked at each other we could see we did have similar eyes, cheekbones, and foreheads. We discovered similarities between ourselves, poor mathematical skills being the first, and we asked over and over again, "is it just chance or is it because we're related"?

Although we both knew not to make too much of similarities that could easily be the result of chance, I suspect we would have been thrilled, and would have attributed the cause to Mullett family characteristics if we had "discovered" we both ate food, or both slept at night in beds! Our conversation was a poignant, happy, exciting time for me, one which too few adoptees are fortunate enough to experience. My desire for other adoptees and their birth family members to be able to share the reunion experience has kept me involved with adoptee rights all these years.

In light of my fears while driving to Sally's, I was relieved to discover the reason only Susan was there to meet me was that Molly (my second oldest sister), was on a vacation in Europe, and Susan had been unable to reach Mary at home that afternoon. Susan had decided to wait to inform her mother and Amy (my 9-year-old sister) until she saw how her meeting with me turned out. Thus, I would be able to look forward to meeting more sisters, and more of Bill's family at some future time, since Susan was reasonably sure all of them would, perhaps not immediately but eventually, want to meet me. Susan, at least, rather than viewing my appearance as an unwanted reminder of an unfortunate transgression in her father's past, saw me as a not totally unexpected gift, a piece of her father to carry on into the future.

"Not totally unexpected" is the clue to some of the questions I had raised earlier that afternoon with Bill's colleagues at the courthouse.

"Did Bill himself even know about me? Who, if anyone, else knew?" Susan reported that around two weeks after her father's death, her mother had told all three older daughters they had a half-brother "out there somewhere" and perhaps they should search for him. Susan had more or less dismissed the statement as idle talk, but was therefore not totally surprised to hear from Sally earlier that evening about my appearance at her father's office.

Susan and I were brought back to reality by Sally, who came out to the front porch to tell us that the folks in the back yard were going crazy wondering how we were getting along. We were getting along so well we had forgotten all about them! We decided we should probably join the others waiting for us, and we went into the garage where Sally, Sally's husband, and Susan's friend Gary were waiting. There we talked until nearly midnight with everyone sometimes talking at once. At length we decided to call it a night, but I had learned still more about my "new" family. Susan would call Mary (in the morning?) and tell her about me, and the next morning I was to call Susan at 9:00 a. m. and find out what the plans were for the day (Thursday, June 23). Other than probably meeting Mary, I didn't know what the next day might hold in store, and I had learned not to try to anticipate.

On the way back to Mike's, I realized that given the day's developments, my commitment to be in the child abuse play in Stevens Point the following Tuesday was even more of a problem than the commitment had been barely 12 hours earlier that same day. Now I *really* did not want to be forced to go to Stevens Point before I was ready to leave Buffalo. I resolved to call the play director as soon as I got back to Mike's house rather than wait to call until the next evening, as we had agreed to do during my conversation with her from Rochester that morning. Thinking back over the day, the fact that only that morning I had been looking for a Buffalo paper in the Rochester library seemed impossible. I had been totally unaware of my four sisters, totally unaware of who my father was as a person, totally unaware of what he did, and totally unaware of how he died. Overall, I had experienced quite a day!

When I got to the Indians, Mike and Karen were both up waiting for me, wondering how the evening had gone. As I tried to tell them everything at once, my thoughts jumped from one topic to another, and the fact that I was, to say the least, in an unusual state of mind must have been obvious to Mike. As I told Mike and Karen some of what I had learned that evening, another set of coincidences appeared. Mike and I had both graduated from Kenmore East Senior High School in

1964, and for several years Mike had taught at our "rival" high school, Kenmore West. After the Mullett family moved back to Buffalo in 1969, the two middle daughters, Molly and Mary, had graduated from Kenmore West. I had lived about one quarter mile east of the railroad tracks that divided the Kenmore-Town of Tonawanda district in two, and on the extreme south end of town. Since 1969, the Mulletts had lived about one mile west of the tracks, also on the south end of town. Both families lived within a few blocks of the northern Buffalo city line.

As I was telling my story Mike got up and left the room for a few minutes. I wondered if he had gone to bed, exhausted by my non-stop babbling. Shortly, however, he returned with a Kenmore West yearbook in his hands and asked if one of my sisters was named Mary, and might she have graduated in 1976? When I answered yes, he said "would you like to see her picture?" There, smiling out at me, was another sister (C4). Since Susan had not known what to expect when she went to Sally's, she did not have any family pictures with her. Therefore, though I had heard about many of my birth relatives earlier that night, Mary's photo was only the third person (after meeting Susan, and Bill's obituary photo), that I had ever seen, who looked like me because they were a birth relative. As I stared at her photo, Mary's smile haunted me until suddenly I realized her smile was the same as mine! I had long noticed there was what I thought of as a rather unusual difference in the lengths of my upper front teeth—nothing bizarre or ugly, but nonetheless, the kind of thing one notices while staring intently at one's face six inches from a mirror. And looking at her picture, I saw the same pattern in Mary's front teeth!

There are simply no words to describe how I felt to see Susan, to see Mary's picture, and to know why these people looked like me. I do share some features, notably naturally curly salt and pepper hair, with my adoptive father, and I'm sure I have unconsciously "adopted" many postural and speech habits from both of my adoptive parents. For as long as I can remember, people who did not know I was adopted, upon meeting me with Mom or Dad for the first time, have often been struck by these similarities (and no doubt by the expectation that a son *should* look like his father). Sometimes they would say things like "You two certainly do look alike." or "I sure don't have to ask who you are." We always replied in such a manner as not to call attention to the fact that any physical similarity was just chance. Just perhaps, especially when I was younger, I think I would actually sometimes "forget" that any resemblance was only chance. Especially during the last few years however, as I became more aware of my adoption and my consequent lack of any knowledge of my physical history or birth family, I became also more aware of how there was no one in my life who was "like me" on any basis other than chance or environment. Now, seeing one sister's picture, and having just met another, I began to feel, in addition to a sense of wonder at the speed with which things were happening, a sense of being connected, of having found the rest of "my place" in time, space and history.

I had yet one piece of business to conduct before trying to go to sleep for the night—calling the director of the child abuse play to make the strongest attempt possible to get out of my commitment to return to Stevens Point for the play. At any other time, I would have especially wanted to be a part of that performance. I had been involved in the play since its inception, a request from the Portage County Council for Human Sexuality that a local playwright create an educational play about child sexual abuse. I had been a technical advisor in the rewriting of the script, had been in the three premiere performances. I believed in the concepts the play promoted, and wanted to perform again in my home community where only one of the approximately 25 previous performances of the play had taken place. In addition, I had made the suggestion to hold a performance during the extended Fourth of July weekend as part of Stevens Point's 125th anniversary celebration in the first place. I am not in the habit of backing out of commitments, and I had considerable guilt as I set out to do exactly that. In the context of what was going on in my life I felt there was little difficulty in making my choice as to what I wanted to do. Fortunately, I was able, through the director of the play, to find Mike Delain, a student of mine, who had played the part before, and who was willing to return to Stevens Point and perform in my place, if I paid his travel expenses. Although these arrangements were not really finalized until the next evening, I hung up the phone that night feeling freer to pursue my unfolding search without external time pressure.

I finally crawled into bed at close to 1:00 a. m., too excited of course to sleep. One of the many things for which I will always be grateful to Mike, was his idea to leave a pad of paper and a pen next to my bed, suggesting I might want to preserve my feelings and thoughts for the future by writing something down. I jotted ideas and feelings at random on the page. Everything I wrote that night is presented below, in much the same format as I wrote it. The writing represents as closely as possible some of that evening's sensations. Somewhere around 4:00 a. m. I laid the pad aside and fell asleep.

* * *

June 22, 1983

Too many coincidences lead me here—who is the guide?
   Words lose meaning—my "new" father dead 3 1/2 months
                  too soon, or is this how it was
                  meant to be?

Apprehension   \
                \
Hugging   \
               \
Staring   __I'm real!
           /   There are more like me
Laughing   /   are they
         /   as strange—should I hope
Crying _____/   or fear?
               as smart—does it matter?

Disbelief   who do they want me to be?

We're both lousy at math!

Drinking   is it Irish blood?
         is it a coincidence?

Nature vs. Nurture in real life rushing past me

Sadness/fear—   how will I tell my parents?
      All feelings together jumbled
      Put these on hold.

Am I? Am I? Are You Me? Am I you?

* * *

Perhaps, since my parents appear in my writing ("sadness/fear—how will I tell my parents?"), I will raise now what was for me a very sensitive issue: the probable reaction of my adoptive parents to my search and reunion. When I committed to doing my search, I had decided now was the time for me to be "selfish," defining selfish as taking care of my own needs. I realized my search might result in some level of pain for me as well as for others. However, I also believed the pain which was definitely arising in me by not knowing my history was greater than the pain that might be caused to my parents (as well as to members of my birth family) by my searching.

I had become clear that my motivation for the search was not to hurt my parents or my birth family, or to gain some sort of revenge for the pain I felt. I was searching in order to ease the pain caused by some of the decisions made for me by members of my adoptive and birth families, as well as by the legal system. These decisions had been made in my best interest at the time they were made, however, the results of those decisions were no longer serving me well. I came to see my decision to search as not unlike my decision to stop drinking. When I decided I had to stop drinking, I knew that I had to do what was best for me, even if my abstinence made others uncomfortable, and even if my abstinence cost me some friendships. Putting one's own needs ahead of those of others requires a certain level of self-confidence, a commodity which had been rather scarce in my life. I was happy with myself for having had the courage and self-confidence to make the decision to stop drinking, and I came to see my decision to search in much the same way.

Early on in the process, well before I left Stevens Point, I had decided I was conducting *my* search and that until the search was complete, and until I had time to digest the results, I would keep the process largely to myself. The discovery that both sides of my birth family were living in the Buffalo area, some of them less than 20 miles from where my adoptive parents now lived, raised a problematic issue for me. I knew my parents had always had difficulty talking about my adoption, and three weeks earlier, when we had talked about my need to know all of the remaining information they had, I had not shared with them my almost immediate decision to begin my search. I did not share my plans in part because I thought knowing I was searching would be painful for them. In addition, mixing issues from my birth and adoptive families at the same time, let alone people from them, was more than I wanted to take on, at least until I had a sense of having completed and at least partially digested the search process. Although I did spend some time thinking about my parents, the worry did not significantly affect my enjoyment of the reunion experience. The overall effect of the worry was not much more than a small cloud, peeking over the horizon of an otherwise gloriously clear sky.

CHAPTER 7

Part of the Family?

On Thursday morning, June 23, I was up by 7:30 a. m., showering and looking forward to what the new day would bring. I called Susan at 9:00 a. m. as we had arranged. She told me she had contacted Mary, and I was to meet Mary at Susan's house as soon as I could get there. When I got directions to Susan's home on Orchard Place, the proximity of my childhood home to Susan's home (two miles) was again fascinating. Susan lived about two miles southwest of the Buffalo Veterans Hospital, and I had grown up about a mile northwest of the same hospital. Before I hung up, I told Susan I had seen Mary's picture and I had found a similarity in appearance between Mary and myself. I was waiting to see if she (Susan) and I also had the likeness. What was a short drive to Susan's house by Buffalo standards (15 minutes) seemed to take forever, especially since, by my Stevens Point standards, ten minutes of driving will generally get you from one end of town to the other!

I am sad the experience of meeting Mary was not as profound as meeting Susan had been the night before. Susan was the very first blood relative I had ever seen in person. I had less time to prepare to meet her than I had to meet Mary, and I had not seen her picture beforehand, as I had with Mary. Nonetheless there was much of the same disbelief, staring, hugging, and loss for words I had experienced the previous evening. The three of us stared at each other and asked each of us—in pairs—to take off our glasses and sit together so the third could look at us. Poor vision appears to be an unfortunate family trait!

I noticed Mary's smile right away, and after the initial excitement had calmed, asked Susan to smile so I could look at her. Sure enough, there was the same tooth pattern in Susan's smile also! We got out cameras and went outside to take pictures of ourselves (H1). I, especially, felt at a disadvantage being unable to directly see my own face next to those of my sisters, and I was looking forward to seeing photographs of all three of us together. Remember that this all was happening in a time when nearly all cameras had film that needed to be developed and printed. Selfies had not yet been invented. At one point Mary went upstairs and, after coming back downstairs, said she had been staring at herself in the mirror. Unfortunately suggesting we all look in the mirror together never occurred to any of us!

While sitting in Susan's front room, we were discussing the obituaries in the Buffalo and Lockport papers, and Susan gave me a copy of the Lockport newspaper obituary since I had only seen the Buffalo version. I looked at Bill's picture, agreed the Lockport photo was better than the one in the Buffalo News, and started to read the obituary. Shortly I stopped in favor of talking to Susan and Mary, assuming that I could always read the obituary later. Shortly thereafter, another amazing coincidence surfaced. Susan mentioned the obituary again saying something like "The St. Lawrence thing was sort of an inside joke. Dad always wanted to go to college and would have gone there if he could have." I was somewhat confused by the remark and asked her to clarify what she had said, since I had still not yet read the entire Lockport obituary. She replied that her dad really hadn't been a student at St. Lawrence but he had attended several summer training institutes there and loved the campus.

Rather incredulously I told her I had gotten my BS at St. Lawrence. Susan told me she had started her freshman year at Potsdam State (just 11 miles from St. Lawrence) partly because her father was so enthusiastic about that area! I then read the Lockport obituary, and right after the spot at which I had stopped reading earlier, was the statement "He was a 1947 graduate of Lockport High School and attended St. Lawrence University in Canton, NY." Further comparing of memories revealed Bill's attendance at St. Lawrence was at the regular summer law enforcement seminars St. Lawrence sponsored. He had been in Canton during the summers of 1965, 1966, and 1967. These just happened to be the three summers between my four years there as an undergraduate! I can only imagine what my reaction would have been had I not skipped my planned stop in Lockport before going to Buffalo, the day before. If I had found the Lockport obituary first, I probably would have been no more amazed than I was to find that my four sisters lived within five miles of my Claremont Avenue home, and that two of them went to Kenmore West.

Our finding that Bill "just happened" to be on the St. Lawrence campus during the three summers between my four years there led us to wonder whether he had perhaps known who, and where, I was. If he had any such information about me, his presence at St. Lawrence may have been no coincidence—he may have been there not necessarily to "spy" on me, but perhaps to "just be" where his son had been. When I thought I was walking on the street where Pearl grew up, I certainly felt a strong sense of connection with her. Perhaps Bill was in Canton seeking the same type of connection, but a much more simultaneous one, with me. However, neither Susan nor Mary that morning, nor anyone else in the Mullet family who I have talked to in the intervening years, ever got the slightest hint from Bill that he knew anything about who I had become, or what had happened to me. The definitive answer to this question may be one of the things Bill took to his grave with him.

As Susan, Mary and I talked about what we did for a living, we discovered all three of us had very similar work interests. Had Susan and Molly (the third of the three older sisters who was out of the country at the time) and I all worked at our jobs in the same community, I might well be placing my university students with them to gain practical experience. Susan was then working in a sheltered workshop for the developmentally disabled, and Molly was counseling abused women and children. Two more of the themes I had written about the night before were again arising: the high number of "coincidences" we were finding, and the question of whether these could be explained by heredity or environment, or some other cause.

Overnight Susan had gathered some family photographs for me to see, and we spent a while looking at them. I saw pictures of my other two sisters, Molly and Amy, their mother, Bill's mother and his brothers. There were also photos of Bill at several different ages. Although everyone said I looked most like Molly, I immediately fell in love with Amy. She had dark expressive eyes, and in two of the photos I saw had long hair and seemed shy. Much to my surprise, a strong protective urge that I can't really explain arose.

As we continued to talk, I began to learn more about my sisters' family life, their mother, Bill's drinking, and his divorce from their mother. I also learned more about what sort of knowledge my sisters had previously had about me. After Bill's death their mother had told the oldest three sisters they had a brother "somewhere out there." Though

Susan and Molly chose to dismiss the story as some sort of figment of their mother's imagination, Mary told me she had believed the story, but had never been sure of what if anything to do with the information.

For many years Mary had been the "baby" of the family, and was her father's favorite companion, with whom he shared a lot. When Mary was in her early teens, her mother got pregnant, and the pregnancy was clearly not an accident, but was instead consciously planned. Mary told me about a time she had gone shopping for baby furniture with her parents during that pregnancy. Their mother was shopping elsewhere in the store, and Mary found her father standing in the toy section of the store, holding a football, with tears in his eyes. Although she didn't know the meaning of the tears, she remembered the incident. Later, after Amy's birth, her father told Mary that before he had met their mother, he had a son with another woman, and the son had been adopted away. She then understood the meaning of his tears. He made her promise not to tell anyone else about his son.

In retrospect, both Mary and Susan thought the pregnancy which produced Amy was probably an attempt on Bill's part to have a son. They also agreed his drinking problem worsened significantly after Amy's birth. By the time the drinking really got bad Amy was in elementary school, and had been growing up during a time of increasing tension in their home due to Bill's drinking and the associated marital problems. As things worsened, their parents divorced and Bill moved into an apartment, ultimately living with a woman friend he had met in the bars. Mary and Susan told me Amy had taken their parents' divorce and Bill's death hard. In light of the recent history, we discussed when and how to tell their mother, Jane, I had found them, and whether, when, and how to tell Amy about me.

In the midst of this discussion, the phone rang and their mother was on the line! Susan talked about some routine matters, then covered the mouthpiece and beckoned me to come and listen at the phone. She said to her mother "Mom, remember after Dad died, when you told me I had a half-brother? What was that all about?" Getting my ear up to the phone took me a second or two, and when I did, Jane was telling Susan about how her father had planned on marrying a girl he was dating, and that she had gotten pregnant. They were too young to get married right then, and so the girl—named Pearl Belschner—had moved to Lockport, and then had gone to Niagara Falls to have the baby, which was then given up for adoption! Jane thought the adopting family was from the area but she wasn't sure. She said Bill and Pearl even dated for a couple of years after the baby was born, but Pearl had ultimately married another man. She added that she still saw Pearl once in a while.

Hearing Jane's story, absent a couple of small differences, was really the first independent confirmation I had that what Pearl had told me was true, touched off the tears again, and I sat down stunned, but happy. Susan caught Mary's and my eyes and mouthed "I'm going to tell her." She said "Mom, are you sitting down? What would you say if I told you he was here? Now. In my living room." I heard a muffled "What?" come over the phone and Susan said "He found us yesterday, Mary met him this morning—it's too complicated to tell you over the phone." A short time later they hung up and Susan said we were going to go to the house to meet her mother, if I wanted to. Of course I did, and we were off on yet another adventure.

I drove my Jeep to Jane and Amy's house, with Susan and Mary next to me in the front seat. The experience was surreal: big brother Doug driving his sisters so he could meet their mother. As my sisters gave me directions to the home that had been theirs since 1969, I felt the strange sense I had been there before, which, in this case, was probably true! Still more of my birth-family's life had been centered close to where I grew up. We drove over streets on which I had often ridden my bike as a child, past the home of an old high school girl friend, and ended up a mere three miles west of my childhood home, on a street which, although I cannot specifically remember being on before, I might well have traveled. Several areas about which I DO have clear memories were just a few blocks away.

Meeting Susan and Mary's mother was not as emotional as meeting my sisters had been, but we shortly began to talk, and as I told Jane the story of how I had found them, there were tears all around the table. Susan was now hearing my story for the fourth time (once from Sally, then from me, again as I told Mary, and now yet again as I told their mother). Susan seemed not to tire of listening, which was good, since she would get the chance several more times in the next few days.

We discussed how and when to tell Amy about me. Jane's initial reaction was to go slowly, not wanting to shock her too much, especially so close on the heels of Father's Day which had been very hard on her. I was disappointed, wanting of course to meet everyone as quickly as possible, but I also knew Jane was Amy's mother and knew her best. Her decision would have to be respected. I tried to set my personal feelings aside and speak as a professional, suggesting that if they were not going to tell Amy while I was in town, they should think about delaying in telling her the news for only a few days or weeks, not for months or years. Based on my own reaction to "not knowing" I believed Amy would feel left out if she were to learn only long afterward of my existence and my visit. I told Jane the probable negative effect from delay should be balanced against the additional stress telling her immediately might produce. Of course, in order for her to understand how we could be (half) brother and sister, she would have to understand how I came into existence in the first place, and the discussion of the fact her father had engaged in premarital sex might also be difficult for both Amy and her mother. After lunch, when we left Jane's home, I was under the impression that my meeting Amy would not occur until a time rather far in the future. While a delay in telling her certainly was not my preference, I understood the decision of how and when to tell Amy about me would not, and should not, be my choice.

Susan was feeling overwhelmed by the intensity of the past 18 hours, and so was I, so I had no objection when she suggested we cool things for the rest of the day. She had an appointment in the afternoon which she could not cancel, and so at about 2:00 p. m., only slightly 24 hours after learning they existed, I dropped my sisters off at Susan's, and went to Mike's to collect my thoughts. Susan and I had arranged to go to Lockport, and to the cemetery the next day (Friday, June 24), and so I knew more exciting experiences lay ahead. Tentative plans were made to have dinner on Saturday night at Mary's house.

Back at Mike's, I realized I had not as yet written to Pearl, and nearly two weeks had passed since I had first talked to her, so I sat at their dining room table and wrote her a ten-page letter. What to say in such a letter? I tried to touch on a little of everything: my family; childhood; interests; job; health; marriage; and a summary of 36 years of living. Not really too much to cover in a hand-written letter! I also asked questions which had arisen as a result of talking to Jane, contradictions such as where I had been born (Niagara Falls or Buffalo?), had Bill and Pearl really continued to date after I was born, and so on. I spent the better part of Thursday afternoon writing, and sent the letter off the next day, hoping there would be a response waiting for me when I returned to Stevens Point.

Thursday night sleep came earlier than the night before, and I had the first dreams I can remember having about my sisters, my birth father, and the changes I was experiencing. I can recall few specific details of those dreams, just the soothing presence of people, and the knowledge of who they were, and of who I was. They were pleasant dreams.

The weather was continuing to cooperate, and Friday, June 24, was another beautiful day. Susan and I went to the cemetery, and I found out one reason why Mike and I had been unable to locate Bill's grave on Wednesday evening. There was not as yet a headstone. At the grave-site, Susan wandered off to be by herself. I was alone with my thoughts, my feelings, and a still-bare grave, the dry spring having prevented grass from growing over the broken ground.

I believe asking "What if?" is a basic part of human nature. What if John Wilkes Booth had missed when he shot President Lincoln? What if President Kennedy's car had been just a few seconds late, or early, as he rode through Dallas? As I looked at my birth father's grave, I kept asking myself "what if things had happened differently in 1946?" What if Pearl had not gotten pregnant? Neither I, nor my new-found sisters would exist. Or would we? What if Pearl and Bill had married each other when she became pregnant with me? Then I'd certainly exist, but would I be "me"? If I was not the "me" I now knew, then who would I be? If they had married, at the very least my life would most certainly have been different. What would growing up with a full biological brother, or even more intriguing, with a sister (or several of them!), have been like for me? If Pearl and Bill had married, then what about my sisters? They would not exist as the people they now are either, but would they exist at all? These unanswerable philosophical and spiritual questions had darted about my head throughout my reunion period, but at the site of my birth father's grave they were particularly poignant. I tried not to dwell on them, realizing too much dwelling on the past, and how things might have been different, was where madness lay. If not madness, too much concentration on the past is at least a distraction from the experiences of the present.

At first, I could not be angry with Bill, or sad about his death. To be angry at him for creating me seemed, and felt, wrong. To be angry at him for not marrying Pearl and "doing the honorable thing" felt wrong, too. They were both young and still living with their families. Still more of those unanswerable questions came to me. The question of whether giving me up had anything to do with his later drinking problem was one of them. I thought, if my birth parents had married each other, Bill might not have gone on to father the four sisters I had just begun to meet. Thus, I just couldn't be sorry about his death as I now sat on the ground by his grave because I was still so happy I had found his family. Sadness just didn't seem like the right feeling for the time. I found myself saying "if meeting him was meant to be, you'd have met him before he died. There is a plan here—relax and accept what happens." When Susan came over, and we talked for a bit, the sense of loss finally hit me, but what I experienced was as much a feeling of sadness for Susan, having lost the father she knew, as a feeling of sadness for myself, who lost a father I never knew. I took a pebble from his grave with me, and we went on to Lockport. I still carry that pebble in my travel kit.

On the way, Susan told me we would probably go directly to Shamus' Restaurant for lunch as it was nearing noon. Shamus was her father's favorite place to eat, and during the years he worked in Lockport he had lunch there nearly every weekday. There was a possibility we would meet the son of one of Bill's brothers (the son of my birth uncle, thus a birth cousin of mine) for lunch, but that was not definite. Susan had talked to her cousin the night before, and they had decided to go slowly in telling the rest of the family. As we drove to Lockport, I was struck by what I saw as a miracle: exactly three weeks, after I had driven alone to Lockport to research my birth family, I was now returning to Lockport with my birth sister. A whole new exciting world had opened up, and I knew there was more to come. I didn't have to wait long.

As Susan directed me to the restaurant, I discovered we were kitty corner across the street from the County Hall of Justice. The proximity of the restaurant to Bill's workplace, in addition to the Irish motif, undoubtedly contributed to his patronage. More importantly to me, however, the restaurant was also directly across a small square from the County Civil Service building, where three weeks ago nearly to the hour, I had first "accidentally" come across the name of my birth grandfather, and my search had begun to roll! I was remarking on the amazing twists and turns my search had taken as we sat down in Shamus to order lunch. Susan unknowingly echoed my feelings from just 48 hours earlier, Wednesday afternoon as I waited outside Judge Kane's chambers, when she said "many of these people in here probably knew Dad. Isn't it strange to be sitting here now with you?" I couldn't agree more, and was trying to absorb the feeling of the place when another part of the adventure began.

We had just been served our salad when Susan looked over my shoulder and gasped "Uncle Junie!" (C9–10). I turned around to look as in walked three people: a younger man, an older gentleman, ruddy and tanned, and a pleasant gray-haired woman. Though because of the noise level Shamus was not the best place for introductions Susan presented me with my cousin Tim (who she had talked to the night before), and his father, Bill's oldest brother, my uncle Henry, known to the family as "Uncle Junie." I had thought the woman was Henry's wife, but I soon learned she was Bill's sister Mary Margaret Shanley (C10), known in the family as "Aunt Sis." I realized as the introductions were completed that in one fell swoop I had met an aunt, an uncle, and a cousin too! The number of birth relatives I now knew had just more than doubled! By then we had moved to a larger table, and the meals Susan and I had ordered were delivered. Tim, and Aunt Mary and Uncle Henry also ordered meals. I don't remember eating but I must have since my plate was nearly empty when we left an hour later.

We talked of the past, and of the part Uncle Henry had played. He was the oldest son in the family, and when their father died while Henry was a teen-ager, he took over the role of the patriarch. He had also been the person who took charge at the time of Pearl's pregnancy. She had moved into Lockport with Bill and Henry's family while she was carrying me, and Uncle Henry had driven Pearl to the hospital in Buffalo (Jane was wrong about my birth being in Niagara Falls) and had stayed with Pearl while I was born. Uncle Henry even reported the nurses, thinking he was my father, had urged him to "do the honorable thing" and marry Pearl! He had asked to see me after I was born, and had held me briefly before I was taken away to begin my new life. I believe this was when Uncle Henry told me Pearl had still been in emotional distress at the time of my birth, and had chosen not to see me or hold me.

Uncle Henry agreed with Jane's opinion that I looked more like Pearl than like Bill. I again told the story of my search (we were now at number five for Susan!), and there was more careful observation of my behavior. They agreed that somehow my hands, or my use of them in gestures, reminded them of Bill. Both Aunt Mary and Uncle Henry have "salt and pepper" hair turning to mostly gray, and the question of how I came by my own prematurely gray hair was definitely answered.

I know both Uncle Henry and I were in tears on and off during lunch. I suspect the same was true for the rest of the strangely composed group at the table. The entire meal was a surrealistic experience for me, to be sitting in an Irish restaurant on a Friday afternoon, surrounded by members of my newly found birth family. Surrounded by the happy and oblivious crowd we were talking about the recent death of a man who was a father, brother, and uncle to the family members seated there. And yet at the same time we were talking of the recent surprise appearance of the son who, under different circumstances, might have carried on the family name. We were talking of my loss of the experience of growing up surrounded for all of my life by my biological kinfolk, as I now was for the first time. And yet I was so deliriously happy that, at least for a while, I could have that experience. Such joy and such sadness at the same time. The lunch, though not Chinese, was truly sweet and sour!

We left the restaurant, and Tim had to go back to work, so I took pictures of my four "new" relatives with the courthouse where Bill worked in the background, and the rest of us left for Tim's house where his wife, and Uncle Henry's wife, D'Nelle, heard my story (number six for Susan, and counting!). Aunt Mary said she'd like to have me come to a family gathering at her house the next evening (Saturday, June 25). The gathering planned for (my sister) Mary's house could be moved, and plans were tentatively set to return to Lockport the next night. There were two more of Bill's brothers in the area, and some discussion of when to tell them, and what their reactions might be. Susan's baby sitter was expecting her back at three o'clock, and at five minutes to three she and I left to return to Buffalo.

On the way back we realized again that we were both exhausted from the intensity of the past three days, so we decided to take the evening off from the reunion process. We set a time for me to call Susan on Saturday. Friday night I took my break from my search by visiting Pat, a friend of much more recent acquaintance. Though he lived in the far south Buffalo suburb of Hamburg, Pat commuted across the entire city of Buffalo, some 30 miles each way, to work at a company in North Tonawanda. He was a member of the Air National Guard with Bob, another one of my high school friends. Bob, Pat, and Mike Indian were all pilots, and through Bob and Mike I had met Pat. Getting away from the process of the reunion, which had grown to occupy virtually all of my waking hours for several days, was almost a relief. After a late night of conversation with Pat, I called Susan the next day, at which time I found out the plans had changed again. Aunt Mary had to work unexpectedly, so just the Buffalo branch of the family would be gathering at my sister Mary's at 6:00 p. m. Saturday afternoon Mike Indian and I took a flight in his plane around the Buffalo area. We flew over north Buffalo, Grand Island, Lockport, and Wilson, where I had learned from Uncle Henry Pearl had grown up. From the air I was again struck by the relatively small area within which so many important things in my life had taken place.

When I picked up Susan, her daughter and her infant son for dinner, I found their mother had decided to tell their youngest sister, Amy, about me. I would be meeting her within minutes. We got to Mary's, and at the top of a long flight of stairs, in Mary's kitchen, I met the third of my four sisters. Amy was as shy and cute as I had thought she might be from the photos I had seen at Susan's. We stood looking at each other, she said "glad to meet you" very politely, and I asked her if I could have a hug. She nodded her head, and we hugged. She shyly walked away and said quietly to one of her sisters, "He's cute," and the sister (mercifully I have forgotten which one!) immediately reported her remark to me and to the rest of the room in general. Amy was embarrassed, and I, in mock anger, said "Come on now, that was supposed to be a secret!"

We visited for a couple of hours, talking about Bill, his family, me, my family, and particularly about Molly—now the only sister I had not yet met. Molly was the one who most people seemed to think bore the closest resemblance to me both physically and psychologically. We took a picture—several pictures actually, of the entire family group and various subsets, and then, too soon, the evening was over, and I had to leave (H2).

I had decided that on Sunday, June 26th, I would leave Buffalo and continue with what had been originally planned as the last stop of my vacation, a visit to friends in Columbus, Ohio, so I arranged to stop at Susan's the next morning and select some photographs to take with me, and to say good bye—or rather farewell, since I was clearly aware that I now had more reason than ever to come back to Buffalo, and soon! I hated to leave, but yet I knew I needed some time to react, integrate, and put into perspective the past five days. I had had quite a month since Sunday, May 28, when I finally asked my parents the questions that began my search.

I had but one stop left before I could get back to Stevens Point and really take time to think about the whirlwind activities of the past month, and that was at the home of Ann Johns, a friend and former colleague at my first job as a psychologist. Ann's office had been next door to mine for two and a half years at Columbus Children's Hospital during my first job after I got out of graduate school. I had been looking forward to sharing my experiences with Ann, especially since she was both a psychologist and the adoptive mom of a then-teenage daughter, who I had met in Columbus. Everyone with whom I had thus far shared my story had been directly involved in the search in some way and already knew their part of the story. With Ann I would have a chance to tell the whole story from the beginning, and would have a sophisticated and knowledgeable audience. I had a larger audience than

I had expected because Ann invited her daughter, Anna, and one of Anna's friends, who was also adopted, to listen. I took nearly two hours to go over the whole story, and whether the speaker or the listeners derived more benefits from the telling is an open question. The chance to put my story into order, and to begin to think about the next steps in the process was a chance to grow, and gave me more to think about on the last 11-hour drive back to Stevens Point.

My feelings upon my return to Stevens Point were odd. I felt during the month I had been gone I had changed so much, but the city, my job, my friends: all these had not changed at all. I was still in the midst of a marital separation, and within hours after my return I went out to my old house to pick up some mail. I learned my wife had gone through a cancer scare while I was gone, and had just been released from the hospital that day. I told her of my search, and she told me she was upset that she had not heard about my progress directly from me. Instead, a mutual friend on the faculty (who I had told about my search when I had called back to the department secretary from Rochester) had told her about what I was doing. Sadly, Margaret's happiness for my progress was significantly tempered by feeling left out of the process. I hadn't thought to include her, in part because of our marital troubles, but mostly for the same reason I had still not yet chosen to tell my parents: I was doing *my* search, and I wanted to think the process, and the results, through myself before letting my family, or very many others in on the story. I was still unsure how the long-term effects of the search process would play out, and wanted some time to work through at least the early aftermath myself.

I was to get lots of time to think that summer, as I had sublet my apartment in town and planned on living in my cabin, which is located about 20 miles from town. There was no telephone, only a portable generator for electricity, and Margaret and I had bought 44 acres of land, and selected the cabin site specifically so we could have peace and quiet. I built most of the cabin myself, starting in the fall of 1980. For the next six weeks I commuted to town four days per week, leaving by 6:45 in the morning, to teach a summer school class. I returned to the cabin, usually about mid-afternoon each day, to be alone with my thoughts and my writing. Staying at my cabin for the whole summer of 1983, I wrote most of Part One of this book.

PART TWO
THE AFTERMATH

CHAPTER 8

The Aftermath Begins: Pearl's Withdrawal

When I got back to Stevens Point from the trip, I found there was not a letter waiting for me from Pearl. I had written to her before leaving Buffalo for Columbus, and was hoping she would also have written in the time since we had first spoken. I was disappointed, since we had agreed to write to each other and send pictures, but being on the road, I had no photos to send her. I decided perhaps she was having trouble getting her thoughts together to write them down, or perhaps she was waiting to see pictures from me. So I immediately started to sort through my collection of pictures of myself to select out a group that would show Pearl what I had looked like over the years. I gathered about 20 or so, and sent them off to her, with a letter in which I told her about the various periods in my life represented by the photos I had selected.

I mailed them off to her within a few days of my return, and was surprised when, just a few days after I had sent them, they came back, along with a letter from Pearl. Judging from the time between when I had sent them to her and when they came back, she must have had them in her possession for less than 24 hours, and perhaps she even sent them back the same day she received them. In the letter that accompanied them she thanked me for sending them, and wrote that I looked like I was happy as a child, and I was an attractive young man. One of the pictures I had sent was of me in my summer Boy Scout uniform. I was wearing shorts and my back pack, ready to go on the North Star canoe trip. In my letter I had made comments about my skinny legs. Pearl's letter made reference to my legs, saying they must have come from my birth father's side of my family because everyone in her family was a little heavy. Reading these comments, I knew she had at least looked at the pictures.

However, the rapidity of their return made me very uneasy. I thought if she had felt at all good about seeing them, she would have kept them for at least a few days. In my letter, I even identified which ones she might keep if she wanted, and which of them I wanted to have returned to me because they were one-of-a-kind and I did not have the negatives for them. I had even dared to hope she might decide to show them to her other son, Keith (D5–D7, H3, I2, I4, I6, J6), which also would likely have meant she would have to keep them for a while. Unfortunately, rather than feeling she returned them so quickly because she was highly motivated to write, I got the sense their rapid return was a sign she didn't want them in her house any longer than necessary.

I was trying to decide what to do about Pearl's apparent lack of desire to have my pictures in her home when I got another letter from Lockport. I recognized neither the name nor the address, but since it was from Lockport I assumed it must have something to do with my search. I excitedly ripped open the letter to find it was from Alice Williams, one of the two long-time employees of the Niagara County Welfare Department who were off of work the day I stopped to look up Alice Belschner. Alice had returned to work the day after I left, and was asked by a co-worker (probably the clerk with the nephew who went to UWSP), whether she knew of anyone by the name of Alice Belchner who worked for the Department during the 1950s. For many years Alice Williams had been Alice Belchner, during the time she was married to a man who had passed away in the late 1950s. She had remarried and was now writing to ask me who in her family I was seeking. As an amateur genealogist herself, she thought she knew of all of her relatives, and she was fascinated by the possibility that there was someone she had missed. Alice mentioned several possible routes of connection, including that I might be related to her through her first husband. His last name had originally been Belschner, and he had dropped the "s" to make it more pronounceable. Her ex-husband had several brothers, and Alice mentioned the names of these men, one of which was Clarence Belschner, who I knew, by then, was my paternal birth grandfather. She asked me whether I recognized that day any of these names, and to tell her all of the genealogy I knew about myself.

This letter was both a surprise and a revelation. I *was* on the right track after all! Moreover, had I stayed in the Lockport area, continuing my search for one more day, I might well have completed my search right then, since it is highly likely that if I mentioned Pearl's name, Alice would have known her, and told me who she was. Of course, had I mentioned Pearl's name it would have uncovered the secret of my birth, something I learned, when we later spoke, Pearl did not wish. I was glad I had not been very specific about why, or for whom, I was searching, and had been careful about mentioning names when I was at the Welfare Department.

Now, especially knowing that Pearl still wanted to keep my existence a secret, I decided I had best write to Pearl to ask her advice about what to say in my letter back to Alice Williams. I quickly wrote to Pearl, summarizing Alice's letter, and asked her what she would like me to write back to Alice. Pearl's response to this letter was rapid also. She implored me to please ignore Alice's letter, or better still, to write to Alice and tell her I was mistaken, and that I was no relation to her. According to Pearl, Alice was very judgmental, and was the kind of woman who could not keep a secret. Pearl feared that if Alice found out about me, she would tell everyone. I decided to write to Alice telling her I had found out what I needed, and that I was not related to her (A technical truth Pearl had pointed out to me in her letter about the situation, writing that Alice "is not really a blood relative to you, she's related only by marriage.") Before I could get my letter to Alice composed and sent, another post card arrived from Alice saying she was eagerly awaiting my reply to her letter. I sent my reply, and, thankfully, haven't heard from Alice since.

More than the contact Pearl and I were having by mail, I had wanted to meet in person with both Pearl and Keith. I had hoped she would be the one to offer to arrange a meeting with me. The most logical time for us to meet would be that coming fall when her husband was scheduled to work in Rockford, Illinois, as Pearl indicated he would be doing when we first talked. I had decided not to pressure her by bringing a meeting up again, and to let her be the one to mention a meeting first. With the quick return of my photos, and the wariness that action, and her response to Alice Williams' letter gave me, my decision to let her be the one to bring up any meeting was reinforced. We exchanged perhaps one or two more letters during the summer and fall of 1983. She did not mention coming to Rockford, and I did not either.

In situations where emotion runs high, every word of every letter is likely to be the subject of careful scrutiny. Both the writer and the reader are likely to go over the letters repeatedly, asking "What does she mean?" "Why did he write this" "Why didn't she write that?" I was interested to see Pearl closed her second letter to me with the phrase "One who cares, Pearl." I closed what may have been my following letter to her with "Love, Doug." I signed as I did only after much careful thought. I do not use the word "love" casually, but I am also not afraid to use the word. I have several close friends, both male and female, to whom I close letters with "love." After much thought, I had decided I did love Pearl for giving me life. However, I suspected that if Pearl and Bill had married, I would have taken the brunt of my birth father's anger when he got drunk. At that point I loved her for *not* marrying him, although later I would learn that, had the choice been their own, they would likely have married. In a subsequent letter to Pearl, I mentioned Keith again. Perhaps I just mentioned his name, or perhaps I asked about whether she had yet told him about me. I'm not really sure.

Something in my letter seemed to have been a mistake, or at least the letter triggered a reaction in Pearl. There was a longer-than-usual delay in her response, and when her letter finally came Pearl wrote that she had looked at my last letter, and at my closing words, and had something she needed to tell me. She said she did not want to hurt me, but that she could not feel love for me. She did not have the sense I was a long-lost son, and didn't think she ever would. There was just too much pain associated with me in her life to allow her to feel good about me. She also said again that she and her husband had decided not to tell Keith about me, and asked for my understanding and cooperation in respecting their decision.

I may have written a response to Pearl's letter, but whether I did or not, a month or so passed without any correspondence between us, and by then Thanksgiving had nearly arrived. Helped by the fact that the month between Thanksgiving and Christmas is always busy with term papers and final exams, to say nothing of preparations for Christmas, I decided not to write for a while. I would be home at Christmas, and I would call her from Buffalo to see how things were going.

I made my second call to Pearl just after that Christmas (1983) from a phone booth in a local YMCA, where I swam while visiting my parents. She answered the phone and I said hello and introduced my-self. I asked her how she was doing and she said that she was "OK." There was no joy in her voice, which was flat throughout the conversation. Her answers to a couple of my other attempts at conversation were given in a one- or two-word monotone voice. I sensed she wanted to discourage me from prolonging the conversation, which ended when I asked her if she had changed her mind about meeting me, to which she replied "no." I then said I would call her the next time I was in town, and we said goodbye and I hung up.

A few other calls I made to Pearl on visits to Buffalo in the summer, or at Christmas break in 1984 and 1985, all followed the same basic pattern. I'll summarize what turned out to be the last conversation we were to have for some time, which occurred sometime in 1985. I asked whether I had called at a good time to talk, and she said it was "not a good time to talk." Then I asked if there was another time when I could call back that would be more convenient, and she said "I'll write." I said I would be back home in Wisconsin within a few days, and I hoped to hear from her in the near future. I asked her whether she still had my address, and she again said "I'll write," beginning to sound even colder, now almost angry at having to repeat herself. I said "Well, good-bye then." She said good-bye, and we hung up. Needless to say, she didn't write.

As these rather painful phone conversations were taking place in 1984 and 1985, I wasn't sure what I should do. I didn't want to contact her "too often" or to have her feel harassed, but how many were "too many" calls? Friends in the search and support movement, many of them birth mothers themselves, suggested I just go to her house the next time I was in Buffalo and knock on the door. I was uncomfortable with doing that, but I didn't know what else to do, since nothing I had done so far seemed to be working. Eventually I decided to let her have some time without any contact from me to allow her to find a good way to come to terms with my appearance. I also hoped she would eventually be able to tell Keith about me.

CHAPTER 9

Sisters

M y relationship with my birth sisters over the years, since I found them in 1983, has been hard to describe. I'm sure my appearance so soon after their father's death did not make matters any easier. In a sense I think perhaps the shadow of whatever each of their relationships was with their father fell across their relationships with me. I recall Susan told me that upon first seeing me she was initially let down because she had expected to see someone who looked like a younger version of her father. In outward physical appearance at least, I don't think I have very much in common with him, although all of them have commented on the similarity of Bill's and my speech and gestures, and we are said to look more alike in pictures of our childhood years.

Had I appeared on the scene before Bill died his reaction to me might well have given my sisters some cues as to how they should respond to me. I certainly hope that Bill would have been more accepting of me than Pearl has been, although (as we will learn in Chapter 10), Pearl's son Keith's positive initial response to me was apparently not diminished by his mother's negative reaction.

There are at least a few less-than-positive feelings of my own with regard to my sisters that I can identify. One of the feelings I am aware of is wondering whether they really think I "belong" in their family. After all, I was not there for the (apparently mostly early) good times during the childhood of Susan, Molly, and Mary. Nor was I there during the hard times of Bill's progressing alcoholism, their parents' separation and divorce, his failing health, and his ultimate death. As an adoptee I think I am particularly vulnerable to feeling "apart" from most any group already. As I will discuss in more detail later in Chapter 10 about relationships with women ("Three Strikes and You're ..."), the feeling of being "apart" probably has its origins in the early sense of discontinuity that I think all adoptees experience between their pre: and post-birth environments. To the extent the personality and interests of adoptees differ from those of their adoptive families the adoptee's sense of not fitting in is heightened.

I suspect the sense of being "apart" may be one of the reasons I have always had difficulty letting my sisters know when I was going to visit Buffalo. I initially put off writing or calling them until the last minute, often calling the evening I arrived, and asking to meet them within a few days. After several years of this pattern, in the early 1990s, Susan, Molly, Mary and I talked about the problems we had in getting together. They told me that while they wanted to see me, their lives were so full they needed as much notice of my visits as possible. Without sufficient notice, it was difficult for them to rearrange their schedules to see me when I suddenly appeared on the scene. After this discussion I promised to give them as much notice as possible. Unfortunately, during the following multi-year period when I gave them several weeks' notice of my planned visits, we still had difficulty finding a time when we all could get together. Despite whatever continues to cause us difficulty in arranging meetings, however, when we do see each-other, I have a great time, and I think they do also. This causes me to wonder after each meeting why I resisted or somehow felt uncomfortable about the meeting beforehand.

Perhaps part of my problem is that I don't want to push myself on my birth sisters if they're not interested in me, and so perhaps I am more tentative with them in some way. Additionally, I can certainly see how I might remind them of some aspects about their father upon which they might not want to dwell. For example, the knowledge that Bill died of alcoholism, and I am a recovering alcoholic, might well cause them some discomfort about their own use of alcohol. Jokes have been made during my visits about the amount of drinking that is going on, and perhaps beneath the humor is a certain level of fear of their father's and my drinking problems, and of what those problems might mean for them.

Another problem bothers me as I communicate with my birth sisters, although this may simply be a subset of what seems to be a more general personality trait of mine. In a variety of situations, I sometimes have difficulty remembering the exact source of information, especially when it comes from a conversation with another person. I find myself often beginning a sentence with "Someone told me," or "I heard somewhere," to avoid attributing information to the wrong person. With my sisters, I sometimes have trouble differentiating them from each other. For example, in writing the section below in which I recall some of the many enjoyable times we have had together, I had great difficulty remembering just which combination of them were there at any particular event. I tend to forget with which one I had a particular conversation. I seem to think of them as almost a singular noun: "mysisters."

In the four or five years after we first met, when I would write letters to them telling them I was going to be visiting Buffalo I would send virtually the same letter to all three of them (with an appropriately changed salutation of course), adding a sentence or two to personalize each letter. From the mid-1980s to sometime in the mid-2010s, I sent standard Christmas letters to all of my friends and family. However, for some reason I felt guilty about writing one standard letter to my sisters at any other time. My guilt, and the sheer effort of sending 4 separate letters, sometimes caused me to put off writing to tell them I was coming to Buffalo until so late that I needed to call them instead of write. I was torn between making the call three times, or calling one with a request that she call the others. When Amy became an adult, I should really have made four calls. I don't mean to suggest I don't know anything about them as individuals because I do. Perhaps I feel I "should" know more about them, or "should" know them better than I do.

The bottom line is that I am much less sure where I stand with my birth sisters than I am of where I stand with my birth brother Keith, who I did, of course, eventually meet, as you will learn in the next chapter. I suspect there are many reasons for my insecurity with my sisters besides the issue of the amount of notice I provide them of my visits. One of the reasons may be simply a function of the differences between my ability to communicate with Keith as a man, and with my sisters as women. Additionally, Keith has no brothers or sisters but me, and each of my sisters each has her other three sisters. For whatever reason, I sense a much higher level of anxiety in myself when I contact any of them than when I contact Keith.

There have been a number of memorable events with my sisters that stand out in my mind. One of these was a meeting at another of the Hertel Avenue restaurants in Buffalo where we often get together. Mary and I had gotten there first, and we were catching up on what had happened since we had last met. On that early summertime, evening we were sitting outside under an awning. Mary had worn a light-colored flower-patterned summer dress. About ten minutes into the conversation, I heard her scream, and saw her staring and pointing over my shoulder, from where I heard another similar scream. I turned around to find Molly walking up, wearing the exact same dress Mary had on! After much laughter I learned Mary had owned the dress first, and that dress was one of her favorites, one in which she thought she looked very good. Molly had seen Mary wearing the dress, had been impressed, and had even borrowed the dress a couple of times to wear. She had then found an exact duplicate in a store, which she bought, in order to not have to borrow Mary's any more. Earlier that afternoon they had both independently selected the same dress to wear to meet me. Even before the laughter died down, I was feeling good to know they had wanted to look nice for their meeting with me. That told me I was important to them.

Other times I remember as being a lot of fun were when Keith, Susan, Molly, Mary, and I all got together. Soon after meeting Keith, I asked him if he wanted to meet my birth sisters. He did, and my sisters also indicated to me they wanted to meet him, so such a meeting was arranged at (where else?) a Hertel Avenue restaurant. I had an incredible feeling of wholeness to sit there and look at the four of them, representing both sides of my birth family. Being with the four of them was probably as close as I will ever get to the kind of meeting other adoptees talk of when they are together with their birth mother and birth father. We all got along very well, with much laughter and many jokes. During our first meeting they discovered Keith knew, and was good friends in high school, with their cousin Pat Mullett, one of the sons of my birth father's oldest brother, Henry. (Uncle Henry had taken Pearl to the hospital when I was born and had held me at the hospital before I became a member of the Henderson family.) Keith had also long known Henry Mullett, and therefore Uncle Henry was probably the first person to have known both Keith and me as adults.

Another time when we got the two sides of my birth family together, Susan told us she and her fiancée were thinking of buying a small house on the Lake Ontario beach in Wilson to use as a summer get-away cottage. We discovered Keith not only knew of the place (located about a half-mile down the road from his house) but he also knew the present owner, and could tell Susan a fair amount about the house. Keith had put in the lawn there several years earlier, and had worked on the plumbing as one of the side jobs he takes in the summertime. My brother and sisters discovered they all enjoyed playing cards, and suggested, if Susan bought the cottage, they might get together for cards and Buffalo Bills football games. I just sat back smiling and watched the conversation, happily soaking in the sense of feeling connected.

There was one other especially memorable time when I was together with Keith and a couple of my sisters as well. In late May 1993, I was visiting Buffalo on the way to go to St. Lawrence for my 25th college reunion. I had arranged to meet Keith, his wife, Kathy, my sisters, and Bruce Caley (G1, G2), a friend I had known since high school, in town. Susan, Molly, and I were there, and Bruce arrived looking very somber, which was quite unusual for him. He asked whether my parents had talked to me that evening, and I said no. He took me aside and told me they had called him just before he left his house. Then he gently told me my Aunt Erland, my father's sister, had died, and I was to call home when I could. I called, and found things were relatively OK there at that point. Dad urged me to finish out the evening as I had originally planned, and to go ahead the next morning on to St. Lawrence, saying "Aunt Erland would have wanted you to go." She was in her late 70s, had been in relatively good health, and her death in her sleep two days earlier was totally unexpected. On the night she died, Keith's family had met her for the first time, at my parents' house. Since I drove Aunt Erland home after Keith's family left, I had been the last person to see her alive.

When mom and dad had not heard from her for a couple of days, my father went to her apartment and found her, in bed, asleep. I loved her very much, but learning she had died peacefully and quickly made things a lot easier. Keith and Kathy arrived while I was on the phone, and shortly after I returned from the call, Mary arrived, looking terribly stressed. My parents had also called her, and she had come to the restaurant thinking she had to be the one to tell me the bad news. On the way there, she had worked herself into a state, and was unable to think of any way to give me the message other than to just blurt out "Hello, Doug, your aunt died." We all were actually able to laugh about her relief that Bruce had done the job for her.

This might be as good a time as any to describe Aunt Erland and her part in my life and search. Aunt Erland was my father's younger sister, by only a year or two. After my father and mother got married, she continued to live with her parents for many years, working in the office of a Buffalo heating coal company. Sometime in her later forties, she married Bill, a widower a year or two older than her father. They had, as far as I could tell, a happy, although childless, marriage. Uncle

Bill had several adult children, as well as grandchildren who were about the age of me and my brother, Dave.

Throughout my childhood Aunt Erland would visit our house often, probably averaging weekly. Each time, she would take me aside and slip me a dollar or two telling me to keep it a secret between the two of us. Since she couldn't afford to give Dave any money, I was not to tell him about it either. She always brought both of us many Christmas gifts, and those were always distributed equally between my brother and me.

When I went off to college, she was especially proud of me and came with my parents to the annual St. Lawrence Parents Weekends a couple of times, as well as to my graduation. I loved her, but at the time I didn't give her special attentions much thought. Perhaps not surprisingly, at some point when Dave and I were young adults, we confided in each other that Aunt Erland had all along been giving us both money and telling us not to tell anyone.

I would have always remembered her fondly, but not in any unusual way, until I started wondering about the possible circumstances of my adoption. As I learned about the situations in which adoptions often happened, I realized that in the 1940s, a single woman living with her parents and finding herself pregnant, often put the child up for adoption. And adoptions, both formal and informal, often happened between family members.

Suddenly, Aunt Erland's circumstances came into a very different focus. What if she was my birthmother? That would certainly explain why people so often perceived physical similarities between my father and me. It would also explain her special treatment of me. It might also explain why she never married until she was well past childbearing age. And of course, in the years before I was adopted, Aunt Erland would have been well aware of the child-bearing difficulties her brother and my mother were having.

In the absence of knowledge, we create fantasies. Early in my thinking about a search, I spent perhaps a couple of months wondering how I could go about finding out what had happened to Aunt Erland in the mid-1940s. This was one of the factors in my deciding I wanted to search. Of course, once I found my birthmother, and learned the truth of my adoption, Pearl's situation bore some uncanny similarities to the fantasy I had made up about Aunt Erland. Fortunately, many members of my birth family had met Aunt Erland several years before her death and so on that evening everyone knew who she was. It was not until working on the 2024 revision of this book that I wondered if the timing of her death was in any way related to having just met Keith. Was it possible that she could now rest comfortably, having met both sides of my birth family?

There was one more half-sister, and Amy was just 9 when I found the family. I was especially reluctant to force myself into Amy's world. There was considerable concern on the part of her sisters and their mother that meeting me might be too painful for her so soon after her father's death. She had been the only one living with her parents when they split up, and I understood she had taken her father's death quite badly. I was very glad her mother chose to bring her to Mary's for the dinner on the Saturday night at the end of the week in which I found them. The next time I think I saw her was some years later when she and her mother came to a party at my parents' home on Grand Island. At that time Amy was still in high school, and she knew my friend Mike Indian (who also came to the same party) because he was a teacher at her school. Throughout her high school years, my letters to Amy had always been sent to both Amy and her mother at their home, in order to indicate to both of them that I did not want to come between them. Amy never responded to my letters, and I hope I never pressured her to. With possibly one more exception, during the time she lived with her mother, Amy never chose to accompany any of her sisters when we would get together. On occasion one of the older sisters would explain that Amy was unable to come to see me, sometimes explaining their mother was overprotective of her, and sometimes saying she had other plans. Although I would have liked to have seen more of her, I understood things were different with Amy than with the older three because of both her age and the fact she was still living with their mother. I could live with that situation.

When Amy left for college, I wrote a letter just to her (but sent the letter to her mother's address because that was all I had) saying now that she was on her own, I would be contacting her directly to let her know I was coming to Buffalo. I wrote that if she wanted me to, I would no longer send letters to her at her mother's address, saying all she needed to do was to give me another address. I don't think she ever responded to this letter either, and so my connections with her had, over the years, become almost nonexistent.

When I visited Buffalo in the winter of 1996 we arranged a meeting of Susan, Mary, Molly and I at a restaurant. When I arrived, there were four women at the table. I said hello and sat down, but it took me a few minutes to realize I was sitting next to Amy! In the years since I had last seen her, she had grown up, changing from a shy girl to a poised and confident young woman. Her maturity was an exciting thing to see, but a rather scary one as well, since I was forced to realize just how much time had passed since I had first found my birth family.

CHAPTER 10

Keith: When Is a Secret Not a Secret?

I did not contact Pearl for several years, from sometime in 1985 until 1990, when an unexpected health problem, extremely high blood pressure, arose. Beginning during the 1987–88 academic year I ran into three serious problems at work. In the academic world, there are three levels of rank for Doctoral-level faculty members: Assistant, Associate, and Full Professor, each having performance and time-in-rank requirements. I was hired in 1976, at the usual entry level as an Assistant Professor, and was promoted in 1982 (my earliest eligible time), to Associate Professor. Having continued my previous level of performance, I had applied for promotion to Professor on schedule in the fall of 1987. For reasons I considered broadly understandable, but in my case not valid, I was denied promotion both in 1987, and again in 1989. Both times I obtained assistance in addressing the issue (which was being "below his department's average student ratings") without success. The third time, in 1990, and with assistance from a new Department Chairperson who was knowledgeable in statistics, I received my promotion, but the entire four-year effort was extremely stressful for me.

Had the problem with my promotion been the only work difficulty I was having at the time, I probably could have coped with that problem successfully. However, two additional problems arose toward the end of the appeal process for the second denial of promotion in the spring of 1989. My department was experiencing rather serious personnel issues. Two people, both of whom I worked closely with on a daily basis, began to function increasingly ineffectively. As with most personnel issues, the details remain confidential, and the process was painfully slow. It was personally painful for me as well, but eventually the situation resolved with both individuals leaving their positions.

Perhaps the fact that my blood pressure should have suddenly risen to what was a dangerous level should not seem odd, especially in light of all of the stress I was experiencing, but the problem was, nonetheless, something I had not expected. Stress level aside, I was leading a relatively healthy lifestyle. I had been sober since 1978, never smoked, swam between two and three miles a week, and was slightly below-average in weight. When the problem first presented itself, I stopped drinking coffee, which for many years had been a mainstay of my high activity level. I even attempted to use biofeedback and meditation to alter the pattern and muscular style of my breathing both while swimming and in general, but none of these approaches at reducing my blood pressure worked. Ultimately, I had to go on medication, which I did in May of 1991.

I thought my birth brother, Keith, should really be aware of his potential for a blood pressure problem, and was unsure of whether or not, without the benefit of my experience, there was enough history of high blood pressure in others in his family to make him aware of his potential risk. I had been giving Pearl time to change her mind and tell Keith about me, and at the time the blood pressure problem developed, I had not contacted her for about five years. Susan and I were going to be in the Buffalo area for a vacation in early August of 1991, and I thought the health issue would provide a good reason for me to make contact with Pearl again.

One of the things Susan and I did in New York during the vacation was to take Uncle Henry and D'Nelle up on their oft-repeated invitations to visit them at their summer home in Northern New York State. We drove to just north of Watertown to spend a weekend with them. Actually, their home was only 40 miles from my undergraduate alma mater (St. Lawrence University), but we didn't drive those last miles to see the campus, though I was tempted. Uncle Henry and D'Nelle were very happy to see us, and we spent time driving along the Thousand Island State Park area of the St. Lawrence River on their pontoon boat and had a picnic lunch in the shelter of one of the islands while Henry fished. We had an enjoyable time talking about our lives, and about Bill and his life. He and Uncle Henry had often come to this area to fish together, and I was again struck by the proximity of places that had been important in both my, and my birth father's lives. Uncle Henry also told me more of what he knew about Pearl and her life. After our visit was over, we drove back to Buffalo where we planned visits with both my adoptive and birth families.

On the way to Buffalo, I decided the time was right to call Pearl to tell her about the blood pressure problem I had developed, and to see whether she had changed her mind since I had last talked to her about meeting me. With Susan standing next to me, I called Pearl from a pay phone along the New York State Thruway hear Batavia. She answered the phone (as she had every time I had called). I told her who I was, and, rather than expressing any happiness at my call, she once again became immediately cold in her tone of voice. I said we had not talked in quite a while, told her I was in the Western NY area for a visit, and asked her whether she was perhaps interested in getting together. She responded that she was not. I said I had a health problem that had arisen and I thought her son might need to know he might be at risk. She said to write her a letter about the problem, and she would see what she could do.

I feared she was simply not interested in seeing me, and she might never be, but I also wondered if she had company, or whether, for some unspoken reason, this was not a good time for her. I decided the time had come to speak plainly and end the uncertainty. I said "I don't want to seem dull, but I don't want to misunderstand anything here either. Are you telling me you have no interest in having anything to do with me, now or ever in the future?" She replied "That's correct." I said I was sorry to hear that, and I hoped she would change her mind. I told her I would keep her informed if I ever changed my address, and that I would write about the health issue. I hung up the phone, ending what I feared may well have been our final conversation.

Once we were back in the car, I told Susan about what Pearl had said on her end of the conversation. I was numb, unable to have any reaction, but Susan cried openly, saying she was furious with Pearl for rejecting me and she just couldn't understand why Pearl was doing it. All I had in me at that point was to continue driving to Buffalo. I think to acknowledge the amount of hurt I was feeling would have made continued functioning simply impossible for me.

I had not yet decided whether or not to actually contact Keith myself, but I thought I would at least look for more information about him while I was in Western NY. That way I would be able to contact him if Pearl did not tell him about me herself. A couple of days later Susan flew back to Stevens Point, and I drove the 25 miles to Wilson to begin the process of checking Keith out. I had learned where Pearl lived and driven by her house a couple of times in the previous few years, and I began my visit to Wilson by driving by her house again. She lived in what appeared to be an old farm house, several miles outside of Wilson, and across the road from a fire station. There were no other close neighbors.

Over the years several people had suggested to me that I might at least get to see her if I were to sit in my car outside of, or down the street from, her house. I could, they said, read a book or otherwise kill time waiting for her to come or go. The first time I found where she lived and drove by her house, I knew waiting near her house to see her would be out of the question. Any vehicle, let alone one with out-of-state license plates, would be highly conspicuous sitting at the side of the road anywhere near her house. The most I could allow myself was to slow from my usual country-road 55 MPH to perhaps 35 MPH and look at the yard and house, and wonder whether I would ever get to meet its occupant.

After driving by Pearl's house, I drove on into Wilson itself to begin the task of checking up on Keith. I knew by then, as a result of having helped many people with their searches, that a high school yearbook was an excellent place to start when searching for information about someone. There I could get a photograph of Keith, as well as find out what kinds of activities he had engaged in while a student. I also knew old yearbooks were often kept in the local public library. When I found the library, I also found a sign saying renovations were taking place, and that the essential reference books had been moved to the basement of a nearby church while the library was closed. I made my way to the church only to find another sign listing the library hours. The temporary library had just closed for lunch! My research was not having a very encouraging beginning.

Since I had only a short amount of time to spend in Wilson, I thought I'd stop at the public high school to see if they had a yearbook on file. As I drove to the high school, I remembered my uncomfortable experience at DeSales High School in Lockport several years earlier when I was a "greenhorn," first starting my search for Pearl. These thoughts gave me a chance to appreciate how far I had come in the intervening years.

Not knowing how to find the high school from the place where I was, I stopped a crew who was repairing a road outside of the church to ask for directions. They pointed me in the correct direction, and I was on my way shortly. Later, after I met Keith, I told him about the process of finding him. After I told him the first part of the story, he wondered aloud if he had met me that day! His job in Wilson is Superintendent of Public Works, and his responsibilities include the sewage and water treatment systems, garbage collection, and road maintenance. During the summer, when the work load is highest, he frequently works right along with his road crew, so I might have even "met" him without knowing who he was! At the very least I know I met some of the men who he supervises. I wondered if any of them saw any resemblance between their boss and the man driving the Honda from Wisconsin who asked for directions to the school that day!

I got to the high school and asked in the office whether they had any copies of old yearbooks. The secretary said while they did not have a complete set, those they did have were kept in the guidance office. At lunch time she wasn't sure whether anyone would be there, but she gave me directions. I found a man about my age in the office, and when I told him I was doing genealogy research and asked him if they had yearbooks from the early 1970s, he said he thought they did. He took me back into a file room and opened a drawer to reveal several yearbooks, including those from the years during which I thought Keith might have graduated. He left me alone to browse and went back to his desk. Shortly thereafter I was looking at a senior picture of Keith B. Dixon from the 1971–72 yearbook, and I was aghast (I2)! He looked eerily like me, especially his hair, which was curly, dark, and longish. The curls piled up on either side of his part, giving him an almost Dagwood-like appearance. I was so astonished because from about 1970 to 1972, I was wearing my hair in exactly the same manner (I1, I2)!

Having found his photo, and pouring over his face, I remembered what Pearl had told me about Keith when I first talked to her about him. She had said something about his having had "problems" in school, and that he was going through a "difficult time in his life." These, she said, contributed to her not wanting to tell him about me. The guidance counselor was still sitting in the outer office. Perhaps, given the man's age, he just might have worked at the school when Keith was a student there. I decided to approach him with the real reason I was looking through old yearbooks. I thought I would ask him first if he could hold our conversation in confidence, and if the answer was yes, I would ask if he could he tell me what he knew about Keith, particularly what Pearl might have meant by Keith's "problems."

The counselor agreed to keep our conversation private, and I told him my real purpose in being there and asked him about Keith. He said he did know him when he was a student, and that he still knew him. He told me Keith worked for the village and virtually everyone in town knew him, and liked him. In fact, he had seen Keith just the day before! I mentioned the words Pearl had used to describe him, and the counselor was at a loss to understand what she had meant. He did say Keith had taken the vocational training part of the high school curriculum, but quickly added there was "nothing wrong" with Keith's abilities or intelligence. His interests simply seemed to be more in learning hands-on job skills rather than in going on to college. The information I got from the counselor created both significant relief, and a new puzzle: just what had Pearl meant about Keith, and how was that related to her desire not to tell him about me?

We went back into the records room again and, knowing there might be photographs of Keith as a child in some of them, the counselor took out Keith's elementary school record folders. Though he showed me only the photographs several of them contained, and not any grades or other information, I had now found out so much more than I had ever expected to learn in one place, especially once Pearl had again rejected any contact with me. I thanked the counselor and asked if I might take the yearbook to the office to make a photocopy of the picture, and he assured me I could. I left to return to Buffalo with what I thought of as a real treasure—not only knowledge I had not possessed just an hour earlier, but a photograph as well. Keith was beginning to take shape as a real person, which made me feel more real as well.

When I returned to Stevens Point at the end of that trip, I wrote Pearl a letter telling her about my blood pressure, setting the problem within the context of the stress I had been experiencing. I suggested that if she could find a way to let Keith know he needed to watch his blood pressure, he would probably benefit, especially if he found himself under a good deal of stress. I also asked her to let me know if there was any other information I could give her that would be helpful. My letter to her not only went unanswered but also unreturned.

I spent the winter of 1991–92 wondering what I should do about the situation, and thinking I should perhaps contact Keith myself, since Pearl did not seem likely to tell him about me. I still did not want to dishonor Pearl's wishes, despite the fact that almost every birth mother I talked to couldn't understand why she did not want to meet me. Most people I talked with said I should take the bull by the horns with both Pearl and Keith: just go to Wilson, and meet them. They thought I should let Pearl and Keith solve any possible problems my appearance might create for them.

I was torn between my desire to meet Keith and my desire not to violate Pearl's request. My fear was that if I contacted him, I might decrease even further any chance she would ever want to meet me. I also spent a lot of time in thinking through the old saying "You can lead a horse to water, but you can't make it drink." I believed parents had the right to "force" things such as vaccinations and dentist visits on their children, even if they were against the children's wishes, as long as the parents knew the activity was good for their children. I also knew once children engage in some of these enforced activities, such as eating new kinds of foods, the children often find they like the very food they had only recently disdained.

I thought Pearl might well like me once she met me. At least many people with whom I spoke thought so! While Pearl's liking me was not unimaginable, I still had difficulty with the idea of forcing her to meet me against her will. I felt to force a meeting would be treating her as if she was a child, not capable of making decisions for herself. Although I had not yet fully developed this concept at that time, I think in retrospect I sensed that, with regard to her pregnancy with me, Pearl was like many birth mothers. She had been put in a powerless position. Others were forcing her to do what they said was best for her, and she had little choice but to comply. I could not answer the question whether, for Pearl, surrendering her son for adoption was really best for her, and really best for me, or whether she was just being pushed to place me because adoption was the least embarrassing solution for the rest of her family.

As an adoptee I too certainly had been in a powerless position with regard to being adopted in the first place. Adults made that decision for me. I had no part in that decision, but since I was a newborn infant, having others make decisions on my behalf was entirely appropriate. However, even though I was now an adult, I was still being told other adults in "the system" knew closed records were "best for me." I was not allowed to make my own decision, even if I thought learning the truth was now what was best for me. Knowing how much being treated as a child in such a paternalistic manner had hurt me, I did not want to turn around and treat Pearl in the same way. Whatever the situation had been in 1946, she was now an adult, and had made another decision with regard to not having contact with me. I believed her decision was wrong, but I still had to respect her decision, at least that part of her desire which dealt with a meeting between the two of us.

However, her decision about not wanting Keith to know about me, and the issues of the ability, and the right, for Keith and me to meet, began to seem to be entirely different issues. He and I were both adults, but only one of us, me, was being allowed to know anything approaching the full facts upon which to base a decision about meeting each other. I was beginning to question Pearl's right to make a decision for her other adult son. My ideas began to crystallize around thoughts that told me: "We're both adults—I should be able to tell him who I am, and then he and I should be allowed to make our own decision about what kind of relationship, if any, we want to have." I just did not as yet have enough faith that I was correct to allow me to act.

Beginning in 1986 I had become active in the American Adoption Congress (AAC), a national group whose primary goal was to work toward humanizing the adoption process, particularly by offering support to adult adoptees and birth parents in search of each other, and helping them gain access to their sealed adoption records. I made presentations at their 1986 and 1990 annual conventions. During the summer of 1991, I had submitted a proposal to conduct a workshop on finding death at the end of a search. In November 1991, the list of accepted program proposals for the April 1992 AAC convention in Philadelphia arrived. I was happy to find my proposal had been accepted.

I was equally pleased to see there would also be a workshop for adoptees who had a birth parent who did not want them to contact a sibling. I found myself in that exact situation, and determined immediately I would attend the sibling workshop, assuming it did not conflict with my own. The final conference schedule arrived in January, and I was relieved to see no conflict with the session on sibling searches. In February I was asked to take over a scheduled workshop on the process of denial in adoption for a presenter who had unexpected surgery, and fortunately that new workshop did not conflict with the sibling workshop either.

At the convention, I arrived a few minutes late for the sibling workshop, and for the first half or so I had to stand near the door, since the room was very crowded. Apparently, there were a lot of people in my situation. As I arrived, a woman on the panel was telling about what had happened when she finally contacted her birth siblings against her birth mother's wishes. In her case she discovered the siblings had known all along that their mother had some deep dark secret, and one of them had even surmised the secret had to do with either having had an abortion or having surrendered a child for adoption. When the speaker made contact with her siblings, everything fell into place for them. Mysteries that had been forbidden to conversation now were solved, and the birthmother's other children understood their mother much better once the secret was out in the open. Even her birth mother finally could see the contact between her children had worked out to be for their good, and also for her own.

The next panelist spoke about how, when she went against her birth father's wishes and contacted his other children, they too had already known about her, and were happy to finally meet. They had always wanted to find her, but did not have the faintest idea about whether searching was even legal, let alone about how to go about starting the process. Several other panel speakers told variations of the same story, and then they asked for questions from the members of the audience. I asked a couple of questions about the biggest issues troubling me, which were that I was risking further alienating my birth mother from me if I should contact Keith, and that I was fearful he might reject me too. Such a rejection would be doubly difficult, and was part of what was holding me back from contacting him.

When the panel and the audience heard I had waited eight years for Pearl to change her mind, they were amazed I could have waited that long. They were pretty unanimous in suggesting that if she hadn't found a way to tell Keith by now, she most likely never would. Members of the audience and panel also pointed out that since she had, after eight years, still not softened her stance toward meeting me, what did I have to lose by "risking" her anger and contacting Keith? As to the possibility he might reject me, not a single person in the room who had contacted a sibling under these conditions had been ultimately met with rejection. People suggested the fact he was an only child would make the thought of having a brother even more attractive to him. There was much good-natured urging me to call him immediately, and several people offered me change, and said there was a phone booth just down the hall. I said I probably would call him, but I needed to think a bit more about whether, how, and when, to call.

In discussions after the formal session ended, I met another adoptee, who happened to be, strangely enough, named Keith. He was in the same situation as I, with a birth brother who his birth mother did not want him to contact. We talked for a while, and I encouraged him to make the same decision I was close to making: calling my birth brother and introducing myself.

Although I left the program thinking I would probably call my birth brother Keith within a day or so, I still wanted to get some perspective on the decision. For most of my life, whenever I have had a major decision to make, I always have tried to plan things so that I have time to make the decision, and then wait for 24 hours before carrying the decision out. If I still felt my decision was right after a day of reflection, then I would follow through and take whatever action I had planned. While I could not always wait for 24 hours after making a decision to carry that decision out (and acknowledging this is a pretty conservative approach to decision-making), the process had always worked well for me, and I used this approach with regard to calling Keith.

I had another reason to wait a day to call Keith. At the same time as the adoption conference, which happened to be during our University's spring break, my wife, Susan, was in New York City at a dance conference recruiting another faculty member for her department. We had agreed she would come to Philadelphia when her conference ended to sit in on my presentation on finding death at the end of a search, which was on Saturday morning. We had arranged a dinner that night at which she would get to meet my high school and college girlfriend, Nancy, who had moved with her husband Russell and their three daughters to the Philadelphia area a few years earlier. Susan would also get to meet some of my adoption-related friends while she was there. If I waited until the next day, Saturday, to call Keith, then Susan could be there with me to share what I hoped would be the joy of his acceptance of me. If he rejected me, then Susan would also be there for moral support. In addition, I thought Keith would more likely be home and able to talk on a Saturday than on a Friday afternoon

Susan arrived from New York on Friday evening, and my program on finding death at the end of a search on Saturday morning went very well, so the day had already started out positively. Early that afternoon, as Susan and I were on the way to the telephone booth to call Keith, I ran into Ken Watson, a very special social worker. Ken began his career in the days of closed records, and had practiced long enough to be one of the first to realize the damage the closed system had done to members of the triad. He was now dedicated to undoing, as much as possible, the problems which he had been part of creating, and to preventing the continuation of the closed system. Perhaps most importantly in the immediate context, he is a large, lovable man, a "hugger" who looks a lot like the well-known W.W. II poster of Uncle Sam. I knew he would understand my excitement and trepidation as I prepared to call Keith. Ken was talking with Keith Ronstein, the other adoptee I had met after the sibling search workshop, who also had a birth brother he wanted to contact. I told them what I was on my way to do, and they wished me luck.

Although I felt I was an old hand at telephone contacts, having made my own call to Pearl as well as several others for individuals on whose behalf I was conducting a search, I was going to do at least one thing differently than I had in the past. There were several situations I had been told about in which the persons who had been contacted (whether an adoptee, a birth parent, or another birth relative) had been taken so much by surprise by the call that they said they weren't interested in contact, and terminated the conversation. Then, sometimes within minutes of hanging up, but sometimes days or weeks later, the person who had been called had a change of heart. However, unless they were able to recall (or already knew) the searcher's name or number, they then had no way of calling the searcher back. In some such cases the searcher, having been rebuffed once, had then waited years to make another contact, and time that might have been spent in reunion was lost.

Therefore, I planned to tell Keith as soon as I got him on the line that I was making a long-distance call and I had had trouble getting the call through. I was then going to ask him to write down my name and number in case we got disconnected. Of course, I knew if he recognized my name, that would mean Pearl had told him about me, and I would immediately be saved the trouble of having to tell him who I was. Even if he did hang up on hearing my name, and then had a change of heart, he could always ask Pearl if she had a way to contact me. But I wanted to be sure he would be able to make his decision without being forced to involve his mother, and so I decided I wanted to have him write my name and number down first thing.

Susan and I found the phone booth, and I went inside, with her standing just outside and listening in. A male answered the phone, and it was Keith. He was somewhat puzzled, but agreed to write down my name and number, which he didn't seem to recognize. I then told him I was an adoptee who had been born in October of 1946 to Pearl Belschner. I paused, and he said "That would make you my brother!" I said "Yes it would." I then added I did not want to cause him any problems, but felt I wanted to get to know him if he wanted to meet me. He was extremely happy to hear from me, and enthusiastically said he would very much like to meet.

I was simply on cloud nine! I soon discovered he had known at least something about me for some ten years. He had been told a "deep dark secret" by a cousin, who began the conversation by asking Keith "Do you want to know a secret about your mom?" I find it hard to believe that anyone would respond to this question with "No, thanks, that's all right"! Keith answered the way I would, and found all the cousin knew was that "a baby" had been surrendered for adoption by his mother long before she had met his father. The cousin didn't know anything more, about the time, the father, or even whether the baby was male or female. Keith, an only child, was immediately curious.

When Keith learned I had found his mother eight years earlier, he was dismayed, saying "Doug, that means we've lost eight years together!" I tried to explain my reasons for waiting so long. I didn't want to cause anyone any trouble, and I had not known whether he knew of me or not. I told him I really didn't want to interfere with the relationship between him and his mother. I'm not sure he understood my reasons for waiting all those years right at that moment, but there would come a time before too long when I would remind him about this part of our conversation, and about my reasons for delaying contact.

We spoke for perhaps an hour, with Susan backing out of the increasingly warm phone booth a couple of times to get some fresh air. Keith told me he had always intended to search for me, but he didn't know where to begin, except that he knew he couldn't ask his mother for information. He told me about his family: his wife, Kathy, and their son and daughter, Derek and Stephanie. We talked about how and when we might meet. We both wanted our meeting to be as soon as possible, and talked about doing so in about a month, in mid-May, as soon as my academic year was finished.

All in all, I guess the reception I received from Keith was as positive as I ever could have wanted. We made arrangements for me to call him when I got back to Stevens Point after the conference, and I hung up the phone, again experiencing that very special kind of feeling I suspect few people on earth except adoptees, or other members of separated biological families, can truly appreciate. I was finally being welcomed by a member of my birth mother's family! I had no doubt I would soon be meeting him. For me, once again, the adoption search and support movement had made it possible for me to make the phone call.

I left the phone booth, practically skipping down the hall, and almost leaving Susan behind! Although over an hour had passed since I had seen them, I was barely back into the area of the hotel where the convention was taking place when the first two people I ran into were the last two I had seen before I had made the call: Keith Ronstein and Ken Watson. I almost ran up to them, burst forth with the good news, and got a hug from Ken. They both said they could tell the minute they saw me the reception had been positive.

For the next day or so, everyone I saw whom I knew even slightly heard the story, or at least got a quick announcement of the good news. I was even asked to make an announcement at one of the general convention sessions, that after I had attended the workshop on sibling reunions, I had called my birth brother and been warmly accepted by him. I was sitting in the hotel lobby late that evening, when a woman who was working with Ben Wicks, a Canadian who was writing a book about adoption, found me. She asked whether I would agree to talk to Ben about how I felt to have just had a reunion over the telephone. Ben and I had our interview on audio tape in the lobby of the hotel, with several people sitting nearby taking in what I was saying. I certainly felt like a star of the conference! Ben's book, *Yesterday They Took My Baby: True Stories of Adoption* was published in February 1993, and unfortunately, I have not learned whether I was a star, or even mentioned, in his book!

I ran into Keith Ronstein a couple more times during the last day of the convention, and each time asked him if he had made the call to his brother yet. He ultimately decided not to make his call during the convention, but had in the meantime discovered his brother worked for the London branch of the same hotel chain in which we were staying in Philadelphia. He had even found a couple of employees in the Philadelphia hotel who knew his brother.

While the reader may already have already realized calling my birth brother from Philadelphia was quite appropriate, I did not recall until several weeks later, in a conversation with a friend back in Wisconsin, that the slogan of Philadelphia is "The City of Brotherly Love." As soon as I returned home from Philadelphia, I called Keith again, we talked for nearly two hours that time, and we began a routine of regular phone calls, often lengthy. I met his wife Kathy over the phone and heard more about their son and daughter. We had talked about exchanging photos in our first conversation, and we both sent off a package of photographs of ourselves and our families right away.

When Keith's package arrived, I was in for another surprise. Keith included a couple of pictures of himself in the mid-1970s, when he had been just married to Kathy, and when I looked at these photos, I found out more about his hair. I already knew from seeing his high school picture that we both had curly hair which we parted on the left, and, as fashion had dictated longer hairstyles, our curls tended to form big asymmetrical mounds on either side of our heads. A large lump of hair would protrude from where we had tucked it behind our left ear, and a larger lump grew just to the right of center on top. As my hair grew increasingly longer I did not like the "Dagwood" look (I1, I2), and tried several other hairstyles, looking unsuccessfully for something pleasing.

The first conversation Keith and I had after the photo exchange led to the discovery of another similarity. We both had hated our naturally curly hair, and had discovered exactly the same manner of dealing with it: we washed and partially dried it with a towel, combed it straight back on our heads, and then tied a cloth over it to hold it flat and prevent it from curling as it dried. We could then part our hair and minimize the "lumpy look" which I had immediately recognized in Keith's yearbook picture.

The tied-cloth approach had led me to a disastrous experiment with having my hair chemically straightened. Problem: the "wild" look (B6). Solution: a chemical straightening. Problem: to my dismay, I quickly discovered the newly straight hair had lost all of its body, and hair would cascade across my face every time I turned my head even slightly downward. Solution: wear a headband to keep my hair out of my eyes. Problem: the headband put a permanent wave back into the hair I had just suffered (and paid) to have straightened (B7). Solution: in the short run, I wore my hair in a pony tail. In the intermediate term, the straightened-but-bodiless hair grew out and got cut off. Fortunately, my hair grew back undamaged by the chemical process, and just as curly as before. In the long run, again fortunately, fashions changed and extremely long hair went out of style.

Keith and I also both discovered the benefits of simply abandoning the part in our hair and its attendant management issues for a more natural look. My final change in hairstyle happened in about 1972. I had a roommate who was the first white male I had ever seen who wore his very curly hair in a "natural" or "Afro" style which at that time only Black men were wearing. After my roommate towel dried his hair, he used a pick and hair dryer to lift and fluff it up. I tried this and the technique worked! Finally, I had found a hair style with which I was happy. I was thrilled the first time I saw the TV show *Welcome Back Kotter* because with my naturally curly hair, mustache, and round wire-rimmed glasses, Mr. Kotter (actor Gabe Kaplan) was a dead ringer for me (I3, I4)! As you will soon learn, since I decided to change my name in junior high school in part because my name was the subject of insulting jokes, it was certainly a pleasant experience to have someone popular who resembled me. As Keith and I laughed over our hair wars, we realized we had both experienced nearly the exact sequence of hair-raising events, and had arrived at the same solution. Nearly 25 years later we were both still wearing our hair in the same way.

In that same conversation, Keith told me about his experience when he got my package of photos. He was at work in the village garage (about a half mile from his home) and Kathy called to say a thick envelope had arrived from me. They both knew the letter contained my photos, and Keith said to go ahead and open the envelope while they talked. When she did, Kathy was amazed at what she saw, and said she'd better bring the photos right over. He and Kathy had looked through photos of me at his office during his lunch hour. In several of the photos he and Kathy easily saw the same similarity in 1970s hair styles I had noticed. In addition, our facial hair was the same: during the 1970s, we both had sort of droopy handle-bar mustaches! Several years later, when I was showing these photos to students in my developmental psychology classes, one of my students pointed out there was yet another similarity between Keith and me that could be seen in that set of photos: both of our wives looked very similar to each other. Most striking was their radiant smiles.

As Keith and I established a regular routine of phone calls, we discovered a number of similarities in our interests: building and construction from carpentry to operating heavy equipment, including my renting a skid steer twice (for a month each time), to work on the driveway at my cabin; and owning SUVs/ATVs/UTVs (I5, I6). Among others of the similarities, we found were that we both loved the outdoors, and took every opportunity we could find to spend time outside, especially in the woods. I had only bow-hunted for my first couple of seasons in Stevens Point, first on the land of my friend and colleague, Wayne Lerand, then the next year on my own land. More importantly, I found hunting, for me, was mainly just an excuse to be outside in the woods. I wasn't just sitting there "doing nothing" while relaxing and watching the squirrels and the sunset. I was *hunting*!

When I started to heat my house with wood (another similarity with Keith) in the late 1970s, the fall of the year was the best time to cut wood for the winter that was a year away. I gave up the hunting in order to cut wood, but I was still at least out in the woods, while cutting the woods down! Keith, on the other hand, is an avid hunter in both the bow and gun seasons. We also discovered I spend my spare time in the woods at a cabin I own located about 20 minutes' drive from Stevens Point, and Keith spends his spare time in the woods at a cabin his wife's family owns, located about an hour's drive from Wilson!

In another of our early conversations, Keith indicated an interest in meeting my parents, which made me very happy. I wanted my parents to meet all of my birth family, and my birth family members to meet my parents, therefore allowing me to share my experiences instead of having to keep my families compartmentalized. As we were discussing how and when I would introduce Keith to Mom and Dad, I thought I might as well explain an oddity of my identity. My father's first name is also Douglas, and when they brought me home from the hospital friends, family, and neighbors started to call me "little Doug," "Dougie" or "Doug Junior" to differentiate me from my father.

For a variety of reasons, Dad did not like any of these nick-names, and so fairly early in my life they began to call me by my middle name, Bruce. I came by that name not because of any rich or favorite relative, or any popular screen hero by that name, but because Bruce is "a good Scottish name." Dad wanted me to know of my heritage, both as his son (the "Douglas" part) and as a member of the Henderson family, which is of Scotch ancestry (the "Bruce" part).

When I got to junior high school, several things made me decide to go back to using my first name. First and foremost, there was another Bruce Henderson in the school, and though he was no known relative of my family, he may have been my evil twin! He often got bad grades, which seemed to show up on my report card, and he kept library books until they were overdue, for which I always seemed to get the fines. These things were not good. There was also a Johnny Cash song which was popular at the time, called "Big Bad John" about "a big, big man," a hero who died saving others in a mine cave-in. Unfortunately for anyone named Bruce, another song shortly afterward was a parody of "Big Bad John" called "Big Bad Bruce." In an era when insulting members of minority groups was acceptable, "Big Bad Bruce" was about a man who was, to be kind, definitely not the traditional John Wayne macho-man hero. As a result, the name Bruce became sort of synonymous with "sissy." I also got tired of having to tell the teachers at the beginning of every school year I was Bruce, not Douglas. So, I just stopped making the change, and became Doug.

By the time I changed to "Doug" though, I had been Bruce to my parents for so many years that they were unable to change. Until their deaths, they called me Bruce, and even now, a few of my oldest friends, and most of my Henderson relatives use that name. This has in the past led to some usually funny, though sometimes awkward, situations when friends who know me as Doug met my parents for the first time.

Mom or Dad would be talking about "Bruce did this" or "when Bruce came home" or they would say "Bruce has told us so much about you." I would start to see looks of puzzlement about who this "Bruce" person was, especially if the listener knew enough about my family to know my brother's name is Dave. An interruption of the conversation for an explanation of my dual-name status usually then had to follow.

In anticipation of Keith meeting my parents, I told him the "Bruce story." He was quiet for a minute, and then said "Do you want to know what *my* middle name is?" That was how we discovered we share the same, and rather uncommon, middle name. Upon discovering our common name, at first, we wondered if Pearl had selected Bruce as a middle name for her second son with some knowledge of the name I had already been given several years earlier by my adoptive parents. Although Keith had not directly asked his mother, we believed she did not have any knowledge of my adoptive name, especially since, in my first conversation with Pearl, she did not show any recognition of my name. She told me she was given a different family name and a different county than what was actually true. Sad to say, this was a common occurrence at the time I was adopted.

When Keith told me his middle name, after the shock wore off, I remembered that in his high school yearbook photo, which I had copied the previous summer, his middle initial was "B," but I had never wondered what the "B" stood for. A trip to the library to examine census data, and a talk with one of my colleagues who teaches statistics, have given me the following information. For men born in the late 1940s and early 1950s, the name Bruce was the 72nd most common name given to boys. If one stopped men of our approximate age at random on the street and asked their name until you found the first "Bruce," you would have to stop about 250 more men before finding a second "Bruce." The chances of finding two "Bruces" in a row are about one in 62,500! And yet here were Keith Bruce and Douglas Bruce, born to the same woman, one named by his new adoptive parents, the other kept and named by his mother and father. Having the same middle name was another of those similarities that made us feel "naturally" close to each other even before we had met face to face. The "Bruce" connection was another of those eerie events that had occurred throughout my search and reunion.

We had wanted to have a meeting as soon as possible, and had early on discussed getting together in the Toledo, Ohio region, which is about midway between Stevens Point and Wilson. Unfortunately,

Keith had used up all of his vacation time, and his work schedule was the busiest in the summer, which was coming up shortly. He couldn't take off the several days of work without pay, and at the same time pay for the costs of the travel, the food, the child care and the hotel such a trip would entail. Due to my teaching responsibilities, I was unable to leave Stevens Point until the end of the semester. Ultimately, we decided to meet on August 13 when I planned to be on the East Coast for my more-or-less annual summer visit.

When we began to plan the specifics of our reunion, we thought the best thing to do was to meet away from our parents and families, and in a place where we could have both privacy and freedom. I suggested the resort area south of Buffalo, where my high-school friend, Bruce Caley, had recently purchased a vacation cabin. I already knew Keith's wife's family also had a vacation cabin south-east of Buffalo, but I didn't know exactly where it was located. As we firmed up our plans, we discovered the two cabins are both in the village of Java, within a couple of miles of each other!

Another of the possible intersections of our families was related to the fact that both Keith's maternal grandfather, and my adoptive father worked in the grocery business. They might possibly have known, or known of, each other through their work. They certainly had the *opportunity* to meet, since Grandpa Belschner was a truck farmer who often took his produce from his home north of Buffalo some 35 miles to the Clinton-Bailey Farmers Market co-op in south Buffalo. My family also lived north of Buffalo (by a whole block and a half!) for many years. Dad worked his way up from a heavy laborer to the head of the transportation division of the Loblaws grocery chain, and for some 20 years drove daily some seven miles from our home to his office, which was in the main Loblaws warehouse at the corner of Bailey and Clinton streets in south Buffalo! They worked within a block of each other, and may well have stopped in for a meal at the same restaurant, one that was located adjacent to the farmers market and across the street from the Loblaws warehouse.

In talking with Kathy, Keith's wife, I found that she grew up in the northern end of the Town of Tonawanda, while I grew up at the Town's southern end. Kathy attended a private girls' high school which I also had ridden past on my bicycle. More strangely, as she talked about places she had worked, she mentioned the name of a North Tonawanda company which I recognized. Pat, the pilot friend of Mike Indian, who I visited the Friday night of the week I first found my birth family and met my birth sisters, commuted 60 miles a day from south of Buffalo to work at this same company. Although Kathy had not worked there in several years, she remembered Pat, and when I next talked to Pat he told me that he also knew and remembered Kathy.

Yet another common connection surfaced shortly after I contacted Keith. I received a call from Richard Kenyon, a reporter for the Milwaukee Journal/Sentinel, who was doing a feature story on adoptees, and wanted to talk to a male adoptee. He was given my name by an adoptee I knew from the Milwaukee area. When Dick called me, we talked for perhaps an hour. At some point during the conversation, he learned I was from Buffalo, and he said that he had grown up in a town not far from there—Lockport. Moreover, when they retired in 1989, Dick's parents moved to Wilson, which just happens to be the place where Keith lives, and was the village manager! When I asked Keith whether he knew the Kenyon family he said yes, they moved to town from Lockport a couple of years ago!

Perhaps similarities and cross-friendships such as these are to be expected between any three people who grew up in the same area, but in a city such as Buffalo, with some 500,000 residents, in an area (Western New York) with nearly 1.2 million people, we were fascinated that there were so many places where our paths, or those of family members, crossed.

One of the other really important similarities between Keith and me arose as we discussed how to handle the situation with Pearl. She had not wanted Keith to know about me, when the facts now were that he actually knew about me before I contacted him, and he was excited at the thought of meeting me. We struggled with how to handle that. We found out both of us value honesty very highly, and neither of us was comfortable with carrying our relationship very far without telling Pearl we had made contact. Keith also wanted his children to meet their "Uncle Doug," (a term he used, to my delight), and did not want them to have to keep their meeting me a secret.

We decided the first step should be for Keith to approach his mother and tell her about my contacting him. Although I think he had no doubt that I was the baby his mother had surrendered, his talking to her would also be a chance for the both of us to verify and fill in details in the story I had been told by Bill's family. Keith waited for a time when he and his mother could be alone, which took several weeks from the time I first contacted him. One night when his father was at a meeting and would be gone for the rest of the evening, he had his chance. Referring to the conversation he had with his cousin some ten years previously, but without naming her as the source, he told her he had been told by "someone" she had been engaged to a man and had given up a baby that resulted from their relationship. He wondered if the story was true.

She acknowledged the basic story, and began to tell him in detail about her engagement to Bill, and of the resulting pregnancy. When Bill found out she was pregnant, he agreed to marry her, and she went home to tell her family. She began to cry as she told Keith of her mother's angry reaction to the news she was pregnant. Pearl's mother flew into a rage, raced into town to Bill's house, and in the most unpleasant of terms accused Bill of ruining her daughter, and demanded he marry her immediately. Bill's reaction was to decide that being a part of a family where he was held in such low esteem was not what he wanted, and he backed out of his commitment to marry Pearl. He apparently disappeared, even from his own family, for a period of time.

Pearl's mother then insisted Pearl leave the family home immediately lest her father find out about her pregnancy. When I had first contacted her in 1983, one of her first questions to me had been to ask whether I had told her father who I was. I had told him that my mother was a friend of Pearls in school, and had lost contact with her. In truth the pregnancy seems to have been an open secret between Pearl and her father. The pregnancy and my existence were acknowledged tacitly and indirectly, but never spoken of openly. Bill's family took her in, and she lived with them throughout the pregnancy and delivery. Pearl then told Keith the boy to whom she gave birth had been adopted by a family from Buffalo, and he was now a psychologist in Wisconsin.

Keith asked her how she knew about where I was today, and she said "A few years back I got a call from him." Her answer provided Keith with a perfect opening to say "Well, a few weeks ago I got a call from him too." Pearl's reaction, to both Keith's dismay and mine, was to immediately say "I told him not to do that." When Keith asked her why she felt that way, her response was she was hurt when she thought about the past, and bringing my existence up was also hurtful to Keith's father. In Pearl's view, her husband (Keith's father) had "taken me in when he didn't have to," and had been good to her for her whole life.

They talked for a few more minutes, and Keith told her we had been in frequent telephone contact, we were planning to meet, and that he wanted his children to meet me also. She indicated to him she wanted no part of any meeting, and, still crying, asked Keith to make her one promise: that his children would never call me "Uncle Doug."

Keith told me he had made this promise to her "even though I knew as I was saying it, it was something I could not do." He also told me that at several points during the conversation both he and his mother had been in tears.

By the time he was through telling me about the conversation with his mother, I, too, was in tears. Telling me about that conversation with his mother was very hard for Keith because he didn't want to hurt me. At the time when I first contacted him, Keith had asked me why I had waited eight years to make contact, and I had replied I had not wanted to hurt anyone. I reminded Keith of what I had said back then, and said this was exactly the kind of pain I wanted to avoid. I told him I was sorry I had put him and his mother through more pain. Keith's response was one I wish I could let every adoptee hear, especially those who fear the effects of searching on their birth family. He said "Doug, don't be sorry. That was the best conversation my mom and I have had since I moved out of the house, and I understand her so much better now."

As a specific example of what he meant by understanding his mother better, he told me that before his grandmother had died, she had Alzheimer's disease, and was not able to live on her own. Keith's grandma moved in with his parents for a while, and he couldn't understand why his mother was so irritable and cold toward her. Finally, after only a short time, Pearl sent her mother to live with her sister, Keith's aunt. This was behavior on his mother's part that had been puzzling to Keith for some time. When Pearl finally told him about her pregnancy with me, she said that her mother "wasn't there for me back then, when I needed her, but she expected me to drop everything and take care of her now, and I just couldn't do it." He understood that puzzle at last. Hearing Keith understood his mother better once he had knowledge of the full story was a great relief to me, and I also believe he understood why I had delayed contacting him for so long. It also allowed a good deal of my guilt at having violated Pearl's wishes to dissipate.

Now that Pearl knew I had contacted Keith, however, we had another problem. How were we going to let Keith and Kathy's children, Derek and Stephanie, meet me and know who I was, without creating more unnecessary pain for Pearl? Despite Keith's promise to his mother that his children would never call me "Uncle Doug," he and Kathy did not want their children to think I was just "a friend," as some had suggested. All three of us believed that would be a deception, which would eventually have to be revealed or another "deep dark family secret" would be created. We all believed to create a new secret would just lead to another opportunity for someone to tell that secret to Derek or Stephanie, just as Keith's cousin had told him about me. We also agreed that keeping me a secret would only create a barrier to communication between Keith and Kathy and their children, which was also something none of us wanted.

Keith, Kathy and I spent several weeks talking and thinking about how to balance two seemingly competing forces. We wanted to respect Pearl's feelings (and those of Keith's father as well, since Pearl had told Keith that hearing about me bothered him), and yet we also wanted at least as strongly to be honest with the children. I told Keith and Kathy about what I believed was the healthy decision Jane Mullet had made to tell Amy about me as quickly as she did. She told Amy while I was still in town during the same visit in which I first contacted the family. That way Amy was not kept out of the process of meeting me. We all wanted to find a way to avoid keeping me a secret from Derek and Stephanie, and also to avoid having to tell them to keep meeting me a secret from their grandmother. Both of these potential secrets were distasteful to all three of us.

After much thought I came up with a rationale (or a rationalization if one is inclined to be less kind) which would allow Keith and Kathy to tell their children about me, but at the same time, to ask the children not to talk to, or in front of, their grandmother about meeting me. I suggested to Keith and Kathy that they have the discussion in the context of a talk about the difference between public and private, and also about good manners and kindness. They could point out that being polite often means resisting doing or talking about things we know everyone does (or talks about), in situations where that particular behavior or talk would make others uncomfortable. I suggested using, as examples, picking one's nose, or talking about having to go to the bathroom, at the dinner table. Everyone does these things (well at least we all go to the bathroom!), but we don't do, or talk about, them where the behaviors would make others uncomfortable, and are therefore inappropriate. We don't talk about things in public that are private matters.

They could then let the children know that having to give up Uncle Doug, who was her baby, was very painful to their grandma, and though grandma knew they knew about me (and eventually that they had met me), she felt sad to hear about me. To avoid making grandma sad, they should not talk about me when she was around. I must say I was mildly uncomfortable about my own suggestion that I was still a "dirty little secret" which was implied by comparing discussion of me with discussion of bathrooms and nose-picking. However, I felt that some discomfort on my part was certainly bearable when the alternative was the creation and perpetuation of more deception. Fortunately, Keith and Kathy agreed with me on both the importance of avoiding deception, and the "manners" approach to telling the children, and so Derek and Stephanie heard about their "Uncle Doug." Keith told me the children, too, were excited about meeting me. I was happy.

All that remained now was for all of us to meet each other. In the process of arranging our meeting, we realized the proximity of the cabins belonging to Kathy's family and to Bruce Caley. We decided to meet at Bruce's cabin at the end of a trip Susan and I would be making that coming August to Cape Cod.

On the morning when Keith and Kathy were to arrive, I was in a state of high excitement. Keith and I had, by then, spent much time in telephone conversation, I had seen several of his pictures, and I felt I knew him fairly well, and yet seeing him for the first time face-to-face was definitely going to be a thrill. Having Susan along with me to share the event was also wonderful, since I had not had anyone with me to share the excitement when I had met my birth sisters. We decided to videotape the reunion, not particularly with an eye toward the tape ever being a part of a public display, but more as a personal memento. We got out my camcorder and I gave Susan an operating lesson. Actually, I gave her several lessons. We checked the lighting and focal distance inside the cabin. We rehearsed how and where we might arrange for Keith and I to meet so that Susan could best get our first meeting on tape. We did a dry run of the expected action. Twice. Once everything was ready, I spent the minutes immediately preceding their arrival pacing the floor, wringing my hands, taking deep breaths, and looking out the window in the direction of the main road. I felt like a child waiting for dawn, so I could get out of bed on Christmas morning!

After what seemed like an endless wait, a car finally came up the hill on the gravel road to the cabin. They pulled into the driveway, and I stood inside the living room at the appointed place, at the right distance from the camera, and in the right light. Keith and Kathy got out of the car, I got one look at him through the window, and I immediately forgot all about the video plan and practically ran out onto the porch and down the stairs to meet him. After just a few seconds, I remembered Susan, the camcorder, and posterity, and took them into the cabin.

There we found Susan walking toward the door, a dismayed look on her face, camcorder in hand, with the microphone hanging loose, dangling by one thin wire! In my anxiety about not missing the video of my dreams, I had not allowed her to let the camcorder out of her hands after the rehearsals were complete, and she had been sitting in a chair, with the camcorder in her lap. Apparently, she had been sitting with her arms folded over the top, resting on part of the microphone. For the last couple of weeks I had noticed intermittent interruptions of the sound, sometimes accompanied by static when I was recording, and I now knew why! The microphone had been in the process of slowly breaking, and had picked that moment to finally die. After the commotion caused by both the reunion and the broken camcorder, we decided a "silent movie" of some of our early face-to-face contact was better than no movie at all, and so Susan shot some video of Keith and I sitting on the couch together.

We spent the rest of the morning in excited conversation, leaving the living room of the cabin only to go outside to take photos of Keith and me, brothers separated by adoption, standing together facing the camera, and then both facing to the left and to the right. About mid-afternoon we decided to go out for lunch. We also thought while we were out eating, we might run into Arcade, the nearest town of any size, to see whether the camcorder could be fixed. When we arrived in town, there was only one store in the phone book that listed itself as repairing video equipment, and we found them shortly. They looked at the broken microphone and said repairs were impossible, that they would have to special order a replacement, and the part would take several days to arrive. We expressed our disappointment, sharing with them the story of how Keith and I, brothers separated by adoption, had just met, and that we desperately wanted to have sound recordings of the weekend.

A store employee who had been listening nearby then came over to say they just happened to have a broken camcorder identical to mine in the store that belonged to the Arcade Police Department. Several weeks before one of the officers had accidentally pointed their camera into the sun and burned out the video system. The cost of replacing the damaged part was more than the department's budget could handle, and the camera was just sitting in the store's back room waiting for a final decision to be made on what to do next. If I was willing to take a used microphone at the new microphone price, they could take the microphone off of the Police Department's machine and sell that microphone to me. They would then order a replacement, which then could be put on the police camcorder that was waiting for repairs, and no-one would be the wiser. With yet another stroke of good luck, we were soon on our way with a functioning camcorder.

We spent 12 hours talking the first day, and another six the second, which included a trip to the other side of the valley above Java Lake to see the cabin where Keith spent his time. We realized the cabins would be within sight of each other if not for many years of tree growth. Then, Keith and Kathy had to leave to return to Wilson for his 20th High School reunion. Two days later Susan and I drove up to Wilson and I met his children. The entire experience of meeting a half-brother and his family for the first time when I was 46 years old was another example of that special high, which only a few people could appreciate. The knowledge and experience I was gaining are taken for granted by those in intact biological families, where they have always been surrounded by their biological and social roots.

Another issue had arisen in Keith's conversation with his mother that we wanted to pursue. Pearl had told Keith one of the reasons she was reluctant to have contact with me was that his father was made uncomfortable by discussions of me. She was grateful to him because had been good to her by marrying her, and she did not want her past to hurt him anymore. She seemed to have the sense she was unworthy of her husband's kindness. Though Keith seemed surprised by his mother's reaction, I have observed the sense of being "damaged goods" in many birth mothers from well before the 1940s, and even into the 1970s. Pearl, like many unmarried pregnant women, was sent away to have her baby before their pregnancy would "show" in order to hide her shame from her family and friends.

As Keith and I talked, we realized that at first Pearl had told me she and her husband didn't want their son to be hurt by my appearance. Then, after I had met Keith and my presence did not hurt him, but was instead welcomed by him, she had told Keith his father was hurt by knowing about my presence. Keith decided he would find a good time to have a talk with his father to ask him directly about how he felt about me. The chance to talk arose during deer hunting season in the fall of 1991. Deer hunting was something Keith had done with his father for most of his life, and hunting was a time when he felt particularly close to his father. When Keith asked his father how he felt about my presence, his father's response was "it's something that happened long before I met your mother. It's no concern of mine." Keith and I eventually sadly realized the real person who would be hurt by dealing with me was Pearl herself, and she had first used the alleged hurt feelings of

Keith and then those of his father as a way of protecting herself from something she could not handle.

There was one more detail regarding my reunion with Keith I had yet to take care of, and that was telling my parents in person about what had happened. As had been the case with my reunion with Pearl, I had planned to pursue the actual search and reunion on my own to see where they would lead first. Then, once I had adjusted to whatever I would myself find, I planned to bring my parents and the rest of my family into the process. My plan had been to tell them when I was home for Christmas 1992.

Before I leave for home each Christmas, I try to send out a "computer Christmas Letter" to my friends and family. I try not to make the letter one of those saccharine "we're all stunningly beautiful, happy, healthy, rich and famous" letters that make people gag, but I probably don't succeed all that well! Each year during breaks in my end-of-semester work, I compose my Christmas letter. Some years I am able to begin writing as early as Thanksgiving, while in other years I find I am not able to get to the task until after getting back to Buffalo for Christmas. That particular year I got an early start on writing, and soon realized I wanted to include my reunion with Keith in the letter. This meant calling my parents on the phone to tell them about our meeting before they got the letter, or keeping the news out of the letter completely until I had told them, or writing two versions of the letter, one with the section on meeting Keith, and one without. I chose the last alternative, and was sure not to send the "Keith letter" to any of my friends who might accidentally or otherwise spill the beans to my parents before I got home to tell them myself. I was well aware I was being hypocritical by criticizing those who kept secrets from me with good intention, and then turning around and doing the same to my parents, but I felt creating two versions of my Christmas letter was the best solution given the situation. I rationalized that in only a matter of a week or so after sending my letter I would be telling my parents in person. The two-letter solution seemed like a good idea at the time.

Like many apparently good ideas though, there was an unforeseen flaw: Susan, who had been with me for the reunion with Keith, talked about the experience in *her* Christmas letter, which she sent to my parents, just as I sent mine to her parents. Forgetting totally about the fact that she might have done this, I went to Buffalo, keeping my eye out for a good time to tell my parents. Within a few hours of my arrival there, Mom made a comment about being surprised to read in

Susan's letter that I had met Keith! Talk about feeling badly! I tried to explain my rationale for not telling them sooner about Keith myself. I said I had again planned to talk to them as soon as the opportunity presented itself, but I know they were hurt because I had left them out. There is a lesson here I suppose, but whether the lesson is about both living and dying by the sword of honesty, or about the fact that none of us is perfect, I can't say. Perhaps the lesson is simply that life, rather than being simple choices between black and white, is a series of grey compromises.

Another example of the problem with secrecy (in this case, how secrets can last a long time), and possibly also one of synchronicity, involves a meeting I had while in graduate school. Throughout my childhood, there were several couples with whom my parents socialized frequently. Those years being the baby boom, there was a large group of their children who also socialized frequently, and one of these was a girl named Carol. Our mothers had been friends since high school. Carol was older than I, and was also one of those people who still called me Bruce. Although I'm not positive of her age, she was apparently old enough at the time of my adoption that she understood both the nature of a pregnancy generally preceding a child's arrival in a family, and, I didn't know that I was adopted.

Perhaps some 25 years later, I was a graduate student in Columbus, Ohio. Carol was living in Cincinnati, commuting to Columbus weekly to take classes in a Masters in Social Work program. Both of our mothers had been increasingly vocal in suggesting that we meet while she was in Columbus. Finally, we arranged a dinner meeting and joked almost immediately that now our mothers could get off of our backs about the issue. Of course, our mothers were right, and we enjoyed an evening of conversation, especially since, in psychology and social work, we had many interests in common.

At some point during the meal, Carol was telling me about the son that she and her partner had adopted. Suddenly, after mentioning his name, Bruce, for the first time, she stopped, and presented me with an almost panicked look. Her mouth may have even been open in mid-word.

It took me a second or two to realize what was happening, and I said soothingly "Carol, I know I'm adopted." She released the breath she had been holding and said something to the effect of "oh thank goodness." We then proceeded to a really interesting discussion of our views of adoption, and of how adoption had changed from my birth in the 1940s to the 1970s. At some point after that, we lost contact and I have not been able to relocate her.

Reconnecting with her would be interesting and would allow me to ask her a question I didn't ask at the time. What were their reasons for their selection of Bruce (a still-unusual name), for their son? It might enable us to determine whether her son's name was just chance, or came from some family member on her partners side, or perhaps had some connection to me and my name.

CHAPTER 11

The Importance of Support

There is still a missing piece in my search and reunion story, however. That piece is how did I realize I needed to do a search, and how did I do it? On my internship in 1970, with my therapist in Chicago, I first discussed the effects of adoption on my life, and the possibility of searching for my birth family. Not much specifically adoption-search related happened for some 10 years, as I began my first job in Columbus, and moved into teaching in Stevens Point. Having testicular cancer in 1981 certainly raised my level of awareness of what was missing from my life history. However, I might not have come to the decision to search at all, were not the people and groups which form what, broadly defined, is called the "adoption search and support" movement being both visible and available to me. Furthermore, once I decided I needed to conduct my search, I certainly would never have been able to complete the process as quickly as I did without the significant assistance of people from the search and support community.

For most of my life, a part of my basic philosophy has been that the desirable way of living meant I needed to give good things to the world in at least some proportion to the level of the good things the world had given to me. After I completed my search in the early summer of 1983, I was already clear immediately upon my return to Stevens Point that my search and reunion experiences had been a very good thing for me. During the following year I told anyone who would listen about my search and what the knowledge I gained and the process of reunion meant to me. I began to realize because of the help and support I had received I wanted to do what I could to allow others to have the same kinds of help and support in making their own decisions, and in doing their searches if that was what they wanted. Now that I have described my search and reunion process, I will take a step back in time to describe how I went about returning some of the good things I had been given by sharing my experience with others.

As a result of my having joined the Adoptees Liberty Movement Association (ALMA) in New York City early in my search, I began to receive their regular national mailings as well as special regional communications about activities the group had planned. I began reading their newsletter, the *ALMA Searchlight*, which contained stories of searches and reunions as well as articles about the political and legal activities in which ALMA was engaged. Reading their newsletter was another step toward learning more about how this particular part of the search and support community functioned. In the spring of 1984, I got an ALMA mailing about a conference of a group called The National Council for Adoptable Children (NACAC) that would be held in Chicago at which Florence Fisher, ALMA's founder, would be speaking. I knew about Florence because she had written *The Search for Anna Fisher*, which was probably the first widely read book about adoption search. Though I had not yet read the book, I had heard of it, and I knew of Florence's early role in speaking out for the rights of adoptees. At that time, I was new enough in the adoption search and support movement that I did not really know what the areas of specialization or interests were for any of the many groups involved in the adoption movement. Thus, I did not know NACAC was an organization composed primarily of adoptive parents of special needs children, and the social workers and other professionals who worked on these adoptions.

The term "special needs" here refers to children who have a variety of problems that make them difficult to place including but not limited to physical or mental handicaps, a history of physical and/or sexual abuse, being of mixed race, being older, or being a part of a sibling group. Sadly, these children often belong to several of these categories at once. For a variety of reasons, the adoptive parents in NACAC were not, especially at that relatively early time in the adoption search and support movement, very receptive to the idea of adoptees searching for their birth families. Many of these parents were particularly frightened by the idea of birth parents searching for their adopted-out children. I did not realize Florence's presentation to NACAC was a trip into rather hostile territory, representing what may well have been one of the first times a member of the adoption search movement was ever invited to speak at a NACAC meeting.

Not having knowledge of the historical context of her presentation however, from my point of view the NACAC convention was a welcome chance to meet Florence Fisher, who I already realized was a legend in the adoption support movement. I had not been able to meet her in New York City because she had been out of town at the time of the June 1983 ALMA meeting I attended. As it happened, I was going to be traveling through the Chicago area at about the time of the NACAC meeting on my way to my 20th High School reunion in 1984, and attending the meeting would simply be a matter of moving my departure date ahead by three or four days. Since the notice of the meeting had arrived only a week or two beforehand, I assumed that by then the rooms in the hotel were all taken. I was wondering about where I would stay if I were to attend the meeting, when I got a call from an ALMA member in the Chicago area reminding me of the meeting and asking whether I was planning on attending. We got to talking about where I would stay, and eventually she offered me a place on the floor of a room several of her friends had reserved in the conference hotel. Although she herself would be unable to attend the conference, she assured me her friends were a relaxed and compatible group. She would tell them about my plans to sleep on their floor, and she was sure they would welcome me. These arrangements were just fine with me, and I made my travel plans accordingly.

I arrived at the conference hotel about 6:00 p. m. and the hotel desk called the room in which the person whose name I had been given was registered. There was no answer, and so I left a message that "Doug Henderson was here and was waiting in the hotel lounge. Please meet or call him there." I retired to people-watch in the bar. About every hour for the next several hours, I returned to the desk, asked them to call the room again, got no answer, updated the time on the message, and returned to the bar to watch and wait. As the time approached 11:00 p. m., I became increasingly worried that something had gone wrong. I began to wonder what I would do about a place to stay if they did not call or come into the bar soon. Finally, about 11:15, I got an answer in the room, however, the woman who answered the phone did not recognize my name. She said they had assumed the messages, which unfortunately did not have the recipient's name on them but only the room number, were being left for the wrong room, or were just from some weirdo, especially since all of the residents were women. Worse still from my point of view, they knew nothing about any plans to have a man share their room with them. When I mentioned the name of the ALMA member who had promised me space on their floor, her response was "Oh, it would be just like her to promise that, and then forget to tell us!" A quick poll of the other three occupants in the room led to the conclusion "if you're an adoptee you couldn't be all that dangerous," and I was invited, sight unseen, to take a spot on their floor. Thus began the first of what were to be many nights spent sharing a wide variety of sleeping quarters with other triad members at various adoption conferences and meetings.

The NACAC meeting itself was something for which I had obviously not been prepared. Given what I soon learned about the nature of NACAC, there were many handicapped and mixed-race children there. Often, I would encounter an older, or less handicapped, child, or a group of them, pushing what was probably a brother or sister around in a wheelchair. There was one particular little boy in a wheelchair who I ran into on the elevators several times. He captivated everyone in his presence with his friendly attitude and sunny disposition, and the obvious love his siblings had for him was heartwarming. Nevertheless, I had a heavy heart much of the time, seeing all of these children whose lives had obviously been very hard.

Seeing those children at the NACAC conference turned out to be my first introduction to the fact that the nature of adoption had changed significantly since the 1940s, when I was adopted. Beginning with the advent of widely available and effective birth control, and accelerated by the changes in society which made a single woman raising a child more acceptable (or at least less shameful), the "face" of adoption had been changing. By the 1980s, typical adoptions were no longer of mostly white, healthy, newborn infants as I had been. The overall number of adoptions was in significant decline, and of those adoptions that continued to happen, more and more of them were from three rather new categories: step-children in a remarriage; the "special needs" children I was meeting at the NACAC conference; and foreign-born children. The full implications of these changes in adoption would take me several years to understand, but fortunately I was introduced to the changes fairly early in my involvement with adoption search and support.

I attended a couple of the NACAC conference meetings in addition to the meeting with Florence Fisher while I was there. At these I began to appreciate the level of discomfort there was at the presence of adoptees (and even a few brave birth parents), members of ALMA who were interested in search and reunion. As adoptive parents, the members of NACAC seemed to be fearful of search by either adoptees or birthparents. Acknowledging their adoptee's need to search might signal a rejection by their children of them as adoptive parents, or as a sign they had failed to meet their children's needs. My sense was that the parents might also fear loss of, or at least pain for, their children if they were to search. The prospect of birthparents searching for their adopted-out children, and perhaps trying to take them back, was also a threat to many of these adoptive parents, made worse by media-fueled court cases challenging completed adoptions. I began to sense the social workers were concerned not just at the pain they believed a reunion would cause for all involved, but equally concerned (or even more so) that their promise of confidentiality to all involved was being broken by the search process. The expectation seemed to have always been that birth parents and adoptees would, and should, never meet, and our presence at the conference was a reminder that searches and reunions, which were unexpected and largely unwanted events, were at least a possibility.

Years later I was told a story by an adoptive parent and NACAC member about just how uncomfortable the presence of searching adoptees once had made many of the adoptive parents at NACAC. At a meeting sometime in the later 1980s, a female adoptee in her mid-20s who was interested in searching spoke about up her desire to find out more about the search process at an "open mike" session. There was a murmur of disapproval in the audience, and an adoptive parent rose to the microphone, said he was not interested in hearing these kinds of questions, and asked her "what business do you have coming to this meeting, anyway?" Her response was that she was an adoptee, and that she could be one of their own children once they had grown up. She then asked "Isn't this organization supposed to be about what is good for adoptees?" Her question made at least some of the adoptive parents in the audience realize they needed to rethink their feelings about search and reunion.

Perhaps because of the general discomfort with the topic of searching, the session at which Florence spoke was not particularly well-attended. The audience consisted primarily of ALMA members, who, like me, were not even registered for the NACAC meeting, and were there as a courtesy admission, primarily to see Florence.

At a reception for Florence that evening, I was able to meet her and thank her for her organization's help in finding my birth family. I asked her whether there was a branch of ALMA in Wisconsin, and she told me there was not. After discussions with others that evening I decided to look into establishing an ALMA chapter in Stevens Point, and to perhaps becoming ALMA's Wisconsin liaison, a position that was open at the time. When I told Florence of my decision, she was agreeable, and said the information on becoming an ALMA state liaison would be sent to me.

Perhaps the most important contact I made at the NACAC convention, though I would not realize the importance for a while, was with an adoptee psychiatrist who wishes to be identified as "C. E." He was from Wisconsin, and he and I immediately related well to each other. Perhaps our easy relationship was because we were among the few males at the conference (especially among those from ALMA), or perhaps we got along because of our common mental health and adoption background. At any rate, C. E. was the first person I had met from Wisconsin who was a part of the search and support movement, and we exchanged addresses and agreed to remain in touch.

The day after Florence's presentation and reception I pushed on to Buffalo to attend my 20th High School Reunion. At the "sock hop" held in the school's gymnasium on Friday night I ran into Maureen Kenmore, who had been one of my first "girlfriends" when we were both in the 7th grade. As I recall, our "dating" had been limited to going to a movie, to which my mother had accompanied us on the city bus, but for a while that year we had exchanged surreptitious notes in school, and evening phone calls at home. We remained friends throughout high school, and had kept in touch, and even gone out together a couple of times during the period when I was home for vacations during college and graduate school. Eventually she married Robin Kenmore, who had also been a friend of mine (and obviously of Maureen's!) in high school.

As we talked about what had gone on in our lives, Maureen shared she had recently had breast cancer, and was active with the local chapter of the American Cancer Society. When I told her about my testicular cancer we shared a few moments of quiet sadness, wonder about how our lives had moved in parallel, and gratitude about how lucky we both were to have survived such a frightening and life altering experience. When I told Maureen about how my cancer experience had led me to do my search, she asked me if I had yet run into Jana Tritto at the reunion. Jana just happened to be named Jana Henderson in high school! She and I were not related to each other, and for some reason she had not been in my homeroom, even though homerooms generally were assigned alphabetically. So, although we did not know each other very well, as the only two people in our high school with that last name, we both knew who the other one was.

Maureen told me Jana had become an adoptive mother of a family of 13 children, two of her own, and 11 adopted, most with special needs. Maureen knew about Jana because an article on her family had recently run in The Buffalo News. Both Maureen and I thought the involvement of both of the high school's Hendersons in adoption was pretty unusual, and so we went looking for Jana. When we found her, we discovered there was even more to the story than we had imagined. We uncovered yet another of those strange sets of coincidences that were becoming commonplace in my life.

After high school Jana and her husband had settled in the state of Washington and, in addition to two children of Jana's from an earlier marriage, they adopted 11 more. Other than the considerable task of raising their children, neither of them had "traditional" paying jobs. They supported their family from the subsidies made available by the federal and state governments to parents who were willing to adopt special needs children. Jana's family lived comfortably on their combined income, and she could have flown to Buffalo alone for the reunion, but she wanted to bring her whole family with her. Because of the cost of making a trip across the country, and due to the size of their family and the special physical care several of them required, they were unable to make the trip back to Buffalo to visit Jan's family very often. Flying the whole family anywhere was out of the question. In fact, they had difficulty taking their family on any kind of a vacation at all, for these same reasons.

In order to allow her whole family to make the cross-country trip to her reunion in Buffalo, Jana came up with a novel solution. She and her husband applied for a number of grants which together would fund the purchase and outfitting of a motor home with the special medical equipment and special physical adaptations, such as a wheel-chair lift, that their children needed. The stated purpose of their request for money to purchase a motor home was to allow her family to embark on a cross-country tour to promote special needs adoption. The tour would include attendance at several adoption-related conferences, including the NACAC conference which had occurred the previous weekend in Chicago. As we spoke, I slowly realized the boy who had so captivated me and other people on the elevators was her son, accompanied by several of Jana's other older and younger children! We marveled at the oddity that we had each been in the same place, unaware of the other's presence.

After the rather unusual discoveries of Maureen's cancer and of the story of Jana's family, the rest of the reunion was rather predictable as class reunions go, with the exception of one more surprise. I certainly was interested to meet many of my old high school friends and acquaintances again, and one of those who I met at the Saturday night banquet and dance was Lon Wilson. I had known Lon because we both played in the high school band and orchestra, and he had also been a friend from the youth group at our church. Lon had become an attorney, and as we talked, I was surprised to hear he had worked for many years in the Erie County Court system. My birth father had long been the chief assistant to the head judge there. When I asked Lon whether he knew a Bill Mullet at work, he replied "Sure, he was a good fellow. He died a year or so ago." When I told Lon I was Bill's birth son, he was almost as surprised to find that out, as I was to find one of my high school friends had worked with my birth father!

CHAPTER 12

I Get Active

Upon my return to Stevens Point from my high school reunion, in the summer of 1984, a thick package of documents from ALMA awaited me. I read the material with increasing dismay because of the many legal-sounding requirements and prohibitions I found. I was expecting to start a support group, not to open a law office, and I began to think about whether I really wanted to get involved with ALMA at all, although I knew of no other options.

I definitely wanted to start some kind of support group, and so I also began to ask around in my circle of friends, acquaintances and especially students in my classes, for others who might be either adoptees or birth parents with an interest in starting a search and support group in Stevens Point. Due to my recent experience at NACAC in Chicago, the fact adoptive parents in significant numbers might also be both interested in joining such a group, and an important part of one, did not occur to me at that time. By the start of classes in the fall I had identified several individuals who said they were interested in meeting to talk about adoption search, one of whom was the wife of one of my students. In September 1984, an informal group of three began meeting monthly in my living room. By our third meeting in November, we had begun to discuss whether we wanted take a step ahead and announce the formation of a support group to which we would invite the public.

Early that fall I heard from C. E., the adoptee psychiatrist, who was following up on our meeting at the NACAC conference in Chicago. He told me about an adoption search and support group which had several chapters in Wisconsin. The group had begun in about 1981, when a group of adoptees, birth parents, and adoptive parents got to know each other as a result of meeting at legislative hearings where they were testifying for changes they wanted to see in the Wisconsin state adoption laws. While they did not agree unanimously on what should be changed, they discovered they had one area of agreement. They were all working toward a change which would allow adoptees and birth parents to meet each other once the adoptee was an adult. They began regular meetings to support each other both in working for legislative change and in the search process itself, in which several of them were still involved. By 1984, there were chapters of the group, which they had named Adoption Information and Direction, known as "AID," in Milwaukee, Madison, Appleton, Oshkosh, and Eau Claire.

C. E. told me AID was sponsoring the Midwestern Regional Conference of the American Adoption Congress during October in Eau Claire. AID was looking for a speaker on search and reunion issues as seen by the spouses, children, and parents of adoptees and birth parents who searched. He had given them my name, and told me that based on his recommendation, someone from the group would be calling me to invite me to facilitate a "Significant Others Panel" at that conference. When Linda Day, their state president, called we had an extended, and very pleasant conversation. I was surprised to learn she was a "triple hitter." Linda was herself adopted as an infant, had become pregnant and surrendered a daughter for adoption as an adolescent, and had recently become a single adoptive parent in an open adoption. The timing of her call was particularly fortunate, since I was especially interested in finding out more about her group. Because of the legalistic element of the information I had received from ALMA I had become quite disillusioned with the prospect of affiliating with them, and was looking for an alternative. At the end of our talk, I agreed to chair the significant others session at the Eau Claire conference, and told Linda I might want to become more involved with their group.

The conference in Eau Claire was excellent, much more to my liking than the experience at NACAC had been. One reason I enjoyed the conference, though I was unaware of the exact cause at the time, was that the primary purpose of NACAC was *not* to assist triad members in the search for birth relatives separated by the adoption process. However, that was exactly what Adoption Information and Direction, and the American Adoption Congress, were all about. I clearly liked the fact that due to their inclusion of adoptive parents, all three sides of the adoption triad were represented in both of these groups. This made more sense to me than the primarily adoptee membership of ALMA. In both AID and the AAC, those on each of the three sides of the triad could interact with members of the other two sides. Even better, the interaction was in a context where people could discuss issues with a member of the triad with whom they did not have the emotional history they often had with their "own" family members.

I also liked the fact the members of the group seemed to be friends, as well as working for the same cause. Though I had my own hotel room for the Eau Claire conference, one of the most enjoyable parts of the conference weekend was Saturday evening, when perhaps a dozen of us relaxed in the room of one of the members, told inappropriate jokes and laughed until the wee hours of Sunday morning. I became quite interested in starting a chapter of AID in Stevens Point, and requested they consider allowing me to affiliate my as-yet-unnamed, private, and very small group with them. About a week after the conference, I received a letter from Linda officially asking me if I would like to have the Stevens Point group become a chapter of AID. The other Stevens Point group members agreed to affiliate, and we began to make preparations for our first public meeting, which would occur late in January 1985. I felt a very good match had been made.

History showed I was quite correct in that feeling, since over the following 10 years I was to attend many AID Board of Directors meetings, serving for 10 years as the leader of the Stevens Point chapter, and for four years as State President. Until the early 1990s, our semi-annual Board meetings were held in the Madison home of Ginny Whitehouse, an adoptee and an adoptive parent, one of the group's founders and its first State President. These meetings would typically run from Friday evening until Sunday afternoon, with pot-luck or ordered-in meals, and with everyone sleeping in spare beds or sleeping bags on the floor of Ginny's living and dining rooms. The Board meetings were part business and part a three-day slumber party!

The experiences I have had over the years in the adoption support movement have been some of the most meaningful of both my personal life and my professional career. The only times their intensity and meaning were approached by any other professional experiences were during my clinical work doing full-time diagnostic testing and therapy at the Children's Hospital in Columbus, and part time consulting work after I moved to Wisconsin. Not only was the adoption work personally meaningful and rewarding, but within my Department and University, where all faculty are expected to do a certain amount of professional service to the off-campus community, my work was seen as a valuable application of my professional skills.

As rewarding as my adoption search and support work has been however, during my years of work in the movement, I also experienced many frustrations. Working to open up both the individual closed records of people who came to our group for assistance, and to end the secrecy of the entire adoption system would sometimes wear me down to the point of wanting to quit. Yet whenever quitting began to look appealing to me, it seemed either a particularly rewarding search success, or a particularly infuriating example of damage from the closed system, would come along to re-energize me all over again. Fortunately, several of these rewarding search successes occurred early in my adoption "career," and kept me motivated during the times of challenge.

At that first conference in Eau Claire, I also met Shelley Borreson, an adoptee and adoptive parent, who was the leader of the Eau Claire AID chapter, at that time the newest in the organization. As I gradually learned more about the search process in Wisconsin, I realized Shelley should be in a position to assist Katherine in her search for her birth daughter. Katherine was the birth mother whom I had chanced to meet at the ALMA meeting in New York City who grew up in Wisconsin Rapids, but had traveled to Eau Claire to have her baby. Although I had not gotten all of the information from Katherine that would allow the completion of her search (not knowing at the time I met her exactly what would be important), I believed Katherine would know the information I now knew would be needed. I told Shelley about Katherine, and gave Katherine's phone number to her. Shelley called Katherine, who had continued searching without success, and who was happy to have the assistance. In only a matter of weeks, Shelley had completed a search Katherine had been unsuccessful in completing for years, and Katherine and her daughter had their reunion. Theirs was the first of many reunions in which I would have a part, and the joy of being able to help others to have the experience from which I had benefited so much, and the thrill of "beating the system" which is so much against reunion, have kept me involved in helping people search.

By January of 1995 our Stevens Point group was ready to "go public," and we held our first openly announced meeting on a Wednesday night late in that month. An article in the *Stevens Point Daily Journal* which appeared on Monday of that week featured the story of my own search and reunion, and was accompanied by a prominent boxed announcement of our group's first meeting, which was that Monday night. Carroll Duer, leader of the Oshkosh AID chapter, and also an accomplished searcher, Linda Day (State President), and several members of the

Oshkosh and Appleton AID groups, all traveled to Stevens Point to attend our first meeting. We had about ten local people in attendance, and felt we were off to a good start.

One of those who came to that first public meeting was Lisa Schobert, a Stevens Point adoptee who had been searching for her birth brother unsuccessfully for five years. At our first meeting she gave the information she had to Carroll, who was able, 2 days later, to find Lisa's brother, then living in the Minneapolis area. The day after that, Saturday, Lisa met her birth brother in her living room. At Lisa's request the reunion was photographed by a reporter for the *Stevens Point Daily Journal.* Thus, on the following Monday, exactly a week after the article about our group's first meeting had run, a front-page article and photo told of the group's first successful reunion! We certainly did not waste much time in getting started.

Shortly before our second Stevens Point chapter meeting began, a short, and very slight man who appeared to be in his mid-seventies, walked tentatively into the room and asked if this was "the AIDS meeting." He was met with a nervous laugh from those of us already present, and we explained we were AID, an adoption support group. He had found what he was looking for, but had mis-spoken. When the meeting began, he told us his name was Hilbert Pankonin, and he was a birth father who had, with his wife, surrendered the youngest two of their six children for adoption during the depression. He had been searching for his children unsuccessfully for many years, and had been referred to our group by his state senator, who he had contacted for help.

Fortunately, Hilbert's rather interesting beginning by mixing up the group's name did not portend more bad experiences to come. As he told his story, he said he and his wife had always regretted the fact that they could not afford to keep their youngest two children. He told us the church charitable agency with which they were working suggested what they should do with their children was to keep them in the family rather than to adopt them out. The agency tried to help the family find ways to live more economically, but the financial and emotional burden was finally just too great, especially since his wife was in chronic ill health herself.

Because he perceived the agency's attitude was that the family should not be split up, Hilbert ended up leaving the daughter in her bassinet in the basement stairwell of a church in a neighboring town. He told us that several years previous to his coming to our meeting, the daughter had found out the identity of her birth family, and had learned only part of the circumstances of her discovery in the stairwell. She had maintained some contact with Hilbert and his wife, though the contact was mutually rather unpleasant due to the daughter's perception that she had been "abandoned outside the basement of a church." Her anger about her partially known history had poisoned her relationship with Hilbert's family.

Hilbert told us he was working on a book about the family history, writing in large part so the two adopted-away children would know they were dearly loved, and the decision for adoptive placement was not made lightly. He wanted them to know they had been in their parents' thoughts and prayers ever since they left the family. He had already selected a powerful title for his book: *Magnetism of Blood.*

Hilbert's wife was now suffering from cancer that would, before too long, be fatal. He desired to find their adopted-out son, make contact with him, and hopefully learn he had had a good life. Hilbert wanted to give his wife some degree of peace by sharing good news about their son's life with her before she passed away. Until the search was completed, however, and he knew what he had found, Hilbert did not plan on telling his wife, to protect her from yet more pain if the news was not happy. With what I had learned about the search process in the course of working with Shelley Borreson on the search for Katherine's daughter, I believed Hilbert probably knew, or could find out, the information which would allow me to successfully find his birth son. Shortly after Hilbert's second group meeting, to which he brought the information I needed, I drove thirty miles north of Stevens Point to Wausau, where I believed the birth certificate containing the son's adoptive name would be on file.

As I walked up the steps into the massive Marathon County courthouse I was trembling with excitement. I remembered my own search, the help I had received along the way, and how much finally knowing my truth had meant to me. I already felt rewarded to have been able to offer help to others in search by starting the support group, and I had already seen how happy Lisa had been with her reunion with her birth brother. Now I was about to conduct the first search I had done on my own. I hoped my first independent effort would go well. I found the correct office, signed the necessary papers certifying I had read the "guidelines for conducting genealogy research," and, once I actually began to look at the records, was able to easily identify the amended (adoptive) name of Hilbert's son, and the names of his adoptive parents. The entire process took me less than an hour.

As it happened, the adoptive family lived in the western part of Wisconsin when they adopted him, and I needed help again from Shelley Borreson, who located the adoptive family's current address and phone number, and made a phone call to the adoptive parents. Using a cover story about wanting to contact their son about a school reunion, Shelley chatted with the adoptive mother, who said her son had completed a doctoral degree in a scientific field, and was currently married, had two children, and lived on the east coast, where he had moved in conjunction with his work. I called Hilbert and told him what I had learned. Hilbert was overjoyed just to find his son was alive, and the fact he was a successful professional and had a family was almost more than he could bear. I gave him his son's name and current address, and he asked me what I thought we should do next.

All of the people who taught me how to search had told me to be sure to allow the searcher to make the actual contact, whether that contact was to be by letter or by phone. Adoptees and birth parents have often been made to feel powerless by the adoption process, and allowing them to make the final contact themselves, on their schedule, is a way of empowering them. Having the adoptee or birth parent make the call also assures the person in search is really ready to take that final step, preventing an overzealous searcher from acting prematurely. The experts also told me that making the contact myself, which is called "acting as an intermediary," was risky. The contact by the intermediary might be the only chance the searcher may have to interact personally with the person they have been searching for, especially if the found individual is one of the few who resists further contact. Also, if the contact was made by telephone, which is my personal preference, hanging up on one's actual birth kin calling unexpectedly would also likely be harder to than hanging up on an unrelated stranger. Thus, had I been following standard search practice, I would have left the next step up to Hilbert.

I tried to follow the advice I had been given, and suggested to Hilbert the next step was up to him. I told him that whenever he was ready, he could call or write to his birth son. Hilbert, like Lisa, had been searching fruitlessly for many years. He was so impressed that I had been able to do what so many others had not, he wanted me to "continue with your good work" and call the son myself. He also thought as a fellow adoptee, educated at the same level as his son was, I might get a better response from his son than he. I tried to explain the reasons why I thought he should be the person to make contact to no avail. He wanted me to make the call.

So, knowing in my first search I was "breaking the rules" by serving as an intermediary, I called Hilbert's son. As I would learn later in my contact with my own birth brother, Keith, totally complete secrets are few and far between. Hilbert's son was not entirely unaware of the story of his adoption, having been contacted several years earlier by his other adopted sister. She had previously told him her angry and hurt partial version of how they had been adopted away from their four siblings and their birth mother and father. Probably because he had heard about his birth family only through his birth sister, he, like his birth sister, also had bad feelings about them. He listened politely to my description of the story Hilbert had told of the family's problems, and as I told him about my perceptions of Hilbert as I had come to know him. The son said he would be willing to send me a letter telling of his life, and some photos of himself and his family, but he did not wish to be "harassed" by his birth family, and wanted to have no further contact with them. He asked me not to tell them of his identity and whereabouts, and, knowing I had already done so, I said I didn't think that would be possible. I did say I would pass on his desire not to be contacted again.

I realized as we talked that the contact was going badly, and our conversation might be the only one that would be taking place, and I remembered the advice of my search-expert friends that serving as an intermediary was a risky activity. I wondered whether the son might have responded more positively to a call from Hilbert himself, and I began to wish I had turned on the tape-recording feature on my answering machine before I had placed the call. At least then Hilbert and his wife might be able to hear their son's voice, even though what he was saying would be painful for them to hear. I had decided against making a recording only partly because recording without the permission of the person being recorded is illegal. More importantly to me, recording the call would have created yet one more instance of deception and secrecy. Even though I might be making such a recording with the best of intentions, I did not want to engage in more of what I believed was so destructive in the adoption process. I gave the son my name and address so he could mail the photos, and my phone number, in case he should change how he felt about contact, and said good bye.

The next call to Hilbert was difficult. Looking back, I think it was the most difficult call I had to make in my entire time as a searcher. I felt so sad to have to give him what I considered to be the bad news of his son's hostility and desire not to be "harassed." Hilbert, however, was not as hurt as I had thought he might be. Perhaps, as I had experienced when I heard about my own birth father's death, the joy of knowing *something* took on greater importance than the actual content of what I had learned. Hilbert was happy he would be receiving a letter and photos, and he would have nothing of my apologies for making the call myself, and for not having better news.

Shortly before our next group meeting the letter and photos arrived, and I brought them to the meeting to give to Hilbert. Tears were in his eyes as he held the photos and read the letter. He passed them around to the group and many of us cried with him, partly out of joy that another round of secrecy had been ended, and partly out of sadness that his search had not ended on a more positive note. A couple of months later Hilbert, who continued to attend group meetings for several years, asked me if I thought sending his son a birthday and Christmas card each year would be considered harassment. I told him I didn't think so, unless his birth son told him not to send any more. He began to send two cards a year, sometimes containing a small note.

Over the next few years, he reported receiving occasional calls from his adopted-out daughter. She remained angry for that entire time, and even called me at one point. I tried to explain to her what I saw as Hilbert's dilemma at the time he left her at the church. Little either Hilbert or I could say seemed to reduce her hurt and anger. Several years later, when *Magnetism of Blood* was finally completed and published, I read Hilbert's description of the night he left his daughter at the church.

He selected a well-lit place, the only exit from the church basement where there was a regularly scheduled weekly meeting going on. Based on watching the church for several weeks, he knew when the meeting would adjourn, and waited in the stairwell, with his daughter in his arms, holding her and talking softly to her until he heard the rising of voices that indicated the meeting was ending. He kissed her, wished her well, and left her, running off at the last moment as the sound of footsteps approached the door. He waited in the shadows to be sure she was found, then made his way home, alone.

Reading his description, especially when I did, after having known Hilbert for several years and having assisted him in finding his birth son, was a sad, yet enlightening experience. I could see an act that can be made to sound as cold and uncaring as being "abandoned outside the basement of a church" could, from another point of view, be one of extreme sadness, motivated by love. Hilbert clearly deeply loved not only the two children who he surrendered but also the four he kept, and their mother. I only wish that Hilbert's daughter might someday learn to perceive things that way.

In one of the cards he sent to his son, Hilbert mentioned that he had collected an extensive family genealogy, and had offered his son a copy. The last I was to hear from Hilbert, sometime in the early 1990s, was a joyous letter in which he told me his son had written to him, asking for a copy of the family tree and photos of his birth parents and of his other brothers and sisters. Perhaps the very first search I conducted myself for someone else had not turned out so badly after all.

In the years since that first search I conducted for Hilbert, I have usually seen a different set of choices than Hilbert made. When I identified and located the person they were seeking, and gave them the information, almost every person who asked me to conduct a search has chosen to make the contact themselves. Furthermore, almost all have done so within a few hours of my call to them, even when they said that, before doing anything, they were going to think on what to do next for a few days. I believe the possession of the actual knowledge of who and where the sought-after relative is, is such an emotionally "hot" item that people can't let another moment pass before acting on the urge to finally know everything.

Hilbert's misstatement of the group's acronym, when he asked at his first meeting if we were the "AIDS group," was only one of many similar instances. Our group name created a problem with which the Board of Directors needed to wrestle repeatedly over the years. The group had begun in 1981, and we had been referring to ourselves by pronouncing the acronym "AID" as a word long before we had heard the acronym AIDS, which subsequently became widely known and feared. Over the years, people began to confuse that term with our group's name. Eventually the Board decided to stop using the nickname "AID" spoken as a word, entirely, opting to either pronounce the entire group name, or to refer to ourselves as "A, I and D." Once we became an incorporated non-profit organization in the late 1980s, we began to use "A I D I," pronouncing each letter independently. Now that the confusion with AIDS had subsided, I will use the term AID.

After the Stevens Point group's success with the searches for Lisa's birth brother and Hilbert's birth son, we continued to have monthly meetings attended by three to ten people. Between the searches which I competed myself, and those in which we provided a referral to someone who was successful in the search, we probably completed about a search per month for our first several years, giving us an almost continuous run of happy reunion stories to share each month. Another of the aspects of many of our meetings was having a guest speaker or visitor who was an adoption professional. These guests included adoption social workers and administrators from the state of Wisconsin, and adoption social workers from The Children's Service Society, and Catholic and Lutheran Social Services, some of several private adoption agencies serving Central Wisconsin. Through these meetings we learned about the work our guests did, and, more importantly, the guests learned about our problems and concerns.

One of the frequently expressed reasons for opposition to allowing adoptees access to their original birth certificate and the social history surrounding their birth is to protect us from harmful or hurtful information. Examples of such kinds of information are pregnancy by incest, pregnancy by rape, and uncertainty about paternity due to a birth mother having had multiple partners.

Melodie was a member of our Stevens Point AID chapter for about a year. She came to us as a single mother, bringing her recently born infant with her, and wanting to find her birth family. Through her adoption agency, where the staff was very supportive of her search, she had attempted to use the state search program. Melodie's search had been unsuccessful because the program was unable to locate either of her birth parents, without whose permission information could not be released. Her social worker encouraged Melodie to seek out the Stevens Point AID group. I was familiar with her social worker through my previous search and support work.

As Melodie told us the little she knew about her birth, it was clear that her search was going to be difficult. At that same time, we also had a member whose wife was doing her search, and he came to meetings to support her. He was a retired detective from the police force in one of the larger cities in the state. I am unclear whether he asked, or told, anyone that he was going to search on her behalf. When he learned her birth history, he came to me with his concern. He had learned Melodie was conceived in an incestual relationship between her birth mother and her birth grandfather.

We were worried about how this information could be given to her without creating a crisis. I immediately called Marcia Van Brunt, an adoption social worker from Rhinelander with whom I had worked for many years, for her advice. I then consulted with the social worker I knew at Melodie's agency. Together we decided the worker would immediately schedule an appointment at which she would tell Melodie what we had found, and urge her to return to the AID group, as well as to continue in counselling, if she needed to.

When Melodie came to the first meeting after she met with the social worker, in the course of talking about her new knowledge, she told us tearfully, "now I really want to find my birth mother because I know what she went through. It was my adoptive father who made me pregnant." She continued to attend meetings for several more months as she pursued her search with help from her agency. We could see in those few months that, rather than destroying her, the new knowledge had given Melodie strength, perhaps through knowing that she was not alone in her situation, and how to cope with it. One example of a positive reaction to distressing news certainly does not prove knowledge is always better than lack of information; however, it does support the right to one's personal information, as well as suggesting that people have the ability to deal with difficult facts.

I continued to be involved in the adoption reform movement, initially at the state, and eventually at the national level. My experiences included spending about 10 years as the leader of the Stevens Point AID chapter and four years as state president of that group, offering written and personal testimony at numerous hearings, and serving on two state-level advisory committees regarding adoption reform. I made numerous presentations at adoption seminars on the state level as well.

I also began to be involved at the national level where I made presentations at conventions of the American Adoption Congress (AAC). In subsequent chapters I will describe in additional detail my gradual movement from working on the state level with AID to the national level with the AAC, as I discuss changes in my career path and the role of synchronicity in my life. Since the following chapters are largely organized by topic rather than by chronology, I'll summarize here the general sequence of what I've done in adoption reform.

Late in the summer of 1994, I took what had become my nearly annual summer trip to the east coast to visit friends in the New York City area and family and friends in Buffalo. It turned out if I cut just a weekend off of that trip, then on the way back to Wisconsin I could stop in Chicago to attend the weekend meeting of the AAC Task Force on Reorganization. The meeting turned out to be not only a lot of intense work but also a pleasant experience. I got to know several new people, and learned a lot more about several others who I already knew. As things would develop, many of the folks on the Task Force were going to be involved with me in the governance of the "new"

AAC that would arise from the work of the Task Force. Eventually the reorganization suggested by the Task Force was adopted by the AAC Board, and serving on the Task Force turned out to be another major step in helping me move into the national adoption scene.

Because of my membership on the Task Force, I attended a meeting of the AAC Board of Directors in Chicago a year later, in late summer of 1995. The results of that meeting led to my being asked to serve on the Board of Directors of the AAC as the Director of Training in September of 1995. I was elected to be a member of the Executive Committee of that organization two months later, and continued to serve on the Executive Committee and in the newly renamed position of Director of Professional Relations and Continuing Education.

For most of the 1994–95 academic year I took an active part in an internet adoptee's mailing list. The list became for me a second search and support group, available on a 24-hour-a-day, seven-day-a-week basis. For people who did not have a local face-to-face support group which they could attend, as I did, the adoptee list was their only source of assistance: a virtual support group. I spent sometimes three or four hours a day on-line, reading messages posted by others, and posting messages of my own. As I became known on the list, people frequently asked me for my opinion as a psychologist about their situations. Occasionally I would ruffle the feathers of people on the list by offering opinions when they weren't wanted, or opinions with which people disagreed. I made several good friends on the list, and began private e-mail conversations with several of them. At the April, 1995, AAC convention in Las Vegas members of the adoptee list wore special badges, and we organized a dinner so that we could meet face to face, "IRL." Seeing people who I had known only online was fascinating.

In the summer of 1995, I attended a party in the Chicago area at the home of one of the Internet adoptee list members and met IRL with even more people I had grown to know very well on line. An adoptee at this party, when she heard I taught at the University of Wisconsin–Stevens Point, asked me whether I knew Jim, an English professor on our campus. She, also an English professor, had met Jim at several conventions, and they were good friends. Though I had not ever met him personally, Jim and I had talked on the phone just that spring. He had seen articles about our AID group in the local paper, and had decided to try to contact the son, now a young adult, who he had fathered at 18 in the military and who had been placed for adoption. Since he had told me he was no longer hiding his birth father status, I decided to share this information with his friend who I had just met. She was fascinated, and said "Tell Jim we now have another thing in common to talk about at those deadly convention business meetings!" Connections I had through the adoptee mailing list allowed me to put Jim in touch with searchers in California, and he had a successful reunion with his birth son. These types of synchronous interactions are fascinating, and, as you will learn, the adoptee mailing list was a part of several more synchronicities.

My university expects members of its faculty to be professionally active in their field, which means both publishing and performing professional service in their area of expertise. The book you are now reading is one of these areas of service. As you will see when I address synchronicity shortly, my choice of professions (psychology) and specialty fields (behavior problems in children and adolescents) was probably no accident. I have been extremely lucky that my personal interests and my professional development have been so closely related. Sometimes I have a hard telling at any given moment whether I am working, playing, or engaging in personal development and growth. Typically, the same activity fits into all three categories. I realize, though sometimes I forget, that few people are as lucky as I am. In the 1970s, *Saturday Night Live* comedian Garret Morris portrayed an Hispanic baseball player whose only apparent knowledge of English, and whose stock answer to any and all questions, was the carefully spoken phrase "Beisbol been berry berry good to me." To paraphrase Morris, I can certainly say the adoption reform movement has "been berry *berry* good to me!"

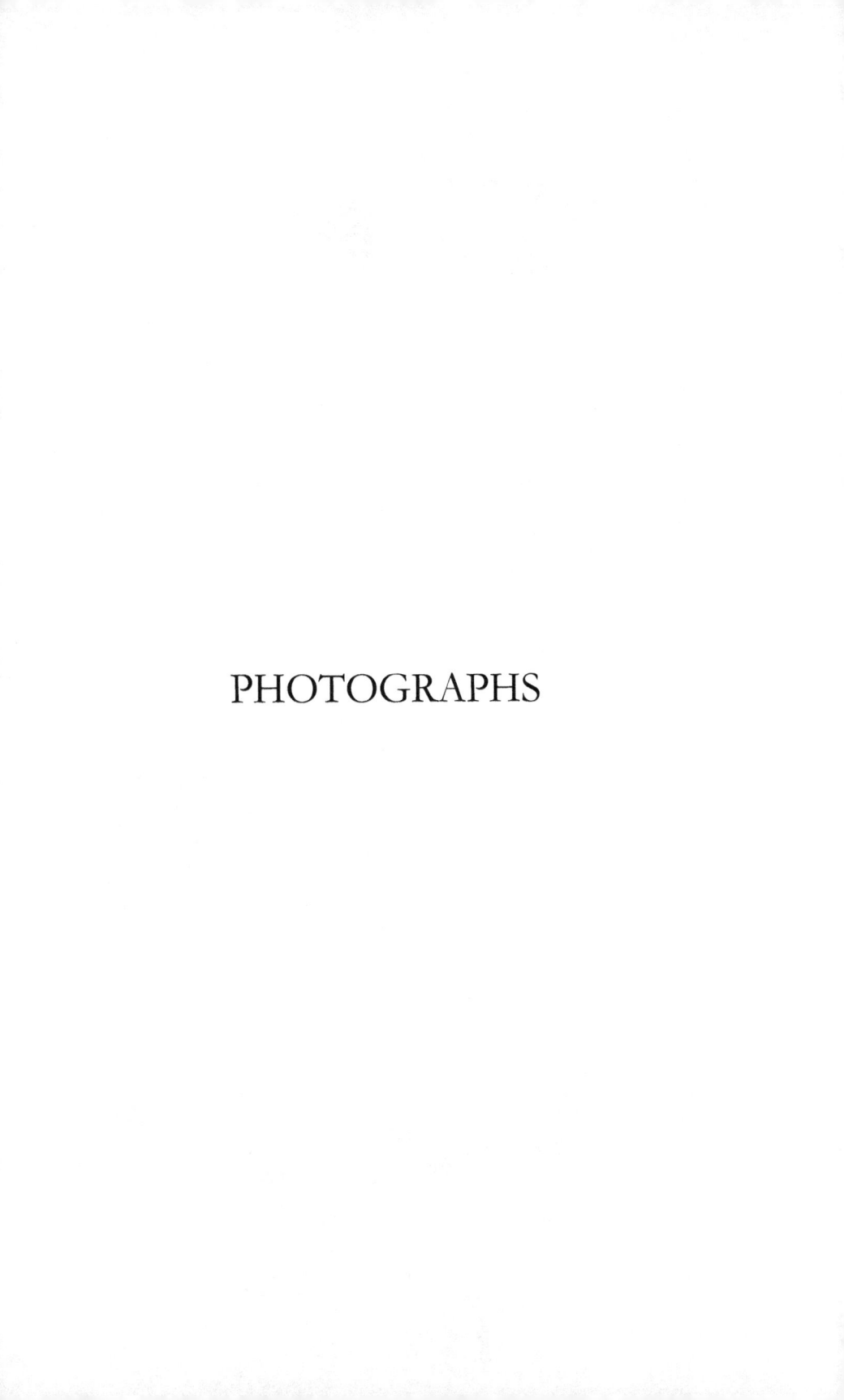

PHOTOGRAPHS

A1. Henderson family, summer clothes in Buffalo, 1952.

A2. Big brother Bruce scares little brother Dave, Fall 1952.

A3. Bruce, about 8, Dave, about 3, *ca.* 1954

A4. On the boat,1963.

A5. Dave's HS Graduation,
1968.

A6. Those were the (hair)
days, 1978.

A7. Dad with beard,
and Mom, 1988.

B1. Bruce, 10th Birthday
Picnic, 1956.

B2. Doug, HS Junior,
on the boat, 1963.

B3. Doug, ROTC
Honor Guard, 1965.

B4. Doug, college graduation,
*I said I'll never be a bearded
weirdo*, 1968.

B6. Doug, *hair so big I couldn't stand it*, 1973.

B5. Doug, *things change. Peace, brother*, 1970.

B7. Doug, *I had it straightened*, 1973.

B8. Doug, *one of my favorite photos*, 1975.

B9. Doug, *a photographer before cell phones*, 1977.

C1. Molly, about 3,
Susan, about 6.

C3. Molly, about 10,
Susan, about 13,
Mary, about 6.

C2. Molly 9, Susan 12, Mary 5, Jane and Bill, mid 30s

C4. Mary, High
School Senior.

C5. Mary 20, Amy 4,
1978.

C6. Amy, about 7.

C7. Bill on his
wedding day.

C8. Bill, age 38.

C9. Bill and Henry.

C10. Susan Hannen, Sister; Henry
Mullett, Uncle; Mary Margaret
Shanley, Aunt; June,1983.

C11. Molly and Jim, 2020.

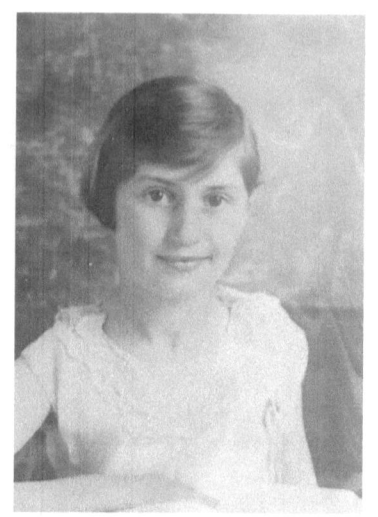

D1. Pearl at 9.

D2. Pearl at 17.

D3. Pearl's Wedding, 1950

D4. Pearl, *ca.* 2021.

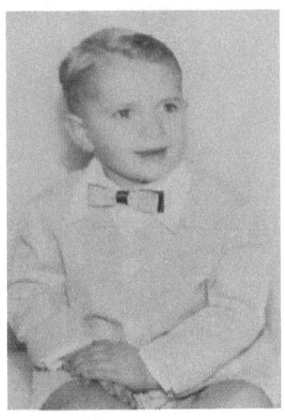

D5. Keith, *ca.* 3, 1956.

D6. Keith and Kathy's Wedding, about 29, 1979

D7. Keith, mid-1990s.

E1. Doug and Susan. 1986. Early on.

E2. Dougie and Susie, 2010, Later on.

F1. Dave and I had pet rabbits. Our house is behind Kath. Her house is behind me, *ca.* 1954.

F2. Werrick girls, Henderson boys. Sue a year older than me, Kath a year older than Dave, *ca.* 1958

G1. Class of 1964, Kenmore East High friends, 1973, Mike Indian, Frank Hermon, Bruce Caley.

G2. Class of 1964, Kenmore East High friends, 1995, Mike Indian, Doug, Bruce Caley.

H1. 1983, Susan, Sister; Doug; Mary, Sister.

H2. 1983, Lower: Mary Mullett Flynn, Susan's Daughter, Alissa; Middle-Amy Mullett; Susan's Son, Michael; Top- Jane Mullett, Doug, Susan Hannen.

H3. *Seated*: Molly, Susan, Me. *Standing*: Keith, Mary. Mid-1990s. Why so glum?

H4. Molly, Susan, Me. Mid-1990s. We DO know how to have fun!

I1. Dagwood Doug, 1971.

I2. Dagwood Keith,
HS Graduation, 1972.

I3. Big Hair Doug, 1972.

I4. Big Hair Keith, 1982.

15. Boy's toys Doug, 1994.

16. Boy's toys Keith, 1979.

J1. Susan Hannen,
Sister, 2024.

J2. Molly Gold,
Sister, 2022.

J3. Mary Flynn,
Sister, 2022.

J4. Amy Mullett,
Sister, 2024.

J5. Doug Henderson,
2024.

J6. Keith Dixon,
Brother, 2024.

PART THREE

SYNCHRONICITY: IT JUST SO HAPPENED

CHAPTER 13

Life and Work Come Together

In the late summer of 1985, I was contacted by the office of the Northern Region of the Wisconsin Department of Health and Social Services (DHSS) in Rhinelander. Perhaps they came to me because members of their staff had met me at our Stevens Point AID meetings, or at one of the regional conferences I had attended. They asked me if I was interested in presenting a program on "combining the past, present and future in the adoption process" to a group of adoptive parents and their early teen-aged adopted children. The program would take place at a resort in northern Wisconsin as part of an "Adoptive Family Weekend." All of the speakers that weekend were to be videotaped, with copies of the tape made available to each of the DHSS service regions across the state. I was excited about being asked to speak because I might be able to reach a new and important potential audience. I would also have a chance to expand my contacts within the community of adoption professionals.

In 1984, I had applied for a faculty development grant to obtain training for the course in the Psychology of Sexual Behavior which I had been teaching. As part of my training, I spent a month during the summer of 1985 at the University of Minnesota Program in Human Sexuality. It turned out I was to complete my training on Friday afternoon of the weekend of the conference. Although my DHSS presentation was scheduled for Saturday morning, I was invited to come on Friday afternoon and stay for the entire weekend. I knew the conference would be a good place to broaden my background by meeting the adoptive families who would be there, and by hearing and meeting the other speakers, so I decided to take advantage of the offer. I drove directly from Minneapolis to the resort in Eagle River, Wisconsin. On Friday evening I met many new people and attended the opening programs for the weekend.

My presentation on Saturday morning, about integrating the adoptive and birth families (and for many of these children, foster families) was well received. There were many questions from the 20 or so adoptees and adoptive parents who attended. On Saturday during the late afternoon and evening there was no planned activity in order to allow the families to enjoy some private time at the resort facilities, and therefore the staff also had that time off. There were about a dozen social workers in attendance, and as it happened all of the women in the group chose to go into Eagle River after dinner to find some entertainment. The men, five state social workers and I, decided to remain at the resort to enjoy what promised to be a warm but beautiful summer evening on a northern Wisconsin lake. However, shortly after dusk a ferocious thunderstorm arose, and we were more or less imprisoned in the staff cabin until late that night.

We were seated on a couch and chairs in a small circle in the living area of the cabin. Since all of the other men knew each other already, early in the conversation I was asked "So what do you do, Doug?"

"I'm a professor in the University of Wisconsin–Stevens Point Psychology Department."

"And what courses do you teach?"

"Oh, a number of them, Introductory Psychology, Developmental, Testing, Behavior Problems in Children, and Sexuality. Actually, I just finished a month of training for the sexuality class in Minneapolis." I had learned to mention the sex course last because it always led to interesting, but usually predictable, reactions in my listeners. I thought mentioning the training in sexuality to this particular group might add some new responses to the list I had already heard many times.

Several of the men made the usual comments about the college class, such as:

"You mean they actually teach a college course in *sex*? For credit?"

"Boy after I got out of the Army, I could sure have taught that course."

"Is there a laboratory with that class?" "Yeah, out behind the barn!"

In response to mentioning the training in sexuality that evening, I recall mainly one comment intended to be funny: "You must be pretty slow to have had to get training in *sex* of all things!"

After the laughter had died down, eventually the discussion turned more serious. Several of the men wanted to know what topics I included in the course. In the list of areas, I mentioned that I talked about sexual abuse. One of the men said "Now there's an area I could really use some help with." A general murmur of agreement accompanied by nodding heads led to the discovery that all of the men present had worked on sexual abuse cases. Some of the cases had involved repeated and often bizarre ritual abuse of child, adolescent, and even adult victims. I could tell from the suddenly quiet tones of the men's voices, the silences, shaking heads, and deep breaths, they were all deeply troubled by the topic.

I had long been aware sexual abuse within the birth family was one reason why a significant number of children were removed from their birth families and made available for adoption each year. As we discussed the issue, several members of the group said some of the children in the adoptive families attending the conference that weekend had been removed from such abusive families. This was why one of the other presentations that weekend was on parenting children who had experienced sexual abuse. The men began to talk about their feelings about the sexual abuse cases with which each of them had worked. Some of these cases were so horrific, that even removing all identifying information, the men had not felt they could share their feelings about them with anyone, not their fellow social workers or their wives. In many of the cases they had worked on, the minor status of the victims resulted in the case files being closed, further inhibiting their ability to talk about their own reactions to what they had seen and heard.

As part of my just-completed training in Minneapolis, I had done some readings, and watched some videotaped interviews and therapy sessions with both the sexually abused and their abusers. Some of that material was so disturbing I too had not felt comfortable talking about what I had seen and heard except with my supervisors. I had also worked on preventing child sexual abuse with the Portage County Council on Human Sexuality. With my background I knew what some of the activities these men had dealt with were likely to be. I shared my thoughts on child sexual abuse with them, and commented, based on my own admittedly limited real-life experience, working with sexually abused children was terribly difficult.

Perhaps what evolved that night was because the fierce storm raging outside gave us a feeling of isolated security and a sense of camaraderie, or perhaps the conversation developed because most of these men did not normally work together, though they all knew each other. I would like to think perhaps the discussion also occurred because I somehow facilitated the process. Whatever the cause, we had an extended discussion of our feelings about working on these cases. In a very real sense, we had a group therapy session. Several of us discussed in detail both the actual events, and our personal reactions to the people involved, abused and abusers alike. We vented frustrations about the legal system, the investigative process, and the difficulty of treating both the victims and the victimizers.

Fortunately, the storm caused the women to delay their return to the resort until much later than they had planned. By the time they rejoined us we had used most of the evening to discuss and perhaps to begin resolving many of the feelings about their work that several of the men had locked away and tried, unsuccessfully, to forget. I thought at the time it was occurring the discussion had been an important event, and I was quite touched when, the next morning, several of the group members confirmed my feelings when they went out of their way to thank me for "last night."

One of the social workers in that group was "Bart" Bartholomew, who worked in the Rhinelander DHSS office. Although I did not know at the time, Bart was married to Marcia Van Brunt, also a social worker, who owned and operated Northern Family Services, a private clinic in Rhinelander that was both a certified outpatient mental health clinic and a state-licensed adoption agency. A significant number of Marcia's adult clients were the childhood victims of the same types of abuse Bart, the other social workers, and I had discussed during the storm that Saturday night in Eagle River. At that time, Wisconsin state mental health clinic certification rules required a psychologist or a psychiatrist to serve as a consultant for all clinics run by social workers. Marcia just happened to be in need of a consulting psychologist, and Bart returned to Rhinelander after that weekend quite impressed with my background and skills. He told Marcia about me, and when the videotape of my presentation was available, she watched the tape. Marcia decided she had found the psychologist with whom she wanted to work.

Bart made the initial call to me sometime during the spring of 1986 to describe the clinic and Marcia's desire to hire me as a consultant. I said I was not particularly interested, especially since I was going through a busy time at the University right then. I told Bart he might try calling back early in the summer if Marcia was still interested at that time, but I made no promises. When Marcia herself called me again in May my schedule was more open, and I agreed to at least drive the 90 miles up to Rhinelander to meet her and talk about what my duties might involve. After meeting Marcia, and having dinner with her and Bart, I decided working with Marcia was an experience I wanted to pursue.

For the next three years I traveled one Friday a month to work at the clinic in Rhinelander. I spent a typical day reviewing Marcia's treatment notes, often seeing a patient with whom she needed some assistance in diagnosis or treatment planning, and talking with her about a wide variety of clinical and philosophical issues. We began to spend Friday evenings together, continuing our conversation over dinner. Often Bart would join us. As has been the case in many areas of my life, as our conversations evolved, I began to have a hard time distinguishing when I had stopped "working" and started what more resembled personal growth, or even "playing." As I got to know them, I learned Bart and Marcia were both quite extraordinary people, and together they made an extraordinary couple. Both of them were divorced after long first marriages, and both also came into the profession of social work later in their lives. Marcia became a social worker after many years spent as a self-described "mouse" in an abusive marriage, which she finally worked up the courage to leave, taking her three young sons with her. She supported them as a single mother while she finished her undergraduate and graduate degrees. Bart and Marcia also shared a deep spiritual dimension, although their beliefs included non-traditional concepts such as reincarnation, soul travel, and other mystic, holistic and alternative ideas. Bart, was an ordained minister before he took up social work, and he still preached as a fill-in minister at several northern Wisconsin churches.

I found the monthly trips to Rhinelander became increasingly valuable both professionally and personally as I began to do considerable re-evaluation of my own beliefs about the meaning of life in general, and about my specific purpose in the world. Through the discussions with Bart and Marcia I first began to understand and appreciate the concept of synchronicity, which I had first heard about while studying the work of Carl Jung in graduate school. Jung defines synchronicity as the experience of a personally meaningful event so rare that its occurrence by chance alone would seem to be impossible. I began to recognize the synchronicities that had happened throughout my life, but especially during my search and reunion.

As I discussed the ideas I was being exposed to in Rhinelander with Susan, she became interested in meeting Bart and Marcia to share in the discussions we were having. We were ultimately able to turn my monthly trips north to the clinic into weekend mini-vacations. I would leave Stevens Point around 6:00 a. m. on a Friday for Rhinelander, and Susan and her son, Carch, would come north after school ended that afternoon, meeting me either at the clinic or at Holiday Acres, a nearby resort on one of the many lakes in the area, that Bart and Marcia had recommended to us.

The first night we stayed at Holiday Acres, in January 1987, we had barely checked into our room when there was a knock at the patio door. We let in a well-bundled-up child who introduced himself as Jamie, said he was seven years old, and asked how old Carch was. When Carch answered that he was seven also, an immediate bond was established, and they shortly went outside to play in the snow. Jamie's grandparents owned the resort, and his parents, who lived right next to the resort, were the managers. Each time we returned to Holiday Acres for the next couple of years, the two boys entertained themselves. Carch often spent one of the nights, typically Friday, at Jamie's house, thus making the trips enjoyable for him, as well as for Susan and me.

Meanwhile, the wide-ranging discussions continued, now including Bart, Marcia, Susan, and me. Gradually I began to appreciate the important role synchronicity had played not just in my search and reunion experiences, but in my life in general. The four of us explored the topic of spirituality in general, including the meaning of our lives, reincarnation, and even such concepts as out of body experiences and channeling. I began to see the chain of events leading to my association with Marcia, Bart, and Northern Family Services as an example of synchronicity. Yet another of the fortunate chains of "chance" events in my life seemed to have been "arranged" in order to work out in just the "right" way. By meeting these particular people, at this particular time in my life, I was presented with information and experiences that were the perfect growth opportunity for me. The areas of synchronicity and adoption (and their relationship to each other) have become for me both a professional specialty and a personal growth area. Thus, in another very meaningful way the separation between "work" and "play" that is so clear in the lives of many people, is rather indistinct for me. I feel extremely fortunate.

One of the more meaningful growth experiences I had in Rhinelander was related to the fact that Northern Family Services was, in addition to being a mental health clinic, a state-certified adoption agency. The reason for my professional position there was to provide state-required supervision for the mental health clinic portion of Marcia's work. On occasion, however, Marcia would use some of my consulting time to discuss both general adoption issues, and specific children, birth mothers, or families on her adoption caseload. One Friday she told me over lunch about "Alice," a teenage single mother. Alice had worked with Marcia during her first pregnancy on the decision of whether to raise the baby herself alone, or to place her son for adoption, and chose to raise the boy herself. Recently, when Alice learned she was pregnant again, she had contacted Marcia, and decided to place the second baby for an open adoption. In Wisconsin, as in most states, while an adoption *plan* may be made while the birth mother is pregnant, the legal adoption *process* cannot begin, and the adoption cannot be finalized, until after the baby has been born. Alice had already picked out a family into which she wished to have her child adopted.

Alice had made arrangements for the infant to be placed directly from the hospital into a foster home until the adoptive placement could be finalized. Once the baby had been born, however, and Alice had actually seen and held her daughter in the hospital, before the girl went to the foster home, she began to have second thoughts about her decision. Earlier that week she had called Marcia to say she wasn't sure about continuing with her adoption plan, and she wanted to try having her daughter at home with her and her son for a few days. She picked up the baby Thursday at Marcia's office to take her home for the weekend. She called that Friday morning to say she didn't think she could manage the extra responsibilities involved in keeping her daughter, and perhaps she would carry out her adoption plan after all.

Marcia told me Alice would be bringing her daughter back to the office that afternoon, and asked if I would be willing to meet with Alice if she was interested. I knew immediately working with Alice would be difficult for me personally because such a meeting would bring up a lot of my own issues. From my many conversations with birth mothers over the last few years, I also was aware that whatever I might say in the conversation would be remembered by Alice for the rest of her life. I remembered the many birth mothers who said they had felt pressured to do what *other* people wanted them to do. I prepared myself to listen ever so carefully for what *Alice* wanted to do, and reminded myself that I must not let my own personal issues interfere with what Alice wanted, and what her daughter needed. Based on the history Marcia had related to me, I felt the decision to place for adoption was probably the better one for both Alice and her new-born daughter, as well as for the son Alice was already raising. I hoped as I talked to Alice, I would be able to serve what I perceived as both her and her baby's needs, while at the same time being careful not to impose my own feelings and needs on the situation.

I was reviewing records when Alice arrived. Marcia told Alice she worked with an adoptee who had become a psychologist, and he was in the office at that time and willing to talk with her. Alice immediately said she wanted to talk to me. Marcia took the baby so we could have fewer distractions while we talked. I mostly listened, and learned as I had hoped I would, that Alice had realized, in just one day, the task of trying to raise two young children on her own would be nearly impossible, at least for her. What Alice wanted most from me was to hear what I experienced growing up adopted.

We talked about not only my own experiences as someone born and adopted in the traditional closed adoption system of the mid-1940s, but also about the experiences of children who were adopted under some form of an "open" system, as had evolved in recent years. I already knew from my extensive discussions with Marcia that she would not conduct an adoption which would be of the old-fashioned "permanently closed" variety she could see had produced so much pain for so many people. The closed system typically involved lifelong separation between adoptees and their birth parents, and lifelong uncertainty for all involved. I believe the uncertainty is the cause of many of the problems adoptees and birthparents experience. Therefore, I could reassure Alice her daughter would most likely not suffer any serious damage from an open adoption. I emphasized the importance of openness and honesty, and added that any problems her daughter did have would be significantly lessened as long as there was no secrecy. I told Alice she could reduce the likelihood of problems especially if she would be available to the adoptive parents while her daughter was growing up, and to her daughter once she became an adult.

Having lifelong access to her birth mother, and to other birth relatives, including the birth brother she already had, would allow Alice's daughter to know where she fit in to the world biologically, and to become aware of any subsequent developments in Alice and her son's health that might affect her daughter.

Talking with me seemed to reassure Alice, and we went to find Marcia and the baby. I went back to reviewing records, and Marcia and Alice talked for a short while. Then Marcia's office door opened, and I heard Alice say she had to leave to get home to care for her son, and so the time had come to say good-bye to her daughter. I came out of my office to wish Alice good luck, and was the witness to what must be one of the hardest tasks a human being must have to endure: a mother saying good-bye to her child who she is surrendering for adoption. My only consolation was my belief that unlike so many closed adoptions of the past, for Alice and her daughter good-bye would not be permanent. Nonetheless, the scene was still a heart-wrenching process for me to observe, let alone for Alice to experience.

After Alice had left the office, Marcia told me that because Alice had initially asked to keep her daughter with her until Monday, Marcia was having a problem in contacting a licensed foster home to take the baby. It was four o'clock on a Friday afternoon, and there were only a couple of foster homes in the county licensed to take such a young infant. As soon as Alice had called that morning, Marcia had called one of the foster homes she regularly used and left a message on their answering machine to call her back. They had not as yet done so and a call to a second foster home resulted in a conversation with a teen-aged child who said the parents were out and would not be back until around dinner time. State licensing law prevented Marcia from taking the child home with her, since her home was not a licensed emergency foster home. Thus, there was, at that time, no place to legally put the baby, and Marcia would have to remain in the office that afternoon (and evening if necessary), until an adult from one of the properly licensed foster families was able to come and pick the baby up.

However, there was a much more immediate problem. Marcia had one more client to see, and her secretary had gone into town to get office supplies. So, when Marcia's client arrived, I was elected to hold the baby until the secretary returned. I sat in the office, holding an infant who was so young that she probably would have no conscious memory of this time or of me in her life. I no longer needed to concern myself with being "professional" or with preventing my issues from interfering with my obligation to meet other people's needs. I was overcome by a rush of emotions related to my own adoption. I recalled that Uncle Henry had held me, but Pearl had not. How many people had held me when I was an infant? Had they known what my life would be like, where I would be placed, or even what my name was then, if I even had a name, or what my new name would be? How many more people would hold Alice's daughter before she got to her permanent home? Would any of the people who would hold her, even her adoptive parents, ever understand what she was experiencing in the way I did? As I gave up fighting back tears, I wasn't really sure for whom I was crying, or whether they were tears of sadness or of joy, or whether I was simply in awe of the immensity of the process of adoption. I said a prayer that she would live a life free of the pain caused by ignorance and secrecy, that her life would be happy and healthy, and that we, who were making life-altering plans for her, and all the others like her, would make the right choices. As Alice's baby and I rocked that afternoon, I felt I was in touch with something much greater than I. I was rocking for every adopted infant, every birth parent, every adoptive parent. I was rocking for every birth and adoptive brother, sister, aunt, uncle, and grandparent. And I was rocking for myself.

CHAPTER 14

Synchronicity: Not Only in America

In the spring semester of 1988, I took leave from Northern Family Services and my regular job at the University to spend five months in Spain, as the faculty leader of the UWSP International Program in Madrid. While there I had, at times, some of the loneliest experiences I have ever had, and at other times some of the most ecstatic ones. During my travels in Madrid and around the south coasts of Spain and Portugal, I had numerous experiences of "déjà vu," that uncanny feeling that "I've been here before." or that "I know what will happen next." Throughout history philosophers and more recently psychologists and cognitive scientists have argued about what, if anything, these experiences mean. But regardless of how or whether they can be explained, most people have had them at one time or another. Often, they give us pause: we have a mental jump, our spines tingle and typically we may not even have time to shake our heads in wonder before the sensation is over.

The largest number of my déjà vu experiences in Europe occurred around Valencia in southern Spain. Valencia is a beautiful old city historically having been under periods of control by both Moslems (the Moors) and Christians (the Roman Catholics). The streets are lined with orange trees (Valencia oranges originated there), which were in a ripe or near-ripe stage when we visited, making Valencia a colorful and delightfully fragrant city. Several times as I walked through Valencia, I had the very strong sense that I knew, almost in the sense of being able to see, what lay ahead around the next corner. When I turned the corner, my feeling was very often proven to be correct. Although I have had déjà vu experiences in other places before, previously the experiences would almost always cease at the instant I became aware of them. Those I had in Valencia were of unusually long duration and were very intense. I had an unusual sense of comfort there, and while there were few if any places in Spain where I felt uncomfortable, Valencia was somehow more than just comfortable for me. I almost felt as if I belonged there, and I hated to leave.

Some weeks later, we traveled to Granada, location of the Alhambra palace. I explored the palace itself, and marveled at the beauty of its intricate geometrically designed plasterwork, and its many fountains, and gardens. Then I hiked alone up into the mountains overlooking the palace, which spread up the mountain from the town of Granada at its base, to watch the sun set. I had heard a legend about a Moorish king who realized the battle for his castle at Alhambra had been lost to the invading Catholic armies. He went up into the mountains overlooking his palace and wept over the loss of such beauty. One of his advisors rebuked him, saying he was ashamed of his king who would cry like a child rather than fight and die like a man.

For whatever reasons, I identified with that king, and I, too, wept at the beauty which lay out below me as the sun set. I have a hard time describing the depth and spiritual intensity of the experience I had there. I felt connected to the universe, close to God, deliriously happy and yet also profoundly and painfully aware of a deep sadness at least part of which was because I was there alone. The humanistic psychologist Abraham Maslow describes what he calls "peak experiences," and watching the sun set over the Alhambra was but one example of several peak experiences I had while in Europe.

Just a few days prior to the experience at the Alhambra, I had another similar experience at the beach in the Portuguese town of Praia da Roca, on the southern Portuguese Atlantic coast. We had rooms in a modern high-rise apartment hotel a few hundred feet back from the golden-colored sand beach. The beach was a half-mile wide in places, curving for perhaps a couple of miles between two high points of land jutting into the sea. The town sat on a sandstone cliff some 75 to 100 feet high overlooking the beach, which had obviously been carved out of the cliff by the waves.

Simply put, the beach was the most interesting and most beautiful natural scenery I have ever seen. The water and wind had eroded soft sandstone at the shore-line to make huge natural sculptures which dotted the beach and continued out into the water. Some of these natural sandstone sculptures rose nearly as high as the top of the cliff which was their origin. There were many natural arches, some of them large enough to walk through, and also many crevices and caves which the wind and waves had dug into the face of the cliff itself.

The students and I spent virtually all of our time in Praia da Roca on the beach, playing football, sunning, and walking up and down the beach exploring the rocks, which changed their appearance hourly as the sun moved and the tide changed. One of the days we were there I took a long walk by myself down the beach. I felt particularly lonely that day because, even though I was surrounded by people, they were all either my students, a mix of fun and responsibility for me, or non-English or Spanish-speaking adults. I wanted to get away from the crowd where I was lonely in public, and be alone in private. Earlier I had seen several dark places hidden in the rocks in a relatively deserted area which was located much farther down the beach from the vicinity of the town where we had been spending most of our time. I headed off to explore these shadows.

As I approached the first of them, I realized I was seeing a cave. I was initially put off by thoughts of bats and spider webs. However, I had never seen anything like these caves before, and my curiosity gradually overcame my fear of the beasties I imagined might lurk inside their darkness. Although the openings of many of them were too small to admit an adult, eventually I found one of them which had an entrance large enough to allow me inside. As I stooped slightly to enter the cave, and my eyes adjusted to the dark interior, I noticed some green plants on the back wall, and looked up to find the source of the light I could see entering from the top of the cave. I had to move around a bit inside the cave, but eventually I could see where the action of the waves and wind had hollowed out the cave all the way up to the top of the cliff, perhaps 50 to 75 feet above. I could also see there was a patch of bright blue sky at the top of the cave, framed by flowers and grasses gently waving in the breeze. The view was an unexpected and very beautiful surprise that took my breath away. I was immediately glad I had not allowed my initial reaction of fear to predominate, and I had listened to the little voice inside me with the message to explore.

I did not spend all of my time in Praia da Roca exploring the beach, however. At the time we had first driven toward the town, we noticed from the distance a large number of high-rise buildings. As we got nearer, we saw they appeared to be under construction. Once we actually arrived in the town, however, I could see many of the buildings had not been worked on for some years. I later learned most of them had been abandoned by their builders. The mortgage-holders, by and large land speculators according to the story, had in many cases lost large sums of money.

From my fifth-floor room in our hotel I could see directly into the nearest abandoned building, and on the first day of our visit I had seen several people walking around in the lower floors, so I decided to do some more exploring myself

I followed a path from the main street toward the rear of the building. I found partial walls built out of scrap lumber and cardboard, remains of fires built up against the concrete walls, some of them still warm, bedding on old mattresses, and a couple of ropes with clothes drying on them, and the strong smell of human waste

A particularly sad sight was the young mother carrying an infant who walked up and into the place late one afternoon. Later on, as I cooked my steak in my fancy air-conditioned private apartment, I could see her cooking their dinner over a fire made of scrap lumber, built against a wall on the third-floor level. At one point she walked to the edge of the building, and looked out in my direction, and I wondered if she saw me watching her. I had a hard time eating in peace as I watched her, wondering what life path had brought her there. I gave some thought as to whether I should try to go to her and offer her food or money. Then I remembered the fear I had felt earlier, while exploring an area of the building where homeless people lived, and that was during the day, when most of the people were away. I decided I had best keep to myself.

As I ate my steak sitting on the porch, I found myself thinking about my life, the things I took for granted, and the ironies of our existence. I wondered about the woman as I watched her. She was quite possibly caught in a trap, perhaps one of her own making, or perhaps she was the victim of someone else's decisions. There she was, living her life in the abandoned wreckage of someone's dreams, living within mutual sight of others, like me, whose dreams had been much more fulfilled than hers might ever be.

I especially wondered about her baby, who had not chosen to live that way, but was there because that was where her mother lived. I wondered what kind of a future that baby would have. The baby girl I had held in my arms in Rhinelander, whose mother, Alice, had decided to place her for adoption, came to my mind. I thought about the decisions we make as a society about what constitutes a "good" life for an infant. The fact that babies are so resilient, and so able to adapt to such a wide variety of life experiences, is pretty remarkable, and pretty fortunate for us as a race. I was glad I had the group's final beach party later that evening to look forward to. Sleep might otherwise have been difficult with the image of that young mother stooped over her cooking fire, and her baby with an uncertain future, fresh in my mind.

At the end of the academic portion of the semester in Spain the student group was scheduled to take an approximately two-week tour of Europe by train, with me as their tour guide. The tour, and my formal responsibility as group leader, ended on May 20 in Amsterdam. I had the option to delay my return to the U.S. at that time if I wanted to remain in Europe for a personal vacation, and I did so. I traveled around Europe for four weeks on a Eurail pass. For the first two weeks of the trip, my friend, Bruce Caley, joined me. Susan then came to join me for the last two weeks of my vacation, and the three of us spent some overlapping time traveling together.

Throughout my time in Spain, I had kept in touch with Susan by spending an hour or so a week on the phone with her, and I had already told her about a fair amount of my peak and déjà vu experiences. During our travels in Europe together I filled her in on more of the details about the unusual experiences I had been having, particularly those in southern Portugal and Spain. We decided we couldn't wait to share the stories with Marcia and Bart. Even though we were anxious to return to Wisconsin to discuss these things, June 20th, the day of our return, came too soon. After teaching a four-week summer school class, I had the rest of that summer to think about and make sense of the special experiences I had while I was in Europe.

CHAPTER 15

Synchronicity: Not Only Here on Earth?

M any of the ideas I am about to present may sound strange, and the experiences I will be describing might even make me appear crazy. I can assure the reader that some of the ideas certainly sounded odd to me at the time I first heard of them! As I began to experience some of what I am about to describe I was afraid at times I was losing the levelheaded logical thinking ability about which I had always prided myself. As I move into the areas of synchronicity and psychic experience, I may lose some of my more rational/scientific readers. More likely some of you will think I am the one who has lost something! But whenever I am tempted to dismiss things I do not understand or experiences that do not seem to conform to my version of reality, I try to stop. I remember that many ideas we take for granted as "truth" today were once regarded as extreme, heretical, or just plain crazy when they were first proposed.

The classic example to give now would be the concept that the earth revolves around the sun, a concept that was not easily observable, and of the condemnation Galileo received when he suggested the idea. However, a modern example, which I like much better, has to do with our perception of the world around us right now. Assuming you are not reading this book in a room with walls lined with lead, I can state, with confidence, some facts about your environment. Likely present in the room with you are several forms of music, heated discussions on all sorts of issues, sporting events, advertisements, news, and even phone calls. How is it you are able to concentrate on your reading amidst all of that distraction? Because you can't sense *any* of these stimuli unless there is a proper translation device (in this case a radio, television, or cell phone) operating nearby. We now know about radio frequency waves.

They are real, and are not made any less real by our inability to perceive them without the assistance of an operating device. Before this form of energy was discovered, or if we had not yet learned of the discovery, we might think someone who insisted on the presence of all of these things in the room had a rather serious mental disturbance. Our inability to perceive a stimulus, or our lack of knowledge about a concept, is not proof that the stimulus is not real, or that the concept is false.

We may become aware of new stimuli or concepts in at least two ways: *discovery* of something that has always been there; and *invention*, the creation of something which is (presumably) "new." To believe we have discovered all there is to discover is as naive as to believe we have invented all that can be invented. To automatically dismiss the beliefs of those whose experience of reality seems different than ours as either mental illness or as an unexplained, and unexplainable, exception to the rules of reality, places us at risk. We risk later being proven wrong, closed-minded, or at least appearing foolish. However, I also believe that to uncritically accept everyone's reported beliefs and experiences is equally risky. I try to look at other people's reported life experiences with an open mind, and try to choose skeptical openness to their experiences over either the extreme of uncritical acceptance, or of self-assured denial.

Shortly after I returned from my semester in Spain, I resumed my monthly trips to Rhinelander, with Susan and Carch again coming up to share the weekends. I had the opportunity to share with Bart, Marcia, and again with Susan, my experiences in and around the Mediterranean Ocean. One of the topics we discussed often was the idea that there were many dimensions or levels that made up what we call reality. We talked about the implications of the idea that time and space might exist in different ways than traditionally perceived in our culture. We came to understand these particular dimensions might not be as constant and objective as many, or even most, in western society currently believe.

While I was in Spain Marcia had met Phyllis McCoy, from the Minneapolis-St. Paul area who was a channel. "Channels" are people who are able to cross the dimensions of time and space, or to contact one of those other dimensions Marcia, Bart, Susan and I had spoken about. Channels may speak with the voice and thoughts of someone who is dead and wishes to contact living relatives or friends. Channels may also contact spiritual beings from another dimension of time or space, and may speak to us today with knowledge from the past or the future. Marcia had seen Phyllis both in a workshop setting and for an individual "reading" session. In addition to talking about these ideas with Bart and Marcia, Susan and I read about Phyllis' understanding of reality in a small book written by Phyllis that Marcia lent to us: *The Primer: Channeled Guidance from God and the Masters.*

In the fall of 1988, after my return from Spain, Phyllis was scheduled to present a session about some of her beliefs as part of a weekend series of workshops in spirituality which was being held in northern Wisconsin. It just happened to be scheduled on a weekend I would be traveling to Rhinelander to work with Marcia. When I heard about the workshops, I decided to attend the Friday evening and Saturday morning sessions, and then take advantage of Phyllis' availability for private consultation on Saturday afternoon to schedule a channeling session with her. I had not met Phyllis before the workshop on Friday night, and did not really get much of an idea of what to expect in our session Saturday afternoon from what she presented on Friday. The Friday session I attended was mostly about Phyllis' general understanding of reality, of the relativity of time and space, and of our place as human beings in the physical and spiritual world. Much of her presentation was a review of what Marcia, Bart, Susan, and I had been discussing all along, and what we had subsequently read in her booklet.

We had our private session in a vacation home lent to Phyllis for the weekend, built into the side of a hill in a heavily wooded area. The weather was typical for late fall in northern Wisconsin—cloudy, calm and cool. The stark beauty of the woods was reinforced by the open design of the house. As I waited in the glassed-in front hallway for Phyllis to meet me, I began to think about the fact that the house was surrounded by tall trees. The leaves had all fallen, and the ground was brown with them. I have always loved the woods, and these trees were beautiful, powerful, aged, and very much alive, although their appearance on the surface was deceiving. They were merely asleep for the winter.

Their now-leafless branches intertwined, becoming less distinct the higher or the farther away I looked. Each tree, and all of its branches, as well as its invisible roots, became less an individual, and more a part of an incredibly complex and interrelated forest—a pattern of individuals, merging into a whole. I thought the trees in the forest were not unlike the lives of we humans as we get older, becoming more complex and inter-related, and less individually important when viewed as part of the whole.

As I thought about how the lives of trees and people are alike, I remembered a story I had once heard about the difference between oaks and pines under the weight of heavy snow. They are like two kinds of reactions people can have to the weight of stress. The oak is rigid and hard, trying to hold up the weight of the snow without bending. In fact, the oak simply can't bend very much at all, and although oak is very strong wood, when the weight gets too great the oak breaks with a CRACK heard far and wide, which often destroys the tree. Pines, however, are softer and more flexible than oaks. They bend with the weight, and when the snow gets too heavy their branches drop and let go in a soft and beautiful avalanche of snow after which their limbs reach back to the sky again. As I experienced the various kinds of stress in my life, many times I had tried to be more like the pine than the oak. That aspiration was intentional. I'm not sure how well I have succeeded. Looking out at the woods, I also thought of the importance of having roots, those hidden but crucially important bases upon which we build our lives. My search had shown me this was a fact of life as important and true for people as it was for trees.

One of the essential beliefs in Phyllis's understanding of the spirit world is that our souls return many times to take on different human lives. She believes souls are involved in gathering the wisdom of experience with each life through which they pass, and souls become more complex, more aware, and more mature as they get older. When a soul has become sufficiently complex and mature (or "old"), there is no longer any need to experience any more of life as a human, and the soul moves on to another plane of existence. I looked at that forest, with its continuous cycle of life, growth, decline, and death, followed by rebirth from the remains of the lives of many previous forests. I wondered if I had always understood Phyllis's ideas, even though I had heard of them only recently. Perhaps this is why I have always loved the woods.

My thinking was interrupted by Phyllis's arrival in the front hall. We walked to a different part of the house, located on the house's high side and overlooking the valley below the hill into which the house was built. We worked in a room that was mostly windows, and being in that room was almost like being in a bird's nest, surrounded as we were by just the tree tops. We began the session seated facing each other, knees almost touching, with Phyllis taking my hands in hers. I looked at her as she closed her eyes and took several deep breaths, and then I closed my own eyes. There was a short period of silence, after which Phyllis shuddered a couple of times, and said "There is another here with us." She let go of my hands. "He is showing me a wide, long expanse of sand, perhaps a beach. There is one set of footprints leading down it. I sense a deep loneliness. Yes, you are all alone here."

I immediately thought of the beach at Praia da Roca in Portugal, and I began to experience a profound sense of wonder, and of deep union and communication with Phyllis. I sensed she really understood me, and she had somehow connected with one of the more powerful experiences I had while in Europe the previous spring. She went on to describe how I was walking down the beach, and came to "an opening, low in the rock. It is a natural opening, not a man-made one. You have to duck down to enter, and once inside you look up, and," (here she seemed genuinely both pleased and surprised) "oh, your spirit guide is up there, wearing a brilliant white robe."

By now I was so moved I had begun to tear up, and had to take deep breaths to keep from breaking into sobs, since Phyllis had just described almost the exact experience I had on the beach at Praia da Roca in Portugal. As far as I know I had only told Susan any of the details of my experience on that beach. I believe I had not told Marcia anything at all about it, especially anything as specific as what Phyllis was now telling me. How had Phyllis known of this image?

The session continued with Phyllis giving me a name for my spirit guide, and telling me he had always been there, serving as a protector and source of strength. She told me he would continue to be available to me in times of trouble should I ask for his help. The idea of having a spirit guide also resonated with me, since as a child I had been taught in church that we each had our own special guardian angel watching over us, and keeping us safe from harm. I had always thought that I was especially lucky to have such an angel keeping me safe and helping even bad situations to turn out all right. One of the issues I had been working on in my various therapies as an adult was to regain that sense of being special, and the confidence I once had that things would always work out for the best.

Phyllis also told me my soul had past-life connections to the Mediterranean region. I told her about the déjà vu experiences I had had in Spain, and she suggested these were perhaps places where my soul had experienced previous lives. She suggested that farther east, in the area of Greece and Turkey, there were more such connections.

There was one more bit of information she provided. I asked her about what previous connections there had been between Susan and me. She responded slowly, after a long pause. "I see hard, hard work—stooping, repetitive work. There is sweat in the hot sun, and a sense of love and kinship. Ah, it is the American south. You are Black slaves, a brother and sister, working on a plantation together picking cotton. You know,

I'm not sure whether I'm seeing you as the male. It seems you were the woman, and Susan was the man."

Susan's area of specialty within dance is tap, which has its roots in both Irish clogging and Black folk dance. For as long as I can remember, watching tap dancing has sometimes led me to a very surprising and intense emotional place. Susan and I as brother and sister immediately struck several responsive chords deep within me. Several of my friends, as they had gotten to know Susan and seen her interact with me, had said to me they saw our relationship almost as more like a brother and sister than like lovers. I have also always noted I have several characteristics more traditionally found in women, most notably my pattern of superior verbal skills compared with my significantly lower level of mathematical skills. Somehow, Phyllis had again touched on important aspects of my life.

When I returned to Stevens Point, I shared the channeling experience with Susan, and with a couple of close friends. When I told one of them of my "soul history" as a Black person, he told the story to his wife, who is from the American south. She then remembered what had been for them a very puzzling incident had occurred when I first visited their house. The couple collects the work of a Black artist who is famous for painting scenes of slavery. They had several works by this artist displayed in their dining room, including at least one painting of a heavy Black woman picking cotton. When I saw these paintings, they recalled I had an unusual reaction. I had become quite upset with them, not exactly accusing the couple of being racist, but saying I thought they were only perpetuating biased stereotypes to display these sorts of pictures. They had talked about my reaction after I had left and thought I was unusually strong and emotional. The incident and the intensity of my reaction were things that I had long since forgotten, until they told me of them again. Perhaps those pictures had touched a sensitive place in my past. Whatever the case, my friends and I discussed how odd it was that Phyllis should have seen me as a Black woman, not having known of the painting incident at all.

CHAPTER 16

Whither My Career?

In the spring of 1986, the annual national conference of the American Adoption Congress was held in Milwaukee, with AID as the host group. By that time the Stevens Point chapter of the group had been operating nicely for over a year. I was beginning to feel as though I had some good ideas about the adoption process to offer to both mental health professionals who worked in adoption and to the adoption community at large. I had been to a couple of state and regional conferences, and had met other mental health professionals who were also members of the adoption triad. One of these was Linda Yellin, an adoptee social worker from Michigan. Linda approached me about co-leading a workshop during the Milwaukee conference on the post-reunion process with her, and I agreed to do so. C. E. and I had remained in contact, and he and I decided to combine our talents for a workshop at the same conference titled "A Psychiatrist and a Psychologist Look at Adoption." These were my first forays into the national adoption scene, and I felt they were reasonably successful. Linda and C. E., as well as others at the conference, also seemed to share my opinion. Perhaps as a result of the Milwaukee workshops, or perhaps because of my involvement in other adoption support activities, I was asked to present workshops on "Issues of Denial in Adoption" and on "Counseling the Adult Adoptee After a Completed Search" at the 1990 AAC annual meeting in Chicago. Those workshops also were well-received, and attending the conference allowed me to meet still more activists in the search and reunion field.

At the Chicago convention C. E. and I met two other adoptees, one who was a psychologist (Dorissa Flanagan, from Milwaukee) and one who was a psychiatrist (Bob Andersen, from St. Louis.) I had heard from Bob earlier that spring because he was having a difficult time dealing with the woman who was the head of the Wisconsin Adoption Search Program, which he had contacted for assistance in his search. C. E. and I had lunch with Dorissa and Bob, and we began to jokingly refer to ourselves as "the adoptee shrinks." Bob had been born and adopted in Milwaukee, and had been unsuccessful in finding any information on his birth mother. He had previously gone to Milwaukee to search, and was interested in returning to do further investigation. At lunch in Chicago, we decided to have a conference phone call, which ultimately took place in August of 1990. During this call we decided to meet again in person. Since three of us lived in Wisconsin, and Bob wanted to return to Milwaukee, we decided to get together at Dorissa's home in Milwaukee for a weekend in the fall of 1990, to talk about our experiences in adoption from our unique professional perspectives. The weekend, while not resulting in any formal publications, was an important event, at least for me, in developing my ideas about the adoption process and its long-term effects. At the time Bob was writing a book about his adoption and search experiences and how being adopted had influenced his life. I agreed to review an early draft of his book, and in doing so was further motivated to write my own book. (Bob's book: *Second Choice: Growing up Adopted*, was published in 1993.)

One of the more memorable experiences I have had in my involvement with the search/reunion process was sitting in a car with Dorissa and C. E. outside of the black-market maternity home where Bob believed he was born. Bob was inside a neighboring house, talking with a man who had lived there at about the time Bob was born. He returned to the car after perhaps a half-hour, visibly moved by what he had just heard. Taxis would arrive at the home, often at night, bearing pregnant girls and women. Then, some days later, a taxi would leave, now bearing a lone and non-pregnant occupant. The neighbor also told Bob about hearing the screams of the women giving birth and the cries of the babies, especially in the summertime, and about seeing the well-dressed couples who arrived in fancy cars, often on Sunday afternoons. The couples in these cars left a short while later, carrying a tiny bundle wrapped in a blanket. The history of this house, and the reaction all four of us had to hearing about it, remains for me a poignant representation of both the pain and the joy of the adoption process.

C. E. and I enjoyed working together, and have seen each other at conventions and exchanged letters and calls periodically over the years. In the summer of 1991, he again served as my "angel." The American Adoption Congress was looking for someone to present a session at their 1992 annual conference in Philadelphia on what to do when one finds a death at the end of a search. C. E. knew I had found my birth father only three months after his death, and he again spoke up on my behalf. He mentioned my name to the AAC Education Director, and she contacted me to ask whether I had any interest in presenting such a workshop. I told her I surely did. Perhaps because of my strong personal interest in the topic, I tried harder than usual to make my presentation as academically respectable as I could. I did not want to be just sharing my personal experience and feelings, and so I included a literature survey and a review of the theories of attachment and of the reaction to death in general before I discussed finding a deceased birth relative. A number of people have since told me they found attending that workshop, or listening later to the tape, was very meaningful to them. While there I also expanded my circle of friends still further within both the grassroots and professional members of the AAC. And of course, at the 1992 Philadelphia conference, in "The City of Brotherly Love," you will recall I first talked to my birth brother Keith.

At the same convention in Philadelphia, I attended a program on sexuality and adoption. This program was an unfortunate example of what happens when professionals share their knowledge of a subject they may know very well, without at least some knowledge of their audience. The person who presented the workshop had very good credentials as a sex educator, but was not a member of the adoption triad. They had not thought about how being a triad member might affect one's sexuality, and may not even have known very much about the dynamics of adoption. They also underestimated the level of sophistication of the audience, and presented traditional sex-education material on about a senior-year high-school level. The presentation was about half way through the allotted time yet the speaker hadn't mentioned anything about how adoption might affect one's sexuality. I raised my hand and asked if the presenter was planning on doing that. The answer was: "Of course. We are all sexual beings." And the presentation continued. It was ultimately virtually devoid of anything specific to triad members. During the latter part of the program, I had noticed others in the audience who were also clearly disappointed with the absence of adoption-specific content.

After the workshop was over, I struck up a conversation with Tom Matlock, an adoptee from Washington state, and Kim Wassermann, then a doctoral candidate in counseling psychology at Temple University in Philadelphia. As a result, we felt we could do at least as good a job as the presentation we had just attended. We submitted a proposal for the 1994 AAC program in New Orleans which would contain useful and relevant information about how sexuality effected triad members because the presenters would all *be* triad members. The proposed program evolved into two sessions, the first in which an adoptee (myself), then a birth parent, and then an adoptive parent, all of us also mental health professionals, would each present a section on how their sexuality had been impacted by their triad position. Then separate follow-up discussions would then be held for each side of the triad. Although Kim was ultimately unable to go to New Orleans, Tom and I co-led a slightly revised program.

As my name became more well known in the support movement, and because I was listed in several reference sources as the leader of a search and support group, I began to get all sorts of mailings regarding various adoption-related programs, other search and support groups, and research projects related to adoption. One of the more interesting of these appeared in 1990. I received a request from LaVonne Stiffler a doctoral candidate in counseling, regarding her dissertation project, which was on synchronicity and adoption search. I had begun to become aware of synchronicity as I told my search story over the years, and had learned a lot more about the concept in my discussions with Bart, Marcia and Susan. I was quite certain many of the experiences I had were examples of synchronistic events.

LaVonne was collecting examples of synchronicities from a sample of triad members she was recruiting by contacting search and support groups. For her dissertation she was going to attempt an analysis and classification of these synchronicities, and she wanted people who had experienced such events to write them down and send them to her. Her letter mentioned the fact that she eventually planned to include the stories in a book, as well as to use them for her doctoral research. While the idea of writing to her about my own synchronicities was appealing, and while I might well have had experiences which she would find useful, I did not, in the end, send her my information. My reasons were in part because of time pressures from work, which made fitting something else into my schedule difficult but also selfish because I was reluctant to send material to someone else that I hoped someday would be in my own book!

Perhaps a year later I received a notice in the mail that LaVonne's book, *Synchronicity and Reunion: The Genetic Connection of Adoptees and Birthparents*, was available for purchase, and I immediately sent for a copy. Once I began to read the book, I could not put it down, and I immediately regretted I had not sent her my information, especially since I had as yet done nothing concrete about moving my own book (this one!) any closer to completion. In LaVonne's book were descriptions of various kinds of synchronistic events that in many ways duplicated those I had experienced in my own search. My reading had two immediate effects: I wanted to meet LaVonne and find out more about her work, and I became even more determined to one day write my own experiences into a book for publication. I began to recommend *Synchronicity and Reunion* to others both in informal conversations and when I was asked to speak to groups about adoption-related topics.

I was notified in November 1993 that the two programs on sexuality had been accepted for presentation at the April 1994 conference of the AAC in New Orleans. A list of the other programs accepted for presentation in New Orleans was included, and I was happy to see LaVonne would be presenting a workshop on her book. I decided immediately I would attend her session no matter what else I did at that meeting. That was, of course, unless by some incredible stroke of bad luck, one of my own two sessions on sexuality was scheduled at the same time! In January 1994 the convention announcement brochure came with the final schedule of events. I was relieved to see that our sessions were not going to overlap, and I could attend LaVonne's workshop.

Earlier that semester (the fall of 1993) I had been approached by Tom Rowe, a Psychology Department colleague with whom I had a long friendship. He was at a decision point in his career, and was thinking about pursuing a new line of research related to a phenomenon that had long sparked his interest: synchronicity. Tom knew of my interest, and wondered whether I might want to cooperate with him in some research. We had already talked about the striking similarities being discovered in reunited identical twins separated by adoption and raised apart, and about my own experiences in my search and reunion. The director of the best known of these research programs, the Minnesota Study of Twins Reared Apart and Adoption, had served on the AAC Board of Directors, and I had met and talked extensively with Nancy Segal, the program's Associate Director at a couple of AAC conventions. Having just completed reading LaVonne's book, I was very interested in Tom's proposal for a research project, and I gave LaVonne's book to Tom to read. We also read the article in which psychoanalyst Carl Jung first introduced and described the term synchronicity, and began a series of discussions about how we might use traditional scientific methods to investigate just how unusual some of the curious coincidences of synchronicity really were. Tom developed the basic methodology we have used, and has done most of the work on the project, but our research has proven for me to be just the right project in which to have become involved.

In our basic methodology, we ask random pairs of university students who do not know each other to pretend they are reunited birth relatives, and to spend an hour of discussion trying to find and list similarities between themselves. We then ask another and much larger group of university students to read over the list of these discovered similarities, and to identify those similarities that are also true of them. Let's say as an example the members of a pair of "pretend" reunited adoptees discovered, among many other things, they both ate with forks, and both had broken their left arm in (separate) pick-up football games. When the large group of students is asked whether either of these events is true for them, presumably all will say they eat with a fork, and likewise relatively few would say they had broken their left arm in a football game. "Common" similarities (eating with a fork) are identified, and we drop them out. We are then able to identify similarities that are infrequent enough to be statistically unusual (such as breaking one's left arm playing football). We are finding there are patterns of similarities that exist between random strangers, against which we plan to compare the patterns found in reunited birth relatives. A difference in the patterns for the birth relatives that couldn't be explained by genetics might be evidence of the existence of some "noncausal" connection such as synchronicity. As of the end of 1997 our project had generated two published studies, and had assisted three of our four undergraduate research assistants to obtain admission to graduate school.

As the AAC convention in New Orleans approached, I realized I wanted to do more with LaVonne than just attend her convention session. I wanted to be able to meet and talk with her personally. I thought meeting with her might be best done at some point before the beginning of her session. As soon as I arrived in New Orleans, I began to ask people I knew if they knew her. At a hospitality hour the night before the conference began, I was able to meet her, and we talked about her book, and about both my own search synchronicities and the research Tom Rowe and I were conducting. Even though Tom and I had not at that time had any of our work accepted for publication, LaVonne was fascinated with what we were doing. She asked me to take a few moments at the end of her session to describe our project. I was very flattered, and of course agreed to do so.

The next day, the first day of the convention, and the day before my program on Sexuality and Adoption, I was looking for a quiet place to have lunch with a friend. I had just over an hour to eat before needing to be at a convention session I wanted to attend, and all of the restaurants in the convention headquarters hotel were full, so we left the hotel in search of a quieter, and hopefully quicker, place to eat. We thought we could find such a restaurant in a nearby Holiday Inn, but when we got there, we discovered the restaurant was only partially open due to construction in the building. The lunch hour was almost over, and therefore only one other group was seated in the restaurant. As we got closer to them, we saw they just happened to be a group of eight people from the AAC convention, primarily adoptees, and most of whom I knew. One of the group was Tom Matlock, who would be helping with my adoptee sexuality discussion group the next day, and two others were Joe Soll and Jack Marvin. You will read more about Jack shortly. We joined them and when someone asked about the program we were going to be presenting the next day, a lively discussion of sexuality ensued. During the discussion at least one and often several of those at the table confirmed virtually everything I had planned to say in my part of the workshop. The discussion had the effect of giving me much more confidence that what I would be saying in my session about adoptees and sexuality would be well received by the adoptees in the audience. The discussion got so intense I lost track of time. When I suddenly realized I was going to be late to the next convention session, I decided the present conversation was valuable, and was happening for a reason. I decided I needed to follow the synchronicity that had brought that particular group together, and to remain where I was to bring that conversation to a close. It seemed not to be wise to leave one productive conversation unfinished only to rush off to a session for which I was already half an hour late.

The decision to follow the synchronicity and to stay where I had found myself was especially interesting given the topic that was being covered in the session I was missing. I had been in a hurry to eat in the first place because the first session after lunch that afternoon just happened to be the one led by LaVonne on the role of synchronicity in adoption! With the invitation LaVonne had made the night before to speak at the end of her session about my research in synchronicity and my own recent synchronistic lunch experience, I still wanted to attend her synchronicity presentation, even though I would arrive late. The occurrence of a synchronistic event which resulted in preventing me from being on time for a session about synchronicity was really rather amusing, and I shook my head and laughed aloud as I rushed to find the room where I feared LaVonne's presentation would be nearly over before I arrived.

When LaVonne saw me come in she smiled and nodded in my direction, acknowledging she had seen me enter. She had finished her formal presentation by the time I got there and had already begun asking for people from the audience to contribute their thoughts and experiences. With about ten minutes left in the session she introduced me and asked me to come to the front of the room and say a few words about my experiences and my research. I felt I gave a fairly good accounting of myself, and LaVonne seemed to be very happy also with what I had to say.

After the session LaVonne and I talked for a while, and she asked me if she could give my name to the producers at *Unsolved Mysteries*, who were doing a segment on the types of synchronicities between adoptees and their birth families she described in her book. They were looking for an "expert" of whom they could ask some questions about the concept of synchronicity. I was pleased LaVonne thought that much of me, and somewhat awed at the thought of perhaps being on national television, but I did not allow myself to get too excited about the idea. After all, I was just a plain old psychology professor from a small state university in the middle of Wisconsin—of what interest would I be to Hollywood?

There was one more very startling synchronistic event which occurred during the convention in New Orleans. Two years earlier, on one of the evenings of the 1992 AAC convention in Philadelphia, I had dinner with a group of people that included Joe Soll, and Jack Marvin. I knew Joe was an adoptee social worker who was the leader of a large adoption support group in the New York City area, but I had not previously known Jack. During the course of that evening, I recall learning only that Jack was an adoptee. We all had a good time, and I was left with a very positive opinion of Jack.

At the 1994 convention in New Orleans, as I arrived in the hotel on the evening before the beginning of the conference, and just before the cocktail party at which I met LaVonne, I saw Joe across the lobby and walked over to speak to him. As we were talking, Jack walked into the lobby arm in arm with an older woman who was using a cane. He saw us, they made their way over, and Jack introduced the woman as Peg, his birth mother. I made note of the fact they were approximately the age of me and my birth mother, and decided to get to know them, with an eye toward perhaps understanding my own birth mother, and any possible relationship I might have with her, better.

On the second day of the convention, I was in the book room and noticed Jack and Peg were also there. Later I saw she had gone into a corner and had seated herself on the floor with her back against a wall, while Jack browsed at the book tables. I sat down with Peg and introduced myself, telling her I wanted to know how she and Jack had met, and how their relationship was working out. Peg told me their story, and in the process mentioned Jack was a psychologist. Surprised, I commented that I was a psychologist too, and we laughed at such a strange coincidence. Shortly she asked me to tell her my story, and late in the process of telling her I mentioned my birth mother by her first name, Pearl, which is how I think of and refer to her. Peg suddenly leaned forward, grabbed my arm, and said "What did you call her?" When I replied her name was Pearl, Peg said "I don't believe this— Do you know what my REAL first name is? It's Pearl! Peg is just my nickname, made up of my three initials."

By then I surely should not have been taken so much by surprise by Peg's revelation, but the nature of such synchronicities is that they *do* jump out at you and "grab" you. Had I been asked, prior to that moment, if I thought there was another male adoptee psychologist with a birth mother named Pearl in the whole country, let alone in the same room with me, I'd have thought I could safely say no! When Jack came over to see how Peg was doing, we shared our discovery with him. Jack seemed to take the news much more in stride than either Peg or I did, seeming to have the attitude "these things happen."

Jack's and my paths were to cross again, and in a way which, at that time, neither of us might have guessed. As a result of a major reorganization of the AAC which occurred in the fall of 1995, Jack became the new Vice President of the organization, and a month later I became a member of the Board of Directors, in charge of the AAC continuing education program. Shortly after that I was also elected to be one of the at-large members of the organization's Executive Committee, and I continued to serve in these roles for about 5 years. At the annual AAC convention in the spring of 1997, while I was on a semester abroad in London, England, Jack was named as the interim Executive Director of the AAC, and I was elected to fill his old role as Vice President!

Unfortunately, in order to be able to complete this book during my sabbatical leave from the University, I had to decline the position, and though I remained in my positions on the Board and Executive Committee, I had to take a reduced role for much of 1997. Jack and I became good friends and occasional roommates at conferences, and for the next few years, in weekly, and sometimes daily contact via e-mail.

I returned to Stevens Point from the 1994 Philadelphia conference, largely forgot about *Unsolved Mysteries*, and jumped back into the usual end-of-the-semester rush that always greets me on my return from the AAC convention. April, the month in which the AAC convention always takes place, is also a month in which I have always been busy. Term papers come in and must be graded. Advising for the fall semester occurs. Our Psychology Department Annual Student Awards Banquet, which I had chaired since it began, occurs in the later part of the month. On the last Saturday of April there is always a student research program in Madison to which my research students typically submit at least one paper for presentation. Often at the end of the year the Faculty Mediation Subcommittee, of which I was a member or chair from the mid-1980s to the mid-1990s, needed to hold hearings for grievances filed by members of the faculty.

The entire 1993–94 school year had been particularly busy for me. I had an unusual amount of committee work on campus, a couple of new activities in adoption, and I was also becoming active in alcohol and other drug abuse, a new area. Therefore, one of the troubling aspects of that particular spring had been that even before I left for the convention, I could see I was fast facing a critical level of overload at work. I realized I could not continue my increasing level and variety of professional involvement. I was going to have to make some decisions about narrowing down the future direction of my career within a very short while.

One of the new adoption-related activities that I began to get involved in around the spring of 1994 came about as a result of a statement I had made the previous year in Madison. At a legislative hearing into the functioning of the Wisconsin Adoption Search Program, I had experienced a sudden insight. The Search Program had been set up in the early 1980s, as a result of lobbying by AID, of which, by the time of the hearing, I had been elected state president. There had been problems with the way the Search Program was operated from almost its very beginning, and things had finally come to a head with an investigation by the Wisconsin Legislative Audit Bureau in 1993–94. I had been at a public hearing, listening to testimony by people who were unhappy with the program's services. Suddenly I realized since its inception the program had been run without the direct formal and official input of a single member of the adoption triad, the very population of people who the program was designed to serve!

When my turn to testify came, I pointed out the absence of input from members of the triad, and suggested the situation was analogous to the state sponsoring a program offering services to the Native American community, and having the program operated entirely by whites, without even an advisory committee made up of Native Americans. In front of me within the hearing committee I saw several of the committee members' responses. Several heads nodded and several pens made hurried notes. In the audience behind me there was a general murmur of approval. I had obviously made an important observation. Early in 1994, when the final report of the Legislative Audit Bureau on the Adoption Search Program was released, there was only one major change from the draft version of the report. A recommendation was added that the Adoption Search Program develop and meet regularly with an Advisory Committee to be made up of consumers of the program's services: adoptees, birth parents, and adoptive parents. Just before I left for the New Orleans AAC convention, I received a letter from the Wisconsin DHSS, asking me to serve as a member of the newly created Advisory Committee. I served on this committee, which reviewed the operations of the program from April 1994 to November 1995.

One of the benefits of being a university faculty member (a benefit that is sadly disappearing as higher education budgets tighten) is the sabbatical leave. Periodically (generally not more often than every 7 or more years), faculty members can apply for time away from their normal duties to pursue special professional development projects. These are most often used to refocus one's career, update one's research, or engage in other professional development that would not be possible without stepping away from usual duties. As the 1993–94 academic year drew to a close, after not feeling the need for a sabbatical leave since starting at UWSP in 1976, I felt it was time to refocus. There were three distinct roads my career could take: continuing work with my students that had started in the mid-1980s developing a sentence completion test for children; moving into alcohol and other drug abuse, an area which had recently become a strong focus of interest for me, and in which I had a personal as well as a professional interest; and continuing my work in adoption, which began with my personal search in 1983, and had developed into a significant aspect of both my personal and professional life. Quite clearly, I could not take all three of the roads, and I knew doing justice to even two of them would be very difficult. With the emergence of my interest and research into the relationship of synchronicity and adoption, there was the possibility of increasing my adoption involvement significantly, and of adding the research component that I, along with virtually everyone else in the adoption movement, believed was necessary.

I had already run into conflicting schedule problems in trying to follow all three of the paths. Both the AAC national conference and the Madison Psychology Honor Society paper session where my personality test students presented their work, occurred at about the same time in late April. The conflict forced me to miss the presentation of several of my students' papers in order to attend AAC meetings, and having to give up seeing my students' presentations was something I really did not like to do. I simply had neither the time nor the energy to continue to follow all three roads, and I doubted that even a sabbatical could be stretched to cover two major projects. I decided to apply for a sabbatical anyway, and began to ponder which of the roads I should take.

One thing I had learned by that time was to listen for the messages life was sending me. At about the same time, just after returning from the AAC meeting in New Orleans, I got a call from the man who had been the AAC vice president for many years. When I recognized his voice, I wondered if his call was going to be one of those life messages. I knew there had been an increasing level of discontent within the membership, and he told me that at the Board of Directors meeting after the New Orleans conference a Task Force on Reorganization was created in response to the discontent.

I had sat in on the early part of that same Board meeting for an hour or so before my train left to see for myself how the board functioned, having heard a good deal of criticism over the years. It is possible I was the only person present who was not already a member of the Board. In his call, the vice president told me that the purpose of the Task Force was to reassess the structure, membership, and goals of the organization, and to make recommendations to reset the group's course as needed. My name was one of those mentioned by the Board as a good candidate for membership on the Task Force, and he was asking me to serve if I was willing. I was willing, and decided perhaps I had been given the message I had been awaiting.

The message got even more clear when within a few days of agreeing to serve on the Task Force I got a call from a staff member at *Unsolved Mysteries*. She asked me some questions about LaVonne's book, *Synchronicity and Reunion: The Genetic Connection of Adoptees and Birth Parents*, and about the concept of synchronicity in general. Within the week I received a couple of extended phone calls from a segment producer for the show. Later I learned that in the process of these interviews with me on the phone, the producer had asked me essentially all of the questions she planned on asking in the interview for the show itself, and she had liked my answers. Eventually we began to talk about arrangements for me to be filmed for an *Unsolved Mysteries* segment which they were going to call "Adoptee Coincidences." I now definitely believed I had a message about which road might become important in my life.

However, the way was still not clear for me to follow the adoption road. I realized the time frame they were discussing for filming the *Unsolved Mysteries* episode was almost certainly going to conflict with a summer school class I had been scheduled to teach on the developmental aspects of alcohol and drugs. I contacted the outreach education office on our campus and found out the enrollment in the class was still low enough that I might not be allowed to teach the class at all. Even if we were going to be able to offer the class, it was unlikely I would be able to teach at anything approaching an appropriate pay level. After some discussion, they offered me the option of canceling the class if I did not want to accept the full pay rate. After a day or so of thought, I decided to cancel the class. The cancellation took a large chunk of work off of my schedule (preparing for and teaching a new course) and also freed me to be interviewed for *Unsolved Mysteries*.

Thus, in early May 1994, I felt I clearly had the answer I had been waiting for. I was to continue my work in the area of adoption and synchronicity in my search and reunion experiences. I set myself to the task of applying for a sabbatical to finish my book, for which I already had the first part of the title: *There Are More Like Me*. This was part of my free writing the night of June, 22 1983, the day I first met a birth relative. I also had a direction to take for the next few years of my career. My sabbatical request was approved and the coming years took the following form. I would have two fall semesters, 1996 and 1997, of full-time leave (at three quarters pay) to write my book. For the semester between the sabbatical semesters, the spring semester of 1997, Susan, Carch, and I would be in London, England, as faculty leaders for the UWSP International Studies Program (at full pay).

CHAPTER 17

Hollywood, Here I Come!

In my next conversation with the *Unsolved Mysteries* producer, she told me I would be identified, with my degree and academic affiliation, as an expert in explaining the types of similarities they would be featuring. She said they would rather not reveal I was an adoptee who had also had some of these experiences myself. I also learned one of the individuals they would have on the show was an adoptee from the south-western area of New York State named Don Larkin, who had searched for and located his birth mother, Betty Landers, in nearby northwestern Pennsylvania. The first time he saw her house, Don discovered his birth mother and he had the same two fairly unusual objects in the front windows of their houses: a crystal sun-catcher; and a carved wooden hummingbird. Since Don and Betty both lived in the same area of the country, the show would most likely be filming their portion of the segment close to where they lived. The producer gave me a choice: I could be filmed either on the east coast or in Hollywood at the *Unsolved Mysteries* studios.

I had noted that out of the whole United States, the area of the country where Don and Betty lived was within 100 miles of my childhood home in Buffalo. I asked the producer whether I might drive to the filming and be reimbursed for mileage rather than having them fly me. I could then make the short drive to Buffalo and visit my family after the filming was complete. She agreed and said their travel agent would be in contact with me once a definite place and time for the filming of Don and Betty was set. I even began to wonder if I could invite family or friends to observe the filming, though I didn't ask about that possibility!

180

I knew LaVonne and her two daughters would be another of the families on whom the segment would focus. In talking with the producer I learned both the daughter LaVonne surrendered for adoption and the daughter she raised were called Lorie, and both had remarkably similar interests, including playing the flute, riding horses, and learning sign language, even though neither of them knew a single deaf person! I suspected the reason why they were not going to interview LaVonne as their expert was because her family experience was being featured on the show.

I never got the chance to ask whether family and friends could watch my interview being filmed. For reasons which were not clear to me, but may have been related to Don's family situation, all of the filming for the entire segment was ultimately done in Hollywood. The studio flew me out a couple of days early in order to be sure I would be available when I was needed, and at my request, let me stay for an extra day at the end of the filming. They offered to pick me up at the airport and drive me to the hotel, or to rent me a car with unlimited mileage so I could drive myself. I asked them to rent a car for me and they told me the car was mine to use as I pleased while I was there. On one of the extra days before the filming I drove to the beach at Malibu. There had just been another in the long series of fires there that destroyed hundreds of luxurious homes, and I wanted to see both Malibu beach itself, and the damage.

Unsolved Mysteries uses the Beverly Garland Hotel, located near the major studios in Universal City area for its guests. When I arrived, I was asked to call the studio to tell them my room number, and the production assistant I spoke to told me Don and Betty were also staying in the same hotel. I decided to try to meet them, and called Don's room. I think they were a bit nervous about meeting me when I called, but they agreed they would be interested in talking. They were to be filmed during the day on Saturday, and I was to be filmed in the evening, and we weren't certain whether or not we'd see each other again, so we decided to meet in Don's room on Friday night. As I took the elevator up to his room, which was on one of the highest floors, I wondered what a large, California-style earthquake would be like.

I had only been in one earthquake, and that was a very small one while I was in Chicago on my internship. I was in the elevator of the John Hancock building, on my way down from a visit with friends who lived on the 89th floor, when I noticed the elevator seemed to have bumped against the side of the shaft. The next day I asked my friend about it. He told me they had felt the building sway just after seeing me on to the elevator. They had been surprised because while such building movement was commonly caused by high winds, there was no wind that night. The next morning they read of the mild earthquake, and wondered whether I had noticed it in the elevator. I had. And I was thinking about it again in the elevator ride up to Don's room.

While I arrived at Don's room in mild anxiety from thinking about an earthquake, any anxiety Don and Betty may have had about meeting me seemed to disappear as we got to talking about our search and reunion stories. In addition to discovering their similar window ornaments, there were many other similarities between Don and Betty. One of these was that they both liked railroad trains. Long before their reunion, they each had read in the papers about a proposed dam in the Kinzua and Allegheny River area of northwestern Pennsylvania. As they talked, I remembered parts of the Kinzua dam story from my own childhood, when the controversies had spread to the media in western New York.

The waters rising behind the dam would have destroyed several small towns, flooded Native American burial grounds and forced the abandonment and dismantling of an iron railroad trestle a mile long, and 300 feet above the Kinzua River near Mt. Jewett, Pennsylvania. At the time of construction, the Kinzua Bridge was the longest and highest of its type in the world. To get there required a drive out into isolated country, followed by a hike along the tracks, a journey that sounded daunting to say the least. Upon hearing the trestle might be destroyed if the dam were built as planned, both Don and Betty had visited the site, unknowingly within a few weeks of each other. Perhaps as a result of the controversy around the bridge, the design of the dam was changed, and the Kinzua River Bridge was saved and became a tourist attraction which was knocked down in 2003 by a tornado! In 2011, a large remaining section of the original bridge was reopened as the Kinzua Bridge State Park Skywalk. Don and Betty were both impressed, however, that the other had cared enough about seeing the bridge to make a trip to the site.

Were this all of the story, the common visits of Don and his mother to the bridge alone would be impressive. However, at Christmas of 1995, about 18 months after my conversation with Don and Betty, I added my own surprising connection. I was visiting Lancaster, California, to help my partner, Susan, and her family finish cleaning out the house that belonged to her recently deceased aunt. Virtually all of the furniture had been removed before our arrival, and our task was to sort through her aunt's antique collection and personal effects, deciding what to keep as mementos, what to sell, what to give to the local charity store, and what to throw out. In a cupboard beneath the family room wet bar, I found a lone plastic place mat, set aside and kept apparently because it had some meaning to Susan's aunt or uncle. The mat was plain on one side, but on the other side was an aerial photo of the Kinzua Bridge! Hand-written above the photo were the following comments: "1 mile long, 300 feet high, railroad now out of use, built in 1896." The photo makes abundantly clear just how isolated and just how majestic the bridge really is. I saved the place mat for myself, and it has become a personal footnote to Don and Betty's story, as well as an interesting visual aid when I speak about synchronicity.

The filming of Don and Betty's *Unsolved Mysteries* segment was scheduled to take all day Saturday since they were to be shooting some scenes outdoors. I was picked up at the hotel and driven to the shooting site for my interview at 6:30 Saturday evening. I have to admit I was slightly disappointed my ride was in a Jeep Cherokee rather than a limousine, but I made good use of the rental car! On the way there we took a route from which I could see the Hollywood sign, and I joked to the driver that now I really felt like I was a movie star! We took what seemed to be a circuitous route to the shooting site, and I have always wondered whether she took all of her passengers out of the way just so they could see the Hollywood sign. Or perhaps every drive in Hollywood is circuitous!

When we arrived they were still filming scenes with Don and Betty, so I had a chance to walk around exploring. The set was actually a rented house, located at the base of the hill on top of which the dome of a large observatory could be seen. I could see immediately I was going to have a true "Hollywood" experience. There was quite a large crew: about eight or nine people, a large truck, some four or five vehicles, and all sorts of specialized equipment such as boom mikes and steel tracks on which the camera rolled. They had a sound man who sat at an elaborate set of portable electronic equipment. The sound assistant used an electronic clapboard with a digital clock to synchronize the sound and visual recordings. The director used those familiar phrases such as "roll picture," "roll sound," "action," and "cut." I learned that even though the actual final product of their work would be shown on television, rather than using videotape, the crew used easier-to-edit traditional 35 mm movie film. I had purchased a Sony High 8 mm camcorder especially for the trip west, not wanting to repeat the sad experience I had when my old VHS model died at just the time I was to meet my birth brother Keith. I was flattered that the camera operator hurried over to me at his first opportunity to ask whether mine was "the new one with the color viewfinder." When I answered yes, he spent some time carefully examining the camcorder, making approving comments all the while. With technical superiority being as fleeting in video as in computing, I greatly enjoyed my moment in the technological sun.

Watching the filming process was a pretty exciting experience, made only slightly less so by my gradually mounting anxiety over how my own interview would go, if we ever got to it. My anxiety grew as the filming of Don and Betty, which was to have been completed by about the time I got there, ran long. I watched as they filmed some seven or eight takes of an actress playing Don's birth aunt walking him in front of Betty's house, which was the time he first saw the front window decorations which they had in common. Then they filmed Don walking up onto the front lawn and looking into the window, from several different angles, several times each.

At one point during the filming of these scenes, a beautifully restored old car pulled up and parked in an empty space right across from the house, but hidden from view of most of the crew by one of the equipment trucks. I walked over to the car, and saw it was a Chrysler. One of the things Don had told me the night before at the hotel was that one of his hobbies is restoring old Chryslers! During a break in filming I told Don about the car's presence, and we walked to the other side of the truck so he could take a look. He immediately told me the exact year and name of the model, but he also told me his interest was only in a particular narrow span of years in the 1920s. Perhaps, since the car was from the early 1930s, Don was not particularly interested, and instead, he was rather disdainful of the restoration job that had been done. I thought we had just experienced a pretty weird "coincidence" anyway, especially since we were there for the purpose of filming a program on coincidences!

They then filmed several takes of Don meeting Betty for the first time, greeting her with a hug in her front doorway. The recreation of Don and Betty's reunion scene was really moving for me to watch, since I had only talked to my own birth mother on the phone and had never met her in person. I couldn't help but wonder what the experience was like for Don and Betty to act their reunion out again (and again, and again!). I wondered what my own reunion would be like, and even whether I would ever get to have such a scene with my own birth mother.

I realized I was jealous of Don and Betty, and a layer of sadness grew on top of the anxiety over my upcoming interview.

The next filming I watched was several takes of Don driving up to Betty's house for their reunion. For this scene Don drove the director's car, and on the first take he came into the driveway too fast, bumping the underside of the car loudly on the slight hump made by the sidewalk. A check for damage was performed, and Don backed the car out onto the street for another try. During the second take, which was stopped because of a barking dog, I noticed the front California license plate on the car was clearly visible. I wondered if that was important since I knew the real reunion took place in north-western Pennsylvania, and Don was from neighboring western New York state. I had even been told earlier by a crew member that the particular house being used was selected because the house resembled those in Pennsylvania more than those typical for Southern California. However, since these people were the film-making professionals, and not me, I decided not to say anything about the license plate. As Don was getting out of the car at the end of the third take, which seemed to have gone well, the director shouted "cut" and announced she had just noticed her California license plate, and the fourth take was delayed while the plate was removed, and several other attempts to shoot this scene were made. I was unclear whether even after all the takes they had made they had something they would be able to use.

The scene in which Don walked up onto Betty's front lawn and looked into the window turned out to be the only segment from the two or three hours of filming I watched that they actually used in the show. Perhaps the final broadcast segment didn't include anything else from the whole day's outdoor scenes because of what was going on in the neighborhood. There was a noisy party across the street and two houses down, with cars continually coming and going. Somewhere a dog was constantly barking, car alarms periodically went off, and a woman two houses down the street in the other direction from the party was having a screaming fight with her husband that could be frequently heard everywhere in the neighborhood. The film crew told me the screaming had been going on and off for the entire day. Occasionally she came out onto the street to complain loudly to the crew about the increased traffic and parking congestion she felt the filming was caus-ing. Their explanation to her, repeated several times, was that they only had four or five vehicles, and the congestion was caused mostly by the large and noisy party a neighbor was throwing. That information did not seem to help. I wondered if I was observing a typical Los Angeles Saturday afternoon, and thought, if so, I was glad I lived in Wisconsin! The crew frequently had to stop their filming due to these interruptions, and then they had to begin the whole scene over again once the disturbance settled down. Nonetheless, I couldn't believe they spent a whole day working and used only that one short segment of Don in front of the house. Investing all of that time for one short scene must have been very frustrating for the crew and the cast alike. It certainly frustrated me to watch! The crew continued filming Don and Betty until dusk forced them to stop.

Then we all went inside the house: the time for my interview was at hand. They had set up a mock office in the kitchen and dining nook area of the house, using a poster board backdrop, some law and consumer-finance books, and a bunch of dried flowers. I was worried the titles of the books would be seen, but they told me they would "soft-focus" the background so all the viewer would see was a wall with books and flowers behind me. I own only one decent sport coat, and due to middle age spread I couldn't fit into my only suit, and so I wore the sport coat to the filming. The coat is maroon in color, and as it happened they had selected a maroon backdrop to create my "office." Since they didn't have another backdrop on location with them, I had to remove my sport coat and do the interview in just my shirt and tie. During the lighting adjustment and make-up phases, one of the crew, perhaps wanting to try out the newest electronic toy from Sony, grabbed my camcorder and made some video of me (just as I was about to ask if someone would do exactly that), so I had some more souvenir footage, except now I was in front of, instead of behind, the camera.

The interview itself took between 45 minutes and one hour. During the interview I tried to make the points that some of the "coincidences" of similarities between adoptees and members of their birth families could be explained by the genetic tie, that some may be early or even prenatal memories, and that some of them might well be "just chance." But my important point was that we need to consider the possibility of connections through a dimension of reality we just don't yet understand. I suggested the terms "spiritual" and "extra sensory perception" might be those some people would use to describe this dimension, but said this other dimension of reality might be of a nature as yet totally unknown.

The first time I used the term "synchronicity" the director stopped the camera and said she did not want me to use that term, joking "we're not PBS here." They did not want to have to take the time to explain the term, so I had to stay with the word "coincidence." She also had to stop me every time I used phrases such as "as I mentioned earlier," or "this is another example of . . ." She said since my interview would be edited, the order in which I spoke might not be the order in which I was heard, so every answer I gave, or statement I made had to be independent of anything else I had said. Everything had to be able to stand alone. I think she only had to stop me to correct my language about four more times! Then I began to catch myself, but it took me a while to become comfortable with that way of speaking.

Throughout my interview, as had been the case for the entire time I was there, we all had a lot of fun, with the crew laughing and teasing each other. They all seemed to like what they do, which allowed me to more easily relax and just be myself. "Just be yourself" is advice I have given many a student who was worried about job or graduate school interviews, and of course being yourself is easier advice to give than to take. Actually I felt much more relaxed while the interview was being filmed than I had while anticipating it in advance. I also felt pretty good about the interview afterwards, though I must say I was relieved the work was done. Pizza was ordered in for dinner after the interview was over. The crew began wrapping up the day's work, putting my "office" and the other equipment back in the truck, and moving the furniture in the house back into place. The pizza arrived about 10:30, and the crew ate while they worked.

While I was munching on pizza I was asked to sign a release to allow the show to broadcast my "likeness." I noticed with amusement I wasn't asked to sign the release until after the interview was filmed. I thought of being asked to sign a permission for surgery after awakening from the anesthetic! With the film "in the can" the damage, if there was going to be any, had already been done. I wondered if perhaps the purpose of their timing was to allow me a chance to say "no thanks" if I thought I had been "ambushed" or the interview had gone badly. I wondered if I'd have to walk back to Stevens Point if I didn't sign! I signed the release.

I asked when the segment was going to air, and the director said that decision was not made by her, and frequently they did not know until a week or two before the planned broadcast date. She added sometimes they even switched segments within days, or even hours, of a show's broadcast, especially if they had a segment related to a breaking news story ready to air, but not yet scheduled. She told me I would get a call from the studio when the decision on a broadcast date was made.

During our conversation she also mentioned a topic I had heard the crew talking about earlier. The NBC network had decided to move *Unsolved Mysteries* from what had been its long-time Wednesday evening time slot to a time one hour earlier, and on Friday night, beginning with the upcoming new fall season. The crew had made nervous references to the time and date changes a couple of times, wondering if as a result they'd all have their jobs in the future. The director explained their concern was they would be facing a different audience "mix" with more families and children watching than in the past. A different set of competing shows on other networks or on cable might also change the success level of the show. They had already realized they would have to change their balance of stories to include more human-interest stories such as the one we were filming, and fewer crime mysteries, so predicting when my segment might be broadcast was particularly hard for her.

Finally, the equipment was put away, the house returned to order, and my Hollywood experience was over. The young woman who had picked me up, and had been there all evening working as a production assistant, dropped me off at the hotel about midnight. All in all the entire experience was quite a thrill. Because of my request to stay in the Hollywood area a couple of extra days, I was not scheduled to return to Stevens Point until the Monday afternoon after the interview filmed.

I spent Sunday morning, the day after the filming, driving along the beach at Malibu again. In the afternoon I drove to Northridge and took pictures of the damage there from the major earthquake that had happened on January 17. Just two weeks before the quake, Susan and I had spent a day visiting graduate school friends of hers who lived in Northridge, the northern Los Angeles suburb that was the epicenter of the quake. Returning to the area after my filming, for the first time I directly observed the results of an earthquake. Seeing the damage to the very same places Susan and I had visited just five months earlier in January was especially eerie. After a brief visit with Susan's friends, who lived within blocks of the epicenter, I toured their neighborhood. I saw many of the buildings featured in TV news reports that had collapsed on top of ground-level parking lots. Despite the fact that the quake had been several months earlier, many of the heavily damaged structures still had not been razed, and parts of crushed automobiles stuck bizarrely out from under them. I walked up to, and easily looked into what had been second floor windows, but were now sitting at ground level. I couldn't help but wonder what it would be like to be in an earthquake, especially when I thought about my own hotel room, which was on the ground floor of the hotel building. Fortunately I had only one more night to stay there!

There was one more activity I had planned in Los Angeles before I returned to Stevens Point. Barely two months earlier that spring at the AAC conference in New Orleans, I had noticed an interesting woman in the lobby of the convention hotel on the night before the convention started. I made inquiries about who she was, and found, to my surprise and delight, she was another adoptee psychologist. Her name was Marlou Russell, and she became someone I wanted to get to know! Not surprisingly, we attended a couple of the same programs during the convention, and at one of them I struck up a conversation with her. Although we had a chance to meet briefly at the New Orleans conference, we had not had time to really get to know each other. We had exchanged business cards with the intention of meeting "someday." Just two months later, when I had completed the arrangements for the Unsolved Mysteries taping, I called Marlou to talk because "someday" might have just arrived, and much sooner than either of us had anticipated. Marlou just happened to live in the Los Angeles area!

We made arrangements to meet for breakfast on the Monday morning after my taping, before I was to leave for Stevens Point. We talked first about my search and reunion, and the process that had lead me to the Unsolved Mysteries show, as well as a little about the upcoming AAC Task Force meeting at the end of the summer. Toward the end of the conversation Marlou told me about her reunion experience. She had come into touch with some feelings about her birth mother that, once the reunion was made, turned out to have most likely been prenatal memories. Our conversation was pleasant, and too short. We parted with me wishing we had more time to talk. Little did I realize we would have another chance quite soon!

Things returned to normal rather quickly when I got home. Just after the fall semester began the University news service did an interview with me, covering both my experience as a guest on Unsolved Mysteries and my search and reunion story. A copy of the article was sent to the Stevens Point paper, and one to my home town paper back in New York state. On October third, the day after the news service article was mailed, I got a call from the Unsolved Mysteries studio.

"Hello, Dr. Henderson this is Janet Jones from 'Unsolved Mysteries.' I'm calling to tell you when the 'adoptee coincidences' segment will air."

"Great, I've been wondering when it would be on."

"I first want to tell you we are very pleased with the segment. We think it is among the best we have done in a long time. In fact we're so happy with it that it will air as the first segment in the very first show of our new fall season."

I said I was happy to hear that and asked, "When will that be?" Then she added the clincher.

"It will be on Friday, October 14."

I couldn't believe my ears and said, "You're kidding."

"Why would *I* kid *you* about this?"

"Because October 14 is my birthday!"

The tables turned, and she said, "Now *you're* kidding!"

"Why would I kid you about this?"

"October 14 is my sister's birthday, too!"

We both made excited comments expressing our general amazement at this turn of events, particularly given that the show we were discussing was itself about coincidences. As the excitement began to ebb, I said jokingly "Okay, so she and I have the same birthday, and that's pretty weird. Big deal! I have a good friend here too who has the same birthday, but just *how old* will your sister be?"

The assistant said aloud to herself "let's see . . . forty-six . . ."

I interrupted and said "Well, no dice, I'll be forty-eight."

"No, *nineteen* forty-six is the year she was born." and she started again to calculate her sister's age aloud.

I interrupted her. "Don't bother, that's the same year I was born—we were both born on the very same day!" We talked for a few more minutes about the wild improbability of the situation and hung up.

Now I had work to do! Within the next few days I made several dozen calls to family and friends, and notified the local paper, who changed the last lines of the University News Service article to include the air date, and the fact that the show would air on my birthday. Then I sent an email out to the friends and relatives on my Christmas card list. I also posted a message to the several hundred adoptees I "knew" through the adoptees internet mailing list. That message, no doubt, was forwarded to many other members of the triad who have connections to the internet, further adding to the number of people who knew about the show.

I had more than enough anxiety about how I would come across on the actual show. After careful consideration of my performance in the interview, I was still fairly comfortable with what I had said, and how I had come across, but I did not know how I would be portrayed once the interview was edited and integrated with the rest of the segment. I joked with friends about how in the hands of a good editor, a film of the infamous Richard Nixon statement "I am not a crook," could be edited to have Nixon appearing to say "I am a crook." And this was many years before the advent of Artificial Intelligence! Over the previous few months several members of the internet adoptee's list had appeared on various radio and television shows, and the appearances had been greeted by spontaneous rave "reviews" from the list members. Jeff, who was the founder of the mailing list, had appeared earlier that fall on a National Public Radio show. One of the post-appearance messages to the list about his performance began with the enthusiastic subject line "Jeff's a stud!" In my message to the adoptee's internet list announcing the air date of "my" show I had written "Hopefully I will conduct myself (or be edited to appear!) in the same great manner as have our other recent media stars. Gee, it's been a long time since anyone said 'Doug's a stud'!!!"

As it happened, the night of my birthday was also the night of a concert in Stevens Point by singer Melissa Ethridge, and I had thought early on I might like to attend her performance. Those plans were stopped by my TV appearance, but I consoled myself with the thought that I'd certainly have another chance to see her some time, and Unsolved Mysteries would probably be my only chance to be on national TV. Susan and I decided to have my birthday dinner as planned that night, but we moved meal time a half hour earlier than usual to be sure to have the meal over by 7:00 p. m., which was the local broadcast time for the show. There was also a Boy Scout camporee going on that weekend, scheduled to begin about 4:00 p. m. that Friday about ten minutes' drive north-east of my house. I had already planned because of my birthday not to be there until Saturday morning, so I did not anticipate the television appearance would cause any additional difficulty with those plans.

When the big day finally arrived, I got up as usual and went to the YMCA where I did my routine one-mile swim. Work that day was a good distraction from my concern about how things would go, and I came home from campus about 5:00 p. m. to prepare for my birthday dinner, and to set up my video recorders to record the show. I had two of them, and had also asked several friends in other cities to record the show for me in case something went wrong. I recalled an incident earlier that fall, during a football game the entire state of Wisconsin seemed to have been watching. A driver slid off of the road and took down a telephone pole, knocking out cable TV service for over half of

Stevens Point until almost the end of the game. I'm told you could hear the screams all over the effected part of town as the televisions went black. I also remembered, and cared not to repeat, the experience with the broken camcorder at the moment of my reunion with Keith. I even planned on taking my telephone off of the hook during the show so as not to be interrupted by anyone calling. I was determined not to let *anything* interfere with watching my national TV debut.

That determination seemed to be for naught when just after getting home from work I got an emergency call to take some equipment that was locked up in the storage area in the basement of the church out to the Scout camp. No other adults with keys to the locked church were available to bring the equipment out, and they wanted me to come immediately. I would have to run the errand during the time I was planning to set up and test my VCRs. I scribbled a note to Susan, who I expected to show up to cook me a birthday dinner to find I was not there, explaining what had happened. I got back from the Boy Scout camporee just about the time that dinner was ready, and we ate quickly, holding off having my birthday cake and opening my presents until after the show. We finished dinner about ten minutes before show time, and I rushed to get my video cassette recorders set to the correct channel and ready for one-touch recording. When the show began I was still not entirely certain the recordings were going to proceed properly, but it was too late, and we sat cross-legged on the floor in front of the living room TV to watch. As promised, the adoptee coincidences segment was the first to air, and by about 7:15 my segment was complete. By 8 o'clock, I was really quite happy with both my own performance and with the way in which the whole issue was presented. I concluded it was not a bad birthday present at all!

In all the rush to get ready, I had forgotten to take the phone off of the hook, and shortly after the show ended it rang. A voice that was vaguely familiar introduced himself as Brandon Tartikoff, a name I also vaguely recognized. He said he was calling from New York City, he had just seen the *Unsolved Mysteries* show, and he wanted to talk to me about doing some work for him. I stalled for time, knowing something was fishy. It took me a few seconds to place the name the caller used, which I recognized was that of the head of programming for the NBC TV network. Then, more importantly, I recognized the voice. The caller was really Tom Little, a college fraternity brother, calling to play with my mind! I had been best man at Tom and Cindy's wedding the winter after we graduated, and I visited them frequently on my trips to the east coast. We talked for a bit, he congratulated me on my appearance and said I "at least *looked* intelligent" and then he said he had to go because it was Cindy's birthday, and he was taking her out to dinner. I had forgotten (if I had ever known) that Cindy and I were both born on October 14! I asked to talk to her and wished her a happy birthday. Several years later I discovered Cindy also was born in 1946. Maybe the coincidence of sharing the October 14, 1946, birthday with the sister of Janet (the staff member from *Unsolved Mysteries*) wasn't so unusual after all? Or maybe we had an even MORE unusual event, with THREE people born on the same day of the same year somehow involved in that show on coincidences! The only other call I got that night was from my parents, who had of course watched the show, and wanted to wish me a happy birthday and tell me they were proud of me.

Later that night I played back my video tapes of the show (both of which worked, despite the interruption) and timed the three brief segments of my interview they used. They ran for just 19, 20, and 21 seconds each! It's amazing to me that the show probably paid well over $1000 to get me out there (round trip airfare, three nights in the hotel, four days of rental car, and some expense money) plus the cost of the crew and equipment, and yet they used just 60 seconds of me in the show. That works out to paying some $1,000 for a minute of my time! One thing's for sure, I'll never be worth $60,000 per hour again! Now I know why there's so much advertising on TV.

CHAPTER 18

Hollywood Calling, Again!

On Thursday, December 15, 1994, just when I thought life was getting back to normal after my appearance on *Unsolved Mysteries*, the phone rang in my office. It was Paul Taylor, a producer from an NBC show called "The Other Side," a talk show, similar to Phil Donahue's popular model, which featured psychic, metaphysical, and spiritual topics. I had not heard of the program because it normally ran during the hour after the Today show, and the three NBC stations which were available on cable in central Wisconsin all ran the Donahue show in that time slot. I asked some questions about the approach the show took, and Paul's description of the show's host was intriguing. The host was an "ordained minister and licensed therapist with a doctoral degree in psychology who used to be a stand-up comedian." I was immediately interested in this fellow!

Paul asked me whether I could fly to Hollywood early in the next week to tape an adoption-related segment for the show. The segment about psychic or spiritual connections between children and their parents would be part of several segments broadcast together under the episode title "The Link of Love." However, as interesting as another national TV appearance, and "The Other Side" in particular, sounded, we were in the last week of classes, which is always a very busy time of the semester. Though most of my term papers were graded, I was scheduled to give final examinations the following Saturday, Tuesday and Wednesday, and I then had to assign course grades. The producer wanted me to fly to California on Monday. I said reluctantly that I could not do the interview, and Paul asked if I could recommend any other people who had my expertise. I thought I'd return LaVonne Stiffler's favor and so I mentioned her name, and Marlou Russell's, but he then told me it was LaVonne who had given them my name.

He also said they had only a limited budget with which to work, but they still needed a couple of adoptees who had unusual connections with their family members to fill out that segment of the show. He asked if I knew of any such people who lived on the west coast, since they couldn't afford very much airfare. Although I could not think of any such individuals right away, I offered to put out a call for such people on the adoptees internet mailing list. He gave me his phone number to put in the message, and I wished him luck finding people for the segment, and expressed my regrets at not being able to take part in the show.

A few minutes after the conversation ended, I was in the Psychology Department office, and mentioned the call to my department chairperson. She was surprised I had said I could not participate, and I explained that although two of my final exams were on Saturday and would not have been affected by the proposed trip, my other two final exams were on the days they wanted to have me there. She asked if those two exams were ready to give (they were) and if there was any other work that had to be done besides scoring those exams and assigning the final grades for those classes (there was not). To my surprise, she then said "Well, I think we ought to find a way to help you go!"

With the chairperson's approval to be off-campus during exam week (an absence that is normally frowned upon) and help from her and other colleagues, I was able to arrange faculty coverage for my tests. My work-study student would then score the multiple-choice exams, and send the final scores and grade book to me. I would assign the grades and fax them back to the appropriate office on campus. These arrangements were all made within about an hour, and I called the producer back, hoping in the meantime he had not found someone else to do the interview. He had not, and so plans were made Thursday afternoon for me to fly off once again to Hollywood on the following Monday, December 19.

As it happened, I already had a round-trip ticket to Los Angeles departing on Friday December 23 which I had purchased previously. Susan and Carch were going out to visit her family who live in Lancaster (north of Los Angeles), and I had decided to go with them. We were able to arrange for the studio to pick up the extra cost of moving my Friday departure ahead to Monday, and they agreed to let me stay at the hotel until Susan and Carch arrived, at which time we would go to her parents' home. I would use the return half of my ticket as I had originally planned. A series of short-notice travel arrangements which might have seemed improbable, especially during the week before Christmas, fell together with minimal difficulty.

When I arrived in Los Angeles Monday at dinner time I was instructed to go to a hotel near the airport. The production assistant for "The Other Side" told me there would be a room for me there, and I was given a third-floor room at the front of the hotel. I had just begun reading *The Primal Wound*, by Nancy Verrier, then the newest book to have hit the adoption market, and was quite content to hang around the hotel room and lobby, reading and enjoying the unexpected early freedom from the end-of-the-semester rush. It always takes me a while to get used to suddenly having nothing pressing to do, after the gradually increasing demands of each semester, and so this was a good chance to wind down.

On the first morning I was there, which was the day before the shooting, I made it a point to be in my room at 9:00 a.m. to watch that day's segment of "The Other Side." This would be the first time I had ever seen it, and I thought it might be a good idea to see the show before I was a guest on it! I decided to make a video of the show with my camcorder from the TV screen in my hotel room. I began recording just before 9:00 a. m. by shooting the not-particularly-impressive view from my hotel room: the hotel parking lot, with the Los Angeles airport in the background, and two palm trees in the foreground. Then I focused on the TV screen to catch the opening credits and the first few minutes of the show, after which I turned the camcorder off. Watching gave me a pretty good feel for the way it was conducted, the nature of the audience, and the type of guests. The host was, as I had thought he would be, an unusually interesting fellow.

I also wanted to make video of the credits at the end of the show, since they usually run by so fast a speed reader would be hard-pressed to keep up with them. I thought I would play them back, stop the tape, and get the correct full names of several of the staff people I had talked to, or might meet, since I assumed these would be in the credits. As I started my camcorder toward the end of the last commercial, I was amazed to see a promotional slide of the hotel I was staying in. Over the photo, the usual mellow announcer's voice was saying: "Guests of 'The Other Side' stay in the beautiful Continental Plaza hotel, convenient to Los Angeles International Airport." As I looked at the picture, I could easily identify the window of my own room! In the photo there was only one open set of blinds in the entire front of the hotel. They were located on the third floor, just to the right of the center of the building above two palm trees. As it happened, the open blinds were, if not in my room, in the one right next to it. It was a pretty odd sensation, but at least I knew enough not to run to the window and wave, expecting to see myself on TV!

For the rest of that day I lurked in the hotel lobby, waiting for it to be time for the interview, reading, and watching people. One of the people I noticed was a woman, who, based on her accent, must have been from England. She seemed to have a lot of time on her hands, since she spent the larger part of the morning sitting in or walking around the lobby, and was the only other person, besides hotel employees, who I remember seeing more than once. I struck up a conversation at lunch with the young man who ran the lounge/bar in the lobby and learned his wife was an adoptee, part Native American, who was searching for her birth family. He and I continued that conversation at dinner that night, and at lunch the next day, when I met his wife briefly, and told her I thought the Native American Child Welfare Act might be helpful to her.

When the van came to take show guests to the studio, I discovered the British woman I had noticed in the lobby, Cassandra Eason, was also going to be on the same segment as I! There were several other guests for the "Link of Love" segment staying in the same hotel, who were also in the van, and we got to know each other during the 45-minute drive to the studio. While we waited for the show to begin, Cassandra and I struck up a lively conversation. She had written several women's books in Britain, and was working on another on psychic children at the time. We talked about my experiences and my understanding of synchronicity and of the spirit world in general.

The experience of taping "The Other Side" was much more exciting than my Unsolved Mysteries segment filming had been. It's not that I found the Unsolved Mysteries experience uninteresting, but since that interview was filmed in advance and edited, and was not in a studio, I didn't have the immediate experience of knowing there were many more people in the "audience" than the members of the crew. For "The Other Side" there was a live audience in the studio, and, though this show was also taped in advance and edited, the experience was much more similar to what I had thought appearing on television would be like. For example, there was a "green room" stocked with snacks where guests waited to be called on stage. More importantly to me, however, the show was taped on a sound stage in the NBC Studio building.

When the van had arrived on the studio grounds and parked, the driver told us we would be walking into the building past the parking spaces for the Tonight Show staff. I had my ever-present video camera going as we walked by a space with a "Jay Leno" sign, which had a large and shiny old automobile parked in it. We entered the studio, and on the wall, I was thrilled to see the larger-than-life brown-toned photographs of old movie stars I had seen in "backstage" segments of the Tonight Show over the years. We turned to the right down a hall, and I missed looking into the open door of the studio for the Tonight Show because I was looking through the viewfinder of my camcorder, trying to get a picture of the environment while also trying not to trip. (I only know I missed looking into the studio because when I played the tape back later I could see an open double door on my right and hear the sounds of the show coming through it as I walked by!)

We were taken into the "green room" for the show and were told to make ourselves comfortable. An "Other Side" show on a different topic was already being filmed in the studio, and there were monitors on the walls showing what was going onto the tape, and soundproof windows through which we could watch the activity in the studio itself directly. The segment on adoption-based connections was at the end of the "Link of Love" show, and the entire day's taping was running a little late anyway. Waiting together in the green room allowed those of us who were going to be on the show, and especially the adoptees, a chance to find and meet each other. I had already talked to one, Al Monderas on the telephone, and I had been given the name of the other, Hildy Mott, and I wanted to find them both.

On Saturday, between my grading the final exams I had given that morning and packing for the trip, I had gotten a call from Al. He was an adoptee, though he was not on the adoptees internet mailing list where I had posted the request for potential show guests. However, the searcher who helped Al find his birth father was an adoptee from Colorado who I knew through the internet list. When the searcher saw my request, she immediately thought of Al, and called him. Rather than giving him the show producer's name and number, she had given him mine. Al called to ask for more details about just what the show was looking for. Neither of us had ever seen the show, though he had at least heard of it. We talked about his search and reunion experience, and I told him I thought his experience was just what the producers wanted. I encouraged him to call to volunteer for the show.

On Sunday, the day before I left, I had gotten a call from an Oregon-based adoptee searcher, a member of the internet list, who was calling on behalf of Hildy Mott, a California adoptee with whom she had worked. Hildy had found her birth mother and a birth sister. Hildy, like Al, was not on the internet list, and she had many of the same kinds of questions Al had. I answered them as best I could, making it clear I had never seen the show and could not vouch for the motives or approach of the producers. After hearing about Hildy's story, I also thought the synchronicities in Hildy's reunion were just what the show was looking for. Just before leaving for California, I saw on the adoptees list that Hildy and Al had agreed to be on the show, so I knew I had been able to recruit two people for them. Although the two searchers who saw my internet request and had referred Hildy and Al to the show, are friends of each other, that was the extent of any connection between Al and Hildy.

As soon as I got into the green room, I started asking likely candidates if they were Hildy or Al. Once I found Al, I asked if he had met Hildy, the other adoptee on the show, and he asked me if I wanted to sit down because he had an unbelievable story to tell me. He was an Emergency Medical Technician, and was originally scheduled to be on duty at the time of the taping for the show. When the searcher called to tell him about my internet call for volunteers, he wanted to be on the show, but first he had to rearrange his schedule. Al and his ambulance partner arranged to switch shifts with another team so Al and his wife could travel to Los Angeles to tape the show. As they were getting ready to leave the house, Al, on a last-minute whim, suggested to his wife that they call his partner to see if he wanted to take a ride to the studio and watch the show's taping. "After all," Al said, "I knew he'd be free!" The three of them had driven to the studio together.

As far as Al knew, he did not know any of the other guests on the show except me, and that, only by phone. As I had, when Al arrived in the green room, he began asking people whether they knew me. As he worked his way to the back of the crowded room, he spied a pair of familiar faces—a young woman and her handicapped daughter. Al, his partner, and Al's wife made their way back to say hello to them. They struck up a conversation trying to determine how, and from where, they knew each other. After a short while they realized Al and his partner had recently been to their house on an ambulance run to take care of her daughter, who was having trouble breathing. The mother, Hildy!, still had one of Al's business cards in her purse. He had given her his card because he teaches classes in CPR which Hildy had been interested in taking. They found they both lived in the same suburb of Los Angeles, about an hour's drive from the studio.

When the topic of "what are you doing here?" arose, they were astounded to discover they were both going to be on the adoption segment of the show, and they were both looking for a fellow by the name of Doug Henderson who was responsible for their being there. Further excited discussion revealed both Al and Hildy had their birth parent reunions on the very same date: August 6, 1994, and both had experienced a 33-year separation from the birth parent with whom they were reunited! Before Al had even finished telling me the details, I wanted to meet Hildy myself, and he took me to the back corner of the room, where I met Hildy, her daughter, Al's wife, Al's partner, Hildy's adoptive mother, and Hildy's birth sister. While we waited for our segment of the show there was lots of animated conversation about the unusual connections we had discovered, and what it all could mean.

Staff members from the show then arrived to take Cassandra and me to makeup. I asked someone in the room to make video of me as I was getting made up, and as the video was being shot, I noticed the Tonight Show was playing on a monitor in the room. I asked whether the show we were seeing was being taped at that time and was told it was. Then I noticed Melissa Ethridge was singing, and I realized that the only other time I knew I had been in the same city with her was earlier that fall, on the night of October 14, when she had a concert in Stevens Point. Melissa is one of my favorite singers, and I might well have gone to see her then, except for the fact that October 14 was my birthday, and I wanted to stay home to watch myself that night on "Unsolved Mysteries!"

As I left the make-up room, there were a lot of people milling around in the hall, and a cable laying on the floor which ran past the make-up room door. I noticed a small dressing room across and just down the hall with a camera man standing outside the door. As I walked past the door, I could see they were filming a young couple wearing white bathrobes and sitting on a convertible couch that had been made into a bed. I thought I should watch the Tonight Show that night to see what that was all about!

Back in the green room while waiting to go onstage, I noticed there was one lone advertisement the size of a business card, torn from a newspaper and taped to the wall. It looked so out-of-place I was drawn to examine it more closely. It was a going-out-of-business ad for a metaphysical specialty store in Lancaster, California. Lancaster, about 50 miles north of Los Angeles, is the town where my partner Susan grew up, and to which I was traveling to begin our long-planned two-week vacation in just two days! When I asked, none of the staff of "The Other Side" seemed to know how the ad had gotten there.

Then it was time to begin taping our segment of the show. Hildy's birth sister accompanied her on stage, and Al's birth father was interviewed by telephone from Florida. Both of their searches had been accompanied by many of the same kinds of synchronicities I had experienced. In the time since my Unsolved Mysteries appearance, I had heard even more of these stories. Hildy and her birth sister had lived within a mile of each other throughout their high school years. A bakery in which Hildy worked at night and on weekends had become a magnet, drawing her birth mother in almost weekly to shop. Both Hildy and her birth sister had started their searches, stopped in frustration, and started searching again, all in the identical years. Al, and many of his birth kin, had experienced dreams of each other at the same time. Al, who didn't previously know he was adopted, was led to this discovery, and to his birth family, by the content of these dreams.

Cassandra and I were brought on to the stage about 45 minutes into the show, after Al, and Hildy and her sister had told their stories. I was rather uncomfortable when the host introduced me by saying I had "missed his father's love all of his life," something I had never told the host (since I had not yet met him), or his staff, and simply wasn't true. This proved to be the only even slight problem though. Unlike my sixty seconds of air time on "Unsolved Mysteries," I spoke for a total of nearly four and a half minutes on "The Other Side," with the first segment being two and a half uninterrupted minutes in which I was asked to tell of my own synchronistic experiences. Especially because of the nature of my introduction, I felt very strongly I wanted to point out my desire to search had nothing to do with the love I felt in my adoptive family, and right away found a way to say that. After I told my story the host asked me to comment on Al and Hildy's stories, which gave me a chance to say I thought science would soon have to look at a whole other dimension of knowledge to explain the kinds of experiences more and more people were having. There were several questions from the audience to me, and I commented on other questions and answers given by others on stage.

That evening, I got back to the hotel in time to see the last three quarters of the Tonight Show. I saw Melissa Ethridge singing (again!)

and was able to put the robed couple I saw in the bed into context. They had won a "contest" to see which couple from the audience had the worst accommodations in Los Angeles for a Grateful Dead concert that week-end, and the couple had won because they were sleeping in the back of his pick-up truck which they had driven from one of the southeastern states. The prize was a free stay in the "Tonight Show Hotel," which was a back-stage dressing room. Jay walked them back to their "luxurious accommodations," going out of the studio doors I missed looking into, and right down the hall through which I had walked as I entered the studio. On their way to their dressing-room hotel suite, Jay gave them a "tour" in which he pointed out the make-up room. The cameraman walked in and quickly panned a portion of the room, but alas, I had not quite yet arrived there. I guess it would have been too much to ask to appear on the "Tonight Show" accidentally!

When I had arrived in Los Angeles before the taping of "The Other Side," I had called Marlou Russell again to tell her I was in Los Angeles to be a "TV star" one more time, and to ask whether she wanted to continue the conversation we had started after the Unsolved Mysteries taping. She was agreeable, and available the morning after the taping, and so we had arranged to meet again for breakfast. Before, during, and after the taping of the show Cassandra Eason and I had struck up a friendship, and as I got to know her, I thought Marlou and Cassandra might be interested in meeting each other, so I invited Cassandra to join Marlou and me for breakfast. For several hours we discussed the connections we all sensed between ourselves and those we were related to. Marlou told Cassandra in more detail the story she had told me in our first meeting, about having been in therapy during which she was encouraged to recall earlier and earlier memories. Marlou had recurrent images of being trapped and of being angry at someone. When she was finally reunited with Sara, her birth mother, and shared these images, Sara told Marlou she had been very overdue by the time she was born. Although I did not know it at the time, it would not be long before I would have the chance to meet Sara also.

Cassandra pointed out her belief that genetic-biological connections were not the only way to achieve "The Link of Love." She believed strong emotions such as love could produce the psychic connections even in the absence of biological ties. Cassandra told Marlou and me in more detail about a dream-based connection she had mentioned briefly on "The Other Side," between "Linda," an adoptive mother she had worked with in England, and the infant who "Linda" later adopted.

Before "Linda" had even decided to adopt, she had a strikingly vivid dream about the birth of a dark-skinned dark-haired child being born to a light-skinned light-haired mother in a far-away land, both of whom she saw quite clearly. Because the dream was so powerful, she wrote in her journal the date and time of night when she had the dream. Later she decided to adopt a child, and when she first saw her adopted son, she recognized him immediately as the boy about whose birth she had dreamt. She checked her journal against his birth date, and found an exact match between her dream and the time of his birth.

We talked more about how science could explain such connections. I suggested there may be a form of energy of which we are as yet unaware, and used my favorite example of radio waves, which are real, but which we can't perceive without a translating device. They have always existed, but we didn't know about them until the radio was invented. Cassandra told me she would be writing me from England to ask some questions she might use in her next book, which was to be titled *Psychic Families*. When the book was published, in 1995, chapter nine contained things both Marlou and I had said during that conversation, as well as information I had sent in response to Cassandra's letter. The book also contained ideas from the work of LaVonne Stiffler, who Cassandra had met while taping a previous segment for "Unsolved Mysteries."

As Marlou, Cassandra and I talked about LaVonne and the *Unsolved Mysteries* segment in which Cassandra had appeared, another odd coincidence surfaced. Cassandra was talking about the filming process and mentioned she had been staying at the Beverly Garland hotel. While she was there, in a room on an upper floor, the Northridge earthquake had happened. The questions I had when I was being taped for *Unsolved Mysteries* about what it would be like to be in a California earthquake were answered, and by someone who had been in an earthquake in the same hotel I had stayed in, and who was being taped for an episode of the same show! Cassandra told of the building shaking, of running from her room into the darkened hall, and wondering whether she would live to see her children again. She was finally able to take the stairs down to the ground floor. From her report I decided a major earthquake was an experience I didn't need to have first-hand. We all clearly enjoyed the conversation, and unfortunately the time for Marlou, Cassandra, and I to part came too quickly.

I was anxious to see a tape of the show, and was disappointed when I got to Susan's family home in Lancaster to discover her parents' VCR timer had misfired, and their tape was incomplete. For a variety of reasons I had great difficulty getting an intact tape of my appearance on *The Other Side*. Since it doesn't run in Stevens Point, two other people beside Susan's parents had taped it for me (in Madison, WI, and Youngstown, OH) and both of the other tapes had flaws as well! It took some careful editing on my part, but between the three tapes I was finally able to get a reasonably good quality tape of my second big chance at television fame.

In the fall of 1995 I had my third shot at national television, when I received a call from the syndicated show *Sightings*. They were planning a segment on synchronicity, and wanted me to discuss synchronicity from the point of view of a researcher. What made this show different and exciting was their ability to film me on my own campus. After perhaps an hour of telephone pre-screening questions, they arranged to send a film crew up from Madison to do the actual interview. I spent several hours cleaning my office. Although a certain amount of clutter might make my environment look intellectual, I didn't want it to look like a rats' nest, which is its usual configuration. No offense meant to rats! Unfortunately, once the crew arrived on campus and looked at my office, they decided it was too small, and we had to "borrow" a larger office from a colleague. By the time the scene in the borrowed office was arranged there were extension cords running out into the hall and to the office next door, bright lights shining out onto the hall, and some disruption had been caused—enough to call attention to the fact that something was going on. Several people, both students and faculty, had noticed that I was unusually well dressed, and had asked me what was happening. I used the phrase I enjoy using when people ask me why I am wearing a coat and tie: "I'm playing doctor today." I greatly enjoyed the chance to be able to add: "I'm not a real doctor but I'm playing one on TV."

After the interview portion of the filming was complete, they wanted a shot of me in front of a class, so we "borrowed" a class that my colleague was teaching, and they shot a few seconds of me in front of the class, and looking over a student's shoulder. Then the crew set up outside the building where I work, and filmed me walking up, and entering the door under the large "Science Building" sign. It was fun being the center of attention as people walked by.

Now, having been taped for national television shows three times within a year and a half, I was beginning to feel rather comfortable with the process, and thought that the *Sightings* interview had been my best. I was anxious to know when I would get to see the interview. The camera crew, stringers for several shows, had no idea when the segment would air, and referred me to a Hollywood number. The assistant at the *Sightings* studio gave me the now-familiar response: I would get a call just before the show aired. A year went by, and in the fall of 1996, I called the number again, this time encountering an answering machine. I left a message with my name and phone number, asking whether they yet had an air date for the interview they had filmed with me. I got no return call, and concluded the *Sightings* producers must have decided not to use the piece.

Susan, Carch, and I had been increasingly busy with preparations for a semester in London, and the three of us left Stevens Point for England on January 11. It took several weeks for me to get an e-mail account set up, but when I did, and retrieved my queued-up mail from the University, there was an e-mail message sent in mid-January from a fellow in Chicago. He had seen an interview with me on the "Sightings" TV show the night before and wanted to share some experiences he had with me! I responded, asking whether he had happened to videotape the show, and he had not, nor did he know anyone who had. Then I tried to find an e-mail address for *Sightings* without success, and sent messages to friends on the internet asking whether anyone had taped the show. Ultimately, I was able to find a friend who had taped a re-run of the show, but I could not watch that tape until I got home from London in June of 1997. When I finally saw the segment, nearly two years after shooting was completed, my feelings about having done well in the interview were validated.

CHAPTER 19

Just Add Some Music: Jack Quist

Other important things beside the "Sightings" interview happened in 1995. A very special synchronistic event occurred at the American Adoption Congress annual convention, that year in Las Vegas. I had presented workshops for the previous several conventions, which meant I was under considerable time pressure in the weeks before arrival at the convention, and some performance-related stress prior to the presentation at each convention. Therefore, my plan was to take the Las Vegas convention "off," and I had not submitted anything for the program. I had also decided to go to workshops which would have benefit to me as an academic psychologist and adoption professional, and thus I would not have to worry about either presenting a paper or getting into a lot of potentially stressful personal issues. I had also served the previous summer on the AAC's Task Force for Reorganization, and I thought the emotions associated with watching the organization begin what I hoped would be a major change would be quite enough excitement for one convention.

The first session on the conference program was an academic presentation by psychologist Thomas Bouchard, Ph.D., Director of the Minnesota Study of Twins Reared Apart and Adoption. He spoke on the reasons he thought were behind the striking similarities which the Minnesota research team had discovered between both identical and fraternal twins who had been separated by adoption and raised apart from each other. I also attended a follow-up discussion with him, which was scheduled for one of the small-group sessions immediately after Dr. Bouchard's presentation. I covered the work of Dr. Bouchard in my developmental psychology classes, and I thought it would be good to be able to tell my students I had not only heard Dr. Bouchard speak, but had also discussed with him the role of synchronicity in the similarities his research was uncovering. I also wanted to talk with Bouchard about the synchronicity research Tom Rowe and I were conducting. Since there were only about ten people at the discussion session, I felt as though I got some "quality time" with him. Although Bouchard was openly skeptical about the possibility of synchronistic connections, he agreed to read a copy of the paper Tom Rowe and I had recently written.

The follow-up discussion with Bouchard was in the first session after lunch, and so the first regular convention workshop I attended was not until late Monday afternoon. I had believed the topic for the session would be a presentation on infant crying, more information I thought I could use in my developmental psychology class. Once the session began, however, I realized the topic was much more personal and experiential than detached, intellectual and professional, as its description in the convention brochure had suggested it would be. While I was somewhat uncomfortable, having wanted to avoid anything personal for a while, I felt it would be even more uncomfortable for me to leave after the session had begun, and so I stayed. As I looked around the room, I recognized several adoptee friends I had met at previous conventions: Tom McGowan, a psychologist, who I recognized from the researchers' discussion group I had led in 1994 in New Orleans; Shannon Poole, a master's degree candidate in counseling who I had also met in New Orleans; and Catalina McClone, who was becoming an expert in the process known as co-counseling and who I had met at an AAC conference several years earlier.

The session dealt with why adoptive parents sometimes report their adopted infants cried more than usual, and they seemed exceptionally hard to console. Diana Ensley York, the session leader, believes the early losses suffered by the adopted infant may explain these problems. For one of the activities during the session itself, Diana asked the participants to imagine a number of our favorite things, such as our favorite place, person, food, music, etc., and to write each of them on a slip of paper. Then we had to "give them away forever and never see or hear or have them again" by putting one designated slip of paper (such as the one listing our favorite food), in a basket each time the basket was passed around the room. As each of the favorites was given away, we were then asked to concentrate on how we felt to have to lose these favorite things. By the end of the session virtually everyone in the room was in tears. The session stirred up feelings in me that surprised me, and I realized I had not as yet resolved issues of loss about my adoption, particularly about my birth mother. When the session was over, I was emotionally wrung out, and feeling lost and lonely as I said hello to Catalina and Shannon. Discussions between the three of us then, and later with Tom, revealed all four of us had attended that particular session in error, each thinking we were going to an academic presentation about infant crying!

Prior to the convention Catalina and I had been discussing the co-counseling process through the mail and on the telephone. The co-counseling process involves a mutual listening technique, and does not require any particular mental health training. Since we were both upset as a result of the workshop we had just attended, Catalina and I decided to have a co-counseling session with each other right there in the meeting room, which turned out to be empty for the next hour. During our co-counseling session, and after more tears, I realized what I needed to do at the Las Vegas convention was not to "live in my head" by attending a series of academic exercises which would have benefit to me as a psychologist and adoption professional. What I really needed was to deal with my emotions and engage in some further exploration of the unresolved feelings about my adoption, and particularly about my birth mother. Thus, listening to what the universe was telling me, I changed my goals for the conference, and decided to attend sessions that were more personal than professional in nature.

One of these sessions occurred on Tuesday morning, a workshop, by Shannon, which I attended on the use of visualization to achieve what we desired as an outcome in our searches. Tom and Catalina were there also. I was deep in thought at the end of Shannon's presentation, looking forward to what I hoped would be a chance to talk with her more about my reactions to some of her ideas. During and after the workshop, I was beginning to wonder whether, through the mental images I was creating, I was somehow inhibiting the chances of a successful reunion. I suspected I might have some fears of not only the possibility of another rejection but also, surprisingly, fears of a highly successful reunion. These fears might be contributing to the ongoing stalemate in our relationship, and I wanted to talk with Shannon about my feelings. However, elsewhere another series of events had been unfolding in which I would play an important, if unintended, part. I was not to have the chance to explore my personal issues further, at least for a while.

Jack Quist, an adoptee and an accomplished country and western singer-songwriter, had come to the AAC convention from his home in

Salt Lake City to get support in approaching his birth mother, Sharon, who he had recently located and who lived in Las Vegas. Doreen, his therapist, an alcohol and drug abuse counselor, had brought Jack to Las Vegas because even though she had little prior specific knowledge of adoption search and reunion issues, she realized contact with his birth family was of extreme importance to him.

On the Sunday before the convention began, Jack asked Doreen to take Sharon a bouquet of flowers and an audio tape of a song he had written for her. The song, called *"Dear Mom,"* begins "Dear Mom, it's been forty years, I think it's time we met. Please don't tell me that you're just not ready yet." The song covers Jack's adoption and his growing up in a loving adoptive family. He sings about his love for his birth mother, and about how he had always wondered where she was and why she had given him up for adoption.

After giving Sharon time to listen to the tape, Jack had then asked Doreen to call Sharon and ask if she would like to meet him. Sharon had said Jack's contact was a surprise, and she needed time to adjust, and to tell her other children, who did not know of Jack's birth. Sharon also said Jack had a birth sister who worked at a nearby Perkins restaurant. Arrangements were made for Jack to call Sharon the next morning, Monday.

On Monday morning, while Tom Bouchard presented the opening address at the convention, Jack called Sharon at the prearranged time, and got no answer. He tried to sneak a peek at his birth sister by going into the Perkins where she worked, only to find she had not come to work that day. On Monday afternoon, beginning to feel apprehensive about the situation, Jack attended some conference sessions, but happened to select those in which only happy reunions with few complications were described. His already-uneasy feelings that something had gone wrong with his own reunion were only heightened.

Tuesday morning, he again tried to call Sharon, only to discover her phone had been disconnected. He called the Perkins to find his birth sister had now missed her second day of work in a row, something her fellow employees said was highly unusual for her. Jack found himself mid-morning Tuesday in a highly agitated state, convinced his birth mother did not want to see him, and fearful of the worst: that she had taken her daughter and fled the city, and he would never get to meet them. He decided to have an early lunch and head out of town. Someone had noticed and been concerned about Jack's mood, and had notified Pat Sanders, the convention coordinator, that there was an adoptee in trouble.

Then Jack's and my paths crossed. As soon as Shannon's session ended, at around 11:00 a. m., Pat entered the room and came directly to my seat. She explained only that there was "a fellow in a cowboy hat" in one of the hotel's restaurants who was very upset that his birth mother had rejected him. Pat said people were worried about him. She wanted me to speak to him to make sure he was going to be all right, and didn't leave the convention in his current state of mind. I agreed to meet with him, but was privately concerned, hoping whatever I needed to do with him would not take more than an hour and a half because I was scheduled to have lunch at 12:30 p. m. with Marlou Russell and her birth mother Sara. I had been looking forward to that meeting ever since I had learned Sara had come to the convention with Marlou. I wanted to hear Sara's side of the story of Marlou's long-delayed birth, as Marlou had told Cassandra Eason and I at breakfast the previous December in Hollywood.

I found Jack hurriedly eating a meal before leaving to go home. Doreen, was trying to calm him down without much success. He was feeling discouraged and fearful about what he saw as a rejection by his birth mother, but, as people sometimes do, he was covering his fear with anger and bravado. As Jack was wolfing down his food he was angry at his birth mother, saying things like "why did I ever think she would be interested in me—she didn't want me then, she doesn't want me now. *I don't need her.*" He told me he was going to leave to return home to Salt Lake City as soon as he finished his meal.

Very quickly I recognized a familiar thread in Jack's speech. The fear of yet another rejection is common as many adoptees conduct their search. I had seen the very same fear in myself just an hour earlier that morning in Diana Ensley York's experiential workshop on loss. Unfortunately, the result of fearing rejection is often the desire to reject the birth family first rather than to face the possibility of the feared rejection from them again. I sympathized with Jack's fears and told him they were certainly understandable. Then I suggested that while *he* had been searching for a long time, his appearance was a surprise to Sharon. Though his birth mother had undoubtedly not ever forgotten him, *she* probably needed some time to digest his unexpected arrival. For her, his appearance might well revive the pain she had experienced herself on his surrender, and might bring up any fears she might have had about her past returning to haunt her. His birth mother would very typically want some time to come to terms with the meaning of his arrival, and to arrange her affairs a bit before she met him. I encouraged Jack to stay at the convention, where I knew there were many others who shared his fears before and during their searches. I told him there were relatively few adoptees who were permanently unable to break through a birth parent's pain and fear to gain acceptance. Even if he were going to be one of those relative few who was rejected, I knew most of the people who were rejected believed that what they found during their search experience was still worth the pain of rejection. I told him a little of my own story, marveling to myself about how uncannily appropriate my story was.

As I learned more about Jack, I realized that, of the perhaps a couple dozen various mental health professionals at the conference, when Pat came to me, she just happened to have selected someone with a lot in common with Jack. Even though my particular practice specialty in psychology is child and adolescent behavior problems, Jack and I shared several important personal issues as adults and specifically as adoptees. The most immediately critical of them was that we were both in recovery from alcohol and/or drug abuse. I was also one of those few adoptees whose birth mother had been unable to accept him back into her life. As someone who had experienced that which Jack feared most, I could tell him with conviction that even though I had been rejected, the search and reunion experience, though painful, had been unbelievably valuable to me. Later, when I asked Pat how she came to decide to look for me, she could only say she really didn't know why. Even though she really didn't know much about Jack, a voice just said to her "get Doug." She listened.

Eventually Jack calmed down and decided to stay on to see things through, and he left the restaurant in search of a conference session he had earlier been interested in attending. His counsellor, Doreen, and I talked for a while after he left, and she filled me in on what had been happening over the last few days that had led up to Jack's near-panic state. She told me about "Dear Mom," and asked me if I would like to listen to the song. We went out into the parking lot, and in her car, she handed me a tape player with "Dear Mom" cued up. I heard a beautiful song with an even more beautiful message, and after I wiped my tears away, I insisted we bring the tape inside and play the song for as many of the members of the AAC board as I could find. I strongly felt somehow the whole convention needed to hear the song. In the next half hour or so I had several more chances to hear *"Dear Mom,"* and each time it again brought me to tears.

Eventually I left Doreen and the tape of *"Dear Mom"* with Pat Sanders, and found Sara and Marlou waiting for me back in the same restaurant I had just been in with Jack. It was fascinating to see the similarities between Marlou and Sara, and I was (I hope not too openly) jealous of their relaxed ability to be together, something I feared I might never experience with my own birth mother. Sara told of worrying Marlou would not be delivered healthily because she was so overdue. We concluded the difficult delivery might well have occurred because of the emotional strain felt not only by Sara, who knew she would be surrendering her baby for adoption, but also perhaps by Marlou, who may well have sensed Sara's tension. As always seems to be the case at these conferences, too soon the time came to move on to the afternoon conference sessions, and we had to end our conversation.

For the rest of that afternoon, each time I walked past the conference registration table, I saw a different member of AAC, including more Board members, frequently in tears, sometimes wearing headphones, and listening to *"Dear Mom."* By the end of Monday afternoon, there had already been, as I knew there would be, considerable discussion about asking Jack to sing his song at the Wednesday evening closing conference banquet. While the enthusiasm for Jack's song was high, there was a problem in that a rising young singer from Salt Lake City, the daughter of a well-known Hollywood personality, who was also a recent birth mother in an open adoption, had already been scheduled to sing as the post-banquet entertainment. There was a good deal of concern over what her reaction might be should she suddenly have to share the stage with an older and much more experienced artist. When the request was made to have her share the stage with Jack, she agreed, and arrangements were then quickly made to have Jack sing *"Dear Mom"* for the entire convention. However, we still had one last obstacle. Jack would have been totally happy to sing, except for the fact that in the throes of withdrawal-induced depression he had sold his guitar! While Jack would have been willing to sing the song without any accompaniment, it turned out that singing acapella was not necessary, since the scheduled singer agreed to let him borrow her guitar. The combination of songs by a birth mother and an adoptee, both singing about the pain of separation and of their love for the person they had lost, moved many in the audience at the closing banquet, including me, to tears again.

I had long planned on staying in Las Vegas for a couple of days after the convention, due to the return train schedule. However, the first AAC male adoptee workshop was held at that conference. During the extra days in Las Vegas, I joined several of the men who got to know each other through that workshop, and who stayed after for some bonding and sightseeing. Each evening when I got back to the hotel, I was treated to a recorded phone message from Jack or Doreen giving me an update on the progress of Jack's reunion. It turned out Sharon, his birth mother was in the midst of moving, and had not wanted Jack to see her house in a mess. His birth sister had taken off from work at Perkins for two days to help in the moving process, which explained both Sharon's disconnected phone and his birth sister's missing work. The day after the convention ended, Jack met Sharon, along with the birth sister, who he had already met when he "spied" on her at Perkins the day before.

When he called the restaurant and found she was working, Jack and Doreen went in and seated themselves in her area. He drew out the ordering process by feigning difficulty deciding what to eat. At the end of the meal, he complimented her on her good service, and left her a big tip. She said to him "You're such a nice man." Jack had said to her "Well, maybe I'll see you again sometime," savoring the thought that he knew he would. Before I left to go home, I already felt Jack's reunion was going to work out just fine, and all of his fears, like those of so many adoptees and birth parents, had been unnecessary.

"*Dear Mom*" has been made into a video, in which Jack, Doreen, and Sharon play themselves, and every person seen in the video is a member of Jack's birth family. At the end of the video Jack explains the story depicted is true, and asks those who want assistance with their search to contact the American Adoption Congress. "*Dear Mom*" is also the title song of a CD which has been released on Yellow Moon Records. "*Dear Mom*," along with "*He Would be Sixteen*," sung by Michelle Wright, are almost enough to make an old folk/rock lover (that would be me) like country music! They certainly are the best two songs I have ever heard in terms of speaking to the feelings of the adoption triad.

I remain struck by the sequence of events which occurred, ultimately covering more than a year, and I believe it is an excellent example of synchronicity. Here again are the highlights of what happened before, during, and after the Las Vegas meeting. Two singers, unknown to each other but both from Salt Lake City, came to a conference in Las Vegas. One was a searching adoptee and the other was a new birth mother.

There they made a joint appearance at the national conference of an organization dedicated to ending the lifelong separation of adoptees and birth parents. Although the birth mother had come to Las Vegas specifically to sing at the banquet, the adoptee was in Las Vegas not to sing, but to reunite with his own birth mother. His misinterpretation of his birth mother's behavior had made him upset, and placed his sobriety at risk. This brought him to the attention of the convention planner, who selected me, a psychologist, to help him. I was another adoptee in recovery from substance abuse, who had already experienced the very rejection Jack feared. I helped Jack get through his anxiety about his reunion with his birth mother, and also helped arrange for him to sing the song he had written for his birth mother at the convention's closing banquet. After the conference he had his reunion, in which he found a family full of musicians and song-writers, and his birth family appeared in a video of the song he wrote for his birth mother. At the end of the video Jack praises the organization that helped him in his search. The fact that not only was I a part of these events, but also that I study the nature of just such "coincidental" events as these, made the situation even more synchronistic.

PART FOUR

ADOPTION: LOVE, INTIMACY, AND SEXUALITY

CHAPTER 20

Three Strikes and You're . . .

The original title for Part Four was going to be "Sex, Love, and Intimacy." I put off working on this Part until almost the very end of the initial writing process, probably because these topics are perhaps the most difficult for me to address of any I wanted to cover. These topics are the most personal of all of those in the book, and I have given a great deal of thought to just how much I should reveal about myself. While facing a sort of writer's block about this material in the summer of 1997, I had a very clear and frightening dream. In the dream, my book had been released in paperback, with a half-naked woman sprawled across the cover, and a title reading something like "Sex, Lies, and Adoption: The Secret Sordid Life of an Adopted Male Psychologist." Okay, so I made that title up *after* I awoke from the dream, but I DID see my book in the dream, and there really WAS a half-, well, okay, a fully-naked woman on the cover! A steamy sex book was definitely not what I wanted to create.

Balanced against my fear of revealing too much or of being sensational, however, is another important fact. I want my book to be helpful to other male adoptees, to our wives or partners, our adoptive and birth parents, our siblings, perhaps also our children, and to anyone who wants to understand some of "what makes us adoptees tick." To be optimally helpful would seem to require me to be as open and revealing as possible. Of course, the idea of openness leads me to experience some conflict about the amount of disclosure of my own sexuality with which I am comfortable. But, should I censor too much, the utility of the book may be diminished. In an attempt to compromise between these competing desires, I decided I needed to place some limits on the content of this chapter. Thus, there are certain aspects of my sexuality, and of what I have come to believe is the relationship of my sexuality to my adoption, that I have omitted. Perhaps I will write or talk about these issues one day, but for now, even though I generally believe in honesty and self-disclosure, I will reserve some personal privacy. Also because the women I will write about here who were a part of my life deserve to have their own privacy respected, I have changed some of their names, though the general situations remain true-to-life.

In addition to being very personal, in some ways the issues covered here are also among the most speculative in the book. Sexuality research is as difficult, emotional, and filled with pitfalls, as is adoption research. Many of the ideas I will present here are new enough, or narrow enough in scope, that little or even no scientific data is specifically relevant to these issues, especially as they interface with adoption. Yet in many ways I feel the topics of love, intimacy, and sexuality are for adoptees probably the most important issues I will cover. Of all of the effects being adopted has had on me, the most important effects have been on my self-concept and on my ability to trust women. Self-concept and trust are not necessarily unrelated to each other, and both of them are related to sexuality. How I feel about myself has a clear relationship to how desirable I see myself as a partner in a relationship, and to how I will view the role of sexuality in that relationship. If I don't feel valuable, how can I feel desirable? The relationship between my ability to trust women and my sexuality needs even less explanation. Trust is a necessary part of intimate sexuality. I believe my adoption has affected my ability to become emotionally close to women, to maintain long-term relationships with them, and to have some semblance of a satisfactory sexual relationship with them. While the writing of the present chapter causes me a fair amount of distress, I nonetheless want to share my perspective and experience on these topics.

In order to understand how I believe my adoption affected me in the areas of my ability to love and be intimate with women, I need to present a brief lesson in the development of the infant-mother relationship. In this lesson I will attempt to differentiate between three kinds of information which I will present. First, there are those ideas that are supported by some level of data from formal research. The second kind of information is ideas which are based on the personal experiences of many people whom I have encountered during my 50-plus years of experience in the areas of adoption, adoption search and reunion, and adoption research. The second group of ideas seem to me to have some general applicability. The third kind of information I will present is those ideas which seem unique to my own life experience as a male adoptee who is also a psychologist. I believe, but cannot prove, my ideas about my own life experience have general applicability to other adoptees.

I will limit my lesson about the development of the infant-mother relationship as it applies to adoption to those adoptive placements which, like mine, occurred within the first few weeks of life. However, adoptions which involve a period of placement in a foster home or a period of living with the birth mother will have many similar dynamics to those which I believe operate in the situation which I, and many fellow adoptees of the 1930s to 1960s, and likely later, experienced. The legal process of my own adoption started within a short time of my birth, and I went from the hospital to my adoptive family within a week or two after I was born.

Let the lesson begin! As I write about early development, we need to be aware of what developmental psychologists and medical personnel are talking about when they use the terms bonding and attachment. In keeping with emerging differences in the meaning of these terms, I will use "bonding" to refer to the largely biological aspects of the parent-child relationship, and "attachment" to refer to the more psychological or social processes within the relationship. John Bowlby, one of the premier attachment theorists, describes attachment as parent-child activities involved with making the child feel safe, secure and protected. Since both bonding and attachment are significantly impacted during the adoption of an infant, let me briefly describe them as they occur in a "traditional" or "typical" birth. By the terms "traditional" and "typical" I mean a birth that is the result of a more-or-less planned or anticipated pregnancy, and in which the couple who carried the child is the same couple who raises the child. I also include single parent births where the child is raised only or primarily by the mother (or the father), as long as the pregnancy was more-or-less planned or anticipated, under the terms "traditional" and "typical." Then I will discuss how the processes of bonding and attachment are different in an adoption, how I believe these differences created problems in interpersonal relationships and sexuality (for me and perhaps for other adoptees), and how I believe these problems have played themselves out in my life. Of course, we must always remember that these process (sometimes also identified as arising from "nature" and "nurture"), interact in complex ways with each other

Research suggests rather conclusively that both the processes of bonding and attachment begin well before birth. Exactly how far in advance of birth, or even in advance of pregnancy, these processes begin, we don't yet know. With regard to attachment, for example, the doll-play of young girls might be seen as more than just play at taking care of a baby-doll. Doll play could also be seen as the beginning of the general attachment girls will eventually develop, in much more specific form as they mature, to the infants they may not conceive or bear for many years.

As a couple begins to develop a serious relationship, they may talk about having children one day, and their general attachment as a couple to these future children may begin then. The occurrence of a pregnancy leads to another development in the attachment process. In the traditional situation the couple typically makes yet more detailed and specific plans for, and develops a specific attachment to, their coming child. Of course, the birth of the infant opens another whole broad aspect of attachment, which continues well into childhood and beyond.

Years ago, one of my older "non-traditional" students told our developmental psychology class of frequently talking to his unborn child by laying his head on his wife's stomach. He attended the birth, and throughout it he was silent, overwhelmed and close to tears by the process he was observing. When the baby was born and on the mother's chest, he spoke for the first time, saying something to the effect "It's so nice to see you after all this waiting." As soon as he spoke, the baby turned his head and upper body in the direction of the father's voice, and the father described that moment as an incredibly powerful connection.

Attachment also occurs between an infant and its mother (and to the father, if one is present and involved with child-rearing). We believe infant-mother attachment heightens at, but perhaps even begins before the child's birth, and the process is enhanced to the extent nurturing care-giving is provided by the parent(s). Currently we believe, rather than being specific to one set of individuals (the parents), the infant can become attached to any individual who provides the necessary elements of care-giving, thus making adoption a possibility. Care-giving includes such easily identifiable, and often quantifiable, behaviors as visual and verbal attention to the child, responsiveness to the child's needs, and an overall positive emotional attitude toward the child, as well as much less easily definable attributes such as "love" and "caring."

While we may prefer to think of "mother love" in humans as a purely psychological, social, and nearly spiritual process, one largely included with the attachment process as described above, there are also biological aspects which contribute to the mother-infant relationship. Clear evidence from animals and humans suggests there are biological (often hormone-related) dimensions to behaviors related to the raising of young (such as nest-building) and to biological processes (such as nursing). The protectiveness which female animals show toward their young is well known. Professionals who study the mother-infant relationship apply the term "bonding" to these biological (either genetic or hormone-based) dimensions of the human mother-child relationship.

Mother-infant bonding in humans does not likely begin until a pregnancy occurs. Once she becomes pregnant, hormonal and physical processes in the woman prepare her body for the pregnancy, delivery, and nursing processes. These changes likely also affect her emotional state in ways which increase the strength of her connection to the fetus she is carrying. Bonding in the fetus takes place as its developing senses react to aspects of the mother's bodily environment. We know that the fetus is able to hear, feel, taste, and to some extent "smell," with taste and smell operating on the amniotic fluid. The fetus's eyes even register changes in light levels. Hormones associated with the mother's emotional state, such as fear, or joy, cross the placenta and have a physiological effect on the fetus. In addition, the foods a pregnant woman eats, the kind of music she listens to, and her general level of emotion, all reflected in her physiological state, are transmitted to the fetus. Moreover, we believe the fetus has the ability to register and recall many of these pre-natal stimuli after its birth. We can thus say the infant already "knows" something about its mother by the time of birth. At the very least infants "know" the environment in which they developed.

There are some other important aspects of the early mother-infant relationship that would seem to fall outside either the strict definition of attachment or bonding processes. For example, by the time an infant is born, the new mother already "knows" a good deal about her baby through its pre-birth behaviors such as its general activity level and its waking/sleeping cycle. To the extent she has knowledge of other babies born either to herself or to others within her family, and knowledge of the general family history, the new mother also "knows" about what to expect from her baby, and even on into childhood. Thus, in the typical birth, there is a broad continuity and connection between the mother and infant which typically remains unbroken throughout at least the early life of the child.

Adoption causes significant changes in the processes of bonding and attachment. To the extent the pregnancy which will result in an adoption is less than a happy experience, the birthmother will present her fetus with a different hormonal prenatal environment, and possibly a different nutritional one as well. Depression, anxiety, poor nutrition and poor medical care all may have a greater impact on pregnancies that will ultimately result in an adoptive placement than on pregnancies where the child is more-or-less planned, and will be raised by the family into which it was born.

In adoption, the continuity of the pre: and post-birth attachment and bonding experience is disrupted because the mother with whom adoptees are expected to develop attachment is not the same mother with whom they bonded before birth and with whom they likely began to attach. The maternal-fetal-attachment process in a traditional birth would smoothly transition to after-birth attachment, however, in an adoption, it would be interrupted at the time of separation for placement

The seriousness of the pre-post birth discrepancy and the duration of the consequences of the discontinuity are still a scientific unknown, but we believe the infant is at least aware of the disruption. An example of this might well be the increase in adoptee infant crying reported at the AAC Las Vegas Conference workshop on infant crying by Diana Ensley York. One prominent adoption theorist, Marshall Schecter, MD, has suggested prospective adoptive parents might ease the transition from birth to adoptive environment for their adoptee by learning the type of foods and style of music preferred by the birthmother of their to-be-adopted infant. Schecter then suggests the adoptive parents "adopt" these preferences along with, or even prior to, the baby's arrival in their home. The adopted infant would then experience the adoptive home as an environment where at least some of the sounds, tastes, and smells were familiar.

Once a traditional pregnancy is discovered there is perhaps a six-month anticipation or adjustment period before the birth, during which the attachment develops still another dimension, which occurs with some variability as to the timetable. On the part of the adoptive mother, she might lack many of the prenatal amplifications of the process of attachment to the infant that occur in the typical pregnancy. There may not be time for baby showers, shopping trips, outfitting a nursery, and other such traditional social support rituals. The "pre-birth" adjustment period may be shortened to a matter of days or even hours. On the other hand, there may be years between the initial commitment to adopt a child and the arrival of a child in the home. Both the shortened and lengthened adjustment periods have an as-yet unknown effect. The adoptive mother's pre-adoption attachment experience is likely to be emotionally ambivalent, especially if there is a history of unsuccessful attempts at achieving her own pregnancy, such as stillbirth or other child losses. The experience of application, home study, approval, and then waiting for an available child is also likely to cause the adoptive mother's attachment to be significantly different in quality from that of the mother in a traditional-birth.

The discontinuity of attachment and the disruption of bonding in an adoptive placement is only amplified in the presence of the secrecy that accompanied many adoptions in the past. Thus, there is likely a much different, and probably shakier, basis for beginning a relationship between adoptees and their adoptive parents at the time of their arrival in their new adoptive home than there is between traditionally born children and their parents at the time of their return to the home their mother occupied during her pregnancy.

One piece of information is important here, relating to the social-emotional learning believed to be taking place in infants during their first year of life. This dimension of our lives is being given attention with the work of Daniel Goleman and others on the "Emotional Quotient." However, developmental psychologists have long known of the importance of the emotional dimension. The widely accepted developmental personality theorist Eric Erikson and his many followers (myself among them), describe the first year of life as being critical in the development of "basic trust." When basic trust is established, the infant begins life with three core beliefs: the world is essentially a safe and good place; people can be depended upon to "be there" for me; and others may be safely depended upon to meet my needs. Absence of the establishment of basic trust leads, in Erikson's view, to the development of a person who feels the world is not a safe place, feels isolated from, and does not trust, others, and who prefers to depend on no-one else.

Perhaps the initial emotional response of the mother-to-be on learning of her pregnancy might provide the simplest way to sum up the overall difference between two very different gestations. In the "typical pregnancy" which does not involve thoughts of adoption, the common response might be an excited "Oh my God" followed by happy conversations, phone calls, and a period of joyous planning. In pregnancies which are to be followed by adoption, a more common response might be "Oh shit, now what?" followed by perhaps tears, depression, or fear, and a rather different sort of planning.

In my own case, before my adoption, my parents had been married for six years, and had been attempting to have a baby for all of these. They had been unsuccessful, losing five pregnancies in the early stages, then, with a sixth, a boy very near to full term, in October 1945. They expressed a desire to adopt, and in October 1946, they received a call from my mother's physician telling them a baby was available if they were interested. They immediately said they were, and I was ultimately discharged directly from the hospital to them at about two weeks of age, having had some medical complications that kept me there longer than I otherwise might have been.

My parents followed the prevailing advice given to adoptive parents of that era, and did not use the word "adopted" around me. They told friends and family members to keep the adoption a secret, and planned not to tell me I was adopted until I would be at an age when they thought I would be able to understand the process. Thus, although my and my parents' recollections of just how I found out about my adoption differ, I did not "officially" find out I was adopted until I was about 12 years of age.

Given the information I have reviewed about attachment and bonding, I would suggest, however, that I "knew" on some very deep level that things were different within my first few weeks of life. At the very least, I most likely experienced a different type of bonding and attachment than a biological child would have, whether or not I actually sensed the how or why of the experience. I know full well my parents loved me with all of their hearts, and the fact that they did is extremely important to me. However intense their love was, though, and no matter that they did not use the word adopted around me, they could not erase the discontinuity of care in my life. I likely experienced this discontinuity before I even had the words to express my feeling that something was amiss. Looking back on my life from the perspective of 78 years of life experience, I strongly suspect that my development of basic trust was compromised. Moreover, I suspect this is an aspect of every adoption.

Then (regardless of whose version of how I found out is correct), at the beginning of my adolescence I learned I was adopted. Perhaps being told of my adoption relieved me of the unconscious feeling there was something "different" about myself I might well have had since my first weeks of life, although I was not conscious of having realized any difference during childhood. However, and more importantly, the conscious discovery I was adopted then created a second set of problems, in addition to those of attachment and bonding.

I was now confronted with two questions, both of which I don't believe I ever really faced until much later in my life: "Why did my birth mother surrender me for adoption?" and "Why didn't my adoptive

mother tell me I was adopted long ago?" Because of the secrecy surrounding adoptions, an answer for the first question was not available
to me at the time. I knew the second question would present both my
parents, and me with a very difficult situation, which I avoided by never
acknowledging I had the question in the first place. This is an example
of the process known as denial, a way of reducing anxiety. The result of
even having these questions, however, was to put into my mind, although
at a very unconscious level, a question that led to a modification of my
lack of a sense of basic trust: "If I can't trust the mother who gave me
birth to keep me, and if I can't trust the mother who adopted me to
tell me about my adoption, what woman *can* I trust?" Thus, I started
my dating years with a deeply held, but totally unconscious, sense that
women, at least two who had been very important to me, can't be trusted.

Perhaps because of my unconscious sense of mistrust, throughout
high school and my first two years of college I never seemed to date
girls for more than a few months, or perhaps most of a school year.
When I was in ninth grade, I met a seventh-grade girl at our church
youth group named Nancy Masters. We spent a lot of time at her house
talking, and even dated several times, but never seemed to be able to get
a serious relationship going. Several times during high school I dated
other girls. I went off to college when Nancy was a junior in high school,
and during parts of my freshman and sophomore years had two different "girlfriends," but at the end of each school year those relationships
ended. Each of those summers, when I returned to Buffalo, I spent
time with Nancy, often while she was baby-sitting her younger brothers
and sisters by taking them to Beaver Island State Park, a beach near
Buffalo. When she entered Harpur College in Binghamton, NY, in her
freshman year (my junior year), we started to date more seriously, and
by later that year we were "pinned," the equivalent of a pre-engagement
on the St. Lawrence campus. "Pinnings" were even announced in the
weekly College newspaper.

Since neither of us owned a car, Nancy traveled from Harpur to St.
Lawrence by Greyhound for the major weekends, and I did the reverse
for major events at Harpur. We even spent many of the nights at St.
Lawrence staying in a motel together, which was pretty scandalous, as
well as risky, in the late 1960s. Several students at colleges like ours were
suspended for the same behavior during those pre-sexual-revolution
years! We remained virgins since we were "saving ourselves for marriage." During the summer before my senior year, I think, we discussed
marriage, though I wasn't ready to commit to that just yet.

My lack of readiness to commit to a future with Nancy could certainly have been a function of the world situation at that time. The war in Viet Nam, and the drafting of soldiers for the war, were looming larger in the future of all college age men. I was in Army ROTC and thought I would be eligible for a deferment from immediate entry into service on graduation in 1968, so I likely would be able to attend graduate school. However, the rules, and the fortunes of the war, seemed to be changing all of the time, and the future was always unpredictable. Unfortunately, a deeper reason for my unwillingness to commit to Nancy could have been due to the playing out of the message from my basic lack of trust: "you just can't trust people, especially women, to be there for you when you need them." I pretty much assumed a script in which we would probably get married after she graduated from Harpur in the spring of 1970, at which time I anticipated I'd have my Master's degree in psychology completed. Whether I'd be able to continue on for my Ph.D. directly, or whether I'd have to enter the Army at that time was another unknown.

Toward the middle of my senior year, however, the easy conversation that had always been the hallmark of our relationship began to ebb. We would sit in silence for long periods when we were together. We talked the situation over, and decided our relationship had just entered another stage, one in which we could be comfortable just "being together." We decided we now knew each other well enough that we didn't need to talk all of the time. At least that's what I thought we'd decided.

During what was called "Senior Week" at St. Lawrence, while the continuing students took their final spring semester exams, graduating seniors in good standing were exempted. Some seniors used the week to party on campus, while others took road trips around the north-east coast. Fraternity brother Tom Little and I decided to take an impromptu trip to visit Washington, DC, and stopped on the way at Harpur to pay a surprise visit to Nancy. Unfortunately, I was the one who got the surprise. As Tom and I walked into her dormitory lobby about ten o'clock on a Sunday morning, I ran into her roommate, apparently returning from breakfast. She nearly swallowed her teeth with shock, asking whether Nancy was expecting me. I told her no, the visit was a surprise, and we could stay for just a few minutes because we were on our way to Washington. She offered to go and get Nancy from the dining hall, and I said no, I'd rather surprise her. I discovered her holding hands across a table, her head leaned forward in close conversation with another man. Her embarrassment and extreme discomfort at my appearance told me all I needed to know. After being introduced to her companion, Russell, I awkwardly made my escape in a state of great distress.

Even though it was a Sunday morning, I got good and drunk in the car on the way to Washington. I stayed drunk for most of the rest of the time until graduation, never calling Nancy for an explanation. When I got home for the summer, I called a mutual friend who told me that when Nancy talked to her at spring break about her relationship with Russell, she had told Nancy to tell me about him then. Astounded and deeply hurt that their relationship had been going on so long without my knowledge, I then called Nancy. She told me she didn't know how to tell me about Russell without hurting me, and since she didn't want to hurt me, she just didn't tell me. I suppose there was a certain logic to her thinking. As for my thinking, I didn't do much logical thinking at all. I stayed depressed and drunk for much of the rest of that summer, and left for graduate school at Ohio State in the fall, determined to devote my time to graduate work, and to stay the hell away from women.

Although I would not realize the full impact of these events for another ten years, I eventually came to see Nancy's protective deception was the "third strike against me" by a woman I thought I could trust. For my first two years at Ohio State, I dated hardly at all. I really did succeed at throwing myself into my studies, and this probably had some benefits, though I was more and more aware of being lonely, and was starting to spend more of my socializing time by drinking.

At the beginning of my third year at Ohio State I met an attractive but shy freshman woman named Mary at a campus area bar. She and I began to date, increasingly seriously. By then I had come to view my continuing virginity as an unpleasant embarrassment, of which I wished to rid myself ASAP, but I had also decided I did not want to do it in a casual relationship. I did not want to have to be dishonest, and to pretend as though I knew what I was doing. The relationship with Mary, also a virgin and ready to change, was eventually right, and we lost our virginity together on a mid-winter night in my North Fourth Street apartment. After that "first," we spent many nights together, making up for lost time as it were. That summer, although we lived together in the empty married-student apartment of a friend, I remained essentially uninvolved with Mary (except physically of course). All along, as our relationship began to develop, I had told her I was going to leave the following fall for my internship year in Chicago. As we got more deeply involved, I added that, if things were right when I came back, we could start dating again. I think I had decided having lost my virginity,

I would now lay waste to the fields of eligible females who I imagined awaited me in Chicago. After all, Chicago was then the home of "The Playboy Club!"

That September I left Columbus, and Mary, for Chicago, just as I had long said I would. Sometime before Thanksgiving, mutual friends told me Mary had met another older graduate student, a dead ringer for me in looks, about a month after I had left, and she was dating him. I returned to Columbus for Thanksgiving, arranged to see Mary on my first night back, and tried to take up where we had left off. I am ashamed to admit I got drunk, and got her drunk, and then forced myself on her against her will. Today I would be considered guilty of sexual assault, the variety commonly called "date rape," since that is what I did. Back then I was at the least guilty of being insensitive and stupid.

Not surprisingly, Mary was uninterested in seeing much more of me after that night. From mutual friends, I gradually learned Mary had been very much in love with me. I was almost completely unaware of her love, or perhaps it is more correct to say the depth of her love was something I had been unwilling to acknowledge. Mary herself told me several years later that when I had left for Chicago she was so madly in love with me she would have gladly dropped out of Ohio State and gone with me. I think she always hoped I'd change my mind at the last minute and ask her to come. She apparently cried long and hard when I actually left without taking her along.

As a result of insights about my relationships with women I got in therapy (though the major issue of my "triple strike" situation with women had yet to become clear) I realized I had made a serious mistake in leaving Mary, especially in the way I had, and I compounded the mistake by my behavior at Thanksgiving. At Easter, while I was still in therapy, I went back to Columbus to see Mary in an attempt to win her back. Surprisingly she agreed to see me. I explained myself as best I could, and apologized for leaving her the way I did, and for forcing myself on her at Thanksgiving. I asked her to give me another chance. She told me she was no longer interested in me, and she was still very seriously dating the same fellow she had met after I went to Chicago.

Her rejection of my attempt to win her back had a very unexpected effect on me. After she left the mutual friend's apartment where we had our meeting, I threw myself on his bed and cried. I cried uncontrollably for perhaps two hours. I sobbed. I held myself. I rocked back and forth. At first I feared I was going to die or to disappear, and then I wanted to do so. The more I cried the worse I felt, until I didn't even know why I was crying, or who I was crying for. I got scared. I felt empty. I wondered whether I was going crazy. I cried through all of the feelings and the wondering, and then cried some more, until I was exhausted.

Back in Chicago, in my next therapy session with Mrs. Spaulding I told her what had happened, and about how surprised and frightened I was by the intensity of my crying. We decided I was crying for all I felt I had lost in my life, and talked a little bit about doing a search for part of what I had lost: my birth family. The talk, however, did not lead to any meaningful search activity. I asked my parents to tell me about my adoption again, but they told me only about how I entered the Henderson family. I did not yet have the self-confidence, or the need, to inquire further about how I had come to leave my birth family.

Yet another important development occurred during this, my first therapy. I had gone to Chicago with the rather conscious idea I was going to, while in the Playboy city, make up for the lost activity during my years of virginity (during which I was "saving myself" for marriage to Nancy), by playing the Casanova role. Unfortunately, the hard reality was that I was hardly God's Gift to Women. I wasn't even sure I was a greeting card! For about the first six months of my Chicago year I spent virtually every Friday and Saturday night, and most Wednesday nights, relentlessly "hunting" for women at what was then already being called the "meat market": singles bars in the area around Rush and Division Streets. On the vast majority of these nights, I would drink too much, get shot down by the women I attempted to pick up, spend all of my money, and then drive home late, drunk, and still alone. I'd wake up the next morning feeling terrible physically, and terrible emotionally. Yet, curiously, I would immediately make plans for my next hunting expedition, which I was always sure would be more successful.

Perhaps once every other month or so, the "hunt" would be "successful," and I would go home with a woman, or take her back to my apartment. Frequently the outcome of a "success" was in some ways worse than the more common alternative of going home alone. I would be too drunk to remember the woman's name, or too drunk to perform, or the woman would be proof of the saying "everyone is interesting at bar-closing time." (Of course, having said this, I have to acknowledge I was likely proof of the same maxim to *her*.) Even under the best of outcomes, on the perhaps three occasions over six months when I was still sober enough to remember the woman's name and to perform acceptably, the quality of the sexual activity still paled in comparison to what I had experienced with Mary.

With Mary our lovemaking had been long and passionate, and I took great pride in my ability to bring her to multiple and intense orgasms, and to have them myself. We typically enjoyed a long period of foreplay, and an equally long afterglow. However, after the success-ful conclusion of a "Chicago hunt," whatever sex might occur with the woman I picked up was often mechanical, quick, and emotionally (and often physically) unrewarding. And then there was the problem of getting her out of my apartment, or getting myself out of hers, after the event was over. The post-sex escape was best performed that night before going to sleep because the next morning the problems were even worse, when I couldn't blame not remembering her name on still being drunk, and we had to deal with each other sober. Adding in the effects of sobering up, whether that night or the next morning, I am surprised I considered a hunt that resulted in sex with a woman to be a "success" at all! However, I believe for many men of my age, and especially at that time in the early 1970s, our upbringing and the culture were such that sexual success was a large part of how we defined ourselves as men. This feeling of manhood we got after a successful hunt was probably what kept the hunt alive.

After perhaps six months of nearly compulsive activity, I gradually began to get tired of the hunt, and I brought my feelings about the hunt into therapy, where we identified many problems. These included the drunken driving that always seemed to happen during each of these evenings, the money I was spending, the assault to my self-concept of getting repeatedly turned down by the women I tried to pick up, the rather bad quality of sex when the hunt did succeed, and the bad feelings I had the next morning no matter how the hunt ended, to say nothing of the risks of pregnancy and disease. In an attempt to address these problems, I made a quite conscious decision, one I think had short-term positive effects, but, unfortunately, also had significant, and negative, long-term effects. I decided instead of going on the hunt I would go to one of Chicago's many adult bookstores, buy a porn magazine, come home, and "take care of myself" by masturbating.

If I stopped the hunt and started the new approach, I thought the result would be safer, cheaper, and less of an insult to my ego than the hunt. Sexual satisfaction would be guaranteed, and, for that matter, the sex would be better too. After all, no-one knew what I liked better than me! The new program was, in a sense, a success. I did much less drunken driving, felt much better about myself, and had more money to spend. I also then had the time to go to folk music clubs and listen to the music as many as three or four nights a week, which I discovered I much preferred to spending my time in the hunt.

I believe the history and causes of this decision to, in a sense, replace real women with paper ones are important, and so a look at my history may help explain the decision. Masturbating was certainly nothing new to me, since I can't remember a time in my life when I didn't do it. I had also been buying adult magazines ever since I went away to college, where my nickname, "Dirty Doug," did not refer only to the messy state of my room. I was the porn lending librarian for the fraternity house. What was new, what changed in Chicago, was how I felt about masturbation.

Probably largely as a result of my religious upbringing in the 1950s, I had always felt guilty about my frequent participation in "the secret vice." I "knew" (because the church had told me, and of course I believed it) masturbation was wrong, even "sinful," but that knowledge did not stop me. I just masturbated, and then felt guilty. There's a verse in the Bible (1 Corinthians 13, verse 11) that says "When I was a child, I spoke like a child, I thought like a child, I reasoned like a child; when I became a man, I gave up childish ways." I think in the translation of the Bible the church of my youth used there was something about behaving like a child. That phrase was almost certainly *not* intended to differentiate masturbation from intercourse, but regardless of the Biblical intent, that verse pretty well expresses how I had come to feel about these two activities: I thought masturbation, though wrong, was for children, and intercourse was for adults. Throughout my childhood and adolescence, I had always thought "once I lost my virginity I would never need to masturbate again." Of course, I also "knew" I would not be married until I was a man, and I "knew" I would not have intercourse until my marriage night. Masturbation, the childish activity, was meant to be replaced by the adult activity of intercourse, which was, of course, only acceptable within the context of marriage. This was quite the corner to be painted into!

During my third year of graduate school, while I was still recovering from the trauma of the end of my relationship with Nancy, I decided my values had changed, and I no longer needed to "save myself for marriage." As I have described, I met, and ultimately lost my virginity with, Mary. Much to my surprise, however, once I was having regular sexual intercourse with her, I still had the desire to masturbate. And worse, I still felt guilty. Because I believed masturbation was a childish behavior and "second best" to intercourse, I felt more guilty after I masturbated than I felt after having intercourse with Mary! My guilt was probably also related to the fact I was hiding the masturbation from her.

After some thought (or perhaps rationalization?), about why I continued to want to masturbate, I had decided I just had a higher sex drive than Mary. Yet I also had wondered whether the masturbation somehow filled a different need within me than intercourse did. Though the frequency of my masturbation went down once I started having intercourse with Mary, I continued to masturbate and to feel guilty, both while I lived with Mary the summer before I left for Chicago, and after I went to Chicago and began the hunt in earnest. Once in Chicago, I continued to use masturbation after a failed hunt but saw it as a childish, and second-best, thing to be forced to do. My decision to replace the hunt with masturbation occurred in large part after I came, through my therapy, to view masturbation without most of the guilt with which I had long associated the practice.

Once we began dealing with my feelings about my adoption in my therapy, I realized I still felt like a child on the inside, and outside I was still treated by society as an "adopted child." I told Mrs. Spaulding I did not feel like a man. She observed that at nearly 25 years of age I certainly *was* a man, and she asked me if there was ever a time when I felt like one. After some thought, I realized the only time I really felt powerful and "manly" was when I was thrusting my penis into a woman during intercourse. As we discussed the issue further, I realized part of the reason for my repetitive, and self-destructive pursuit of the hunt was the desire to find a woman who, if I were to be lucky enough to have sex with her, would enable me to feel, for a few exhilarating moments, like a man. Thus, two of the goals of my therapy became: 1) to allow me to find other, hopefully more healthy and less risky, ways of sensing my masculinity, my power, and my adulthood; and 2) to allow me to remove the guilt I had learned to associate with masturbation as a child.

Related to the term "adopted child," many years later as I wrote this book, I recalled the issue of seeing myself as an adult was to arise again in the late 1980s, after I had become an adoption search activist. I became incensed that a proposed change to the Wisconsin law about adoption search referred to adoptees, who had to be *over the age of 21* in order to use the Wisconsin Adoption Search Program, as "adopted children." I made a point of attending a legislative hearing to object to what I considered the offensive language of the bill, as well as to the entire change in the law that was being proposed. In my testimony I asked the committee members to look around the room to see whether there were any children in the room. There being none, I then stated the proposed bill defined me as one, and added emphatically "I am no longer an adopted child, I am an adult adoptee!" The law change was eventually passed (although I, and many triad members, still objected to parts of it), but in both the final bill and the new law that resulted, the term "adopted child" was changed to "adult adoptee." I have a letter from the chairperson of that committee telling me the language change was solely the result of my "compelling testimony." At 43 years of age, I had finally been granted adult status by no less than a Wisconsin State Senator!

Meanwhile back in Chicago, although the therapeutic goals of interrupting my compulsive pursuit of the hunt with the attendant dangers and costs, and of removing or at least reducing my guilt about masturbation, were probably desirable, they did have a serious side-effect, one about which I would like to think Mrs. Spaulding was not aware. Replacing the hunt at least in large part with less guilt-ridden and safer masturbation took me a step away from seeking my gratification with real women, and pushed me toward seeking gratification with fantasy women. This is one of the generally understood problems with pornography. Despite that problem, perhaps, for an individual who did not already have my "three-strike" history with women, replacing the hunt with masturbation might well have been an overall positive goal, or at least a less undesirable one.

However, for me, giving up the hunt served to strengthen my still-largely unconscious belief women could not be trusted. My therapy in Chicago had the effect of reinforcing my feeling that I could take better care of my own sexual needs alone than I could in any relationship with a real live woman. While the ending of the compulsive hunt and the reduction of guilt over masturbation might have been two steps forward, the consequent backing away from depending on real women to meet my needs was one giant step back, the full implications of which would take me many years to realize.

CHAPTER 21

Marriage: Not Happily Ever After

With my internship over I returned to Columbus and began my fifth and final (dissertation) year at Ohio State in September 1972. At the official get-together at the beginning of the year I checked out the new group of graduate students, and my eye fell on two of them: Margaret and Marjorie. Both of them had very long hair I liked, and one (Marjorie) was tall and slender, the other (Margaret) was shorter and more amply built. At the student gathering I was asked, as one of three or four advanced students who had just returned from their internships, to give a brief presentation on my experience, and so I figured both women would already know who I was, and a little bit about me.

Over the next couple of weeks, I made a point of running into and chatting with both of them. I found that though both were equally interesting to talk to, Marjorie was more physically appealing to me than Margaret, so I asked Marjorie for a date. We went out often during September, October and November, and seemed to have a lot in common, especially loving the outdoors and camping. But, although I thought we were getting along well, and although we had slept together in my tent while camping, and although she would kiss me passionately, Marjorie would go stiff and begin to shake and cry as soon as I attempted any more intimate physical contact. I suspected she had probably had some very traumatic sexual experience, and I tried to be understanding, asking her if she didn't want to talk to me about what was so obviously bothering her. She repeatedly said nothing was wrong and she didn't want to talk about it. After a while I decided I wasn't interested in continuing to date a woman with such problems, especially if she didn't want to even talk about them, and so I set my sights on Margaret. Upon reviewing parts of previous chapters, and the beginning of this chapter in the final book editing process I was struck once again by how shallow I am, or at least was at that time, in judging women by their appearance. It almost sounds like was still in the "hunt."

Margaret and I first really talked in depth at a Christmas party for graduate students in the Developmental Psychology Area. Our Clinical Child Psychology program was located in the Developmental Area, and Margaret and I had the same academic advisor. Perhaps prophetically I was quite drunk at the Christmas party, so drunk that the next day I couldn't remember her last name or phone number, which she had given me. The next day I had to call the party host (a friend who it turned out had also just asked Margaret for a date!) to get her last name and number again. We began to date steadily, and, as our relationship developed into a physical one, I discovered I was not as strongly attracted to Margaret as I had been to Marjorie. This was another early warning of future problems in our relationship. Eventually I realized that, while the closer my relationship became with Mary (with whom I had lost my virginity), the better our sexual interaction was, with Margaret, even though our relationship was developing, I continued to get more satisfaction from my masturbatory activities than I got from our lovemaking.

Though the situation did puzzle me, I failed to fully appreciate what should have been the difference between "making love" within the context of a developing emotional relationship with Margaret, and the basically empty and mechanical "one-time sex" I used to have with my "prize" after a successful Chicago hunt. While masturbation might have been better for me in many ways than the hunt (followed on occasion by mechanical sex with a woman I hardly knew), lovemaking with a partner I knew well should have been better than it was. Unfortunately, the lack of improvement over time in our sex life did not deter me from continuing to date Margaret. Perhaps hope sprung eternal, or perhaps I was just afraid to face the end of yet another relationship.

We became "serious" rapidly, assisted by several occasions on which one of us would pick up the phone to call the other one, find no dial tone, tentatively say "hello?" and find the other one already on the line. We had called each other at the exact same time! We chose to interpret these events as a sign we were *really* in love and "on the same wave-length." Years later, in marital therapy we would both come to realize the common wavelengths we really had were: we were both lonely; we were both fearful of remaining alone; we both wanted to have a relationship that would lead to a marriage; and that marriage would save us from our loneliness.

I suppose many marriages begin for worse reasons, but by February (just two months after we started dating) I was telling friends I intended to marry Margaret. She was rather surprised and upset I told others about my plans before I told her. She heard about my plans from them before she heard about them in a proposal from me, let alone even in a discussion about our future! Nonetheless, we eventually set the date for the following September. We were to be married just a year after we had first laid eyes on each other, and barely more than nine months after our first date.

Even the road to the altar was not without warning bumps. Late in the spring I came to fear the marriage was a mistake, though I couldn't really say exactly why. After spending an evening thinking about what to do, I went to Margaret's room in the graduate dorm in tears and told her I could not marry her. She managed to talk me out of my fears by telling me I was only having normal premarital jitters, and besides, "we have already booked the hall, the music, and told the monsignor." There were too many plans made by then to back out of the marriage. So, we went ahead with the plans.

Then in the week before the service I again balked. I was presented by Margaret's local Parish Monsignor with a document I was expected to sign in which I literally swore an oath with my hand on the Bible attesting to several things I knew were not true, and promising to do things I knew we had no intention of doing, for example that we would not use artificial methods of birth control. Of course, the Church assumed we were not already having intercourse, and so no questions were even asked about prior or current behaviors! I became especially uncomfortable when I realized only I, as a non-Catholic, was being asked to sign such a document. The Church, in its wisdom, assumed Margaret, already being a Catholic, would naturally be following the expectations contained in the document, and so she was never even asked the questions, let alone forced to attest to them under oath. This problem too was resolved, with me agreeing to sign the document after her father and a cousin of Margaret's, who was the priest who would be conducting our marriage, presented me with a series of rationalizations about the document's contents. On September 15, 1973, just two weeks after I received my Ph.D., Margaret and I were married. In retrospect, I realize even during our first year of marriage, though at times things were generally quite pleasant, there were continued indications of some fairly major problems.

The Viet Nam war had ended during the latter part of my five-year deferment from entering active duty in the Army. The deferment, which allowed me to complete my Ph.D., was given because, at the time of my graduation from St. Lawrence in 1968, I had been commissioned through the Reserve Officer Training Corps Program as a Second Lieutenant in the Army Medical Service Corps. Upon receipt of my Ph.D., the Army intended to bring me in for my two years of obligated service as a doctoral-level psychologist, at which time I would also be promoted to the rank of Captain. However, by the time I got my Ph.D. in August 1973, the war had ended, and my services were no longer needed. I was given the option to spend only three months on Active Duty for Training at the Army Medical College at Fort Sam Houston in San Antonio, Texas, and I took the three-month option. Margaret took the fall quarter off of school, and after our wedding we had six weeks free until I had to report for duty in San Antonio.

We took about five weeks to travel for our honeymoon, camping our way west from Columbus through Yellowstone, south to the Grand Canyon, then back south-east to San Antonio. On many of those evenings I chose to sit and drink alone by the campfire in front of our tent rather than to go into the tent, where I knew my wife was waiting for me to make love to her. Often, I sat there for so long that by the time I crawled, drunk, into the tent she was asleep, or perhaps pretending to be. Our marriage did not have an encouraging beginning.

The largest problem we had that first year, and probably the most serious of our entire relationship, happened less than four months after our marriage, and again involved a problem made worse by my drinking. We had an apartment a mile or so from the base where Margaret stayed with me until early January 1974, when she returned to Columbus to start the winter quarter. My tour of duty was not over until mid-February, and I was to drive to Columbus when I completed my 3 months duty.

The week after Margaret left, I went to Nueva Laredo, Mexico, with a group of five fellow students at the College. All five of them were 21-or 22-year-old new second lieutenants, fresh out of their college ROTC programs and all were single. Because of my graduate school deferment, at 26, I was the oldest member of the group. And of course I was married. We stopped in Laredo, on the Texas side of the border, and got good and drunk, then left the car we had driven there, and took a taxi across the border to find some "wimmin." The taxi driver knew exactly what we wanted, and where to find them (surprise, surprise!), and took us to a one-story adobe bar located within a dusty walled compound off of a back street. Behind the bar we could see a row of small huts. There were chickens scratching in the yard outside, and several ragged young children playing ball. The setting could not have been more classic had it been part of a movie scene.

We entered the bar full of piss and vinegar, increased (for the others at least), by just having spent two months in an all-male residence, and nearly an all-male environment. Our short military haircuts revealed our identity despite our civilian clothes. There was a group of what appeared to be the very kind of "wimmin" we were seeking, sitting around a rear table. Since our Mexican adventure was to be just a day trip, our arrival at the bar was at about two in the afternoon, and there was not much business for them. In fact, we were the only customers in the place, and there were probably two or three women for every one of us. We ordered another round of drinks, and I drank mine quickly as we took increasingly less furtive looks at them. They seemed to come in all ages, shapes and sizes, but most of them certainly were older and less attractive than the women about whom I suspect many of us had fantasized.

Suddenly the group came to our table. Until then I really had intended to only look, and not to touch. In hindsight I was foolish to have even gone on the trip with these fellows, let alone to have accompanied them to this place in Mexico, and, of course (cue up the recording), I was drunk. The other guys sort of looked up to me as the oldest, or so I fancied, and I wanted to be a part of our group. By the time the sorting-out process was over, each of us had a woman, and sometimes two, seated either in his lap or on a nearby chair. The youngest, and to my mind most attractive of all of them, had come directly to me and had immediately begun rubbing my penis through my pants. Shortly she was sitting in my lap, rubbing herself shamelessly against me. All of my buddies' eyes were on me, and between the effects of an afternoon of beer and the intimate massage I was getting I lost whatever reluctance to participate I might have had left. Shortly I suggested we should go someplace more private, which we did. There were many expressions of what I thought was admiration from my friends, as we were the first in the group to get up to leave. In retrospect I suspect they were not expressions of admiration, but of surprise, or perhaps something worse.

I am not proud of having visited a prostitute within a mere four months of my marriage. This event was one of those I considered omitting from this book altogether, but it is too important to ignore. Violating my marriage vows, especially in the manner I did, was something I would not have thought in advance I would, or could do, and was something I certainly had not planned to do. In the drunken and aroused state I was in, however, I found it easy to rationalize I was "only masturbating with a woman's body rather than with my hand." I further told myself that since I had "no emotional connection with her" having intercourse with her was okay. While being drunk is not an excuse for unacceptable behavior, either legally or morally, I had by then already amassed a long history of doing things while I was drunk which I would never have done when sober. Most frequently these behaviors had centered around driving, often over 100 mph, when I was "too drunk to walk, so I'll drive." There had also been numerous sexual activities in the same category. Unfortunately, I would need another four years to develop enough awareness of just how bad alcohol was for me to cause me to stop drinking permanently. Meanwhile, my guilt about my behavior in Mexico, which began as I sobered up that night on the way back to San Antonio and only got worse with time, was intense.

In the two or so weeks remaining before I was to return to Columbus, I obtained a prescription for an antibiotic from a psychiatrist on the base who I knew from my internship in Chicago, completing the course of treatment on the drive north. In 1974, AIDS was unheard-of, and the public, and my own, awareness of herpes was dim, and so I believed the antibiotics could relatively easily prevent any medical complications of my behavior. The psychological complications were harder to deal with. I remained guilt-ridden and ashamed. Against the advice of the same psychiatrist friend who prescribed me the antibiotic, I decided to confess my sinful deed to Margaret when I got back to Columbus.

The confession was perhaps an even worse mistake than going to Mexico in the first place. The news seemed to absolutely destroy her. It certainly destroyed her faith in me. It may well have destroyed any chance of a future for our marriage. Years later during one of the many courses of marital therapy we entered into, Margaret would accuse me of telling her about the event for exactly the purpose of destroying our marriage. At any rate, her immediate reaction to the disclosure was a pain so great and so deep I made myself the promise I would never do anything to cause such pain to any human being ever again.

The promise not to ever be unfaithful to Margaret again which I had made to myself was one that I would be successful in keeping, but probably only my ultimate sobriety (not begun until 1978) allowed me to do so. Unfortunately, the mental tricks I used to help me keep the promise led to further destruction of my marriage. I was by then a university faculty member, and was in daily contact with many female students. There were a very small number of them who acted as if they were interested in a relationship with me, or so I thought. I knew even though I was aware of the existence of liaisons between faculty and students, if I were to take these women up on their imagined availability, I would risk losing both my job and my marriage. I remained faithful to Margaret. However, I did not fully take on the responsibility for my decision myself. Instead, I "blamed" Margaret for my lack of ability to have the affairs I fantasized were available. I made her the "bad guy" by saying to myself "if she weren't so sensitive I could be running around" rather than taking responsibility for my actions myself, and saying "I think adultery is wrong and I won't commit it." Unfortunately, in that first year of our marriage the realization of what I was doing mentally, and of the serious effect my decision and my failure to take responsibility for that decision would have on our relationship, was still several years down the road.

There certainly was another warning sign of marital problems on my part when, on the morning of our first anniversary, Margaret bound out of bed, ran into the living room and came back with a big smile and an anniversary present and card for me. I realized with horror I didn't have anything for her! I had remembered all week that September 15 (that day) was our anniversary, but somehow, I had thought I'd get Margaret a present later that day and I'd give it to her at an anniversary dinner that evening. I died a thousand deaths as I lay in that bed, trying to think of a way out of the situation. I was unable to find one, other than to tell her the truth, which I'm not at all sure she believed. For her, regardless of whether I had totally forgotten our anniversary or had just planned badly, the emotional reality of the situation was that I did not have an anniversary present for her. We were both left with the uncomfortable message that, like the classic boorish husband from a thousand bad jokes, I had "forgotten" our first anniversary.

Over the years Margaret and I were to spend a lot of time in marital therapy with a variety of types of therapists, both individually and together. I think we probably spent at least five, if not six, of our ten or so years of marriage in one or another form of therapy. Margaret's primary complaints about me had to do with the lack of intimacy and emotion in my relationship with her, my low level of interest in sex with her and contrasting high level of interest in what she derisively called my "plastic ladies." She also had problems with my overall negative attitude, my controlling nature, and my assumptions I was always correct, and I knew the best way to do everything (which was, of course, my way). I am sure, especially in retrospect, many of her criticisms were well justified, and I spent a lot of time in therapy, both during and after our marriage, attempting to address these issues in myself. However, I also believe she went overboard in her interpretation of much of my behavior. Our marriage, of two psychologists, was probably at a high risk of ending up with both of us interpreting the supposed deeper meaning behind each other's every sneeze and hiccup. By the end of our marriage, it seemed to me Margaret would automatically put the worst possible motivation on virtually everything I said or did. It is entirely possible that I did the same thing to her.

Because we already knew and/or worked professionally with all of the marital therapists in Stevens Point, we drove 35 miles north to Wausau to see a therapist there, which more or less put a bandage on the relationship, and we continued on for a while. Eventually we entered marital therapy again, seeing David and Joy Rice, a husband-and-wife team of Ph.D. psychologists in Madison, who were a few years older, and presumably wiser, than we were. They had recently written a book together about therapy with "dual-profession couples." David taught at the university (as I did) and Joy had a private practice in the community (as did Margaret). Visits to them were strangely like going to see ourselves! But it was effective. For a while Margaret and Joy worked individually and David and I did also, then we came back into joint therapy. Trust, intimacy, and the model we each had of marriage from our parents, were the issues on which we worked.

You may recall that in May 1981, I had testicular cancer surgery and spent the summer in chemotherapy. As you have read earlier, Margaret's and my relationship was actually improved for a short time during my treatment. We invited my parents to come for a visit at the end of my chemotherapy and again a few months later when I had physically recovered. It was during that second visit Mom told me about Dad having my birth mother's name, which started me thinking again about my search. Discovering my parents still had secrets from me had a major effect on my marriage. The issues of trust, honesty, and intimacy all came to the fore yet again for me. I believe it was no coincidence Margaret and I separated in January 1983, just six months after my mother's revelation. I remember a therapy session when Margaret looked at me with tears in her eyes, saying "Doug, look at me, I'm Margaret. I'm not your birth mother who gave you up, I'm not your adoptive mother who didn't tell you things, and I'm not Nancy, who left you and didn't tell you. Please stop punishing me for what those women did to you." I realized she had spoken an uncomfortable truth, but I was simply unable to process what she was saying. I heard her words, and knew what she meant, and that she spoke the truth, but I just couldn't respond to what she was saying. I don't remember whether I even cried myself at that time, but years later, in the process of editing this manuscript, I remained filled with sadness for both of us.

At the time of my separation from Margaret in early January 1983, I, like many others at the time of a separation or divorce, was feeling pretty worthless and undesirable. As is also common, Margaret and I had had little if any sex life together toward the end, and I actually wondered whether I could even function sexually with a woman anymore especially after testicular cancer. And, as is also often the case, I attempted to answer my insecurities with a fairly quick affair. Mine, in early spring, was with a twenty-year-old cast member in, of all things, the child sexual abuse prevention play, with which I was involved both as a consultant and as an actor. The affair answered any questions I had about my desirability and functioning, but I also learned that despite the fact 20-year-olds can have an attractive appearance, I really was not interested in a relationship with someone so much emotionally younger than I. Having proved to myself I could still function sexually, for about the next couple of months I withdrew into a shell with my plastic ladies, a shell into which no real women were invited.

I gradually came out of that shell, and started to become lonely. During the spring of 1984, I had noticed, and been attracted to, a woman at a faculty committee meeting on campus. I found her name, Martha, from the meeting attendance sheet, and made inquiries among faculty associates about her marital status. Wayne Lerand, a Psychology Department colleague (and adoptive father) whose office was next door to mine, told me he heard Martha had recently separated, and that she had two elementary-aged daughters. I struck up a conversation with her after the next committee meeting. We decided to go out on a date, and then on several more, and before long we were spending a lot of quality time together. Eventually Martha and I added a strong sexual dimension to our relationship. Although I did not fully realize the consequences of this at the time, I was perhaps the first post-separation relationship Martha had experienced, and especially since she had married at a young age without very much dating experience, when I met her, she was nowhere near ready to settle down with one man. We dated for a few months in the spring, during which time she met two other men, a dentist and an insurance salesman, whom, by summer, she also started dating.

She told me in mid-July what she had been doing, and that there had actually been a couple of times when she had been out with all three of us in the same day! She said she had always been someone's daughter, wife, or mother, and she had for some time wanted to be on her own and to sow some wild oats. Her daughters had left Stevens Point for the summer to be with their father, and being alone, without responsibilities for the first time in her adult life had given her the chance to live her fantasy. She then told me she had started to feel guilty about her behavior and wanted to stop. She described her situation as having "too many lovers, not enough friends," and asked me to stop being a lover, and to be a friend instead.

Martha's revelation nearly led me to a crisis similar to the one which I had when I discovered Nancy and Russell together. Although Martha and I had not ever pledged fidelity or monogamy to each other, I had assumed that we were not seeing other people. The saving grace with Martha, though, was that she said she wanted to remain friends with me, and she really meant what she said. We remained in contact throughout her adjustment period. Although we had a hard time changing the nature of our relationship, we were ultimately able to do so. We remained friends, and still corresponded, even after she later moved out of state to take another job. Martha has remarried (and not to either the dentist or the insurance salesman!) and now has a second family with her new husband.

For the following fall semester (1984) I again laid low, biding my time but getting increasingly lonely. I joined "The Five-Thirty Club" a singles professional group (read "singles" as "recently divorced") that met at a local bar on Friday evenings after work (guess at what time?). There I met and had a few largely unrewarding dates with several women who just seemed interested in complaining about their ex-husbands, and what rats men in general were. I hope that I was not doing the very same thing from the other side, but cannot guarantee that was the case.

In early December I contacted Sarah, a local newspaper reporter who I had known for several years. Two of the main parts of Sarah's beat were the environment and health, two areas in which I was both interested and active. Sarah had written an article about Margaret's employment as the first child psychologist at the county mental health clinic when we arrived in town in 1976. Sarah and I had met and developed a professional relationship while she covered, and I chaired, the Portage

County Health Resource Committee. We also saw each other at various meetings of organizations, such as the County Board of Health, and citizens committees formed to monitor aerial pesticide application in the county, and indoor tobacco smoking, particularly in restaurants. Within just the previous year, Sarah had also written an article about the opening of Margaret's private psychology practice. Sarah thought Margaret and I were happily married, and I had seen the newspaper announcement of Sarah's marriage a year or so previously, and thought she too was happily married.

I was starting the local chapter of Adoption Information and Direction, and asked Sarah whether she could write an article about the group to run shortly before our first public meeting. She agreed to interview me. As it happened, the interview was the day of the first significant snowfall of the winter. At the end of the interview Sarah mentioned she had to go home to shovel her sidewalk, and I laughingly said "Isn't that what husbands are for?" Sarah was somewhat taken aback, surprised I had heard she was married. I told her of having seen her wedding announcement some time ago, and she said the marriage had been a serious mistake, and had only lasted a month. I expressed my surprise and sorrow, and said that such a mistake must have been a very painful experience for her. Although I was sad for her, I was also excited because I had long found her both interesting and attractive. I realized that I now might have a chance to get to know her in a different way. I managed to work into the conversation the fact I too had been going through a difficult time because Margaret and I were separated. Sarah also expressed surprise and sorrow over my situation.

There was an awkward moment of silence, and I suggested that perhaps we might go out for lunch sometime. Sarah said that might be nice, and we agreed to meet two days later, on Monday. And with that, we were off to the emotional races. We saw a lot of each other in about a two-month time period. We spent Christmas together, attended musical performances (Sarah was a pianist), and talked often on the phone, even during the day at work. I found myself doodling her name on papers at the office, and our relationship was a little like being in "*LUV*" when I was a teenager: high on infatuation, hand-holding and hugs, low on much else physical. But I didn't care: I was excited to learn my heart could sing again over a woman, and I enjoyed the singing immensely. However, once the excitement of newness wore off, and before we had gotten physically involved, the relationship ended. I'm still not sure why.

The end was as unexpected as the beginning. At that time, The Butch Thompson Trio was the musical accompaniment for the highly successful Garrison Keillor radio show "A Prairie Home Companion." I had heard they were going to be performing as part of a university concert series in Stevens Point on Monday, February 17. Since Sarah and I both liked the radio show, I just assumed we would be going to see them together. We already had plans to go to an orchestra concert on campus during the last week in January, and late one afternoon I had gone to the Arts and Entertainment Box Office on campus to pick up those tickets. I had planned to pick up tickets for Butch Thompson at the same time, since I was already there, thinking I would ask Sarah to go to the concert with me the next time I saw her.

When I arrived at the box office I found Sarah in line, one person ahead of me. She seemed surprised, and somewhat uncomfortable, to see me. We talked for a couple of minutes, and I told her that I was picking up our orchestra tickets. I did not get, or take, a chance to ask her what she was doing there before she got to the ticket window, where she ordered two tickets for The Butch Thompson Trio. She knew I heard her order them, and yet she did not say anything in explanation. Sarah got her tickets, told me she would see me the next night, when we had planned to have dinner, and she hurried away. I bought only the tickets for the orchestra concert, and realized I really needed to ask her about her plans for the Butch Thompson tickets she had bought.

The next night at dinner Sarah asked me "Can you and I make a promise to each other?" Unsure of what was coming, and half-joking, I said "It depends on what the promise is. Why don't you tell me what you want us to promise?" She wanted us to promise "not to play any games with each other." I said "That certainly sounds reasonable to me. I think you know I don't like playing games." "Neither do I." was the reply. So, we promised not to play games with each other.

Later in the conversation Sarah asked "This is just a hypothetical question. What do you think you would do if I told you that I was feeling very serious about you?" I thought about it a while and said "I would try very hard not to run away as fast as I could." I talked a little bit about my reluctance to get seriously involved with anyone at that point, and added I would be very happy if she said she was serious about me, and that I might even have a hard time *not* wanting to run off and get married. I didn't bring up the Butch Thompson tickets, not quite knowing what to do about that situation.

At the orchestra concert, which was the following week, I asked Sarah about her plans for the Thompson concert, which was then about two weeks away. She said that she was going with a friend, and asked me whether I was going. I told her I didn't know, but I thought probably not. She wasn't clear about what kind of friend she was going with, and I didn't ask her for an explanation because if it was a male friend I didn't particularly want to know. The morning after the orchestra concert we were talking on the telephone, and Sarah told me that she didn't think we should see each other anymore. She wouldn't talk about why she felt that way, saying only that she thought it would "be best for both of us." I still don't know whether she was frightened off by my saying I was tempted to run off and marry her, or by my saying I would not run off with her and get married, but that was the last time we talked. As you will read very shortly, it happened that I did end up attending the Butch Thompson concert, and I saw Sarah there with a fellow.

CHAPTER 22

If Marriage Doesn't Work, Let's Try Another Way

The Monday after Sarah had broken up with me, I found myself next door in the office of Wayne Lerand again, talking with Wayne and Jan, a non-traditional student in her mid-thirties. I was telling them about Sarah, and complaining because I couldn't think of a way to find women to date. I was rather hoping Wayne would have another "dating suggestion" for me. He told me, "Doug, I could name a dozen women right now who would marry you sight unseen tomorrow because you have a good job, you're honest, you don't drink or smoke, and you wouldn't beat them." I suppose his statement, meant as a compliment, made me feel good, but I also knew the women he was speaking about were probably clients from his private counseling practice, so he couldn't *really* name them, even if I were interested in an arranged marriage with a stranger! Jan then volunteered she thought Susan Gingrasso (E1, E2) had gotten divorced recently.

Now, I was interested! Some five years earlier Wayne and I had been sitting in the university gymnasium at the Department's course registration table, and a very interesting woman walked by. After we both watched her walk away, I said to Wayne "*Who* was *that?*" He replied "Susan Gingrasso, but put your tongue back in your mouth, she's married." I told him, "So are we, but there's no law against looking, is there?" Remembering this incident, I thanked Jan for the information and decided to find a way to meet Susan. I investigated and learned Susan was the head of the dance program in our University Department of Theatre and Dance. It just so happened later that week I saw a photo in the local paper of Susan and two other dance faculty members rehearsing a piece for a performance to be held the coming weekend.

She still looked interesting, and so I decided to go to the performance and talk to her afterward.

I went to the Sunday night concert, located in a recently converted church a few blocks from my house, and was quite impressed with what I saw, meaning both Susan, and her work, as well as that of the other performers. I decided to talk to Susan that night, but in the crush of people after the concert I had a hard time getting across the room to talk to her. As I was pushing through the crowd, I found myself face-to-face with, Bob Rosen, a man I had not previously known, but who I learned that night was a percussionist, and a faculty member in our Music Department. He had provided some of the music that evening, including the accompaniment to Susan's choreography. I told him how much I had enjoyed the concert, and then volunteered the highly sensitive and intelligent comment that "I didn't know it was possible to make those kinds of unusual noises." OUCH! I had just called the man's music "unusual noises!" Not "syncopated rhythms," not "auditory effects," not even "interesting sounds," but "unusual noises!" I decided perhaps I was not at the top of my conversational game, and I should probably approach Susan at some better time. I beat a hasty retreat from the church and went home. "Unusual noises" indeed! Lucky I didn't meet Susan that evening and impress her with some equivalent gem such as "I thought your controlled twitching was fascinating."

The next morning (Monday, February 17th) I walked past Susan's office in the Fine Arts Building, which was located right on the route I used each morning from the YMCA to my office. I thought she might be in, but, if she wasn't, I could at least look at her schedule, which I knew would be posted on her office door, to find a time when she would be available. As I looked her schedule over, I realized if we had consciously intended to arrange our schedules to be more incompatible, we could not have done the job better. When she was in class, I was free, and when I was in class, she was free. In the whole week there was only one hour, from 11:00 a. m. to noon on Monday mornings, when we were both available at the same time, and at that time we both had office hours. At least I could telephone her then and we both might be free to talk.

An hour later, just after 11:00 a. m., I called. I told her my name, and said she didn't know me, but I had seen her dance at the concert the night before, and was interested in getting to know her better. She suggested we talk a bit right then, which was fine with me. A short while later we agreed to get together for lunch (always a safe first date), and we began to look for a day we were both free. I was correct about our schedules: it could not happen until Friday of that week. We made the date, and continued to talk. We talked for the entire hour, until one of us (I forget whom) had to leave. As the conversation was winding down, Susan said "Well, Doug, you took a chance by calling me this morning, so now I'll take a chance. What are you doing tonight?"

As it happened, that night I was free, having decided the previous week, for reasons explained above, not to attend the Butch Thompson concert. Susan told me she had two tickets (for herself and her son) for that night, and the three of us could go if her son sat on her lap. I was interested since we had seemed to hit it off quite well on the phone, and so we agreed to meet that night. The night was quite an experience!

I dressed up for the evening in my snow boots, my best polyester pants (only a little shiny) my only sport coat (polyester too) and my down ski parka (beneath which the sport coat extended about three inches). This *really was* dressing up for me because then I was in a blue-jeans-and-blue-work-shirt phase. Around this time, I wore nothing but jeans and a work shirt to work for an entire semester, until the very last week of classes when I had to meet with our College Dean about something. I decided I had best wear nice pants and a sport shirt to the Dean's office! A few months after our first date, Susan told me she took one look at my outfit that evening and almost wished she hadn't agreed to meet! Then, fortunately, she remembered the pleasant conversation we had that morning, and decided if we were to have a future she was going to have to "redecorate" me.

Once we were in the theater, Susan introduced me to her four-and-a-half-year-old son, Carch. I asked again what his name was, and he repeated it. I asked again, and he repeated it again, showing not the slightest indication he thought I was hard of hearing, or slow of thinking. I still couldn't figure out what name he had said, so for the rest of the evening I avoided speaking his name, and called him "little buddy" or "red," (he had flaming red hair), when I had to address him. Carch proved to be a handful in more ways than pronouncing his name. At first that evening he was sitting in her lap, then he was standing on the floor, then to my surprise sitting in my lap, then standing on the floor again, then standing on Susan's lap, and then walking about in the isle, and the concert hadn't even begun yet! Once the music started, he did calm down much more, but he was still one very squirmy, very charming, little boy.

Susan and I enjoyed each other's company, and I might have asked her whether we could get together the next evening but for the fact that I taught a class on Tuesday nights. The following Wednesday at around noon I got a call from Susan asking whether I could follow her out to the place she had her car repaired, which was out in the country south-east of town, and give her a ride back. I was both pleased that she thought to ask me, and surprised that she was comfortable enough to do so after only one "date." That afternoon about 4 p. m. I met her at her house, and she gave me general directions to our destination. As I followed her out of town, I became aware that we were driving the same route that I would normally take to go to my cabin. When we arrived at our destination, about 12 miles south-east of town, it turned out that her repair-man lived only a few miles from my cabin. Although the amount of snow was such that I could not have gotten back to the cabin even had I taken my four-wheel drive Jeep Cherokee, since we were so close, I decided I wanted to drive past the driveway just to check things out. I asked Susan whether she minded taking a little extra drive. Even though the cabin is a mile off of the paved road and not visible, driving past the driveway allowed me to tell Susan and Carch (along because he couldn't be home alone) about my cabin. In the process of this I learned that she liked the outdoors, and when she expressed an interest in seeing the cabin I invited her to come out with me, either on cross-country skis or by driving in, once the weather broke.

On the way back to town she expressed her appreciation for helping her, and asked whether I would be interested in coming to her house for dinner that evening as a more tangible expression of her thanks. I of course agreed, and had dinner at her place that evening (Wednesday) and again on Thursday. This was all before the lunch date we had originally set up for Friday! We also kept that date. We spent time together over that weekend, and I went to her house for dinner once or twice the next week. Susan's office was directly on the route I normally took from my morning swim at the YMCA to my office, and I started cutting through the building. Since she was in class during that time, I took to leaving a note under her office door each time I walked by.

The following weekend Susan was scheduled to attend a dance program at the University of Wisconsin Eau Claire, about 90 miles to our west. She and Carch left just after lunch to make the drive. At about 4:00 p. m., the Psychology Department secretary interrupted my regular Friday afternoon student research meeting to tell me she had a long-distance phone call for me in the department office. It was Susan, who had made it 60 miles, as far as Neillsville, before her Rabbit had broken down. According to the gas station where she had stopped, the car needed major specialized repairs which they were unable to complete, and Susan wondered whether I could bring my Cherokee and tow her car back to Stevens Point. I told her I would have to get a special towing bar, but that she should sit tight, and I would be there as soon as possible. By the time I located a towing bar and brought the three of them (Susan, Carch, and Rabbit) back to Stevens Point, the favor had become a major event. It was well after dark when we arrived back in Stevens Point. I jokingly told Susan that it would take a lot of dinners for her to pay back this favor. I think it was more than Susan's sense of obligation that explains why, from then on, for most of the rest of that semester, I had dinner several nights a week at her house!

We began to see a lot of each other, but soon discovered that we were so busy that if we weren't careful, one or the other of us would be busy virtually every night of the week. Also, since Susan was a single mother with a full-time job, she had to leave Carch at a babysitter during much of the day, as well as many evenings and weekends while she was at rehearsals, giving presentations, or attending performances. The cost of child care was a substantial part of her budget. She wanted to spend as much of her non-working time as possible with Carch, and to keep the child-care costs as low as possible also. Susan had developed the habit of taking him with her virtually everywhere she went, and whenever she possibly could. This included many of the times she and I saw each other, in addition to the dinners we had together at her house. In order to have some private time together we decided to set Thursday evenings aside for each other. Eventually I began to pay for the cost of the babysitter, and for the next ten years of our relationship Thursday nights were "our time."

At several points during that first spring we discussed the nature of our relationship, and our expectations for the future. A problem was immediately apparent. For a variety of reasons, not the least of which was the recency of my divorce, I was not ready to make any sort of commitment to Susan. I was especially not ready to become the instant step-father of an almost-five-year-old. Carch's attitude toward me, especially having had his mother to himself for the first years of his life (since his father was largely out of the picture), was not entirely positive. Although Carch and I got along rather well in general, sometimes in front of me, and more often just to Susan, he would say, with clear disfavor, "Is Doug staying for dinner *again*?" On Susan's part, while she also was too close to her own divorce to want to rush into another marriage, she knew, and clearly told me, that the did not want to remain a single mother forever. We decided to not only acknowledge the presence of this issue but also let it ride until we saw how the relationship progressed.

It progressed very well. Fairly early on in our relationship the issue of my staying overnight when I visited for dinner arose. We discovered that we agreed on two important issues: it would not be good for Carch to wake up in the night and be reluctant to go to his mother because her door was shut, nor would it be good for him to wonder in the morning who was in the house. We also agreed that we both slept better in our own beds, and so each evening I went back to my own house. The first time Susan and I ever slept overnight together was again due to problems she had with her increasingly untrustworthy old Rabbit. Susan, Carch, and I had gone to Madison for what was intended to be an evening at a UW Madison dance program. On the way home, just outside Madison, the engine warning light came on. The mechanic at the gas station we pulled into advised against trying to drive to Stevens Point at that time of night without at least identifying the problem, and so the three of us stayed overnight at a nearby motel.

One other issue came up that first spring. Before the snow was gone (which in Stevens Point is often April!) we began to joke about "the L-word," and how we "feared" we felt it for each other. Probably in the late spring we began to be able to comfortably say "I love you" out loud to each other. We settled into a comfortable routine, especially once we began our regular Thursday evening time together.

Sometime during our second or third year together Carch's attitude toward me changed for the better. He stopped asking whether I was coming to dinner "*again.*" and started asking, in a positive tone, "When is Doug coming to dinner?" The three of us spent several weekends together at my cabin, which Carch really seemed to enjoy. During perhaps our third year as a couple, I brought up the fact that Susan had once said she didn't want to be a single mother forever, and I asked her whether she still felt that way. Her response, that she now realized she was getting from our relationship what she would have wanted in a marriage, both relaxed me and made me feel very good. I too was quite conformable with the status quo. Eventually, Susan and Carch came to Buffalo to meet my family, and I went to Lancaster to meet hers. Although to others by then we were quite clearly together "as a couple," to ourselves we had only made a commitment to not date anyone else without informing each other.

Nearly three years into our relationship, in early January 1988, before going to Spain on a semester abroad which I had planned before meeting Susan, we had gotten out a globe and showed Carch, then about 7, where I would be living in the spring. He seemed to understand that I would be a long way away for a long time. On our last dinner together we again pointed out Madrid and Stevens Point on the globe, and told him I would be leaving the next morning. When I got to Madrid I called Susan to tell her we had arrived safely, and she told me that the evening I had left, Carch got home from school and asked "Is Doug coming to dinner tonight?" I had hardly been in Spain more than a couple of hours, and already I wanted to come home! We talked for about an hour each week while I was there, and after both my and her semester responsibilities ended, Susan came to meet me in Amsterdam, and we traveled together around Europe together for two weeks.

When we arrived back in Stevens Point at the end of June, we had about a week before Susan had to leave to spend the rest of the summer at a Laban Movement Analysis Certification course she was taking in Seattle, WA. Just after she left, I noticed that the house located immediately behind the 100-year-old duplex I owned and lived in, was for sale. At the time of my divorce, I had bought a home I could afford, which had been a duplex, using the income from the upper unit to pay most of the mortgage. The building was a "fixer-upper," located on a major street in Stevens Point, that had been on the market for a long time. I had spent enough time rehabilitating it that I was painfully aware of the saying that "the only thing that works in old house is the owner." For some time I had also been unhappy with living below my tenants and on a busy street, so I thought buying the house behind it would allow me to increase my income from the rental property and get me (literally) out from under my tenants, and off of the noisy street. As it happened, the house had four bedrooms, which might be more than enough for Susan, Carch, and I. I was talking to Susan weekly, and after looking at the house, I told her about it. Discussing buying the house led into a discussion of living together. After a week or so of thought, Susan decided that she was just too old fashioned to feel comfortable "living together without benefit of marriage," with marriage a prospect that neither of us was yet willing to take on. I bought the house anyway, and when Susan returned from Seattle we continued our comfortable but non-traditional relationship.

In the summer of 1989, we began what was to become a seven-year series of yearly week-long rafting/camping trips on the St. Croix River, part of the border between Wisconsin and Minnesota. Although the pre-trip preparation and post-trip clean-up were a lot of work, all three of us enjoyed the trips very much. We took a week's worth of food and floated from Osceola, WI, to an island in the river, where we camped for a week, venturing off the island to civilization only one time, about mid-week, when we crossed to the Wisconsin mainland and hiked a mile back upstream along a railroad track to Osceola, where we had a restaurant meal, a Dairy Queen, and walked back to camp. The next nearest civilization was about a three-hour float down the river to Stillwater, MN. On our second trip we were playing a home-made javelin game, throwing pointed sticks we had made like horseshoes at a circle in the sand. At one point we were standing next to one circle, throwing our sticks at the distant one, and Carch apparently decided to make an easy "bulls-eye" in the circle where we stood. He suddenly threw his stick into the sand right next to Susan's bare foot. I blew up at him, yelling about the fact that "If you had poked your mother's foot with that stick, how do you think we'd get to a doctor?" He cried, Susan was quiet, and I eventually calmed down.

Shortly thereafter, at perhaps the fourth meal we had cooked while there, Carch was poking the fire with a stick while I was attempting to cook on it. I had told him the previous three times he had poked the fire while I was cooking that it was okay to poke the fire anytime at all, *except* when I was cooking. I had explained each time that ashes and sand might get into the food, and that if the food got knocked into the fire we could not go to the store and get more food to replace it-: we'd have to eat it as it was. Yet here he was again, stirring up the fire right under the food, and right in front of me. I again blew up, and started to say "What are you, *stupid* or something?" Fortunately just before the word "stupid" came out of my mouth I heard what I was about to say, paused, and changed the phrase to "What are you . . . doing, poking the fire again?" In a stern voice I repeated my earlier lectures about dirt in the food and our inability to go to the store. The pause in my speech may have kept me from insulting Carch, but I knew, and Susan suspected, what I was about to say. Neither of us was very happy about the situation, and things were rather tense on our little island for the rest of the week. When we returned home we talked about the two incidents, and about the fact that Susan was unhappy with my heavy-handed attempts to discipline and control Carch, and my similar, though less obvious, attempts to control her. Susan announced that they were going to take a break from me, and that she thought I needed to get into therapy to find out why I was so angry. She said "I will not have my son treated like this." and announced that we would not see very much of each other for the rest of the summer. She added that if I had not changed by the time she returned from her sabbatical that fall, our relationship would be over. I sought out a therapist (again) and began to work on finding out what was happening with me.

Susan and Carch spent the immediate next fall semester (1990) in North Carolina. I continued in my therapy, and Susan and I continued to talk weekly on the phone. My therapy eventually uncovered attitudes about parenting that were related to both my adoption and to the way I had been raised. Although I knew I would never be the father of a child of my own, and that I would never replace his father, Carch was as close to having a son as I would get, and I was upset that I was having problems taking on a fatherly role. During my therapy I made some significant progress. I felt that I understood my hypercritical behavior relative to Carch, and that I would be able, with help, to not repeat the unacceptable behaviors again. Susan, who had kept pace with the progress of my therapy over the phone, agreed to give me an immediate warning sign if and when she heard me entering into the criticism/control mode again with either Carch or herself.

As had been the case in our earlier separations, while we were apart, we each had the right to date others, as long as there were no secrets or surprises. At the annual faculty coffee hour that marked the beginning of the school year I had noticed a woman to whom I was attracted, and found out that her name was Debbie, and that she was in the Art Department. Especially since the Art Department is located in Susan's College, and since Debbie's office was in the same building as Susan's, I told Susan I was thinking of trying to meet Debbie. The next week I went to a gallery opening, heard Debbie speak about her work as a landscape artist, and realized we had a common interest in camping and the outdoors, which made me even more interested in her. I told Susan that in our next call, jokingly calling it "the Debbie Report," and added I was thinking of trying to meet her in person. I spent several weeks thinking about the prospect, and each week in our phone call I'd say "Debbie Report: no activity." Eventually I realized, and told Susan, that even considering the difficulty of starting a new relationship, Debbie would have to be pretty special for me to want to leave Susan for her. I had therefore decided not to even try to meet her.

While they were in North Carolina Susan had put Carch in a private school, where he seemed to do better than he had in the public-school classes in Stevens Point. Carch had been unfortunate in having teachers for grades one, two and three that were generally considered to be problematic. He was having considerable trouble with school work, particularly reading and spelling, and I had expressed concern a couple of times along the way. A friend who is a special education teacher and knew Carch told us not to worry, and I decided to let things go.

On their return to Stevens Point, Susan decided to have Carch tested for the gifted and talented program. As a result of the testing we discovered that he was just below the minimum standards for the gifted and talented program. Much more importantly, we learned that he had a severe learning disability. In addition, he was diagnosed with attention deficit hyperactivity disorder, and put on medication. His fifth and sixth grade teachers were both men with excellent reputations, and both his school performance, and his overall behavior, improved significantly.

Carch had taken up Karate in first grade and had begun Boy Scouts. He advanced rapidly in both, becoming a Black Belt in Karate and a Star Scout by 1996. Susan and my relationship continued more or less on an even keel, but the problems over my role in managing Carch's behavior never completely went away. They were made more difficult by the fact that Susan and I were not married and did not live together, so I was not present all of the time to observe his behavior in context.

A couple of years earlier Susan and I had decided to apply to be the faculty leaders for our University's International Program Semester in London, and we were scheduled to be the leaders for the spring semester of 1997. In the spring of 1996, Carch, at the urging of his father, went off of his medication, creating another set of problems. His grades went down (from the Honor roll in 9th grade to Cs and Ds) and his behavior worsened to the point that Susan considered whether he should even come to London with us, or whether he should go to live with his father. We embarked upon a course of therapy in which Carch, Susan, and I in various combinations all saw the same therapist. One of the good things we learned was that Susan and I had a deep commitment to each other. One of the not-so-good things we learned was that for many years Susan's ex-husband had been actively criticizing my role with Carch, but not in front of, or with, Susan. By then the damage had been done. Susan eventually told me to remove myself completely from any disciplinary role with Carch, and I reluctantly had to agree that I was not his father, or his step-father, or anything else that gave me the right to play a parent role with him. Carch ultimately came to London with us, but it may have been more because of his father's inability to take care of him than anything else.

The experience Susan and I had in London was quite stressful. We were not able to just do our work and then have time to enjoy each other, Carch, and London. Instead, we spent much of the time on disciplinary matters with our 39 students, eight or ten of whom simply did not have the maturity to handle living in a foreign culture, even one as similar to ours as Great Britain. Carch, by then 16, lived in the building with the students, while Susan and I lived in faculty housing several blocks away. When we weren't worrying about the students, we worried about Carch, who, while having a great time, was, like several of our students, having trouble doing his studies. Rather than being a relaxing and enjoyable relationship-builder, the trip turned into what, at times, was a nightmare.

We returned from England at the end of May certainly no closer to each other for having lived together for the first time in our then-12-year long relationship, but rather with virtually all of the loving feelings we had for each other extinguished. We had been a good team in London, but that was all. We felt no hate for each other, but no spark either. We decided to break up in July, but after two weeks decided breaking up did not feel like the right thing to do. We spent considerable time after our return attempting to figure out where our relationship was going. We continued to see the therapist we had seen before the London experience, and learned how very well we are able to communicate, but were not really able to find the spark right away. I believed the ball was in my court, and for a while I had not been willing or able to decide what to do with it.

Over the first ten years or so we dated, but especially in the last three or four, Susan began to see more clearly there were problems with me about which she was not happy. She began to resent more and more what she saw as my overall negative attitude, my controlling nature, and my assumptions I was always correct, and I knew the best way to do everything (which was, of course, my way). She began to feel the lack of intimacy and feeling in my relationship with her, and my overall negative attitude, were problems of which she was becoming particularly weary. Unfortunately, as she began to express these criticisms, they sounded all too familiar to me, since they were largely the same as those voiced by Margaret toward the end of our marriage, some 15 years earlier.

One element of Margaret's criticisms of me that was missing from Susan's list was Margaret's complaint about my level of interest in my "plastic ladies." The complaint about my interest in pornography was missing from Susan's list not because I had changed, but rather because Susan had, from the beginning of our relationship, been much more tolerant of this side of me than Margaret had been, even though they both knew about that side of me from very early in the relationship. While Margaret made me feel like a terrible person because I was interested in pornography, Susan had all along been rather accepting of my interest, or at least she had not been openly disapproving. The other element in Margaret's list that was missing from Susan's complaints about me was my drinking. I had been sober for just about seven years when Susan and I met, and I am quite certain that my sobriety relieved a significant amount of pressure on our relationship.

Margaret took about seven or eight years of being married to me to develop her list of complaints. However, Susan took significantly longer, perhaps 11 or 12 years, to reach much the same place. Perhaps I should have taken heart from the fact that Susan took longer to grow weary of me than Margaret did, but taking heart was definitely not how I felt. Instead, I felt a great deal of sadness, and an equally strong level of hopelessness. I thought about all of the therapy I had been through, all of the effort and time I had spent in trying to change myself. I thought about the level of understanding which I believed I had developed about myself. I thought about my reunion experiences, with all of the good I believed they had done for me. All of these important and potentially life-changing things had happened since my relationship with Margaret ended, and I had hoped that through all of these experiences I had changed. As Susan began to voice very similar complaints about me, I realized with great discouragement, and despite what I wanted to think, I had apparently not changed all that much.

I had no doubt I was different at that time than I had been 15 or 20 years earlier. I realized my relationship with Susan, at its best, had been immensely better than my relationship ever was with Margaret, or with any other woman who had been a part of my life. I believed I had never been closer to a woman than I was to Susan. However, I also realized I had never really entered into what I would call a truly intimate and trusting relationship with another woman. I realized I had held back, run off, sabotaged, or otherwise insulated myself from virtually all intimate emotional contact. For all of these years I had been holding on to something, an idea or a feeling, that had destroyed my relationships with women. Several of these women I am sure had a genuine love for me, and might well have made excellent life partners for me. At least they seem to have done so for the other men whom they have all since married. Did I fear trusting myself entirely to a woman? If I were ever to give a woman this trust, and if the woman were ever to leave me, or otherwise to prove unworthy of that trust, I would . . . I would what? Would I be hurt again? Would I cease to exist? Die? Just what did I fear?

Writing this book has been very therapeutic for me. One of the clearest examples of the kind of things I am learning occurred in September 2024, late in the final revision process. You will recall, in Chapter 20, I described the feelings I had in 1972, as I cried during therapy in Chicago. I described the way I felt a few weeks earlier in Columbus, while crying over my loss of Mary, in these words: "*At first I feared I was going to die or to disappear, and then I wanted to do so.*" Then, in Chapter 25, you will learn I was trying to visualize my life without sex, in a 1998 therapy session, using the words "*I feared I would be empty, I could not exist without it, and that I might even, or might as well, die if I were to give sex up.*" Note the similarity in the italicized words. These two feeling states occurred over 25 years apart, and were about loss of different, but likely related, issues. The fear that I was going to die or disappear without something, and the desire to die if I don't have that thing, seems to me to be the essence of my problem both with women and with sex. I can't help but wonder whether this fear is an adoption issue.

While I am now not yet able to give a very clear name to the fear, I do realize fear is what I felt. In a conversation with friends in the early fall of 1997, I said "maybe all I need is a giant dose of courage" to make my relationship work with Susan. Hearing myself put my situation that way was a surprise. I believe I have been able to survive at least three significant challenges during my adult life, any of which might have killed me, and the beating of which required me to have great courage: my drinking, my testicular cancer, and my prostate cancer. Yet the challenge of opening myself to what should be the positive emotions of intimacy and trust had so far succeeded in beating me, or at least in frightening me off. If the cause of my fear was an adoption issue, the origin may have been so early in my life as to predate my possession of language. If so, I may never be able to give a name to the fear. I have come to believe my fear is somehow related to that terrible emptiness, that fear of disappearing, of non-existence I felt in Columbus when I cried myself to exhaustion after I could not convince Mary to come back to me. I also realize that I had not allowed myself to feel that way ever since. Perhaps my feelings about having "lost" my birth mother were intensified by my also having lost my first girlfriend Nancy, and then having lost Mary, the woman with whom I "became a man." Or with whom I thought I would.

This brings me to another unresolved adoption issue that I have learned about in the last few years: the experience of being an adopted male. I believe this issue is strongly related to my relationships with women, and so am introducing it here. At the American Adoption Congress conference in Las Vegas, in 1994, I attended a workshop entitled "The Male Adoptee: Intimacy and Commitment," led by John Patrick McIntosh, MA, an experiential educator and adoptee from Massachusetts. Patrick began the session with several minutes of experience-based exercises designed to break down barriers to communication. The workshop took on a life of its own, and I think it evolved well beyond the plans Patrick had for it, developing into a discussion among eight to ten male adoptees sitting in an inner circle. As we began talking about how it felt to be male and adopted, I realized that, 11 years after beginning my search and my adoption activism, this was the largest group of male adoptees of which I had ever been part. We were surrounded (some thought symbolically) by an outer circle made up of everyone else who had come to the session who was not a male adoptee. The outer circle consisted primarily of birth mothers, but included some female adoptees, spouses of male adoptees, and others interested in understanding male adoptees.

Those in the outer circle agreed not to talk, but to simply listen to the adopted men in the center, as we discussed our life experiences. We men discussed the difficulties of establishing and maintaining intimate relationships, discovering that with only one exception we all had been divorced at least once, and some of the group had several divorces. The one man who was still married to his original wife reported extreme stress in the marriage until "I got my act together," and added that the absence of a divorce was due to her strength, and not to any virtue of his. He believed that any other woman would have long since left him. There was a general sad agreement that we all had great difficulty trusting women, and developing intimacy with them. There also seemed to be an extraordinarily high amount of alcohol and other drug abuse in the group.

I have a hard time describing the feelings I had as a member of that circle. We seemed to all somehow "know" each other, as if we had been brothers in the same fraternity. Or even brothers in the same family. We expanded from the initially scheduled topics (intimacy and commitment) to discuss several additional issues, since for virtually all of us, the ability to converse at a deep level with a group of other adopted men was unique, and very meaningful. One of the unscheduled issues we covered was the difficulty of dealing with the hostility we experienced as directed at males in many adoption search and support groups. We generally agreed that this was due to a generalization of the hostility toward birth fathers. The difficulties of identifying with our widely condemned birth fathers, and the nature of what our birth fathers' (presumed) destructive behavior meant about us as their sons, now men ourselves, were also discussed in some detail. We all had consciously or unconsciously asked some variant of the question "Given the kind of man my birthfather was, what kind of man will I be?" Many of the men stated that they had always felt "left out" in the typically female-dominated search and support movement, and others said that they just felt left out everywhere.

Another unscheduled topic was the discovery that the vast majority of the men present engaged, or had at one time engaged, in what we called "high risk" behaviors. Represented in the group were men who had engaged in sky diving, extreme skiing, technical climbing, motorcycle racing, all-terrain-vehicle driving, wrestling down aggressive mental patients, general drunken driving and speeding, and high-risk business and professional situations. By that time I had already broken my collarbone tipping over my ATV, and was shooting professional fireworks shows. I fit right in! Our general conclusion was that these experiences gave all of us the feeling of being "fully alive." One member of the group suggested that he craved this feeling of "aliveness" because he felt that part of him had died when he was separated from his birth mother.

There was also general discussion of our frustration at trying to deal with our birth mothers, many of whom seemed to have what some sensed as an oppressive need to "understand" us, and to have us "understand" them. Many of the men reported a strong sense of ambivalence regarding their birth mothers. While we wanted to meet and get to know the woman who gave us life, many of us were also angry and/ or hurt at some level because of her having surrendered us, including even those men who reported good experiences within their adoptive families. We wondered whether our difficulty in dealing with women had anything to do with the ambivalence of our feelings toward our birth mothers. Many of the birth mothers there later reported that they had sensed the "anger" side of this ambivalence, and had never before understood it. Several reported that their birth sons had angrily denied that they even *were* angry.

The discussion was so meaningful and intense that we continued nearly an hour beyond the initially allotted two hours. As a participant in the workshop, I felt it was a peak experience, one which had a pivotal effect on my perception of myself, of other adopted men, and also of birth fathers. It was so important to me that I pushed for the inclusion of a similar workshop at the 1996 Baltimore AAC conference, which I ultimately co-led with adoptee psychologist Tom McGowan. With a substantially different group of men in Baltimore than in Las Vegas, many of the same feelings arose, and substantially the same discoveries were made. I understand that at the "Male Adoptee Issues" session at the 1997 conference in Dallas (which I missed because I was in London), similar discoveries about the difficulties of intimacy, the presence of dangerous hobbies, and of substance abuse were made.

Tom McGowan, perhaps the only male adoptee to have attended the first three of these workshops, suggested that the high-risk behavior may also be a form of "tempting fate" arising out of an awareness that our very existence had been on some level "a mistake," and that our existence could have been terminated by an abortion. The life-risking behavior then might be a way of asking "Do I really deserve to be alive?" or "Why am I alive?" Recent research on the abilities of the fetus and newborn infant to learn and remember, as well as theories in the area of attachment and loss, cause me to think again about the statement by one of the Las Vegas group members that he felt that part of him had died when he was separated from his birth mother. Is it possible that the separation from our birth mother might well be experienced by adoptees as in some very primitive way similar to a death? Do adopted men have difficulty developing intimacy and trust with women because, based on our severed relationships with our birth mothers, we somehow equate becoming dependent on a woman and then losing her, with death?

Of course, if separation from one's birth mother was experienced as equivalent to death, adopted women would have the same separation experiences and feelings as adopted men. However, the majority of adopted men will be trying to form an intimate, trusting life-and love-relationship with a woman as adults. Most female adoptees will be trying to form their life-and love-relationships with men. While the birth father is also generally lost to adoptees, the more intense connection is to the birth mother. Therefore, assuming there is some truth to this line of thought, it would be males whose adult love-and life-relationships suffer more than females as a result of the disruption of intimacy and trust with their birth mother. All of this information about the possible effects of adoption on male adoptees *feels* right to me. It is certainly consistent with the ways in which I have had difficulty relating to women. However, the psychologist in me forces me to point out that these are at present only individual observations and untested hypotheses. I hope that, if these ideas have some value, researchers will be moved to investigate them further.

PART FIVE

GETTING IT ALL TOGETHER?

CHAPTER 23

General Issues in Synchronicity

Two couples from out of town walk into an electronic repair store in the small southwestern New York village of Arcade (1992 population: 2,135). They have a video camera with a broken microphone, and ask whether they can get the microphone fixed. The clerk tells them the microphone is beyond repair, a replacement must be ordered, and delivery would take several days. They say they can't wait that long, and leave the store, their camcorder still broken.

You have read about this event already, and know the story didn't end this way. Shortly the group of four left the store with a functioning camcorder. Why did the story end with a repair and not with a disappointment? Perhaps in part because I shared what was happening in our lives with the store clerk. I told her Keith and I were birth brothers separated by adoption, we had just met for the first time, and this was why we so much wanted to get the microphone fixed right away. Another clerk overheard what we were talking about and offered a possible solution.

James Redfield, writing in *The Celestine Vision*, suggests that openness, the sharing of information, and the willingness to let people be a part of one's life, are some of the behaviors that lead people to experience synchronicities. One category of synchronicity is having the right thing happen at the right time, and certainly getting my microphone fixed was both. People who are very "private," who keep to themselves and don't share of themselves, may well be less likely to discover the experiences, traits, fears or other aspects of their life which they share with those around them, and which are the stuff of which synchronicity is made.

Soon you will read about my experience with a store owner who offers to sell me her own copy of a book if I am willing to pay the cost of a replacement book, which she would order and keep for herself. I left her store with the book I wanted because I shared with her more than just my desire for that particular yoga book. Long after I wrote about both the broken microphone and yoga book incidents, I realized that they were both very similar processes. In both cases, strangers went beyond what they might be expected to do because I shared what was happening in my life. I gave the people in both situations a chance to learn about me, and to perhaps discover that they and I had some common elements in our lives. Although in neither of these cases did the salesperson volunteer the nature of any common element, perhaps one existed, or perhaps my openness may have simply allowed the listeners to be a part of something exciting. However, even if there were few common elements in our lives, perhaps the door was simply opened to our joint humanity. Sharing the context changed their perception of an event that, absent my sharing, might have seemed routine, or even an interruption. Either way, my openness allowed the situation to move beyond the normal, the usual, and the expected. Sometimes we create our synchronicities as we experience them.

Other times the elements of the synchronicity seem to have been present for a very long time, or to have been events that happened long ago, and were simply waiting to be discovered. Shortly after we discovered the synchronicity that Keith and I shared the same middle name, I had shared our discovery with Wayne Lerand, a friend and colleague in the Psychology Department. Wayne and his wife, Judy, adopted two children, Christopher and Andrea, as infants. I had known them since they were in preschool. Both were adopted in the traditional closed process. When Chris and Andrea were adolescents, they both attended meetings of AID in Stevens Point, with their parents' approval, and both eventually decided to search for their birth families.

Andrea, the younger of the two, decided to search out her birth family first. By the time she made her search decision she had two children. She had named the older daughter Alexandra because she liked names that began with the letter A, as did her own. The younger she named Andrew because Andrew is the masculine version of her own name. Wayne had previously told me Andrea had applied to have her adoption agency search for her birth family on her behalf. (Wisconsin's adult adoptees are not granted access to their own adoption records to allow them to search on their own, and the right to have their agencies search for them was won in the early 1980s by the founders of AID.) Some months after telling me Andrea was searching, Wayne told me that Andrea had met her birth mother, and that their meeting had been very good for Andrea. I asked him if she had learned anything about her birth father.

Knowing about my birth brother and me sharing the same middle name, Wayne said "You're going to love this—her birth father's name is Andrew, and he has a son named Andrew!" Wayne said that he and Judy had no knowledge of Andrea's birth parents' names when they chose to name their daughter because it was a completely "closed" adoption. Some years later, when I was fact-checking this information, Andrea told me that both she and a birth sister (who she later met) shared the same middle name: Marie! Synchronicities in names, such as these, seem to have been just waiting to be discovered.

The awareness of the term "synchronicity" and of the role synchronicity has played in my life have been an increasingly significant part of my personal conscious experience since I began my search in 1985. However, in looking back over my entire life, I believe there have always been events which could be described as synchronicities. Often, they have involved significant, serious, and even life-altering events. On other occasions, though, there have been events that seemed to defy chance (as do synchronicities), and which also had some degree of meaningfulness to me in that some good came out of them, but which I do not believe had life-altering significance. Can synchronicity sometimes be be "merely" interesting or thought-provoking?

An example of a series of synchronistic events occurred at the AAC conference in Cleveland, in 1993. One afternoon I found myself standing at an extremely slow elevator in the conference hotel, waiting to go two floors up to get to the next conference session. I was debating whether I should wait for the elevator, or take a nearby set of stairs. For no particular conscious reason, other than the thoughts they might be faster and I needed the exercise, I chose to walk up the stairs. At the top of the first flight of stairs I ran into Kate Burke, the AAC President, who was on her way down those same stairs. Although I did not know Kate well, I had been thinking I should introduce myself and talk to her about getting the assistance of the AAC with the legislative situation in Wisconsin. We were trying to pass a bill to allow adult adoptees access to their original birth certificates, and we needed all of the help we could get. A powerful legislative leader, an adoptive father who was very threatened by the idea of reunion, had stated our bill would pass only over his dead body, and he seemed to be in excellent health. (He served in the State Legislature until 2020, and was still living, at the age of 97, as of 2025.)

Although I knew the next presentation would begin shortly, I found myself with a decision: should I talk or not talk to Kate at that particular time? Since she was alone and apparently available for a conversation, I chose to talk, and walked with her one flight back down the same stairs. On the way I asked her how I could go about getting the AAC to help to provide AID with someone of national stature to come to Wisconsin and give testimony regarding our pending legislation. She said AAC had some funding to support this kind of legislative work, and advised I talk to Ken Watson, a well-known social worker from Chicago, and an excellent spokesperson for access to records. I should tell Ken that Kate had authorized his trip if we could schedule one.

I thanked Kate for the suggestion, and walked back up the stairs, only to run into Ken himself at the top of the second flight of stairs, one flight above where I had just met Kate.

Had I not run into Kate when I did, even if Ken had been there already when I reached the top of the stairs, I would have had little reason to stop to talk to him then, since I was on my way to a program. Ken was autographing a copy of his most recent book, and involved in a spirited conversation to boot. I was again faced with a question: should I wait to talk to Ken right then, or should I go on to the next conference session, which by then had just begun, and try to find him later? I chose to talk, and I stood nearby, waiting for him to be free.

While I was waiting, up walked Ginny Whitehouse, one of the founders and the first state president of AID, Sue Anderson, leader of the Madison chapter and the AID legislation coordinator, and Dot, another member of the Madison chapter. While Ken was chatting with the person for whom he had signed the book, I had just enough time to tell Sue and Ginny that Kate had authorized Ken to come to Wisconsin to testify for our bill, and that we needed to tell him of the authorization and to make arrangements for him to visit when the time was right. We did this when the autographing was through. Hearing Kate had authorized his trip, Ken agreed to come, and he and Sue made arrangements for her to contact him as soon as she had a firm hearing date. The perfect set of people had come together at the right place at the right time with the right information to talk with Ken about Wisconsin legislation. This is an excellent example of synchronicity.

Even while the process I have just described was occurring I was aware of the synchronistic nature of the series of events, but as the process unfolded, I began to wonder for what purpose, if any, Dot was present. I must say I was wondering this only half seriously because I really did not expect every person present must necessarily be a part of a synchronicity. As Ken, Sue, Ginny and I finished our conversation, Grace Zaranti, the Midwest Regional AAC Director, walked by, and I found out "why Dot was there." Earlier in the conference I had spoken to Grace about a question Dot had asked me, and Grace had said she needed to talk directly with Dot. So, as a result of Dot waiting for Sue and Ginny while they talked with Ken and me, Dot and Grace were also in the right place at the right time. I introduced them to each other, and they had the conversation they needed to have.

What significance is there to these events, in which decisions were made by a number of people (in addition to those made by me) that allowed us to all be "in the right place at the right time?" I do not know. Perhaps the issues of legislation and of Dot's question were ones that were somehow "ready" to come to fruition, and "readiness," for lack of a better term, is what drove the series of events to occur. Such would be a synchronistic description of the process. Perhaps, however, there is no more profound or meaningful explanation for these events beyond the simple fact that there were a limited number of people with the same general interest in roughly the same place at the same time. Our meeting as we did would then have been no more than the predictable result of the convention environment.

Such encounters, some would say, are the value of having face-to-face conventions in the first place. However, to me, as a participant in the chain of events, I still "felt" like much more than simple random activity was occurring as the events were unfolding. I should also note the sense of "purpose" people often report in synchronicities. There was something meaningful accomplished by that particular chain of events: Ken agreed to come to Wisconsin, and Dot got at least a start on getting her question answered.

As time passes, I am becoming much more aware of other extremely improbable or curious events, yet for these events I can see no higher purpose. I even see little of emotional significance in them, other than a sense of amazement that they could have occurred at all. Carl Jung, who defined the term synchronicity, would say events are not synchronicities solely due to their seeming low probability of chance occurrence (or their "curiousness"). To be properly labeled as synchronicities Jung says these curious events also require a sense of emotional meaningfulness.

Two such "curious" events occurred within week during a vacation in the summer of 1996. I'll name the first of these "men with no necks." Frank Hermon (G1), a friend since elementary school, and I were visiting Judy McCann, a college friend, at her apartment in Hoboken, NJ. Frank and I were planning on visiting a club in lower Manhattan later on that Friday evening, and we decided to treat Judy to dinner as a "thank you" for her hospitality. We went to Arthur's Steak House, a well-known restaurant in the area. Upon being seated, I immediately noticed a couple of extremely muscular young men, perhaps in their mid-20s, sitting at the table next to us. I commented to Frank and Judy about the "men with no necks."

Shortly, an equally well-built Hoboken police officer came up to their table and greeted one of them with an exuberant bear hug. I also noticed the two diners were wearing black T-shirts with a logo of some sort on the front and the word "security" in white letters on the back, and one of them had a spider-web-shaped tattoo emanating from one elbow. I decided wherever they might work, I would, indeed, feel pretty secure with them around! At some point I noticed they had left, and that might well have been the last of my attention to them.

At least I didn't think about them again until early the next morning. Frank and I had checked out the return train schedule, and we left the club in time to be sure we had ample time to walk back to the station. On our way down 28th street, about half-way back to the train station, suddenly I recognized the two security guards from dinner! They were standing with another man in a similar T-shirt, in front of the building we were walking past. I couldn't believe my eyes, and told Frank we simply had to talk to them. He was dubious about taking any time out for unplanned stops, and more or less kept walking, though at a slower pace.

I couldn't resist following up on the reencounter, and so I went up to the men and told them we had been seated next to them at dinner earlier that night at Arthur's. The one with the spider web tattoo said laughingly as he held up his arm "this is pretty hard to forget," and I agreed. We all remarked on how unusual it was that we should see each other again. They said our meeting was especially lucky, since they were only out on the street because they were on their break. I asked them what kind of place they were guarding, and they said it was a private club, and invited us in for a look around. Though I was fascinated with both the chance meeting and the opportunity to see a "private club," I knew there was not time for anything more than the brief conversation we had just had, and so I said we'd take a rain check, and caught up with Frank. Later that morning as we drank our coffee on Judy's veranda overlooking the Hudson, she was amazed to hear Frank and I had happened to run into these men again, a reaction shared by everyone who has heard this story.

The next weekend, another similarly "rare" encounter occurred, that I will call the "tower apartments" experience. Judy and I were spending the day on the beach at Sandy Hook, New Jersey, which is about 45 road miles from Hoboken. Sandy Hook is frequented by people from all over the region. There are beautiful beaches, from which on a clear day one can see the entire classic New York skyline. Hulking concrete gun emplacements remain from World War II. Trains occasionally appear on the far shore. Boats of all sizes continually pass. Planes glide overhead, including in those days the Super Sonic Transport. Sandy Hook is a beautiful and unusual place, where another very unusual event was about to unfold.

While I was off on a walk, Judy lay on her blanket relaxing and reading a book. A woman, Mary Anne, walked by, noticed the title of the book Judy was reading, and asked her if the book was any good. They had begun a lively conversation, during which they had just discovered Judy currently lived in Hoboken, and Mary Anne had lived there for many years, moving away after her recent divorce.

Realizing Hoboken is only one square mile in size, they naturally had assumed they would know many of the same attractions, and they were exchanging their favorites as I returned. When Mary Anne finally asked Judy "Well, just where *do* you live?" Judy's response, "One Marine View Plaza," (MVP1) produced a gasp from Mary Anne, who said "I don't believe it, I lived in Two Marine View Plaza!" (MVP2). The site consists of two identical 25-story towers, inventively named One and Two. When the amazement died down, they began to see whether they had any mutual friends by naming people they knew from the other tower. It turned out, perhaps now not to anyone's great surprise, they had several common acquaintances. They then talked about what a good place that complex was in which to live. As they discussed the views which they had from their apartments, they found the most amazing coincidence of all: they both had lived in the same apartment number, and on the same floor! Judy still lived in apartment 15D of MVP1, and Mary Anne lived for years in apartment 15D of MVP2. Since they were both single and looking for companions for social activities, a friendship began to develop immediately and they made plans for future meetings.

Of course, the topic of my interest in synchronicity came up as soon as they found they had lived in the same complex, but before they learned they had lived in identical like-numbered apartments. After they made that second discovery, Judy and Mary Anne asked me to tell them what I thought it meant that they should meet the way they did, on a beach full of people so many miles away from the building complex they had unknowingly shared for several years. I had to say I didn't really know, any more than I knew the significance of Frank and me encountering the security guards the weekend before in Manhattan. This is one of the problems with trying to understand the concept of synchronicity. I am certain these kinds of meetings occur rather infrequently only by simple chance, yet how might one even begin to attempt a calculation of just *how* unlikely these meetings might have really been if they were truly random?

These meetings were certainly "curious," or "unusual," and likely statistically infrequent, but were they really examples of synchronicity? Jung would ask, "did the encounters also have personal meaningfulness?" While these meetings were certainly statistically unlikely events, I would doubt Frank or I will ever again meet those two security guards, making it unlikely there will ever be much in the way of personal meaningfulness to be found here. I would estimate a greater likelihood of Judy and Mary Anne meeting again, and possibly becoming friends. Does that make the "men with no necks" experience not a case of synchronicity, and the "tower apartment" experience synchronous? What if Judy and Mary Anne do not become friends, and what if someday one of the "men with no necks" saves my life, or even just bumps into me and I recognize him? At what point in a chain of events, and how, do we assign "meaningfulness?"

Jung's definition of synchronicity requires not just the unlikelihood of events but also their having meaning or significance to the participants. Clearly, the many sets of events which transpired relating to my search and reunion have great personal significance and meaningfulness to me, and I believe them to be good examples of synchronicity. However, I must say the scientist side of me is still skeptical of just where the line should be drawn between simply shrugging one's shoulders and saying "amazing," and believing some higher level of significance or meaning is present, thus creating a synchronistic event. Let's take another journey into the world of events that traditional scientists have difficulty explaining.

CHAPTER 24

Michael: The Healing

After I returned from my spring, 1997 semester in London, I spent
a couple of months replacing the roof on my cabin, and then left
for a week in Amana, Iowa, at the annual fireworks convention I had
started attending in 1995. From there I left for my regular August east
coast trip, which I was able to extend into September because of my
sabbatical. I stayed with Judy McCann in Hoboken for just over three
weeks, "paying" for my rent by helping her friend, Joe, install new bathroom cabinets and kitchen plumbing. As usual, Judy and I engaged in
wide-ranging talks about our lives, and, as she had on previous visits,
she again expressed her opinion my involvement with pornography
was part of what was limiting my relationship with Susan. When Judy
had suggested this in the past, I had asked Susan how she felt about
my interest in pornography, and she had said it was not something
that disturbed her. This time Joe also added his similar opinion to the
discussion.

One day on the beach at Sandy Hook, Judy, Joe, and I met Rebecca,
a college professor from Philadelphia. Over dinner that evening, we
got into a surprisingly deep discussion with her about what made relationships succeed and fail. After Judy and Joe drove back to Hoboken,
Rebecca and I sat at the restaurant talking late into the night. Rebecca
had been unhappily married in an abusive relationship for nearly 20
years, and had been looking for a healthier relationship for several more
years since her divorce. As I described my relationship with Susan to
her, Rebecca told me in no uncertain terms she thought I had to make
a decision about what was important to me. She told me she didn't
think I could have both Susan and my attraction to pornography at
the same time. We continued to discuss relationships in an exchange

of e-mail for the next several weeks, and her messages were to play an important role in the not-too-distant future.

On the way from Judy's in Hoboken to Tom and Cindy Little's in Connecticut, I stopped in Pound Ridge, New York, to visit with an adopted friend, Melinda Warshaw. She had contacted LaVonne Stiffler some years earlier about some of the synchronicities Melinda was finding as she worked on her search. They had counseled a bit over the phone about why Melinda wanted to search, and Melinda began to reveal a history of sexual abuse in her adoptive family. LaVonne had then given her my name, knowing I taught a course in sexuality. Over the years Melinda and I had talked on the phone several times, and I had visited her for a couple of hours on each of my previous two August trips. Interestingly, during the time Melinda and I had known each other, it just so happened she discovered she had birth family living not too far away from me in south-western Wisconsin!

I shared with Melinda that my relationship with Susan was suffering. Neither of us was satisfied with what we were getting from the relationship any longer, and I told Melinda I was beginning to wonder whether all of my friends who had insisted Susan must be put off by my sexual interests were correct. I was beginning to feel defeated by the strength of my need for pornography, and by guilt over the lack of an intimate sexual relationship the need might be causing. Melinda asked me whether I would feel less guilty if I were to discover high sexual drive ran in my birth family, and I said I thought that might allow me to feel better. She then asked me if I had ever talked with any of my birth family members about sex. When I said I hadn't, she suggested the obvious: I should talk to at least one of my birth sisters to find out whether my seeming obsession with sex and pornography might be genetic.

I promised her I would do this, but I was unsure of which of them to approach. Eventually I remembered Molly worked with sexually abused women and children. I realized that, knowing about the larger life context in which one's sexuality often occurs, she would probably be the one who would most easily understand what reasoning might lie behind my questions. I promised Melinda I would talk with Molly and ask her whether there might be a genetically strong sex drive on her side of my family background. I realized I had set out on a rather difficult road, even for me, master at open and honest communication that I am (or at least fancy I am!). I was not sure I would have the opportunity to initiate such a conversation, which I hoped could happen when we were alone. Then, even if the occasion presented itself, I was not sure whether or not I would actually have the courage to ask her what her sex drive was like. It's not exactly your run-of-the-mill topic for casual conversation with anyone, let alone a long-separated half-sister!

At some point during the week at Tom and Cindy's I told Cindy (who is an RN), about my conversation with Melinda and my plan to ask Molly about sexuality in her family. Cindy seconded the message that Judy, Joe, Rebecca, and Melinda had been giving me about the possible effects my interest in pornography might be having on Susan. Cindy urged me to continue to examine this issue. Cindy also suggested that perhaps now, as Susan's son, Carch, was about to turn 17, Susan might be realizing a new phase was beginning in her life also. Carch would soon be moving further away from her both emotionally and physically. With the coming change in Susan's life, Cindy thought Susan might be re-evaluating the type of relationship she wanted for the next phase in her life. Cindy suggested even if the pornography had not bothered Susan before, that might have changed now. I had not thought about the issue in quite that way before, and I thought Cindy made a lot of sense.

Taking a break from writing the chapter about my birth sisters, I called to tell Molly I would be in Buffalo in about a week, and to ask when we could meet. We identified the Tuesday night after my expected Monday arrival as the best, and almost the only, night when she would be free so we could get together. My week at Tom and Cindy's was one of the most productive I had ever had in terms of getting material for this book down on paper. The writer's block I had been having was clearly gone altogether, and I almost delayed leaving for Buffalo in order to keep at the work while the words were flowing. I didn't, in part because I had already told my parents I'd be home on the next Monday, and in part because I realized staying in Connecticut any longer would mean I'd have to reschedule my meeting with Molly. I didn't want to have to do that, especially since she would apparently not be free again for the rest of the week.

When I got to Buffalo, I called Molly right away to arrange a specific time and place to meet. We decided on another of the restaurants on Hertel avenue, the area where I had had so many of my meetings with my sisters, and also close to where I had grown up. The late summer evening was clear and warm with a full moon just rising as I drove into town from my parents' home on Grand Island. I thought of the many times, and many places around the world, from which I had watched this beautiful sight. I hoped the evening would go well, and I would have some more answers to my questions about myself before the time the moon set. Molly and another woman were sitting at a table by the sidewalk when I got there. The presence of a stranger with Molly was somewhat distressing, since I wasn't sure whether things would work out to have the conversation I needed to have with Molly if someone else was there, especially someone I didn't know. I also noticed they were the only people in the outside dining area. At least there was privacy which, if not interrupted, would make the conversation easier if I ever got to the topics I hoped to discuss. Molly introduced me to Jane, a co-worker from the counseling clinic at the hospital where she worked.

After the introductions and the usual pleasantries were finished, we began an easy and enjoyable talk about my vacation trip so far, my progress on my book, what Molly was doing, my experiences in London that spring, and my travels around Europe. Jane proved to be an interesting person with a good sense of humor. At a couple of points in the conversation the topic of sexuality came up as I spoke about some of my adventures. Jane made a couple of comments that, as luck would have it, allowed me to move the conversation into the topic I had in mind relatively easily. I told Molly I wanted to ask her some questions, and I wanted to give her some background as to why I was asking them. Fortunately, there were still no other customers in the outdoor dining area, and I talked about my conversation with Melinda, my difficulty with commitment and about some additional aspects of myself I felt were important for her to know.

Eventually I got to the big question: "was there a lot of sexual activity in your family?" Molly's answer did not give me the clear message I was hoping to get. While a couple of members of the family did seem to have fairly liberal attitudes, by and large most of the family was rather conservative. I realized there would be no escaping from my guilt through the claim that a high sex drive was genetic! Then Molly added she thought from what she knew about adoption, and what she knew of my life, the answer to my question was probably within me. Jane, in what seemed to be a sudden burst of insight, suggested perhaps I could benefit from a session with a friend of theirs, Michael Austin. Molly immediately and enthusiastically agreed, saying she thought seeing Michael would be really good for me.

They told me he was a very unusual and talented man, previously an engineer and underwater testing specialist, who had changed his life and become a healer. He had wanted to learn more about the way the human body worked, and had selected chiropractic as the way he would learn. He was also a trained Reiki healer, and Molly had met him when he had spoken in one of her graduate counseling classes. Jane said Michael had an office in Tonawanda, on Niagara Falls Boulevard near Ellicott Creek Park. Hearing this, I realized his office was also close enough to my childhood home that I had ridden my bicycle past the building it occupied many times to picnic and play at Ellicott Creek. I expressed an interest in seeing him, especially since my back had recently begun to bother me again, and Jane volunteered to call Michael right then, tell him about me, and find out when I could see him.

While Jane was away on the phone Molly told me Jane had long had tension-related stomach and leg pain, and just a couple of sessions with Michael had led to a complete disappearance of her pain, and, most importantly, her emotional tension, which she had come to see was a major cause of her pain. Jane returned to say she had reached an answering machine, and so she had just left a message that I would be calling early the next morning to schedule an appointment. Jane happened to have a business card from Michael's practice in her purse which she gave me. Reading the card gave me another hint at what lay ahead. The practice was called "Rainbow Bridge Chiropractic," and his card featured the classic "blue marble" photo of the earth from space surrounded with a rainbow, and the phrase "Healing the planet one soul at a time." Molly said something about how seeing Michael might "open up my chakras" and Jane agreed heartily. Though I had only a vague idea of what they meant, I understood they both thought getting my chakras opened would be a good thing for me. We spoke for some time about Michael's ability to sense the emotional and spiritual bases of pain, and to address these, as well as any physical problems present.

In the parking lot just before we parted, we talked briefly about the fact that yoga had helped both Jane and Molly to relax stress-related muscle tension that had caused them pain, and they suggested I might benefit from yoga as well. For the second time in my recent memory someone had suggested yoga to me, the first having been made a few weeks earlier by a massage therapist at the chiropractic clinic I had just started going to in Stevens Point. Since early childhood I had experienced periodic and sometimes excruciating lower back and leg pain. For some 25 years I had tried to live with or ignore the problem, having been told by a physician my parents took me to in high school my pain was "nothing serious," and having been told by my father at the time that I should never tell anyone I had back pain or "I'd never be able to get a job." In the late 1980s, Susan had suggested chiropractic treatment, and for the first time in my life I had become nearly pain-free. Around 1994, again at Susan's urging, I had taken the standard ten-session series of a deep muscle manipulation technique called "Rolfing," and had gone for a couple of years without needing any further treatment. In late July I had sought out chiropractic treatment again, having experienced a return of a moderate amount of pain. Thus, I felt positively about Michael because he was a chiropractor, in addition to the recommendations about his spiritual healing skills made by Molly and Jane.

The next morning (Wednesday) I talked with Michael and found he was busy all of that day. He had patients in the morning, and in the afternoon, he would be preparing for a presentation he was to make at a spiritualist church that evening. I was encouraged to find Michael was someone who was comfortable speaking both at a university counseling class and in a church. Since I value both the spiritual and scientific approaches, he sounded like he came from a good place. He told me he could see me the next day (Thursday) at 11:00 a. m., or at a couple of times on either Friday or Saturday. By that time, I clearly realized I wanted to get started as soon as possible, and I thought I might even want to see him more than once. Therefore, I made the appointment for Thursday. I spent the rest of Wednesday as I had spent the day before, entering corrections to earlier drafts of this book onto the computer at Mike Indian's house.

Thursday morning dawned sunny and warm, and as I drove to my appointment, I waged a battle between two competing voices in me. One of these, the skeptical and controlling scientist, was saying "Will anything even happen, and if something does happen, what will the cause and effects of it be?" The other voice was telling me to just relax, to give up my need to be in control, and to accept whatever might happen. I knew I should listen to the second voice, and things were more likely to happen in the second mind-set than in the first, but control has always been a difficult topic for me. I generally very much need to be in control, not only of myself, but of my environment. Giving up control has always been challenging, though I generally liked what happened when I did. Actually, that was probably part of what attracted me to drinking: the loss of control being drunk produced in me was enjoyable, though very dangerous, especially when I drove. Perhaps I liked the danger too.

I arrived at the office just before 11, and Michael came out from a rear room just after I had seated myself, picked up, and skimmed through one of his brochures. My first impression was that he was awfully young, but I reminded myself the best of all the therapists I had seen as of that time, was also the only one of all of them who was younger than me. I also reminded myself of the many talks with Bart and Marcia about how an old soul can inhabit a young body. We exchanged greetings, and he gave me a standard chiropractic history form to complete. I looked around his outer office and noticed two features I thought were rather unusual for a chiropractic office: the smell of incense and a carved stone statue of a delicate female form behind a font.

Once I had competed the history, we went into the rear office where there was a massage table set up in the middle of the room, a small desk, and a couple of chairs. We went over the history form and talked for perhaps a half hour. I tried to give Michael an idea of what I was looking for, though beyond relief for my lower back pain I really wasn't sure. He outlined his beliefs about the relationship between body, mind and spirit, the nature of spiritual reincarnation, the existence of many planes of reality, and the validity of many paths to the knowledge of the Divine. I told him I agreed with each of his statements, and felt more and more at ease as he spoke. Michael explained a little about the healing approach he would use, and then asked me to remove my shoes, glasses, watch, and any "lumps" in my pockets such as wallet and keys. At his direction I laid on the table face up.

Although Michael never told me to, I closed my eyes, realizing the fewer distractions I had the better. Only once in the next hour and a half did I "peek," and that was perhaps five to ten minutes into the session. I had been aware Michael was walking slowly around the table, pausing periodically, and when I opened my eyes, I saw him standing above me holding a pendant of some sort on a short string over my chest, and swinging it in a slow circle. I fought the urge to wonder what in the world he was doing, and decided to keep my eyes closed from then on! I told Michael about the two competing voices, one making me wonder what he was doing, and the other urging me to relax and let things happen. He suggested I listen to the second voice as much as I could. A few minutes later he said softly "all of your chakras are open." I would not begin to understand the significance of that message, or how he came to know about my chakras, until later that afternoon.

He urged me to voice whatever images or feelings came to mind, and shortly a deep sense of loneliness overcame me. I said "I feel so alone" and somewhat to my surprise I began to cry. Michael said "We're never alone," to which I replied "I know that, but I'm tired of *feeling* alone. I've always felt alone." I continued to cry, but I was not quite sure of just why I was doing so, other than I felt a sense of both immensity and smallness at the same time, along with a deep sadness. I wanted to curl up in the fetal position, but for some reason I resisted, and instead just retracted myself into the smallest space possible while I cried. I felt as though I was falling into a deep hole. I realized in my head on some level that feeling alone was related to the disconnection in my environment I had felt at the time of my adoption, but I tried to shut off the rational analyst in me as much as I could, and to just be quiet mentally and listen to my deeper inner voice.

There was very little actual talking during most of our session, and I did most of it. I had lost track of where Michael was in the room, as he was not saying very much. After a few minutes of quiet crying interlaced with an occasional sob, I noticed a sense of warmth in my feet. The sense grew to a near-electric sensation, and I thought Michael must be standing at my feet, and perhaps he had his hands close to them. I was not surprised when very gently he laid one of his hands on each foot. A sense of buzzing warmth which was very soothing moved slowly up my body until I was feeling it everywhere, but especially in my hands and feet. At some point he moved to my side and slid his hands under my spine in a manner similar to that used by the massage therapist I had just begun to see in Stevens Point. He also moved my hands and arms, which had been laying straight at my sides, onto my chest, gently folding them in the center.

He stayed motionless by my side with his hands under my spine for some time. The sense of warmth in my hands and feet continued to grow, and I finally told Michael what I was sensing. Suddenly I had a thought, which I also spoke out loud: "I feel like I'm being given a message that no matter where my feet take me, and no matter what my hands do, it will be the right thing." I was very comforted and felt a sense of affirmation and a strong sense of relief. I began breathing deeply and my crying subsided. Michael may have said something in response to my statement, but I don't remember. I do remember thinking "if this message is all that happens here today the visit will have been worthwhile."

I began to sense the presence of the chain of others who had helped me to arrive here, not just physically in Michael's office, but emotionally and spiritually as well. I was more than just thinking about them. In some way they, or their spirits seemed to be right there in the room with me. Their presence, too, was a comforting sensation. Melinda and Molly were the most immediate people I thought about, but Marcia and Bart, Phyllis, and Susan were somehow present also. I felt a sense of gratitude to them because without the experiences which each of them had brought me I would not have been ready for what was happening. And for what I didn't know was about to happen.

Another aspect of the entire session I became progressively more aware of was the music Michael had selected to play: a soft mixture of electronic music and nature sounds such as wind and waves. Part of what made the experience so profound was the music seemed to change with my moods, rising and falling with the tides of my emotions. There was at least one point when Michael changed the tape or CD from one type of music to another, and I was aware of this change, but even that change seemed to be made in a manner perfectly in tune with what I was feeling. I even had the fleeting thought that somehow the music was being activated by my emotional state, but "the scientist mind," still speaking, told me my state was just as likely changing in response to the music.

Shortly I began to cry again, and I felt as though my body was moving rapidly up and down along its spinal axis (head to toe) on the table. The feeling of warmth and tingling in my feet subsided, and at the same time the warmth and tingling became much more intense in my hands. As I cried, I became somehow aware I had the urge to raise my hands off of my chest and into the air. By then I was only vaguely aware of my body anyway, and, unlike the resistance I had earlier felt to my desire to curl into the fetal position, now I just "let it happen." My arms slowly raised vertically, bending at the elbows, with my elbows remaining on the table. With my palms facing each other, my fingers slowly opened. I felt as though the movement was not really voluntary. It just happened.

The strange thing (as if this is only *now* becoming "strange"!) was that I wasn't really certain my arms and hands had actually done what I thought they had done. Had I opened my eyes, or made a more conscious effort to move my fingers, and had I thus found my arms and hands were still folded and resting on my chest, I would not have been entirely surprised. As I lay there in awe of what I was experiencing, a nearly indescribable sensation began to occur. Perhaps the feeling might be best illustrated by reference to a device sold in "head" shops in the 1980s. I have one at home, called "Eye of the Storm," a plasma globe (also originally known as a Tesla globe). It consists of an eight-inch glass globe surrounding a black one-inch ball which is mounted on a glass pillar. When the "Storm" is turned on, beautiful pink-tipped blue "lightning bolts" jump from the ball to the inner surface of the glass globe. If you touch the globe the lightning bolts concentrate on the places where your hands touch the glass. There is very little real "feeling" when your hands touch the glass globe, except a slight tingling sensation when the "power" and "focus" controls are turned up all of the way and one main lightning bolt touches the globe at the location of a single fingertip. I can best describe the sensation in my hands in Michael's office that day as being what I think the feeling would be like if the power level of the "storm" was increased dramatically. I definitely felt as though waves of some sort of energy were emanating from, and between, my raised hands. The image I had was of the little lightning bolts in that glass globe, with my hands as the black ball. I felt as though I was the source of the energy. I think my fingers were twitching slightly, but whether this sensation was real or imagined was also difficult to evaluate.

My feelings, as the sensation of energy and power began to develop, slowly changed from sadness to wonder to joy. I saw what I thought at the time was a silly image of myself as some sort of healer. I felt as though I didn't want to waste all of the power I had. With this power I felt I could do great things, and I wanted to share the power with others. Yet I still cried occasionally. I think the tears were because I had the sense I was unworthy to experience what was happening to me. Michael had been moving around me murmuring words and phrases, many of which I didn't fully attend to or understand. One thing I do remember he said several times and in various ways was "the cup is no longer half empty, it is now half full." I was sure he was referring to the negative attitude Susan saw in me, and with which she was having trouble. Then Michael's voice seemed very close to my head, and he was quietly repeating "you are forgiven, you are healed." At first the phrase made me cry again, but gradually I began to feel a great joy. The sense of joy was so great that for a while I was alternately laughing and crying. I have had a hard time writing about my entire experience that afternoon, since words seem inadequate for the task. Eventually, without the need of any spoken words, I realized the time had come to "return" from wherever I was, and to end the session. Perhaps the fact that in short succession the office phone rang and someone knocked on the outside clinic door helped!

Michael said to remain as I was, and he left to attend to reality. I lay on the table and I tried, gingerly but now consciously, to move my hands. By now I was not very surprised to discover they were actually raised, but I was rather amazed that the feeling of power emanating from them still remained as I moved them around and wiggled my fingers. On his return he suggested I could sit up if I was ready. He helped me to a sitting position and I opened my eyes. I looked both at my hands and around the room, laughed, and commented "my hands still look the same, even though they feel *very* different." Laughing, I said "This is more fun than my laser-light pen!" Michael then left to get me a glass of water. While he was out, I continued to move my hands around my body. I could feel an energy field around me, which changed as I moved my hands through space. I moved my hands closer to each other, and could feel the "lightning bolts" interacting with each other. I couldn't help but to laugh more. When Michael returned with the water, I told him I was amazed at the sensations in my hands, and while I didn't expect that part of the experience to continue, I didn't want to lose the feeling of complete joy I was also experiencing. He told me I didn't have to lose that joy. I again laughed.

By now the sensation in my hands was returning to normal, and we talked about what had happened, how I was feeling, and when we could see each other again. We reviewed some of the ideas and images I had during the session, including the thought that the cup no longer needed to be half empty. I would now be able to see the world was a good place, and my negative attitude would no longer need to prevail. The loneliness and feelings of unworthiness I felt would also no longer have such powerful sway over me. I felt whatever was going to happen with Susan would now be the "right" thing, and if in the future we moved on to the next stage of our lives separately, I was much more certain I would survive. I sensed I had less urgency and concern not just about our relationship but about the future in general.

I asked what sources Michael could recommend for me to read to learn more about what had happened to me, and to help me develop further. He told me there was a metaphysical bookstore near North French Road, the name of which he couldn't remember, and when we went to the outer office, he would look up its name and address. Any book store identified as "New Age" or a store selling crystals would also be likely to have good reference materials for me. He recommended I investigate yoga as a method to attain and sustain the meditative state that would facilitate the spiritual awakening I had just experienced, and identified a couple of books by Richard Hittleman as a good introduction to yoga. Now for the third time in the last six weeks someone had recommended yoga to me, and I realized yoga was obviously something I needed to do. We went to the outer office and scheduled an appointment for 10:00 AM on Saturday, but we forgot to look up the name and address of the store Michael had in mind.

I drove a block north to Ellicott Creek Park where I spent the next hour. After walking slowly through the shady and nearly empty woods, I found a table in a shelter and lay there on my back, closing my eyes and thinking about what had just happened. The experience was something totally unexpected, something almost totally out of the realm of my previous experiences. The only remotely similar events I could think of were the times I had been channeled by Phyllis McCoy, and they had not been nearly as powerful as my experience that afternoon had been. Eventually reality again intervened, and I began to feel hungry. I remembered a restaurant called The Grapevine was located at the corner of Niagara Falls Boulevard and Ellicott Creek Road, and I decided to go there for lunch. While there I had what turned out to be still another completely unique and meaningful experience.

I had spent about an hour in the park, and, at about 2:00 p. m., the last of the lunchtime crowd was just leaving. As I was seated, I noticed there was a rather large group of older men (most appeared to be well into retirement age) just finishing their meal in an adjoining dining area. They walked past me talking and laughing on their way out the door. There was a large fish tank in the restaurant, and I was seated across from it. As I waited for a waitress the fish became a fascinating and relaxing sight to watch. Realizing I had just taken a giant step outside of my own tank, I wondered whether the fish understood anything at all about the world that lay outside of theirs. After the waitress took my order, I realized I had to go to the bathroom, and I got up and headed toward it, located behind me and near the outside door of the restaurant. After I was already walking in that direction, I realized several of the older men in the group were still standing around the door, and guessed some of them were probably in the bathroom. Opening the door confirmed my suspicion: there were two urinals and a toilet stall, and all three were occupied, so I stood near the door and waited. The man standing at the toilet said something about this being a popular place, and I said "It sure is."

A graying, mustachioed, and slightly balding man who was at the left urinal then looked in my direction and said very clearly, and with great feeling, "I *know* you, where are you from?" I was sure he wasn't talking to me since he seemed so certain he knew me, and yet I didn't recognize him, at least on first glance. I looked to either side, saw no-one else was waiting, and realized I was the only one he could have been addressing. I looked back at him, and, perhaps only because of his gray hair and his age, I suddenly flashed to an image of the obituary photo I had seen of my birth father in the Buffalo papers. I wondered whether this man could be related to me, and thought fleetingly of the fact that my birthfather had a couple of brothers who I had not yet met.

I said, "I'm from Wisconsin now, but I grew up in the Buffalo area and lived here until about 25 years ago."

"What do you do?"

"I'm a university professor and psychologist."

"Huh." He shook his head, as if trying to recall something.

At that point the man using the toilet flushed it, and stepped out of the stall saying "There you go, I even left the seat up for you." We all laughed, and I said "thanks," walked into the stall, and returned to wondering what to say to the man who claimed to have known me, who was now washing his hands. Thinking of the advice in *The Celestine Prophecy* to follow up on such "chance" encounters because they have meaning for us, and hoping he would be similarly inclined, I continued the conversation.

"Do you think we should figure out how we know each other?"

By then he was standing with his hand on the door. He looked me directly in the eyes, and in what struck me as the kindest and warmest of voices said, "That's all right, son, let it go. So long." and walked out the door.

I had just had another striking experience on a day already filled with them. I still don't know who he was, and probably I never will. However, such an unusual, and certainly Celestine experience, occurring so soon after my even more unusual, and also certainly Celestine, experience in Michael's office, seemed just "too good" to have happened by chance, and for no reason. I returned to my table and thought more about what message I might find in what would have been an unusual encounter even without the day I had already had. No great flash of insight emerged. Nor did any more flashes of lightening from my fingertips, for that matter!

I began to think perhaps the message for me was to reinforce just how important my search had been for me. Had I not completed my search, and known for certain who my birth father was, and that he was already dead, I might well have wondered, "He called me 'son.' is this man my birth father?" However, having completed my search, and with the knowledge I had gained, I didn't have to wonder. I knew. I could instead wonder, with more certainty and a much greater chance of finding an answer, "Is this man one of the two birth uncles I have not yet met?" Or perhaps some other relative? The experience was also a reminder of just how complex the interactions in our lives are, since one of the birth sisters who I found in my search in 1983 was the person who had led me to see Michael that morning. I wouldn't even have been in The Grapevine that day to have that Celestine moment, and then to ask the question about my search, if I had not first done my search! The way in which various areas of my life had intertwined with each other struck me again. I realized with a smile that those interwoven strands were not unlike—a grape vine!

After I had finished eating, I decided to try to find the book store Michael had mentioned, borrowed a phone book from the restaurant's bar and returned to my seat. There were only a couple of bookstores in the Yellow Pages for the whole Buffalo area that identified themselves as being metaphysical or New Age: Heaven on Earth and Harmony Place. Both of them were in the northern Buffalo suburbs, and thus probably within a few miles of The Grapevine. Unfortunately, neither was on North French Road. I couldn't help but notice, however, that Harmony Place was located at 550 Englewood Avenue in Tonawanda. While I didn't know the street numbering system well enough to locate Harmony Place from the number alone, I did know, since Englewood is only about two miles long, Harmony Place had to be located fairly close to where I grew up on Claremont Avenue. Claremont misses a direct intersection with Englewood by less than 200 feet where they both meet Kenmore Avenue at the north Buffalo city line. In addition, when they adopted me, my parents had lived just a few blocks west of the Kenmore-Englewood intersection, in the first house off of Englewood on Fairfield Avenue, perhaps a couple of hundred yards from Harmony Place. For the first four years of my life, I had lived there too. Given the neighborhood where Harmony Place was located, I could hardly NOT pay a visit!

Harmony Place, I discovered, was located just to the west of the now-abandoned railroad tracks that divided the town's East and West school districts, two blocks west of Fairfield Avenue, and one block west of the end of one of my childhood paper routes. I knew the neighborhood well. As I opened the door to enter the store I hesitated because inside I saw a woman was laying on a massage table and another woman was standing over her. I asked if they were open, and was told to come on in, they were just finishing a healing session. They invited me to relax and look around for a couple of minutes, saying they would be with me soon. I self-consciously examined some of the books nearby while the woman on the table sat up and put on her shoes. They asked what they could do for me, and I said I was looking for a book on yoga by Richard Hittleman that had just been recommended to me.

The owner, whose name I later learned was Kathie, said the book I wanted was rather old, but she could send in a special order for me. When I said that wouldn't work because I was visiting from Wisconsin Kathie asked what had brought me to the Buffalo area. I told them I had grown up on Claremont Avenue and still had family in Buffalo. As we talked about the city, Kathie showed me a book called the *Alternative Health Services Directory*, which was a listing of New Age sources in Western New York, which I decided to buy. I asked about the name of another store in the area, the one that was supposed to be on North French Road, in case they might have a copy of the book. Both women immediately knew it was Heaven on Earth, the other New Age store I had identified in the Yellow Pages.

Kathie let me use her business phone to call Heaven on Earth to ask whether they had the book in stock. While I was on hold, I paged through the *Alternative Health Services Directory*, and found an ad for Heaven on Earth, the very store I was talking to. As I looked through the ad, I saw a list of programs they were sponsoring. I scanned them and found one titled "Discovering and Experiencing Love Over Fear" led by Christian Fisher. Now *that* sounded like just what I needed, and I looked at the date of the program, Saturday the 20, and the date on my watch, Thursday the 18. I realized the program was in just a couple of days, on Saturday night, and I felt I had just been given yet another example of how things were working out in just the right way. When the woman from Heaven on Earth came back on the line to say they didn't have the book but she could place a special order for me, I said not to bother because I was from out of town, and asked if there was still registration available for the Fisher program. My request seemed to confuse her, and I explained I was referring to the program on love over fear which was to be held this Saturday. She said in a rather puzzled tone that program was quite a while ago, and just then I looked at their ad more carefully. I saw I had missed one small detail: Fisher's program had been in *June,* and this was September. I laughed and apologized, making the comment that I guessed I wasn't quite back to Earth yet!

Kathie then offered to sell me her personal copy of the yoga book if I didn't mind a used one, saying she would replace hers with a new one which she would order. I told her that would be great, and she left to get the book from her house, which was connected to the store. I began to talk with the other woman, Barb, a retired teacher, about what I had just experienced with Michael. Kathie came back with the book, and the three of us continued to talk. As it happened, they knew Michael, who they said shopped there. We talked in some detail about my healing, and Kathie and Barb seemed to be genuinely happy for me. I had begun what I already clearly realized would be a new phase of my life. I paid her for the yoga book and the health directory, and we continued to chat.

Eventually Kathie had to leave to run errands, but the conversation I had begun with Barb, who was a substitute clerk and watched the store on Thursdays for Kathie, continued. Another customer entered the store and asked whether they had any charts or books about pendulums. Barb showed the customer several books, started to explain what she knew about pendulums, and showed her several that were for sale. This was great for me, having never heard of pendulums before, but not too far into Barb's explanation the customer said she already had a pendulum at home and already knew the basics. What she wanted now was to learn more in depth about how to interpret the information the pendulum was giving. Barb got out a book and a laminated card with a chart on it, and offered to give a demonstration of how to use the book and chart with the pendulum. The customer laid down on the massage table, and I watched as Barb held the swinging pendulum over the customer's body, identifying which chakras were open. Now the glimpse I had seen of Michael when I opened my eyes earlier that day on his table made sense to me! He had been checking my chakras. Barb found one of the customer's chakras, roughly above her heart, was closed. She said "you're closed here," and the customer laughed and said through her closed eyes "I just closed my heart chakra!"

With that spontaneous demonstration completed, I suddenly realized I had stayed at Harmony Place well past the time I had told my parents I'd be home, and so I said my good-byes and hurried off to Grand Island. My parents were going to go out with friends that night for dinner and a play, and that evening, as had been previously arranged, I took my brother Dave's wife, Patty, and their kids out for dinner and miniature golf—their delayed 1996 Christmas present from me. After the golf, and after the children went off to bed or were on their way, I came back to my parents' house, where I was glad to see Mom and Dad were not yet home. I wanted to talk to several people about what I had experienced that day, and knew that talking would be difficult to do with my parents there. I wasn't ready to share my experience with them yet, and didn't want to have to go to the basement to get privacy.

The first person I wanted to talk to was Susan, especially since I knew she would be leaving early the next morning for a dance convention in Texas, and wouldn't be back until Sunday night. I'd have had another session with Michael by then, and as I dialed her number, I wondered what I'd be like by Sunday evening if the second session was anything like the first. I got her answering machine, and so had to content myself with leaving a message for her. I hoped I was able to convey in the few short sentences, at least something of my excitement.

My next call was to Molly, who had just walked in the door when I called and was starting to prepare dinner while we talked. I wanted to thank her for sending me to Michael. I tried to tell her something of what had happened, and probably thanked her only about a dozen times. Although I was likely a bit incoherent because of the high I was again experiencing as I retold the tale, I believe she understood how important the session had been to me. I asked her to pass the message, and my thanks, on to Jane, and let her finish her dinner in peace.

The next call was to Mike Indian. My excitement grew even more as I told him in considerable detail about what I had experienced. I realized I lacked the vocabulary to express much of what I wanted to describe, but Mike had known me for over 35 years, since we were students at Kenmore East Senior High. He seemed to understand what I was experiencing just as much as Molly had. At one point he said he had only seen me as excited as I was then on one other occasion in his life. I said, "And I know when that was, and I want to thank you again for putting that pad and pen on the bed." I told him the probable title of this book had come to me during the previous four weeks of productive work in the New York City area. As you now know, the first part of the title, the phrase "There are more like me," was part of what I had written in 1983 at Mike's house, on the night I met my sister Susan, the first birth relative I had ever seen.

As I rambled on, I expressed doubts several times as to what I should or might do next with the new person I felt had been born that morning. I told Mike I thought I would not be shaving my head and selling incense at the airport, but even though I didn't know exactly what lay ahead, I still felt confident things would work out. On one of the several occasions I said I was unsure about what to do next, Mike quietly said "Heal someone." I said "Funny you should mention that because that was one of the rather strange images I had today—I could heal people with the power in my hands." Mike's reaction to my report of seeing myself as a healer was eerily similar to Michael's that morning. Mike said the image of healing people didn't seem at all strange to him, since, after all I was already in a healing profession. I fleetingly wondered who Mike had meant I should heal, and guessed he meant for me to heal myself, which was a fine goal as far as I was concerned.

My parents arrived home at just about the time we were drawing our conversation to a close, and Mike said he really wanted to get together to talk more with me. We compared schedules and found the first time we could get together would not be until Saturday about 1:00 p.m. Mike taught at our old cross-town rival school, Kenmore West, and was the coach of the West cross-country team. He and the team would be at a large regional invitational meet at Beaver Island State Park, at the northern end of Grand Island, all day Saturday, but he thought he would have some free time just after lunch. We agreed to meet then, and said goodnight.

After Mom and Dad went to bed, I changed into the green sweat suit I sleep in, and took a beach towel, a candle, and my "new" yoga book down to the basement family room to start my first attempt at yoga. If I was going to change myself, I wanted to get right on with the process. I thought there I could find quiet, and knew there was a thick rug on the floor. I laid out the towel, lit the candle, and had just started the prone relaxation posture when I heard footsteps upstairs. Mom was looking for me, and came down stairs to say good night. I could tell she wondered what the towel, burning candle, and book were for, and I told her I was doing yoga, and kissed her goodnight. On the way upstairs she said she loved me and kept me in her prayers. I said, "Me too," and immediately hoped she knew I was praying for her not for myself. Or was I?

I spent the morning Friday being lazy—sitting around the house and talking with my parents. I was still trying to understand what had happened to me, and didn't have any desire to do anything that required much physical or mental effort. In the afternoon Mom and I went into town to get our glasses adjusted and visit one of her friends who had known mom and dad before they adopted me. All in all, it was a relaxing day, and I enjoyed being with my mom and her friend, Wynn, catching up on old times. Wynn and her family had lived for many years in the same Town of Tonawanda neighborhood as Mike and Karen Indian and Sally Albertson, my birthfather's secretary, at whose house I first met my birth sister, Susan.

I had been trying to arrange getting together with my birth brother Keith late that afternoon and evening. I wanted to watch his daughter, Stephanie, take her horse-riding lesson, and his son, Derek, play in the band at a football game. Mom and I arrived home from our trip to town about 3:30 p. m., and I waited until about 4:00 p. m. to call Keith. Derek answered and told me that Keith had left the house "just two minutes ago" to take Stephanie to her riding lesson, and so that didn't work out. After dinner I walked the short two blocks over to my brother Dave's house, where I spent the early evening with his family. Dave's (only) daughter, Elly, played on a soccer team, and earlier that week I had told her I wanted to watch her playing in a match. That night she told me her game would be at 10:30 the next morning, Saturday. Suddenly I had plans to be in three places during the same period of time. My second session with Michael was in town at 10:00 a. m., and might well last until noon. Elly's soccer game was on Grand Island at 10:30 a. m. Depending on how long the soccer game lasted, I might not even have time for lunch before my meeting with Mike at the cross-country meet at 1 o'clock. At least the soccer and cross-country events were both on Grand Island! I told Elly I would try to get to her game, but because of my appointment with the chiropractor I might not get there until late, if at all. That night I again went to the basement to do yoga and try to prepare myself for my second session with Michael.

At breakfast on Saturday morning the conflict with Elly's soccer game ended when she called to tell me the game had been postponed until an afternoon during the coming week. While I was sad the match was postponed because I would not get to see her play during this trip, the postponement also took away the majority of the time conflict on my schedule, since Beaver Island Park was only about a 15-minute drive from Michael's office.

CHAPTER 25

The Healing Continues

On the way into town Saturday morning, I couldn't help but wonder "how can we top what happened in the first session?" Again, I had to work on myself not to overanalyze things in my head, and not to build up expectations of either success or failure. When I entered the office, Michael was in the waiting area, and he asked me how I was doing. I told him I was still reeling from what had happened, I was still sort of "high," and I was anxious to see where we would go today. He told me Molly had called and talked to him after I had called her on Thursday evening. I think Molly could see that night, and Michael could see then, that I had been, and was still being, deeply affected by his work with me. I told Michael about being unable to locate the store on North French Road, after our first session, and about finding Harmony Place so close to my childhood home instead. I told him briefly about seeing the pendulum demonstration, about buying the book, and that I had started practicing yoga.

Shortly we moved into the inner office, and I told Michael I was experiencing a conflict between thinking and feeling. Michael urged me to let the intellectual part of me fall into the background and to give attention to my feelings in order to increase the chances for whatever might happen. I again laid face-up with my eyes closed on the table, and Michael moved around me, initially silently, later urging me to think of various images and breathe deeply.

He urged me to think about that lonely child we had met in the first session, and described the image of that child moving from the darkness of sadness, loneliness, and fear, into the light of happiness and the comfort of spiritual peace. The image Michael described was very similar to an image of myself I had developed many years earlier in therapy. My own image was of an animal prowling in a dark and threatening jungle. There are dangers in the jungle, and the animal is alone, but the jungle has always been home. The animal knows the rules of survival there, and knows its way around. While not really happy in the jungle, the animal is content. Then one day the animal comes to a clearing. Looking out from the edge of the jungle, the animal sees sunshine, flowers, green grass, butterflies, and other animals playing happily there. The view looks inviting, yet it is frightening because the clearing and the sunlight are new, different, and unknown. Being afraid to go out into the clearing, my animal had always chosen to return to the darkness of the jungle, where there was at least the comfort of familiarity. The jungle image was very sad because I had always wanted to have the courage to enter the clearing, and I never did.

Perhaps because the image Michael selected was so similar to my own image, and perhaps because of the sadness of my image, waves of emotion overcame me, and I began again to cry. Yet even as I cried, I was also grateful, if not happy, that I had been able to return to this space. The first session was not an accident. The magic had happened again! Michael continued to work with the baby image, but inside I was also seeing the animal from my own image. He urged me to take the baby in my arms and walk into the light. After a while he asked me to turn over onto my stomach. He ran his fingers up and down my spine a couple of times, pausing at each vertebra, and working on knots I knew were tensed muscles. A feeling of warmth that seemed to be more than just from his touch began to pass through me.

At length, while he had his fingers low on my back, Michael asked me to breathe deeply three times and to hold the third breath at the top. As I reached the top of the third breath, he seemed to be gathering up threads of something from the vertebra he was touching, and he quickly removed his hands from me as if he was pulling out the threads. Although I could not really see, I could hear he seemed to throw the gathered threads away, perhaps then blowing them out of his hands. After the blowing sound, he told me to breathe, and the exhalation seemed to relax me even more than I had been. As he moved up my spine, repeating his action at each vertebra, I began to feel as if my body was lighter each time he "removed" whatever he was taking out and blowing away. A couple of the times the feeling of lightness was quite pronounced, while at most of the others the lightness was barely noticeable. I sensed something bad was being removed from me, but I did not, and still do not, understand exactly what he was doing.

Our second session, while not as full of whiz-bang new experiences and lightning bolts as the first one, was nonetheless still very moving. Several times during the session I had images come to me that involved the removing of some form of guilt or sin. I had associated these images with thoughts of my sexual activities. I felt I needed to take these experiences as far as I could take them, given my need to head for Wisconsin before too much longer, and so I asked Michael if we could meet one more time. We decided on 10:00 a. m. Monday, and I hugged him and headed off to Beaver Island Park to meet Mike.

Beaver Island State Park is another of the places in the Buffalo area with which I have a life-long history of pleasant memories. The park is on the northernmost tip of Grand Island, which sits in the Niagara River several miles above Niagara Falls. Beaver Island has a wide sandy beach with a boardwalk, and, until a late-night fire in 1992 burnt it to the ground, there was also a huge stately clubhouse with a high cathedral-like ceiling and a beautiful hardwood floor. My first memories of Beaver Island are probably from the time I was in first or second grade. Our family owned a 16-foot outboard boat that we used to anchor in the relatively shallow water off-shore from the beach at "Beaver" and just float there for most of Saturdays and Sundays all summer. During all of those weekends in our boat on the river, I certainly never thought we would one day live just a few miles away from that beach!

Now, some 40 years later, I was again going back to Beaver Island Park. The trip down South Parkway took me past the turn-off for Red Jacket Road, where my parents had lived since I went off to college in 1964, and past Love Road, where my brother Dave and his family had lived since some time in the early 1980s. However, they figured in my thoughts only briefly. I was feeling out of contact with most everything, including myself. In fact, I was wondering just who "I" was. When I got to the park, I easily found the large crowd of high school athletes, boys and girls from seventh grade to high school seniors, suited in a wide variety of colorful school uniforms, wandering about in mostly boisterous, and single-sexed, groups of eight or ten. I recognized some of Mike's team members' uniforms, and asked them where "Coach" was. They told me "Down by the starting line" and motioned toward the eastern area of the park.

I walked in that general direction but didn't see Mike. Because I needed more time by myself to think, much as I had in Ellicott Creek after my first healing session, not finding Mike right away was probably just as well. I was beginning to feel that in order to really feel good about myself I needed to resolve my increasingly guilty feelings about my interest in what Margaret had called my "plastic ladies." I had continued to exchange e-mail about relationships with Rebecca, the college professor I had met on the beach in New Jersey a couple of weeks earlier. She had put the issue of pornography vs. a full relationship with Susan rather clearly: "You can't have both worlds. It just doesn't work." Rebecca's message, so blunt and honest as to be stinging at first, was making more and more sense to me after the two sessions I had had with Michael. And yet, I feared tackling the issue of my sexuality even more than I had feared giving up drinking.

Perhaps the depth of my fear was because drinking, with two memorable high school exceptions, had been an adult-life-only activity for me. Even so, I had had a very hard time giving it up. How could I even think about giving up the form which my sexuality had taken? I had used masturbation, and sex in general, to soothe myself for as long as I could remember. How could I ever give these up? And what assurance did I have that something as pleasurable or as predictable would replace these activities? I wandered through the crowd of students and their families, lost in thought, and found myself out on the boardwalk, with the great empty space that had been the old clubhouse on one side of me, and the beach and river on the other.

I leaned on the railing above the beach and looked out at the river. A breakwater for a "new" marina jutted out almost to the area where we used to anchor our boat, and my mind went back to those days again. From our spot out there, we could see the American shoreline to the east, Buffalo's skyline off to the south-east, the park-like Canadian shore to the south and west, and the clubhouse and the beach at Beaver Island to our north and north-east. Dad would often look over to the crowded beach and say, "Aren't we lucky to be out here and not over there?" He did not like crowds, and until I got into junior high school, I too, was reasonably happy to be out there on the water. Then, suddenly, GIRLS happened! My enjoyment of the boat declined considerably as I became more interested in spending time with my friends, many of whom were over there on the beach, than in spending yet another day on the boat with my family. I remember in high school I felt I had been given a great treat when, a couple of times, Dad let me swim into shore to be on the beach with my friends for a while.

Two weeks before I left home to go to college my family moved from the Town of Tonawanda onto Grand Island. During the summers at home, I would work the night shift at the Loblaws (a grocery store chain) bakery. I would often go to my girlfriend Nancy's house after I got out of work. Her summer job was to take care of her younger brothers and sisters. I would get there at about 10:00 a. m. or so, and we would take one of her father's driving school cars, round up the little ones, and head off to spend the day on the beach at Beaver Island. Around four o'clock we would leave, and Nancy would drop me off at home on the way back to her house. I would sleep until midnight, and then go off to work for another night, and if the next day was a good beach day, we'd repeat the process all over again.

Many times, I had wished we had not messed up the good thing we had going. But who, I wondered, really was responsible for the break-up? My mind wandered over all of the relationships I had had with women in my life, all of which had ended with a breaking-up. Many of those women would probably have made good life-partners. Most of them, including Nancy, had later been able to make a long married life together with another man. The problem seemed to be within me. What was wrong with me? Could I ever get a relationship "right"?

I left the boardwalk and headed back toward the area of the starting line. I thought another race was about to start, and perhaps I might find Mike there. I was correct on both counts, and after a few minutes with his team members and some of their parents, we got a chance to talk. He noted I seemed distant, and much less sure of myself today than I had been on Thursday. I agreed with his observation, and said I had been feeling troubled after today's session. I told him I was increasingly realizing I would need to deal with the sex issue if I was really going to move ahead. Mike gently asked if he could tell me something, and I said sure, wondering what I was about to hear. He, too, voiced essentially the same question that had been raised by several of my other friends over the last few years: "What effect do you think your attraction to pornography might have on Susan's ability to feel comfortable with you?" In reply, I had to say that, even though she had repeatedly said the pornography didn't bother her, at this point I didn't really know, but I thought the porn was probably, at the very least, not a positive factor in our relationship.

Eventually it was nearing four o'clock, and time for me to go home. I said that I was leaving at least four or five times, and then didn't. Clearly, I didn't want to go home, but I knew I didn't want to stay there either. Mike had his coaching responsibilities, and I needed to think some more. When I finally said "I guess it's *really* time for me to go home." for what I had decided would have to be the last time, Mike and I said goodbye. As I walked away, I looked over my shoulder and added, "Right now I don't really know where home is." As soon as I spoke, I hoped Mike wouldn't think I was either playing a "pity me" game, or that I was referring to whether my "home" was on Grand Island, on Claremont Avenue in Tonawanda, or in Wisconsin. I really meant I wasn't sure where I belonged in the Universe at that moment.

I took a slow drive two miles back up the South Parkway to Love Road, turned and drove past my brother's house, and then drove on to my parents. They took me out for a Chinese meal at a restaurant on the Island, and we took things easy around the house after dinner. That night I again went down to the basement family room and tried my third yoga session. I decided about all I was learning from the yoga was how stiff and unlimber I was!

On Sunday morning my parents and I went to church. Since somewhere around 1952, when my family moved to Claremont Avenue, we have attended the University Presbyterian Church. Over the years I have attached various shades of emotion to going to church. These have ranged from viewing going to church as a joy, to dreading it, to seeing it as a rather neutral obligation of being a son. My primary circle of friends was the church's Sunday evening youth fellowship, which I attended from seventh grade through my senior year in high school. I was an officer of the group, and participated in many of the church's youth activities, including a week at the Presbytery's summer camp, where I had my first kiss, with a girl who was also a member of our youth group! During these years I loved going to church (as much because I could be with my friends as for spiritual or religious reasons!) but going to church was also, literally, a pain because I hated the scratchy wool dress pants I had to wear.

Gradually the spiritual aspects of church took more precedence, and for a while in High school I even wanted to be a minister. I assisted in services and preached at least one youth Sunday sermon. In college a required freshman class on the history of western faith and reason pretty much killed my faith in organized religion. I learned how much of what I had thought was "The Sacred Word of God" turned out to be little more than encrusted old customs, primarily from the Jewish tradition. I also realized once the "old customs" were stripped from virtually all religions, they all boiled down to the same basic message, which I saw as some variation of the Golden Rule, or in a broader sense, karma: what you give to the world you will get back. I retained my belief in God, but, perhaps based on the teaching that what we do to the least important of us, we do to God, I decided there was a little bit of God in every human being. I began to believe I could best practice my particular set of religious beliefs on a daily basis throughout my life rather than just on Sunday mornings in a particular building.

But, even as my personal beliefs changed, ever since I left home for college, whenever I was back in Buffalo visiting, my parents expected me to go to church with them. During college it was still enjoyable to go because I got to see many of my friends who were also back for the holidays and were also coming to church with their families. As the years passed, however, the trips to church with Mom and Dad gradually became less enjoyable. I knew fewer people each time I returned, I was often hung over from partying the night before, and I just didn't think much of the whole "church scene." These negative feelings became stronger when I married a Roman Catholic and saw how her church treated me as a non-Catholic, both at the time of the marriage (I couldn't be trusted), and at the time of the divorce (it was all my fault). Thus, I lost even more respect for the organized church.

One other thing happened at my parents' church. Almost every time we went, some friend of my parents who had not known me previously would, when introduced, say something about how much I looked like my parents. I'm sure they meant well, and there may have even been some truth to the statement, but nonetheless, these comments began to bother me increasingly, especially as I became more aware of the place of adoption in my life. Thus, during the majority of my adult life, going to church with my parents was a duty of being a son, and I went pretty much in this frame of mind. When I first moved to Stevens Point, I really didn't go to church very often. Once I bought my land, and built my cabin, I found I often wanted to spend Saturday night and Sunday morning there. I could enjoy the beauty of nature and the quiet. But no matter where I spent my time on Sunday mornings, at least when I was an adult I chose a more comfortable pair of pants to wear!

When I met Susan one of the pleasant surprises I got was that she, too, had been raised as a Presbyterian, although she had remained active in the church her whole life. Over the years I had gone to Susan's Stevens Point church on occasion with her, and always felt comfortable there. I knew the routine of the service, and recognized several fellow faculty members in the congregation. In the mid-1990s, Susan's son, Carch, joined the church, and I finally realized I had been missing something important in my life. I had noticed members of Susan's church seemed to be found in places where I thought good things were happening, such as at Habitat for Humanity. I had been recruited to that group by a neighbor, an English professor, and member of the local Presbyterian Church, who saw me adding a garage and reroofing my house.

I believed many of the faculty who were members there and who I had come to know on campus were good people, for whom I had respect. I had run into their minister at several community presentations on sexuality issues and was impressed by what he had to say. The feeling must have been mutual, since he had invited me to speak to the high school youth fellowship in his church about responsible sexuality. I finally took all of these experiences to heart, and in the fall of 1996, I joined Frame Memorial Presbyterian Church in Stevens Point. I felt much better about the "required" church visit when I was home that year for Christmas of 1996!

Nine months later, on Sunday September 21, 1997, having just had two very moving spiritual experiences with Michael, I was particularly looking forward to going to our old church with my parents, despite Mom's health having deteriorated, and the likelihood someone would comment again on the similarity in looks between my parents and me. I wanted to return to the place where I had received so much of my early religious training. Even though some of what I was taught there as a child was not particularly consistent with my current beliefs, I still felt University Presbyterian Church was "home." The pure white sanctuary with the wooden pews had changed hardly at all since I had preached there as an adolescent. Perhaps one of the purposes the organized church serves is to be a familiar, constant place in a changing world. That church was home for my spirit, even more than the house in which my parents lived on Grand Island, or the house in which I grew up on Claremont Avenue. That morning at church I met a new friend of my father, a man who was dating the now-widowed mother of one of my friends from the old youth group. When he told me, "You look just like your dad," it didn't bother me nearly as much.

When we got home from church, I called Keith to see whether we could arrange a visit that afternoon. Keith and a friend of his had recently finished putting steel roofing on a storage barn he was building behind his house. Since I had just put steel roofing on my cabin I was anxious to see how his job looked. I was looking forward to helping him work on finishing the project up, and with the weather being good that day, he was going to work no matter what. When I got him on the phone, he said his parents were leaving the next morning to take a long trip to the southwest. They were going to come over at about

3:30 that afternoon to say goodbye, and since they might come early, perhaps I shouldn't come over right away. He also wasn't sure how long they would stay, and so he said he would call if they left in time for me to come over later on. If I couldn't come later out that day, he said at lunch time on Monday he was going to be driving out to pick up a gun he had won in a raffle, and he wondered if I wanted to ride along. I would have to be in Wilson, about 20 miles north of Michael's office, by noon to go with him. I thought I probably would want to be alone after seeing Michael, as I had the previous two sessions. Since the first two sessions had each lasted just over two hours, and my appointment started at ten o'clock, I told him I didn't think that would work out. We said somehow we'd get together, and I wished him luck with the barn project.

For much of Saturday and Sunday I had been continuing to think about what should be the topic of Monday's session with Michael. I began to see more and more clearly that if I was going to really achieve peace within myself, I would need to make some changes either in my sexual behavior, or in the way I felt about my behavior. However, I was still frightened by the thought of addressing this major issue so directly.

As I worked over this issue, I remembered a presentation I had made many years earlier. On our campus the students in one of the residence halls used to ask selected faculty members to speak to them with the following set of instructions: "Imagine you are retiring the next day, and the lecture you are going to give us will be the last one you will ever present. Tell us what you think is the most important message you could ever pass on to students." In the late 1970s, I was asked to give one of the presentations in the "Last Lecture" series. After much thought I decided to speak on "The Value of Guilt." My main idea was that guilt was a warning signal. Like pain, guilt told us something we were doing might be causing us harm. I suggested we would benefit from examining whatever behaviors cause us "psychic pain." When we repeatedly engage in behavior that causes us guilt, we might think of the guilt as a signal that we needed to either stop the behavior so we would no longer feel guilty, or adjust our values so as not to feel guilty about things we continued to do.

The fact that I now needed to take my own advice seemed ironic, but that was in large part how I was feeling. Additionally, I suspected more and more strongly that my behavior in the sexual arena was affecting the way Susan felt about me or about our relationship, just as so many of my friends were saying to me, despite her repeated statements that my sexual interests did not bother her. The consequence therefore of continuing to engage in the behaviors and changing my values so I stopped feeling guilty about them carried the risk that the continued behavior might drive Susan away from me, if it had not done so already.

The problem I kept coming back to was I knew what a difficult a time I had quitting drinking, and I had only been drinking for perhaps 12 years or so when I stopped. What would I need to do to change my behavior in the area of sexuality, which had been a part of my life for quite possibly all 50-plus years of it? Would I have to quit engaging in sex altogether, or just in masturbation? Could I be "responsible" about my sexual behavior? Could I "control" it? I knew alcoholics were notoriously unable to engage in a return to "controlled" drinking, and I would never even dare to risk losing my sobriety by trying to go back to drinking "responsibly." I kept making a parallel in my thoughts between what I went through when I gave up alcohol and the task I believed I now faced. The current task seemed impossible. I decided I must seek help with my sexuality in the third session on Monday morning.

I arrived at the clinic a bit earlier than I needed to and went on in, saying a prayer for the strength to be honest with Michael about what I saw as the problem, and about what I wanted from the morning's session: I needed to ask for help in overcoming the power which sex had developed in my life. We greeted each other with a hug, and he asked how I was. I said I was still in awe of what we were doing, but I had some fairly specific goals for our work today. We walked back into the inner office, and while Michael set up the table and answered a phone call I looked at the music tapes and CDs that were on a table by the east window. I had been impressed with the power of the music he had played during our first two sessions, and wanted to get some of the same music for myself. He gave me the names of a cassette and a CD he thought he had been using (I was rather surprised he didn't know for certain) and I wrote them down, thinking I would go to Harmony Place or Heaven on Earth later in the day and see whether I could buy any of them.

After he had the table set up, we sat at the desk and talked some more. Telling Michael in some detail of my history and the reasons for my concern about my sexuality was not as hard as I had feared. When I had finished, he told me he had decided not to work with me on the table today, but rather to ask for a direct intercession from the spirit guides to help me with my problem. He asked me to remove my shoes, and moved his chair directly in front of me, about three feet away. He lit a candle and sat down, and then got up again and asked me to hold a pink stone obelisk during the session, which he told me would serve as a focal point for the energy we needed to call up.

He then invoked the aid of several spirits, mentioning by name some I recognized from the Hebrew and Christian traditions, and many others I did not recognize but sounded Oriental, Indian, and perhaps Greek and Roman. He asked very specifically for their help with my problems with masturbation and sexuality, which encouraged me—he had made clear there was to be no pulling of punches here. He asked me to breathe deeply and to relax, and asked that a beam of golden light be lowered to surround my body. The beam of light would act as a vacuum cleaner to take away the power of my dependency on sex and masturbation.

We began by returning to the image of the baby we had used in the earlier sessions. Michael said that baby was me, and asked me to visualize that baby, and to try to feel what it felt. What I felt was tears again welling up inside me. He asked me to hold the baby. Although I considered cradling the obelisk in my hands in my arms as if I were holding a baby, that didn't feel right, and so I just held the obelisk in my hands gently, and thought of it as representing the baby. He asked me to try to feel what Doug the baby needed to hear from me, Doug the adult. I again began to cry, and the tears continued throughout much of this portion of the session. He asked me to tell the baby what it needed to hear, and I said aloud, but more in the way of a question than a statement "I will always be there for you, baby." He asked me to repeat what I had said several more times. By the third repetition I was strong and confident as I spoke. I felt as though when I said "I will always be there for you, baby," I was Doug the adult making the promise to Doug the baby, but I also had the feeling I was the voice of my higher power, repeating these promises to Doug the adult.

I believe, but am not certain, Michael also had me repeat other reassuring and loving messages to the baby, such as "You need never want for anything again," and "You are sufficient unto yourself." Even though I first wrote about the third session just ten days afterward, I was not then, and still am not, completely certain about some aspects of what we did that day. I believe I remember pretty well what was said and done by both of us in the first two sessions, and what parts of those sessions I only thought quietly to myself. However, I have had great difficulty recalling exactly what I really said aloud to that baby, and what might have been things I was only thinking to myself.

Then we began to deal specifically with the sexuality issue. Michael called again on the spirits to give us assistance. He acknowledged that the column of golden light he had earlier asked for was surrounding my body, ready to take away the power of my addiction to sex. I believe he used that phrase specifically, and that I had also come close to the point of describing my problem as an addiction in our conversation before the session started. Thinking of sex as an addiction was very frightening for me.

He asked me to try to visualize what my life would be like with the power of this addiction gone. I tried to imagine a life totally without sex, which seemed very hard. I feared I would be empty, I could not exist without it, and that I might even, or might as well, die if I were to give sex up. All of these thoughts were frightening. I'm not sure what happened then, probably Michael asked for more help, or perhaps he began to talk directly about the process of change. Suddenly, it seemed out of nowhere, I had the thought, "It might not be so bad after all!" I laughed aloud because this was the first time this possibility had ever occurred to me, and I shared the reason for my laughter with Michael. I think if he made a verbal response at all, he only said that this was good.

Then we started an exercise. He asked me to breathe deeply several times, and then to imagine I was completely surrounded by a shimmering force field shaped like a glass bell jar, which was sitting on the floor around my chair. He asked me to breathe in deeply, to then exhale slowly, and to bend down, slip my fingers under the edge of the jar and pick the jar up by the edge. As I then breathed in slowly, I was to gradually lift the jar up until I had lifted the jar over my head and I had taken in a full breath as I held it aloft. As I raised the jar Michael softly repeated several times that this was the burden of my addiction, and that I was lifting this burden off of myself. He asked me to pause when I had the jar held over my head, and he said the burden was now removed from me. He may have made some gesture or sign of its removal. We repeated the exercise at least once, and probably twice. During the last repetition I had the clear sense I was somehow lighter, and a burden had been lifted from me.

Michael then began to talk about the fact that as we grow, we change. He said some things serve a purpose for a period of time in our lives, and once their purpose has been served, we find they are no longer necessary. The pornography and sex had served the purpose of soothing me and helping me get to this point in my life, and they now no longer were necessary. He said "These things are now neither good nor bad, they just are." And he said they would no longer have the power over me they had previously possessed. I felt the purpose for which I had come to the session had been met, and without either of us speaking, we knew the time for the session to end had come. Michael thanked the spirits for their help, and asked me to seal the cleansing process with three repetitions of "Ommmm," which we chanted together, separated by deep inhalations of breath. I felt I had been given a new power to take charge of my life. The feeling was wonderful.

We stood and hugged, and I thanked him for a truly wonderful experience. I said the work he did must be exhausting for him, and he replied quite to the contrary his work gave him energy, and he learned from every person with whom he worked. I asked a question I had been wondering about, which was along the lines of "Did the kinds of things that happened with me happen often with people who see him?" Michael replied that I had been particularly ready to change when I came to him, and most people did not move as quickly as I had.

We went into the outer office and exchanged e-mail addresses, talked some more about where I might go for further development once I returned to Wisconsin, and about what his plans for the future were. It was time to say goodbye, and I wanted to thank Michael for all he had done for me. I looked at him, said "Michael," and then couldn't think of what words I could use that would properly express my feelings. I just shook my head with my mouth half open. He looked back at me, smiled, and said, "You're welcome," and we both laughed, and hugged again. On the way to the door Michael walked over to the stone font, in which I had noticed a single polished pink quartz crystal on my way into that session. He picked the crystal up and gave it to me. I was touched, especially because of the fact that just a few weeks earlier on the beach at Sandy Hook, I had been collecting stones as I walked, and had spent a day picking up just the pink quartz ones. We went out the door, and standing on Michael's office porch I thought I was experiencing a "new beginning," which might be a good place to end my book. As it happened, there were more important things that would occur within the next few weeks which I ultimately decided to include. Nonetheless, I definitely had the feeling of the ending of one era and the beginning of another during that entire six-day period.

I looked at my watch as I walked to the car, and realized our third session had only taken about an hour and a half. The time was then just 11:30, and I realized I could have gotten up to Wilson to see Keith had I arranged to meet him. I gave some thought to just driving up there, but wasn't sure I would be able to find him, and didn't want to chance making the trip for naught. I told myself "this was the way it was meant to be," and I decided to go instead to Mike's house to sit for a while or maybe to work on the computer. I thought after a while at Mike's I might then go to Harmony Place to shop for some of the music Michael had told me about before heading back to Grand Island. When I got to Mike's the house was locked, and the key was not where he had hidden it for me the previous week. I realized I had not been very clear with him about whether I would want to go to his house that day, not being sure of just how I would feel. So I decided this was okay too, and that I would instead drive to Harmony Place. When I got there I found the store was closed on Mondays. Again I told myself this was okay, that was the way it was meant to be.

I decided I would drive the mile or so from Harmony Place to Kenmore West where Mike taught. I thought I would enjoy having a private lunch with Mike, but then thought that would be unlikely since every time I had eaten at the school with him, we had been in the faculty cafeteria. I thought I really wasn't ready for that, and so perhaps I could just get a key to his house and go there. At 12:10 p. m. I arrived at the school, and I sat in the car for a while, knowing his lunch hour didn't start until 12:30 p. m. I walked into the school at about 12:20, asked at the office where Mike was, and was sent to the third-floor computer lab. There was a sign on the door saying the lab was closed due to technical problems. I asked across the hall at the library where his room was, and found him sitting alone at his desk.

We began to talk, and he told me he thought I looked better than I did on Saturday afternoon. I agreed I certainly felt surer of myself, and was happy about what had happened that morning. I began to tell Mike some of the details when he got up and walked to his closet. I looked at the clock, saw that it was 12:30 p. m. and stood up, commenting "I guess it's time for lunch." Mike said "Yes, but I was going to share my lunch with you and eat here if that's okay." I laughed and told him that eating here was not only okay, it was exactly what I had *wished* we could do, but I had never thought would work out! We joked about the truth of the Celestine idea that we can create our own reality, but I know we both were taking the idea seriously. It seemed to me I created an image of what I wanted to have happen, and I got exactly what I wanted!

Our discussion was of course too short—teachers only get a half-hour for lunch, but during that time Mike did tell me one rather startling thing. He said he could clearly sense my excitement on the phone when I called him to talk about my first session with Michael. But in addition, he said he could feel waves of energy coming from me to him over the phone. When Mike made the suggestion I "heal someone," he had thought he meant either for me to heal myself or to heal someone else. Gradually Mike realized the person he meant was for me to heal was Mike, himself. He said that after we got off the phone, he had experienced something profound happening to himself that he understood as a healing experience. Hearing this brought tears to my eyes again, as well as a whole new level of appreciation for my relationship with Mike. The bell rang in what seemed like no time at all, and Mike's students were filing in. The class he was teaching that hour was psychology, and once they had been seated, he introduced me as a high school friend who was a psychology professor in Wisconsin. As I left, I quietly asked him if his students could handle seeing us hug, and he said no, so we had to just shake hands. It was time for me to return to considering how to address a serious problem that had arisen just a few weeks earlier.

Version One: Pearl and Bill were engaged. When Pearl found she was pregnant, Bill agreed to marry her. When Pearl told her mother she was pregnant and was going to marry Bill, her mother flew into a rage, rushed the few miles into town and into Bill's house and berated him severely. She then went back home and threw Pearl out of the house, accusing her of shaming the family, and saying she hoped neither Pearl's father, nor anyone else, would ever learn she was pregnant. Bill, having been attacked by his future mother-in-law, decided not to join Pearl's family through marriage. Because she had nowhere else to go, Bill's family did the right thing and took her in, and she lived with them while pregnant. She surrendered the infant for adoption immediately after he was born.

Version Two: Bill was sitting at the bar in Shamus, an Irish bar and restaurant near his office in the Niagara County Courthouse. A woman lit his cigarette for him. They struck up a conversation, and he found out her name was Pearl. Eventually she invited him to her quarters in a nearby rooming house. They had relations. Bill was impressed by her attractive body and fancy lingerie, and figured she must know what she was doing. He eventually learned there were several other men with whom she was having relations. Later, when she announced to him she was pregnant, he denied being the father, citing the other men she had been with as more likely candidates. His family, feeling sorry for a pregnant single woman who had no place to live, did the right thing and invited her to stay with them while she was pregnant. She surrendered the infant for adoption immediately after he was born.

We may never know which version of these memories is more accurate, and perhaps we don't really need to. As you now know, I was that infant, but I am now a man. At age 52, fourteen years after hearing version one, and after fourteen years of thinking I knew the truth about who I was, and how I came to exist, I was told version two. Version two comes from a source very "close to the action," a source who was one of the first people to confirm version one at the beginning of my search. After thoroughly investigating version two, I believed this person was of questionable reliability. Unfortunately, I based this book on version one, and the book was virtually complete when I first heard version two. While I was investigating version two, I was once again faced with some of the same questions which caused me to begin my search. I had to again make the difficult choice of balancing my need to know with others' needs for privacy and dignity.

Fortunately, two weeks to the hour before first hearing version two, I had my first healing session with Michael. Fortunately, the work with him gave me both a powerful tool to deal with stress, and a new, larger, and more positive view of life in general, and of my life in particular. After some thought, I decided to just shelve this writing project for a while. With the end of my sabbatical, I had to return to teaching, and thought I'd get back to it at some point in "the future." The future lasted for nearly 26 years!

CHAPTER 26

And, 26 Years Later

This chapter updates my story with information and developments following the suspension of my search and writing in 1998. Since I began the first chapter with a description of Susan and Carch and their place in my life, it is fitting to start this last chapter with a continuation of their part in my story. After that update, and a couple of notes about general changes in technology and society, I will identify additional updates with the chapter(s) in which the material is discussed and/or the year(s) in which the development took place.

Susan, Carch. and I began our time together in London, in the spring semester of 1997. While very educational, and enlightening, and mostly enjoyable, the four months were also very stressful. Sadly, some members of the group were not mature enough to engage in the kind of independent activity in a large city that was necessary for success as a student studying abroad. We had to spend an unusual amount of time with student behavior management, and we returned to Stevens Point rather burned out. From August until December 1997, I continued working on the book during the second of my two semesters of sabbatical leave. We continued to each live in our own houses and to date as we had before my first sabbatical, and the semester in London changed our routine significantly. Eventually, in March 1998, Susan reached a critical point.

Carch had joined the Boy Scouts and Susan and I became troop leaders. After one of the meetings, she asked me to come upstairs to the church library. She sat me down across from her, took my hands, gazed intently into my eyes, and said, "Doug, shit or get off the pot." Speaking her mind has never been a weak point, and, unfortunately, her message was not a surprise. We had both realized, although we had never talked about it with each other, that we had to either move into a new dimension of our relationship or move on with our lives separately. Despite our 14-year history of "dating" my internal reaction was one of panic. What I said to her, after a deep breath, was something to the effect of "I will have to think about this," but my thoughts were more like "Holy shit, how can I do this? I need to get back into therapy!" Over the years, many therapists of various types have been very helpful to me. One that is particularly important, and allowed Susan and me to get to this decision point, was my healing with Michael, reported in chapters 24 and 25. Based on that work, both immediately and over the following years, Susan and I came to an understanding of our relationship that has allowed it to work.

A brief period of therapy helped me realize there was only one way to go ahead with the relationship that was not likely to end unhappily, and that was to give marriage another try. One of the interesting aspects of that therapy was the realization that, had I not spent the past year and a half reviewing and evaluating my life (in the process of working on this book), it is highly likely that I would not have been able to go ahead and make the commitment to marry, or to be able to have a successful marriage.

We were married Sunday, August 23, 1998, at the annual summer picnic of our church, with Carch serving as our best man. It was the right thing to do, since we celebrated our 26th year of marriage, during our 40th year as a couple, in August 2024.

In the summer of 1998, we each sold our houses, and together bought the house we still live in now. Carch attended UWSP getting a bachelor's degree in theater and computer science. He met Liz, a friend while in college, and perhaps in imitation of Susan and me, they dated for seven years before getting married! He now works in Pennsylvania, and they have a small family. Thus, even if the book you are now reading had never been published, the time I spent writing it was certainly a good investment in my own personal growth and development.

Technology update 1. Of the many advances in technology that took place in the 41 years between 1983, when I began my search, and 2024, the time that I resumed writing this book, there are two that are of particular importance. The first advance was the wide availability of cell phones. I'm not really sure when I got my first cell phone, but it is clear that the first few years of my search, at least from 1983 until I contacted Keith in 1992, cell phones were not part of my everyday life. Every time it was necessary to make a phone call I had to find a phone booth, or at least a payphone. I also had to have change, or a telephone credit card to make the call. Long-distance calls carried a per-minute charge, with lower rates on nights and weekends. Recall my response at the ALMA search workshop in New York City, when asked what I was going to do next. "I guess I'll get a roll of dimes and find a quiet air-conditioned pay phone and make some important phone calls." Before the modern smart phone, to verify almost any information that you didn't know, couldn't remember, or had forgotten, or to find an address, you had to find a person who knew the answer, some sort of reference material, or a map. Many of the calls I made during my search were made only after I found a payphone in the privacy of a phone booth, a far cry from just reaching into one's pocket or purse.

Technology update 2. Another advance, which has been much more consequential particularly for adoption search and reunion, is the development of widely available DNA testing services such as 23andMe, Ancestry.com, and MyHeritage.com. In my own search, the question that brought my book project to a halt in 1998, about who was really my birth father, was definitively answered when I, and several of my birth father's family members, appeared on 23andMe. The wide availability of genetic testing has upended the whole issue of protecting birthparent identity and privacy, as was once promised by social workers and adoption agencies. And of course, this can work in both directions since birth parents are more easily able to find their surrendered children as well. The availability of genetic testing has lessened the pressure on states still having closed adoption records to change their laws. However, many adoptees, as a matter of principle and equal treatment under the law, still want to have the right of independent access to their own birth records.

Chapter 23. 1988. The yoga book I bought at Harmony Place (but, with no previous yoga experience, I found challenging to use), was written by Richard Hittleman. My interest in yoga, and the way in which I was able to purchase the book were definitely the result of a series of synchronicities, as I have already described. Hittleman died of prostate cancer in Santa Cruz, California, on my birthday, in October 1991. His death cause and date could be a possible synchronicity, but it is more likely just a coincidence. I never knew about his death, its cause, or of it having occurred on my birthday, until the final preparation of this book in 2024, and there was no connection between Richard and me other than purchasing his book in 1988. However, after yoga was recommended to me by several people, and after relatively unsuccessful attempts to do yoga on my own, I did begin to take yoga class as soon as I returned to Wisconsin. Yoga spoke to me, since I continued some ten years of yoga classes and then switched to a Body Flow class that was both yoga and Tai Chi. The Body Flow class stopped in 2020 due to Covid, but when I returned to class in 2022, I had experienced painful deterioration of both thumb joints. Reparative surgery to the right thumb in early 2023 has not yet allowed me to return to supporting my upper body on my hands. Hittleman's book showed me I really needed to learn yoga from a class rather than a book, and it was the beginning of my yoga journey. The synchronicity was in the multiple recommendations of yoga, in being able to get copy of the book, even though it was not really for sale, and in my finding yoga was what I needed, rather than in the purchase of a particular book by a particular author. But who knows? Someday a member of Richard Hittleman's family may come across *this* book and find it useful. Wouldn't that be interesting? Perhaps even synchronistic!

Chapter 4. The primary content of Chapter 4 is about my involvement with ALMA, whose founding purpose was to protect the rights of adoptees. There were a significant number of birth parents (mostly birth mothers) and a smaller number of adoptive parents involved when I was active with ALMA. There is another well-known national support group in the adoption world, although it did not play a direct organizational part in my own search. However, many of the birth parents I met were also members of a group designed specifically to represent their interest. Founded in 1976, Concerned United Birth Parents is pretty universally referred to as "CUB". As might be expected, their primary concern is with what they refer to as "adoption loss" rather than simply as "adoption."

Thus, in the early history of the adoption support movement, there were groups organized with a primary role of supporting each of the three sides of the adoption triad. ALMA was primarily concerned with adoptees, NACAC primarily with adoptive parents, and CUB with birth parents. Having been exposed early on to two of those three groups, my preference was, and is, to affiliate with groups that support and welcome all three sides of the triad. As such, the AAC, a major player on the national level, and AID in Wisconsin, were both explicitly open to all three sides of the triad. Over the years, each of the three initial groups has broadened their scope.

Chapters 5 and 8. In 1995, 12 years after learning that my birth father had died of alcoholism, and acknowledging my own then 17 years of sobriety, I began to investigate possible relationships between adoption and alcoholism. I soon learned that there was evidence that the connection between alcoholism in birth parents and in their adopted offspring was much stronger than the connection between alcoholism in the adoptive family and in their adoptee. I have recently learned there is now more research on birth parent-adoptee connections in the areas of alcohol and other addictive behaviors. A basic place to start learning more about this would be where I began, in the work of Cadoret (1995).

Chapter 11 and 2024. Hilbert Pankonin and his wife surrendered the youngest two of their six children, a boy and a girl, for adoption during the depression. Our AID group supported him with his search for his son, with me doing the actual search, which was my first. He wrote his book, *Magnetism of Blood*, so that his two adopted children would know how much they were cared about and loved. There was some ambivalence when the two adoptees learned they had been "abandoned outside the basement of a church." Recently I discovered Hilbert died in 1997, at age 91. His obituary lists six children: two female, and four male. While I do not intend to contact his family at this point, the presence of all six names in his obituary strongly suggests to me that there was a reconciliation some time before his passing. At least I hope that was the case.

Late 1998 and 2024. Beginning in April 2024, when I started the revision of this book, I have been in much more frequent contact with my birth brother and my four birth sisters. I am hopeful that this will continue.

Winter, 2006. Susan and I took a driving trip to the U.S. Southwest. We stopped at Joshua Tree National Park and met Roger and Judy Thompson, a couple with whom we hit it off quite well. In 2009, we went back out to visit them again and they invited us to their house, where Roger had a great collection of rocks that he had gathered over the years primarily from that part of the country, as well as rock cutting, grinding, and polishing machines. He was the president of the Shadow Mountain Gem & Mineral Society that met in Palm Springs, in the valley below Joshua Tree, and he took us to one of the club's monthly meetings. I was hooked and remain an active rockhound. We returned to visit Roger and Judy several more times in the next 10 years, but sadly in December 2024, I learned Roger had passed away from cancer.

Susan and I drove on from that 2006 trip to visit her family in Lancaster CA. We arrived on a Friday night tired from our trip and just hung around the house with her family on Saturday and Sunday. In Monday's local paper there was an article about the Antelope Valley Gem & Mineral Club's annual show that had just taken place Saturday and Sunday. It also contained an interview with Jules Ficke, the club president. I was frustrated to have missed the show, but called Jules. After talking a bit, he invited me to come to the next club monthly meeting, which just happened to be the next night. As he gave me directions, I realized the club met in a church only a block or two south east from the house where Susan grew up. You could actually see the steeple of the church when standing in Susan's driveway. I met Jules, and many other club members, and he invited me to come to his house to see his collection. It turned out he lived just 2 miles west of the house in which Susan grew up.

While looking at his collection, we talked about my recent interest in rock hounding and my desire to collect rocks while we were in California. Jules offered to take me out to Lavic Siding, about two hours east of Lancaster to gather some jasper. It is a tiny spot, perhaps a one-time train watering station, but now just an active railroad track crossed by a dirt road in the desert, near the bombing range for Twentynine Palms Marine Base. By this time, I had realized that for all of his rock knowledge, Jules was kind of a quiet guy, and I wondered how we might keep a conversation going in the car for two hours out and two hours back. Turns out I didn't have to worry very long. About five minutes into the trip Jules turned to me and said, out of the blue, "Did I ever tell you I was adopted?" I said "No, but so am I!" and suddenly there was no shortage of things to talk about! We talked all the way out to Lavic, all the while we were jasper hunting, and all the way back into town. And in a sense, we haven't stopped talking since because we still chat on the phone every so often.

The similarities that Jules and I discovered were pretty amazing, including the fact that we had both used ALMA resources in our personal searches, and both were ALMA members for a time. We both were at least somewhat successful in finding our birth families, and the results were so positive for us that we both wanted to share the experience with others by starting an adoption search and support group where we lived, As you have read, I was put off by the excessive amount of legal language when I looked into forming an ALMA chapter, and Jules didn't even go that far, preferring to operate on his own. We also discovered that we had both been active in our current states of residence in trying to change the adoption laws, and Jules continues to be. Sadly, at least for now, both California and Wisconsin, the states where Jules and I live, still allow veto powers for birth parents over adoptees' access to our original birth certificates. Fortunately, both of us were adopted in states (Iowa and New York), which now allow adult adoptees to have access to their adoption records.

Over the next 10 or so years, Susan and I spent a lot of time in Lancaster as her family was in need of significant support and care. Even after she had no more family living in the area, and sold the family home in 2016, we continued trips to both Lancaster and Joshua Tree to visit friends, including Roger and Jules, and for me to rockhound and go to the local rock club meetings and field trips. I also attended meetings of another club, the Palmdale Gem and Mineral Club, which met about 5 miles south of Susan's home. Our regular trips west stopped in 2020 with the onset of Covid, and have not yet resumed. However, not to be outdone by Roger and Jules, from 2021–2023, I was the president of our local rock club, The Heart of Wisconsin Gem and Mineral Society.

Chapters 12, 19, and 21 and 2024. Susan, based on her interest in movement and her certifications in Laban-Bartenieff Movement Analysis and Language of Dance® suggested to me that there might be some movement-related negative effects of the separation of mothers and their newborn children. She believed that these effects might be seen not only in adoptions, but, perhaps to a lesser degree, also in other cases where infants and their mothers were separated for a while at birth, such as premature or health-impaired infants. Her son, Carch, was a premature baby, and he was separated from her for the first month of his life while he was in the nearest neonatal intensive care unit in Marshfield, Wisconsin. Susan commuted an hour each way between her classes to breast feed him, but missed large amounts of contact with him. The topic of early disruptions in the mother-child relationship is particularly interesting to her. We spent some time together searching the literature on movement and attachment and discovered some promising work has already been done in this area. A good place to start to investigate this work is found in an article by Meagan Haase in 2019.

Chapters 10, 11, and 15, and 2020. After losing contact sometime in the late 1990s, C. E., the psychiatrist and one of the "adoptee shrinks" and I met again. We are both members of the same small religious faith, in which three Wisconsin congregations share a minister. Due to Covid-related changes in our Sunday services, C. E. and I reconnected through Sunday morning Zoom meetings! We are still living in the same cities as when we originally met in 1984, about 95 miles apart.

Chapters 1, 5, 11, and 22, and 2023. I received my original birth certificate (impounded and confidential since my adoption was finalized in 1947), from New York State because of a 2020 change in their laws. Even after I had the right to obtain it, it took me a while to decide I actually wanted to go through the trouble and expense. In 1983, I had obtained the information I needed to search in the legal adoption papers my parents had finally given me. Within a few months I had located and contacted both sides of my birth family, although my reunion process had not been fully completed when I put it on pause in 1998. I ultimately decided that I wanted to have that important document from my history, especially since many people had worked long and hard to get me that right. Once I completed the form and paid what seemed like an exorbitant fee for the ordering process, I had to wait to receive it months longer than the legally prescribed time period. When I finally had it in my hands, and before examining it in detail, I was ambivalent. Part of me was angry that I had to wait for 75 years to exercise a basic right held by most non-adopted people. But part of me was also grateful for the work that had made it accessible to me. And of course, I was excited to have proof of my birth in my hands, at last.

Then I began to look at it in detail, and learned that I had actually been given a name, presumably by Pearl, with possible assistance from Uncle Henry. Until that moment, I ever knew I had any name other than "MALE Belschner," as I was identified on the papers my parents had. I discovered I originally had a full name: Clarence (after Pearl's father),

William (after my birth father), Belschner. Until my adoption was finalized on May 12, 1947, that is who I was, at least legally. I was transported back to the 1996 afternoon in Rhinelander, when I held Alice's infant daughter, waiting for her to be picked up by the foster home parents. Again, I had a rush of emotions, and they return each time I think of either of these events.

Chapter 7, 1994, and Winter 2024-5. As the crew had feared, the ratings for *Unsolved Mysteries* slipped when it was moved from its original Wednesday evening timeslot to Friday evenings in the fall of 1994, which was season #7. Two years later, the show was canceled by NBC, and CBS picked up the series. Reruns of the show went into syndication and continue to appear unpredictably. There is also some confusion about which episode of season 7 it is, 3 or 4. It may be tricky to find this show on the Internet, but if you search for "YouTube Unsolved Mysteries adoptee coincidences" below is a URL that brings up a show rerun as of February 9, 2025: **https://www.youtube.com/watch?v=kyDHskPgNfM**

2024. Molly was channeling with Bill (our deceased father) and Jim (her recently deceased husband). She told me they were both helping me from the other side, and would continue if I requested it. I have done so. I always thought I had a "guardian angel" as a child and adolescent, and that belief continues. Now I wonder if Bill has also been somehow helping me all along?

Chapter 22 and Spring 2024. I asked Judy McCann, with whom I have stayed connected over the years, about several aspects of my book. I particularly asked her about the "men with no necks" and "tower apartment" experiences, in which she had both played a role. She reported having no memory of either experience! Even when I sent her the relevant sections of my book, which I had written shortly after they occurred, the descriptions held no familiarity for her. Clearly, they had not had meaning for her beyond a relatively short period of time, after which nothing further developed. My friend Frank, who was with me for the "no neck" event, died unexpectedly a few years ago, so his recollections of the event, if any, are unavailable.

Here, again, we see the difficulties with studying the concept of synchronicity. When I first wrote about those events, I wondered "What if Judy and Mary Anne do not become friends, and what if someday one of the "men with no necks" saves my life, or even just bumps into me somewhere, and I recognize him?" When I initially described these events in this book, I gave my estimates of which of the two was likely to continue to be meaningful, and it turned out, to my surprise, that the "tower apartment" episode had not retained any particular meaning. Of course, it is still possible that one of the "men with no necks" will save my life," but it is increasingly unlikely that Judy and Mary Anne will encounter each other again.

2024. I have maintained contact with Nancy Masters Ghoston and her husband. Nancy and Russell eventually married, are grandparents, and are still together.

2024. After I was unsuccessful in reestablishing a relationship with Mary Towers, she continued to date the man she was dating in 1970. They got married, and we have since lost contact. As far as I can tell, they are still together.

2024. Margaret, my first wife, remarried and had at least two children. We have not had contact in at least 20 years, but as far as I can tell, they are still together.

2024. I learned Jack Marvin, adoptee, psychologist, adoption activist, AAC Officer, and all-around good human, died March 6, 2024, at 88 years of age. I greatly regret that Jack and I lost contact in the later 2010s. You will recall both his and my birth mothers were named Pearl, but his birth mother was known as "Peg," her three initials. In Jack's professional obituary two "mothers" and two "fathers" were named. Elsewhere it was stated "Son of Benjamin Jesse Warrell and Pearl Emmaline Gibson. Adopted."

Chapter 18 and 2024. I looked for Jack Quist on the internet in order to get an update and to get permission to use his name. I finally found a phone number for him, and learned that after the AAC Conference in Las Vegas, he had continued in the country and western field. Because of his startling visual and vocal resemblance to Johnny Cash, Jack had a very successful run as a Johnny Cash tribute artist in the now-demolished Caravelle theater on the strip in Branson, Missouri. The events of Covid caused the venue Jack had been using to close and his life was disrupted for several years. In my conversation with Jack, he updated me on what else had happened recently. With the availability of genetic testing, he was able to locate and learn about his birth father. Even though he learned some difficult things, he reported that he has gone through a turnaround in his life. Jack is again writing and making music back in his hometown, Salt Lake City.

Chapter 12 and 2024. In talking about open adoption with Alice in Rhinelander in 1988, I believed "I could reassure Alice her daughter would most likely not suffer any serious damage from her open adoption." Reading this in 2024, I am concerned about the effects of separation from the birth mother caused by even open adoption. Work by Salisbury and others in 2003 in the *Journal of the American Medical Association* on a relatively new term, "Maternal-Fetal-Attachment" (MFA), is the subject of continuing attention. MFA happens during the time in pregnancy after the fetus starts moving on its own within the mother's body. Researchers believe that the movement initiates a change in the mother's thinking about her fetus. She begins to conceive of her fetus as having an independent identity from her own. The realization that she is going to have a child becomes more prominent and in the ideal situation changes her behavior in the direction of becoming more future-oriented. MFA may result in positive emotions and healthy changes in diet and self-care, and is often the time when the mother, her partner, and other family members begin to talk to the fetus. Some research has also examined the MFA process in fathers, as well. This process in a traditional birth would also be expected to transition to after-birth attachment, but MFA might well be less positive during a pregnancy destined for an adoption, and would be interrupted at the time of separation for placement. This suggests even a fully open adoption with no secrecy might still cause negative effects because of the discontinuity in bonding and attachment. I believe today I would state that Alice's daughter would not likely suffer any *serious* damage from her open adoption. I hope that the adoption remained open, since secrecy, lack of contact, and lack of knowledge do carry some avoidable risks.

Chapter 24 and 2024. Earlier in this book, referring to my healing experience with Michael in 1983, I wrote "How could I even think about giving up the form which my sexuality had taken? I had used masturbation, and sex in general, to soothe myself for as long as I could remember. How could I ever give these up? And what assurance did I have that something as pleasurable or as predictable would replace these activities?" It is worth noting that in 1978, during the process of giving up my active addiction to alcohol, I had a very similar series of thoughts, different from these thoughts about sex, only in that I had not used alcohol in the same way I had used sex, until entering college.

Allow me to quote from an article, published by a licensed psychologist, who for many years taught a university class in human sexuality: myself! "Masturbation may be viewed as a form of self-administered short-term nurturance. It may be the sexual activity of choice for the adoptee who, as a result of disrupted early attachment, has withdrawn from others, developing what Jernberg (1988) calls a 'self-containing life resolve'. Through masturbation the adoptee can obtain reliable nurturance, and pleasure not felt to be available on a dependable basis from others" (Henderson, 1995). Paul Sunderland is a British addiction therapist who speaks on "Adoption and Addiction." This is the title of a one-hour presentation he first gave to the Life Works Community in about 2014, which was still available as of January 2025. Sunderland believes that adoption is, or should be, viewed as a childhood trauma, with low serotonin levels caused by mother-infant separation. The entire video is well worth watching, but at about 29 minutes, Paul describes the important role of serotonin for brain function in assisting with the self-soothing process, which is disrupted in adoption. Addictions (sex, love, alcohol and eating disorders among them), are attempts to meet what Sunderland describes as "the need to self-soothe." Another source of information on this topic is Alexandra Katehakis Ph.D., MFT. One of her 2015 posts to the *Psychology Today* website, titled "Childhood Trauma and Masturbation, For some addicts, masturbation was their first way of self-medicating." pretty much echoes the same idea. Finding the more recent work of Sunderland and Katehakis has helped me to realize I was onto something in my 1995 publication, as well as to understand how and why some of my earliest memories are of masturbation.

Chapter 21 and 2024. My active involvement with AAC ended with my last AAC Convention in 2003. The male adoptee programs at AAC conventions continued for at least a couple more years after that. At some point, the men decided that meeting once a year was not sufficient and began monthly group telephone calls. Many of the members knew me, and I was invited to return to the group to give an historical perspective and a personal update in 2010.

The group continued to meet, and in 2022 they organized the first male adoptee weekend gathering in Colorado. I am happy to have been involved early in a movement that has continued for 30 years, and in October 2024, I began attending the monthly meetings. More information on the male adoptees monthly digital meetup and the MAAIS Retreats (Male Adoptee/Alumni Impact Summit) can be found at maleadoptees.com.

Chapter 22, and 2024. Many of the adopted men had always felt "left out" in the typically female-dominated search and support movement. For a variety of reasons, many of them cultural-social, men in general are under-represented in this movement, and adoptive fathers have been historically probably the rarest male category represented. Perhaps in part, they are absent because of the general hostility towards men that the male adoptees report. Sadly, but obviously, despite their underrepresentation, the attitudes and behaviors of adoptive fathers also play a crucial role in the development of their adoptees.

The adoption process is clearly more complex than the traditional way of having a biological child, with many unique stresses for prospective adoptive parents, not the least of which is stress from scrutiny during the home study. To the extent an adoption is related to fertility issues in the couple, there is also stress, particularly if some aspect of the infertility is traced to the husband. Given the generally poor reputation of birth fathers, many in the male adoptee groups question what kind of father we would be. Female adoptees may have similar concerns, and for all adoptees, their father is a model. As we can see, the role of the adoptive father is significant, but they seem largely not present, and not studied. Perhaps a positive effect of the societal trend towards decreasing gender stereotypes will be an increase in the participation of adoptive fathers in the search and support movement.

Chapter 22 and 2025. On March 3, 2025, we had a long-planned dinner with Bob Rosen. That day just happened to be the first day this book was available in print! He is the percussionist whose music I had called "noise," (much to my chagrin), on the night I planned to meet Susan, in February, 1985. Bob did not recall our first meeting, but of course that had been just over 40 years previously. I read him that section of my book, and all three of us laughed. But then Bob told me that in the process of explaining music-making, he often described music as "noise" which, under certain conditions and expectations some listeners find meaningful, even pleasant, while others do not. It was similar to a plant, which could be perceived as either a flower or a weed, depending on the person and the context. Perhaps I wasn't off of my game at all that night, but who knows how our interaction might have been in a hot, crowded room after a performance, as opposed to the next morning in the quiet of our offices and on the phone?

Chapter 10, numerous others. and 2024. Although I retired from university teaching in 2001, I continued my professional and personal involvement with adoption for several more years. During that period, I worked on the four articles which ultimately appeared in the 2007 *Handbook of Adoption*. When I returned to working on this book in 2024, I made extensive use of the AAC website. It listed the program and participant information for all of their annual conventions, and I found that resource to be very helpful. I noticed, however, that their list of annual convention programs stopped with 2019, and initially assumed that Covid had led to the suspension. But it also seemed they had either not updated their website in a while, or had not resumed having conventions.

At some point in September 2024, when I again tried to visit the AAC website, I found it had been suspended. A Wikipedia search on September 19 revealed the following information. "The COVID pandemic forced cancellation of the conference in 2020, and no further conferences were ever held prior to the organizational dissolution in 2024." The article also quoted a July 25, 2024 letter from the AAC President, indicating that after dissolution, all of the AAC's remaining assets would be transferred to ALMA, the Adoptees Liberty Movement Association. The letter also stated "ALMA has pledged a continuance of legislative advocacy to restore unrestricted access to original birth certificates for all adult adopted persons, a cause the AAC continues to champion."

The demise of AAC is very sad news for me and for the entire adoption community. I had learned a lot from my association with the group and made many friends. Especially after reviewing the details of many years of AAC conventions, I was reminded of the extremely valuable information presented in every one of them. There were often occasions at every convention when there was more than one program occurring at the same time that I wanted to attend. I was also looking forward to returning to AAC conferences to share my book.

The loss of AAC represents the ironic closing of a full circle for me. My first exposure to the organized adoption search and support movement, and finding my birth family, were both through ALMA. Through ALMA I had experience with NACAC. After attending a NACAC meeting I learned about AAC and AID. I was much more comfortable with the approach of AAC and AID, which was to include *all* sides of the adoption triad. Therefore, I spent the rest of my personal and professional involvement with these two organizations. AID ceased its operations in the late 1990s, and AAC closed in 2024. With the loss of AAC I hope that ALMA will expand its horizons to include all sides of the adoption triad. Perhaps it already has, but if not, I believe there is a need for a national organization which fulfills the original role of AAC.

We have now reached the end of this long journey (and equally long book!). I have realized many things during the course of events described here as well as in the process of writing about them. These are most important. Adoption should never be taken lightly by anyone. Separating children from their parents and placing them in a new family, no matter what other aspects of the situation are present, is a serious and life-altering process. Adoption has its place, but it should never be seen as the first response, or as an automatic response, to any problem, personal or societal.

Every adoption represents both gains and losses. Adoption is a multigenerational and ongoing process that permanently affects the lives of all involved. The adoption "story" never ends with the phrase "…the baby was adopted, and everyone lived happily ever after." The adoption process does not end the day the birth parent(s) become "legally" childless, or at least the parent of one less child. The story of an adoption does not end the day the adoptive parent(s) and their new child(ren) walk out of the court as a legal family. The adoption experience for adoptees begins at some point before birth, and likely never really ends. As you and I now know, adoption often causes the separation of siblings and other biological relatives who never knew of or had a part in the process. I have written a more detailed presentation of my beliefs about the nature of adoption in my 2002 article in the *Journal of Social Distress and The Homeless* and in my 2007 article, (#25), in the *Handbook of Adoption*. Although this writing is now some 20 years old, it still represents adoption as I see it.

During and after the active period of my search and writing process from 1983 to 1999, it took me some 15 years to stop tearing up when I described several of the events in this book to others, particularly the experiences of meeting my birth family for the first time. In the spring and early summer of 2024, when I reread some sections of the book that I had not seen in 25 or more years, the emotional impacts came rushing back again. This happened most clearly when I was reminded of the Friday afternoon in Rhinelander, when, for an hour or more, I held an infant whose mother had just decided to place her for adoption. This memory brought me to tears, again, on several occasions. That infant would be about 27 years old now. I hope she has had a good life.

To end on a happy note, please take another look at photos J1 to J6, a recent picture of me, surrounded by my five closest living biological relatives. I smile every time I look at these photos. For me, as for many people involved with the adoption process, these adoption issues are issues of life and death, whether they realize it or not. Fortunately, for me at least, these are no longer issues of life and death. They are issues of life.

APPENDIX

FURTHER RESOURCES

*All online sources available as of January 2025.

Cadoret, R. J. (1995). Adoption studies, *Alcohol Health and Research World*, 19(3): 195–200.

Haase, M. (2019). "Dance of Attachment: Dance/Movement Therapy with Children Adopted Out of Foster Care". *Dance/Movement Therapy Thesis*. 50. https://digitalcommons.slc.edu/dmt_etd/50.

Henderson, D. B. (1995). Sexuality and the adoptee. *Adoption Therapist*, 6, 3, 12-19.

Jernberg, A. M. (1988). The Theraplay Approach to the Self-Contained Patient. *The Psychotherapy Patient*, 4(3–4), 85–93.

Katehakis. A. (2015). "Childhood Trauma and Masturbation, For some addicts, masturbation was their first way of self-medicating." *Psychology Today* Website: https://www.psychology-today.com/us/blog/sex-lies-trauma/201502/childhood-trauma-and-masturbation.

Maleadoptees.com: https://www.maleadoptees.com/.

Pankonin, H. (1984). (written as "Bernard Arthur"), *Magnetism of Blood*. Highland Publishers, Merrill, WI.

Salisbury, A., Law, K., LaGasse, L., Lester. B. (2003). Maternal-Fetal Attachment, *Journal of the American Medical Association*, 289(13):1701.

Sunderland, P. (2010). "Adoption and Addiction: Remembered not Recalled." A one-hour presentation given to the Life Works Community. https://www.youtube.com/watch?v=3e0-SsmOUJI.

ADOPTION-RELATED
PUBLICATIONS AND
CONVENTION PRESENTATIONS

Douglas B. Henderson
(UWSP Students in **Bold***)*

Four articles (contributing author of two, first author of one, and sole author of one) in the *Handbook of Adoption*, Rafael A. Javier, Amanda L. Baden, Frank A. Biafora, and Alina Camacho-Gingerich, Sage Publications, 2007.

> Article #1. Breaking the Seal: Taking Adoption Issues to the Academic and Professional Communities / Rafael A. Javier, Amanda L. Baden, Frank A. Biafora, Alina Camacho-Gingerich and Douglas B. Henderson, P 1-14. Note that I was the only one of the 39 contributing authors that the four editors asked to cowrite the introductory chapter.
>
> Article #20. Psychologists' Self-Reported Adoption Knowledge and The Need for More Adoption Education / **Daniel A. Sass** and Douglas B. Henderson, P 312-322.
>
> Article #24. Adoptees' and Birth Parents' Therapeutic Experiences Related to Adoption / Douglas B. Henderson, **Daniel A. Sass and Jeanna Carlson (nee Webster)**, P 379-398.
>
> Article #25. Why Has the Mental Health Community Been Silent on Adoption Issues? / Douglas B. Henderson, P 403-417.

Sass, D. A., and Henderson, D. B. (2002) Adoptees' and Birth Parents' Therapeutic Experiences Related to Adoption. *Adoption Quarterly* 6(1), 25-32.

Henderson, D. B. (2002) Challenging the silence of the mental health community on adoption issues. *Journal of Social Distress and the Homeless*, 11(2), 131-141.

Houston, David, Perry, Stephanie, and Henderson, D. B. (2001). A content analysis of the life experiences of adoptees and birth parents. Paper presented at the 2001 American Adoption Congress annual convention, Anaheim, CA, April, 2001.

Henderson, D. B., & Javier, R. A. (Guest Eds.). (2000). Special issue: Adoption. *Journal of Social Distress and the Homeless*, 9(4), 261–372.

Henderson, D.B. Adoption Issues in Perspective: An Introduction to the Special Issue. *Journal of Social Distress and the Homeless* 9(4), 261–272 (2000). https://doi.org/10.1023/A:1009416209272

Sass, D. A., & Henderson, D. B. (2000). Adoption issues: Preparation of psychologists and an evaluation of the need for continuing education. Journal of Social Distress and the Homeless, 9, 349-359.

Panelist for "The Triad Experience: A Discussion Among Birth and Adoptive Parents, and Adoptees" and "Challenging the Silence of the Behavioral Sciences in Adoption Issues" at "The Adoption Journey: Socio-Political and Legal Challenges." St. John's University Queens Campus, 2000.

Sass, D. A., and Henderson, D. B. (1999) Adoption Issues: Preparation of Psychologists and an Evaluation of the Need for Continuing Education. Paper presented at Psi Chi Undergraduate Paper Symposium, Madison, WI, April. Also presented at the 1999 American Adoption Congress Annual Convention, McLean VA, May, and at the First Annual University of Wisconsin System Undergraduate Research Symposium, LaCrosse, WI, May.

"Special Issues for Male Adoptees." Workshop presented at the Mid-South/Mid-West Regional Convention, Kansas City MO, October, 1999, also presented at the 2000 American Adoption Congress annual convention, Nashville, TN, the 2001 conference in Anaheim, CA, and the 2002 conference in Philadelphia, PA.

Chaired Workshop "Adoption Education in Therapist Training," at the 1999 American Adoption Congress Annual convention, McLean, VA, May, 1999. Research done by my student, **Dan Sass,** and I was presented by Dan as part of this workshop.

"There Are More Like Me: Search, Reunion, and Synchronicity in Adoption: a Male Perspective" Presented at 1998 American Adoption Congress National Convention, Bellevue, WA.

Rowe, T. C., **Lemke, Jessica M., Pitsch, Eric P.,** and Henderson, D. B. (1997). Motivation and Meaningful Coincidence: A Further Examination of Synchronicity. *Journal of Scientific Exploration.*

Henderson, D. B., and McGowan, T. Special Issues for Male Adoptees. Workshop presented at the 1996 American Adoption Congress National Convention, Baltimore, MD.

Rowe, T. C. & Henderson, D. B. (1995). Establishing Prevalence of Commonalities in Randomly Paired Individuals as a Method for Assessing Synchronicity. *Journal of Scientific Exploration*, 9, 3, 323-331.

"On being Male and Adopted," Invited article published in the Summer, 1995, Adoption Triad Newsletter (TX), and reprinted in the Summer, 1995, Adoption Information and Direction, Inc. Newsletter (WI), and in the Fall, 1995, Newsletter for Origins: An Organization for Women who have Lost Children to Adoption (NJ).

Henderson, D. B. "Sexuality and the adoptee" (1995). *Adoption Therapist*, 6, 3, 12-19.

Workshop Chair, "Sexuality and Adoption" and Presenter, "Sexuality and the Adoptee," American Adoption Congress National Convention, New Orleans, LA, April, 1994.

Leader of support/discussion group on sexuality and the adoptee (follow-up discussion of above presentation) American Adoption Congress National Convention, New Orleans, LA, April, 1994.

Invited presentation on "Involving all sides of the adoption triad in the search and support process," Twin Cities Professional Adoption Discussion group, Lutheran Social Services, Minneapolis, MN, August, 1993.

Panel member: "Triad Awareness Panel," 18th North American Conference on Adoptable Children (annual convention of the North American Council on Adoptable Children) Milwaukee, WI, August, 1993.

Invited Workshop entitled "When You Find a Death at the End of a Search: What Then? " American Adoption Congress National Convention, Philadelphia, PA, March, 1992.

Invited Workshop entitled "Counseling the Adult Adoptee Post-Search." American Adoption Congress National Convention, Chicago, IL, May, 1990.

Invited Workshop entitled "Issues of Denial in Adoption." American Adoption Congress National Convention, Chicago, IL, May, 1990.

Workshop entitled "Post Reunion Changes in the Adoptee" with Wendy Redman, M.S.W., American Adoption Congress National Convention, Milwaukee, WI, May 1986.

Workshop entitled "A Psychiatrist and a Psychologist Look at Adoption" with C. E. (Adoptee Psychiatrist), American Adoption Congress National Convention, Milwaukee, WI, May 1986.

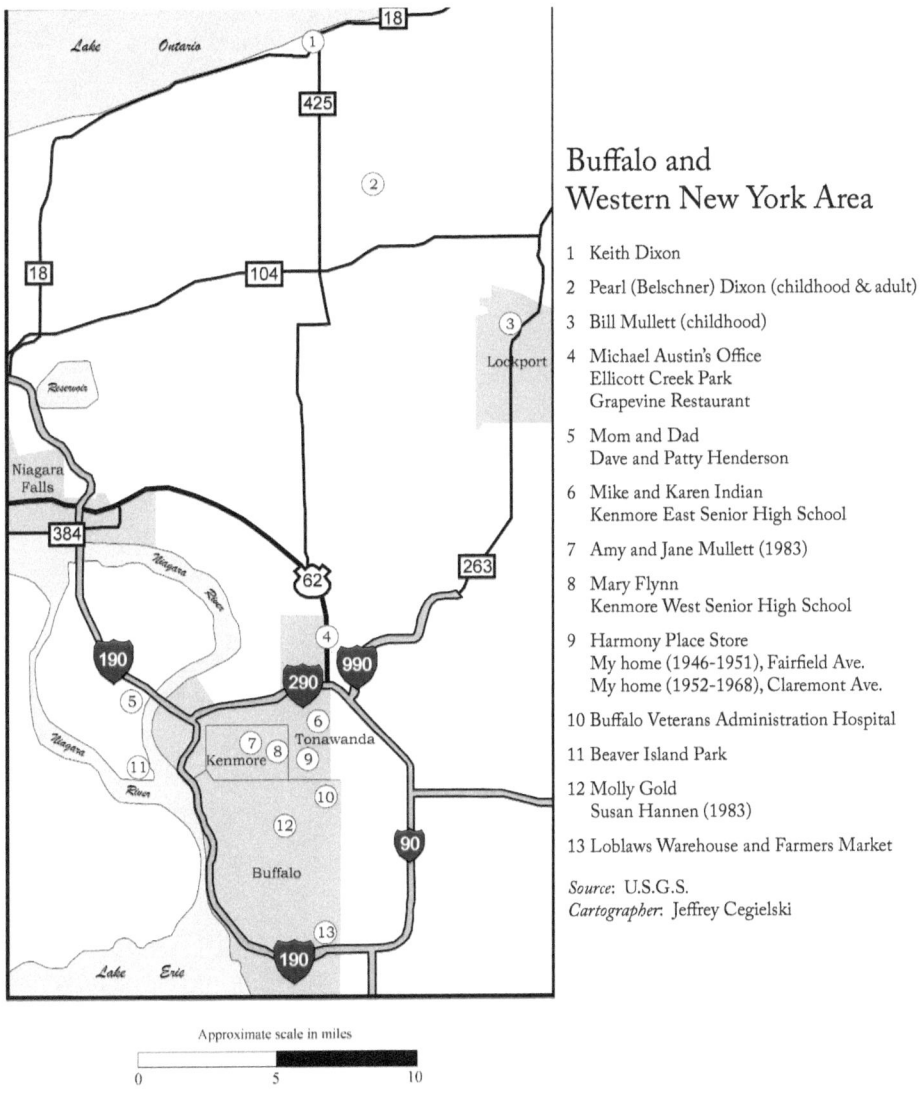

Buffalo and Western New York Area

1 Keith Dixon

2 Pearl (Belschner) Dixon (childhood & adult)

3 Bill Mullett (childhood)

4 Michael Austin's Office
  Ellicott Creek Park
  Grapevine Restaurant

5 Mom and Dad
  Dave and Patty Henderson

6 Mike and Karen Indian
  Kenmore East Senior High School

7 Amy and Jane Mullett (1983)

8 Mary Flynn
  Kenmore West Senior High School

9 Harmony Place Store
  My home (1946-1951), Fairfield Ave.
  My home (1952-1968), Claremont Ave.

10 Buffalo Veterans Administration Hospital

11 Beaver Island Park

12 Molly Gold
  Susan Hannen (1983)

13 Loblaws Warehouse and Farmers Market

Source: U.S.G.S.
Cartographer: Jeffrey Cegielski

Approximate scale in miles

0   5   10

Numbers four, five, six, eight nine, and twelve represent places located too closely together to be represented by multiple markers. All are locations of a home unless otherwise labeled.

ACKNOWLEDGMENTS

I give my grateful acknowledgement to the following organization and individuals.

The University of Wisconsin–Stevens Point Program for the Development of University Personnel for a two-semester sabbatical in the spring semesters of 1998 and 1999, during which I completed the vast majority of the writing process. The University also provided Susan Gingrasso and me with the opportunity to co-lead a UWSP International Program Semester in London in the fall of 1998, during which time I was able to consolidate my thoughts and feelings about this project.

Ross Tangedal, Ph.D. for editing my manuscript, preparing it for publication, and offering all-around advice and support.

The six UWSP Students, identified in the Adoption-Related Publication and Presentation List at the end of the book, who worked with me on adoption research projects and papers.

My wife, Susan Gingrasso, who was beside me for all but the first two years of my search, and after the project stalled, provided me with the motivation to return to and compete the work in 2024.

DOUG HENDERSON grew up in Buffalo, New York, received a B.S. in Psychology from St. Lawrence University, Canton, New York (1968), and a Ph.D. in Clinical Child Psychology from The Ohio State University, Columbus (1973). Doug was a Licensed Psychologist for 25 years, and was listed in the National Register of Health Service Providers in Psychology. His first employment was 2.5 years as a Staff Psychologist at Columbus Children's Hospital, and he is now Professor of Psychology Emeritus at the University of Wisconsin-Stevens Point, where he taught full time for 25 years. Doug was adopted at birth in 1946 in a traditional closed adoption, but despite knowing his adoption had major implications in his life, he didn't seriously consider searching until after he had testicular cancer in 1981. Doug did his primary search between 1983 and 1999, ultimately meeting several members from both sides of his birth family. His reunion process stalled for a number of years until his identity was confirmed through 23andMe.

Doug has mingled his professional and personal interests, authoring/coauthoring 13 publications about adoption in professional journals, including four articles in the *Handbook of Adoption: Implications for Researchers, Practitioners, and Families* (2007). Doug has presented 20 papers or led discussions (five with his students), at 16 different psychology- or adoption-related conventions. He was asked to serve as the Guest Editor of a Special Adoption Issue of the *Journal of Social Distress and the Homeless* (Volume 9, Issue 4, 2000). He founded and led the Stevens Point Chapter of Adoption Information and Direction, a Wisconsin search and support group for adoption triad members, for 10 years. He also served four years as State President of this group. Doug served on the Board of Directors, the Executive Committee, and as Chair of the Nominations and Elections Committee, as well as the Continuing Education Director and a Regional Director, for the American Adoption Congress.

Doug has helped build 24 houses for Habitat for Humanity, as well as most of a small cabin on 44 acres of land he owns near Stevens Point. He is a rock and mineral collector, and enjoys riding, and plowing snow, in his Yamaha UTV. He has also has been a photographer since long before cell phones. Doug lives in Stevens Point with his wife, Susan Hughes Gingrasso, an Emeritus Professor of Dance at UW-Stevens Point.

AUTHOR CONTACT INFORMATION:

If readers would like to contact me with questions or comments about this book, I have created a Substack page for this purpose. To reach it, search for, or go to: "DouglasBHenderson.substack.com" Please understand that I am enjoying retirement, and that the book is the story of a very significant portion of my life. While I want to be available to those with an interest in my book, I cannot promise to respond to every message. I will check the Substack site at least weekly for as long as I am able. Thank you for reading my book, and for understanding.

www.ingramcontent.com/pod-product-compliance
Lightning Source LLC
Chambersburg PA
CBHW021701120626
46545CB00004B/1353